Personal
Insurance

Personal Insurance

J.J. LAUNIE, Ph.D., CPCU
Professor of Finance and Insurance
California State University, Northridge

GEORGE E. REJDA, Ph.D., CLU
V. J. Skutt Professor of Insurance
University of Nebraska—Lincoln

DONALD R. OAKES, CPCU, ARM, RHU
Vice President
Insurance Institute of America

Coordinating Author
ANITA W. JOHNSON, CPCU, CLU, ChFC
Director of Examination Development
Insurance Institute of America

Second Edition • 1991

INSURANCE INSTITUTE OF AMERICA
720 Providence Road, Malvern, Pennsylvania 19355-0770

Second Edition • June 1991

Library of Congress Catalog Number 90-86335
International Standard Book Number 0-89462-061-4

Printed in the United States of America

Foreword

The American Institute for Property and Liability Underwriters and the Insurance Institute of America are independent, nonprofit, educational organizations serving the needs of the property and liability insurance business. The Institutes develop a wide range of programs—curricula, study materials, and examinations—in response to the educational requirements of various elements of the business.

The American Institute confers the Chartered Property Casualty Underwriter (CPCU®) professional designation on those who meet the Institute's experience, ethics, and examination requirements.

The Insurance Institute of America offers associate designations and certificate programs in the following technical and managerial disciplines:

Accredited Adviser in Insurance (AAI®)
Associate in Claims (AIC)
Associate in Underwriting (AU)
Associate in Risk Management (ARM)
Associate in Loss Control Management (ALCM®)
Associate in Premium Auditing (APA®)
Associate in Management (AIM)
Associate in Research and Planning (ARP®)
Associate in Insurance Accounting and Finance (AIAF)
Associate in Automation Management (AAM®)
Associate in Marine Insurance Management (AMIM®)
Associate in Reinsurance (ARe®)
Associate in Fidelity and Surety Bonding (AFSB)
Certificate in General Insurance
Certificate in Supervisory Management
Certificate in Introduction to Claims
Certificate in Introduction to Property and Liability Insurance

The Institutes began publishing textbooks in 1976 to help students meet the national examination standards. Since that time, we have produced more than seventy individual textbook volumes. Despite the vast differences in the subjects and purposes of these volumes, they all have much in common. First, each book is specifically designed to increase knowledge and develop skills that can improve job performance and help students achieve the educational objectives of the course for which it is assigned. Second, all of the manuscripts of our texts are widely reviewed prior to publication, by both insurance business practitioners and members of the academic community. In addition, all of our texts and course guides reflect the work of Institute staff members. These writing or editing duties are seen as an integral part of their professional responsibilities, and no one earns a royalty based on the sale of our texts. We have proceeded in this way to avoid even the appearance of any conflict of interests. Finally, the revisions of our texts often incorporate improvements suggested by students and course leaders.

We welcome criticisms of and suggestions for improving our publications. It is only with such constructive comments that we can hope to improve the quality of our study materials. Please direct any comments you may have on this text to the Curriculum Department of the Institutes.

Norman A. Baglini, Ph.D., CPCU, CLU
President and Chief Executive Officer

Preface to the Second Edition

This is the second in a series of three texts written specifically for the Program in General Insurance offered by the Insurance Institute of America. The first text, *Property and Liability Insurance Principles*, is assigned in the INS 21 course. This text forms the basis for the study of *Personal Insurance*, the INS 22 course. The third text, *Commercial Insurance*, is used in INS 23.

This text begins with an overview of the loss exposures faced by individuals and families and the types of insurance available to treat those loss exposures. The chapters that follow examine the insurance coverages available to help meet the financial consequences of these loss exposures.

Chapters 2, 3, and 4 focus on the homeowners (HO) policy series. The homeowners special form (HO-3) is the basis for a detailed analysis in Chapter 2 of the property coverages provided by homeowners policies. Chapter 3 compares the HO-3 form with the HO-4, designed for tenants, and the HO-6, designed for owners of condominium units and cooperative apartments. The liability coverage provided by homeowners policies is described in the balance of Chapter 3. Chapter 4 deals with the pricing of homeowners policies and with many of the endorsements that can be used with these policies.

Chapters 5 and 6 round out the discussion of coverages related to the property and liability loss exposures of individuals and families. Chapter 5 describes insurance for mobilehome owners and farm owners, as well as other types of residential insurance. The chapter ends with a family residence case that illustrates how the homeowners coverages apply in loss situations. Chapter 6 deals with floater policies that cover various types of personal property, insurance for watercraft, and personal umbrella liability insurance.

Personal auto insurance is the topic of Chapters 7, 8, and 9. Chapter 7 examines the liability, medical payments, and uninsured motorists coverages of the personal auto policy (PAP). Chapter 8 continues the study of the PAP by examining the physical damage coverages under this policy and some of the endorsements used with the policy. The final section of the chapter includes a family case focusing on PAP coverages as they apply in loss situations. Chapter 9 deals with some of the problems and proposed solutions related to auto insurance and society. The chapter concludes with a discussion of personal auto insurance underwriting and rating.

Chapters 10 and 11 examine life and health insurance, respectively. Chapter 12 focuses on a variety of government-sponsored insurance programs designed to meet the needs of individuals and families, with emphasis on the social security (OASDHI) program.

The text was written by J. J. Launie, Ph.D., CPCU; George E. Rejda, Ph.D., CLU; and Donald R. Oakes, CPCU, ARM, RHU. Anita W. Johnson, CPCU, CLU, ChFC, was the coordinating author for this second edition.

Joe Launie is Professor of Finance and Insurance at California State University, Northridge. He has written several texts for the Associate in Underwriting (AU) and Chartered Property Casualty Underwriter (CPCU) programs of the Institutes. Joe was the primary author of Chapters 1, 2, 3, 4, and 5.

George Rejda is V. J. Skutt Professor of Insurance at the University of Nebraska. He is the author of texts in the areas of insurance principles and social insurance, and is a past president of the American Risk and Insurance Association. George was the primary author of Chapters 6, 7, 8, 9, and 12.

Don Oakes is Vice President of the Institute. Don served as coordinating author for the first edition of the text and was the primary author of Chapters 10 and 11.

Anita Johnson, the coordinating author for this second edition of the text, is Director of Examination Development at the Institute. She is also the program director for the Program in General Insurance.

The authors appreciate the many helpful comments received from a number of reviewers on the drafts of the chapters for this text. Reviewers of one or more chapters include Richard S. Cibula, CPCU, CLU, ARP, AU, State Filings Director, Allstate Insurance Company; Donald W. Cook, CPCU, Assistant Vice President, State Farm Companies; Patrick L. Doyle, CPCU, CLU, ARM, Vice President, Office of the General Chairman, Nationwide Insurance Companies; E. Allen Finchum, CLU, ChFC, Officer, Agency Sales, Nationwide Insurance Companies; Patrick A. Gallagher, Ph.D., Employee Benefits Manager, The Graham Company; Edward E. Graves, CLU, ChFC, Professor of Insurance, The American College; Michael R. Hubbel, CPCU, AU, AIM, ARM, ARP, Vice President, Pioneer State Mutual Insurance Company; Thomas B. Morehart, Ph.D., CPCU, CLU, ChFC, Associate Dean, College of Business Administration and Economics, New Mexico State University; Gary K. Stone, Ph.D., CLU, Vice President—Academics, The American College; Barbara A. Taylor, CPCU, Assistant Vice President, Quality Commitment, American States Insurance Companies; Jerome Trupin, CPCU, CLU, ChFC, Insurance Consultant, Trupin Insurance Services; James G. Young, CPCU, CLU, LUTC, General Agent, Allstate Insurance Group.

The authors also wish to extend their personal thanks to several persons. Joe Launie wishes to acknowledge with thanks the support of family and friends that made the writing of this text possible.

For their guidance and the freedom to make choices that eventually led to a career in insurance education, Marnie and Jim Oakes are owed the gratitude of a loving son. To Pam, Steve, and Ken Oakes, sincere thanks for their encouragement and for their understanding of family time devoted to this textbook project.

While we gratefully acknowledge the assistance of the many persons who contributed to the publication of this text, we accept the responsibility for any errors or omissions. Readers are encouraged to provide their comments and suggestions, so that future editions of the text may be improved. Comments should be directed to the Curriculum Department of the Institutes.

J. J. Launie
George E. Rejda
Donald R. Oakes
Anita W. Johnson

Table of Contents

Section II—Liability Coverages ~ *Types of Losses Covered; Exclusions to Coverages E and F; Exclusions to Coverage E; Exclusions to Coverage F; Additional Coverages; Conditions*

Common Policy Conditions ~ *Policy Period; Concealment or Fraud; Liberalization Clause; Waiver or Change of Policy Provisions; Cancellation; Nonrenewal; Assignment; Subrogation; Death of Named Insured or Spouse*

Summary

Homeowners Insurance Pricing ~ *Indivisible Base Premium; Primary Rating Factors; Determining a Homeowners Policy Base Premium; Adjustments to the Base Premium*

Homeowners Endorsements ~ *The Need for Endorsements; Effects of Endorsements; Endorsements Affecting Section I Coverages; Endorsements Affecting Section II Coverages; Endorsements Affecting Sections I and II*

Summary

Homeowners Insurance for Mobilehome Owners ~ *Exposures; Mobilehome Coverage*

Homeowners Insurance for Farm Owners ~ *Incidental Farming Personal Liability (HO 24 72); Farmers Personal Liability (HO 24 73)*

Other Coverage for Residences ~ *The Dwelling Program; Fair Plans; Beachfront Plans*

Family Residence Insurance Case ~ *The Family Situation; Family Residence Coverages; Homeowners Loss Situations*

Summary

Inland Marine Floaters ~ *Meaning of Inland Marine Insurance; Characteristics of Inland Marine Floaters; Floater Policy Provisions; Personal Articles Floater; Personal Property Floater; Personal Effects Floater*

CHAPTER 1

Personal Loss Exposures and Insurance

Personal loss exposures are those loss exposures faced by individuals and families. A personal loss exposure exists when a personal resource is subject to a peril that may adversely affect an individual's or family's financial condition in the event of loss. Personal insurance consists of those insurance coverages designed to transfer the financial consequences of personal losses from individuals and families to an insurer.

Most of this chapter is devoted to descriptions of the major types of loss exposures typically faced by individuals and families: property loss exposures, liability loss exposures, and human loss exposures. The remainder of the chapter provides brief descriptions of the various kinds of insurance coverages available to deal with these loss exposures. These coverages are treated in detail throughout the balance of the text.

PROPERTY LOSS EXPOSURES

A *property loss exposure* is the possibility that a *property loss* could happen.[1] A property loss results when property is destroyed, damaged, stolen, lost, or otherwise suffers a decrease in value because of the action of a *peril,* or cause of loss. All property loss exposures have the following elements:

- Property that may be exposed to loss
- Perils that may cause a property loss
- The financial consequences that may result from a loss

Types of Property

Property is any item with value. For the purpose of identifying property loss exposures, and for legal and insurance purposes, property may be divided into two categories: *real property* and *personal property*. Real property consists of land and structures built on the land. Personal property consists of all other kinds of property. In other words, any property that is not real property is personal property.

Real Property. A family may own several types of real property that give rise to property loss exposures. For most families, their home is the real property that presents the greatest potential for financial loss. Home owners also have a real property loss exposure that arises out of ownership of the land on which their home is built. If their premises include other structures, such as a detached garage or shed, these buildings also represent real property loss exposures.

For some families, other types of real property may create property loss exposures. Condominium owners, for example, have ownership rights to common areas of the condominium property in addition to the unit they own. Some families also own vacation homes or rental properties that need to be recognized as real property loss exposures. In summary, any real property in which an individual or family has a direct financial interest presents a real property loss exposure.

Personal Property. Given the definition of personal property—any property that is not real property—a listing of the kinds of personal property owned by individuals and families could be almost endless. However, for the purpose of identifying personal property loss exposures, and for insurance purposes, personal property may be divided into several categories. The broadest of the categories includes the contents of the family's or individual's dwelling. Other property, some of which is normally found in the dwelling, is categorized separately for reasons that are described below.

Dwelling Contents. A dwelling's contents may include furniture, televisions, stereo equipment, appliances, kitchenware, groceries, clothing, sports equipment, tools, gardening equipment, and many other items usual to the occupancy of a home. All of these items are referred to as the *dwelling contents* or simply *contents*. These items are grouped together for several reasons. First, because they are normally located in the dwelling, they are exposed to essentially the same perils as the dwelling. Second, because many of these items are movable, they also are subject to theft. Finally, the value of these items usually can be determined easily in the event of a loss.

High-Value Property. Some items of personal property, many of which otherwise would be classified as dwelling contents, are worth considerable sums of money. This type of property is categorized separately, especially for insurance purposes, because of the ease with which it may be stolen and removed from the dwelling. Such items include money, securities, coins, silverware, precious metals, jewelry, gems, watches, furs, and firearms.

Property With Intrinsic Value. Property with intrinsic value is property whose value comes from its essential nature or unique characteristics, and it needs to be separately identified in the analysis of personal property loss exposures. An antique chair is an example of this type of property. Such items would need to be separately insured because property insurance contracts typically settle personal property losses on the basis of the cost to repair the item or its replacement cost less depreciation. Property with intrinsic value to the owner may not be replaceable at any cost, and its value needs to be established at the time that insurance coverage is purchased. In addition to antiques, other items with high intrinsic values might include works of art, stamp collections, valuable papers and records, photographs and negatives, and computer software and media on which data are stored.

Business Personal Property. This is personal property owned by an individual's business or employer. Most property insurance contracts written to provide coverage for families limit or exclude coverage for business personal property. An individual who keeps business personal property at home may be financially responsible in the event of a loss to that property. Depending on the type of property insurance the individual carries and the value of the business personal property kept at home, additional insurance may be required to cover this loss exposure.

Motor Vehicles, Watercraft, and Other Mobile Property. Property insurance covering dwellings and their contents typically excludes or provides only very limited coverage for mobile property. Physical damage to motor vehicles of all types, as well as aircraft, usually is excluded from coverage. Limited coverage may apply to watercraft and trailers. If a family owns any of these kinds of mobile property, it should be identified as such so that separate insurance may be purchased.

Perils Affecting Property

A list of all the perils that might conceivably cause a loss to the many kinds of property families own could be almost endless. Therefore, the focus here will be on those perils for which property insurance coverage typically can be provided.

Property insurance on dwellings and their contents may be purchased to cover the perils of fire; lightning; windstorm; hail; explosion; riot or civil commotion; aircraft; vehicles; smoke; vandalism or malicious mischief; theft; falling objects; the weight of ice, sleet, or snow; damage by broken window glass; and volcanic eruption. The following perils associated with the dwelling's mechanical systems also may be covered: accidental discharge from a plumbing or heating system; sudden and accidental tearing apart, cracking, burning, or bulging of a steam or hot water heating system; and freezing of plumbing or of a heating or air conditioning system.

Separate property insurance contracts, as well as endorsements to some property forms, are available to insure high-value personal property items, such as jewelry, and items with intrinsic value, such as fine arts. These contracts and endorsements typically provide coverage for as many or more perils as may be covered under a policy providing dwelling and contents coverage.

An auto may be insured for damage caused by the perils of collision, upset, falling objects, fire, theft, explosion, earthquake, windstorm, hail, water, flood, vandalism or malicious mischief, riot or civil commotion, contact with a bird or animal, and breakage of glass.

Financial Consequences of Property Losses

The major financial consequence of losses to both real and personal property is the reduction in value of the property. In addition, losses to real property may result in increased expenses and lost income.

Reduction in Value of Property. Following a loss, property may be damaged or totally destroyed. The difference between an item's preloss and postloss value is the measure of the financial consequence of the loss. The loss settlement provisions of property insurance contracts typically value property on either a *replacement cost* or *actual cash value* basis. Replacement cost is the amount necessary to purchase a comparable new item at the time of loss settlement. Actual cash value equals replacement cost less a deduction for physical depreciation or obsolescence that has occurred since the item was new.

Home owners usually can choose to purchase coverage for both dwellings and their contents on either a replacement cost or actual cash value basis. Items such as jewelry, furs, antiques, and works of art often are insured on an *agreed amount* basis, which means that the insured and insurer agree on the value of the item at the time the coverage is purchased. Automobiles typically are insured on an actual cash value basis, although some insurers offer auto policies with replacement cost coverage.

Increased Expenses. If a dwelling suffers a serious loss, the owner is likely to incur additional living expenses for motel or hotel rooms and meals out while the damage to the dwelling is being repaired. This is an example of increased expenses that may result as the consequence of a loss. Likewise, if a car is damaged in an accident, the owner may incur an increased expense to rent a substitute vehicle while the car is being repaired.

Lost Income. An additional financial consequence of a property loss may be lost income. Lost income may result if there is damage to property that is owned and rented to others. Some people own vacation homes that they rent to others part of the time. Others rent garages or rooms in their homes. If a loss makes such rental property unusable, the property owner will suffer an income loss until the property can be repaired and rented again.

LIABILITY LOSS EXPOSURES

A *liability loss exposure* is the possibility that a *liability loss* could happen. A liability loss occurs when an individual's financial resources are diminished as the result of a claim for money damages because of injury or harm to another party. Liability loss exposures have the following elements:

- Resources that may be exposed to loss
- The possibility that a claim for money damages may be brought
- The financial consequences that may result

Resources Exposed to a Liability Loss

Liability loss exposures put all of an individual's financial resources at risk of loss. When a court orders an individual to pay liability damages, the amount of the damages is based on the loss to the injured party. The individual's financial resources available to pay such damages are not the court's concern. As a result, all of an individual's savings and property are exposed to loss because of the possibility that the individual might have to liquidate them to pay a large liability damages award. In addition, courts have the power to attach a portion of an individual's wages, if necessary, to pay for liability damages. The fact that all of an individual's assets, plus his or her future income, may be required to pay for liability damages makes the possibility of a liability loss a particularly threatening exposure.

Possibility of a Claim for Money Damages

For liability loss exposures, the peril or cause of loss is the bringing of a claim for money damages. Unless a claim for money damages occurs, an individual's financial resources will not be diminished. In addition, as soon as a claim for money damages is brought, financial resources begin to be diminished by the costs of investigating the claim and preparations to defend against legal action that may ensue. Therefore, the making of a claim against an individual is the action that brings about a liability loss.

Claims for liability damages are governed by *civil law*. Civil law deals with the rights and duties of citizens with respect to one another. The settlement of disputes between individuals and the redress of wrongs committed against individuals are within the scope of civil law. There are several bases for claims for liability damages under civil law. Individuals are most likely to face claims arising out of tort liability, contractual liability, and statutory liability.

Tort Liability. A *tort* is a wrongful act committed by one party against another. When injury or harm results from a tort, the injured party has the right under civil law to seek payment from the wrongdoer. An individual may face a claim for tort liability damages on the basis of intentional acts, negligent acts, and acts for which absolute liability may exist.

Intentional Torts. Individuals may face liability claims that arise out of the following intentional torts.

Defamation. Defamation, which includes *libel* and *slander*, is the dissemination of an *untrue* statement that damages a person's reputation. If such a statement is written or printed, it is libel; if spoken, it is slander. The following is an example of slander that could lead to a liability claim.

Bob and Tom are neighbors. Tom is an accountant for a business firm. As a sideline, he also earns several thousand dollars each year by preparing tax returns for friends and neighbors. Following an argument between Bob and Tom over a matter unrelated to Tom's business, Bob told a number of his neighbors that he had to pay $5,000 in interest and penalties to the government because Tom incorrectly prepared his tax return. Bob's story was false, but it spread throughout the neighborhood. As a result, Tom's earnings from the preparation of tax returns declined by $2,000. Under civil law, Tom could make a claim against Bob for slander.

Malicious Prosecution. Civil law also protects individuals from damage to their reputation caused when another person brings false criminal charges against them with malicious intent. In order for liability damages to be awarded for malicious prosecution, the injured party must show that the charges brought were false and that they were brought with the intent to do harm. Criminal proceedings must have been brought for which there was no other probable cause and then terminated in favor of the accused party.

Assault and Battery. *Assault* consists of a threat of bodily harm under circumstances that lead the threatened person to believe that he or she will be harmed. *Battery* occurs when an individual makes physical contact with another person in an unlawful way. For example, if Mary threatens to hit Betty, and Betty believes that Mary is ready and able to carry out her threat, Mary has committed an assault on Betty. Mary has committed a battery if she carries out her threat and hits Betty. Betty may sue Mary for damages because of the assault and battery.

Conversion. Conversion is the act of appropriating the property of another, thereby depriving the rightful owner of the use or enjoyment of that property. For example, if Harry borrows Fred's garden tractor and then takes it with him when he moves to another town, Fred may seek damages from Harry for the conversion of the garden tractor.

Trespass. The owner of land has the legally protected right to the exclusive possession and use of that land. Trespass is the unauthorized possession or use of the land by another person. For example, Bill and Joe are neighbors who own adjoining properties, and each feels that a ten-foot-wide section of land is on his property. Bill builds a brick grill in the disputed territory. Joe has his property surveyed and determines that Bill's grill is, in fact, on Joe's property. Joe may bring suit against Bill to remove the grill and restore the land to its original condition.

Nuisance. The owner of land also has the right to enjoy the use of that land without disruption from outside sources. If an individual continuously creates a nuisance to his or her neighbors by letting dogs run loose or hosting noisy parties that last late into the night, the neighbors may seek an injunction against such activities or damages under civil law.

Negligence. Liability based on negligence requires four elements. First, an individual must have a legal duty to act or refrain from acting in some way toward another person. Second, the individual must have breached that duty— acted in a way that is different from the actions of a reasonably prudent person under the same circumstances. Third, some kind of injury or harm must have come to another person as the result of the individual's breach of duty. Finally, the breach of duty must have been the direct cause of the injury or harm to the other person.

Liability resulting from automobile accidents is a significant negligence liability exposure for most individuals largely because of the types of injury and damage that such accidents can cause. However, the potential for negligence liability claims exists in many other activities. Serving contaminated food to friends, starting a fire that spreads to a neighbor's house, allowing ice to build up on a sidewalk and thus causing a passerby to fall and break an arm, and accidentally shooting a fellow hunter are just a few examples of actions that may lead to negligence liability claims.

Absolute Liability. Some activities are so inherently dangerous that if they result in injury or harm to another, the individual who engaged in the activity may be held absolutely liable. The injured party need not prove that the responsible individual acted negligently. All that must be shown is that the individual was responsible for the activity that caused the injury or harm.

Claims based on absolute liability may stem from keeping dangerous pets. If a dog is known to have a vicious temperament, a claim based on absolute liability could result if the dog injures a neighbor or visitor to the home.

Individuals who own guns may be held absolutely liable for their use regardless of safety precautions taken to keep them locked away. Use of explosives may also result in claims based on absolute liability regardless of how careful an individual may have been to avoid causing injury or damage to others.

Contractual Liability. The possibility of contractual liability arises when an individual enters into a contract or agreement that transfers the financial responsibility for a liability loss from someone else to that individual. Leases for homes and apartments, as well as rental agreements for autos, power tools, and other equipment, typically contain provisions that transfer the financial consequences of liability losses that occur during the rental period from the owner of the property to the renter. Such provisions may require that the renter assume the liability for *any* injury or harm that results to others, even if the owner of the property was the party at fault. While leases and rental agreements are among the most common sources of possible contractual liability for individuals, any contract that requires an individual to assume liability on behalf of someone else creates a contractual liability loss exposure.

Statutory Liability. Liability may exist because of the passage of a specific statute or law. Most important to individuals and families is the passage of various state laws dealing with liability arising out of automobile accidents. These laws vary from state to state and a detailed explanation is beyond the scope of this text. However, it should be noted that such laws may redefine the way in which legal doctrines relating to negligence liability apply in auto accident cases. In addition, the enactment of "no-fault" auto insurance laws in many states has placed some restrictions on suits to recover damages when auto accident injuries are relatively minor. Under "no-fault" laws, instead of seeking damages through the tort liability system, drivers are reimbursed by their own insurers for minor medical expenses.

Financial Consequences of a Liability Loss

The two major financial consequences of a liability claim against an individual are the costs of (1) investigation and defense and (2) money damages awarded if the defense is not successful. Many liability claims, however, are settled before they reach a court of law. For cases settled "out of court," the costs of investigation and defense may be reduced, and the amount paid in damages is negotiated between the parties to the claim, rather than being determined by the court.

Investigation and Defense. In a liability action, the party seeking liability damages is called the *plaintiff*. The party accused of causing the plaintiff's loss is called the *defendant*. Even before the plaintiff files a formal complaint with the court, the defendant may be aware of the plaintiff's intentions. If so, the defendant may incur costs to secure advice from an attorney, investigate the circumstances surrounding the loss, and obtain statements from witnesses.

When the plaintiff files suit in court, a copy of the complaint is given to the defendant. The defendant must answer the complaint within a prescribed period of time, or the plaintiff will win the suit by default. Additional legal expenses must be incurred at this point if the defendant decides to continue his or her defense.

The next pre-trial step is called the *discovery process*. During the discovery process, attorneys for both the plaintiff and defendant may obtain relevant documents from the other side and interview key witnesses under oath. Each side tries to secure as much evidence as possible to support its case. Depending on the complexity of the case, the discovery process can be both lengthy and expensive.

When the case goes to trial, additional expense may be incurred by the defendant to pay fees charged by expert witnesses. Expert witnesses may be needed to testify on technical matters relevant to the defense of the suit, or they may be needed to refute testimony offered by expert witnesses brought in to testify on behalf of the plaintiff. Thus, a defendant's legal fees continue to mount as the defense moves from the discovery process into the trial at which the defense is presented. In addition, at the end of the trial the defendant may be required to pay court costs associated with the proceedings.

Of course, all of the investigation and defense costs mentioned above are not required for all liability defenses. Nevertheless, the possibility exists that an individual will be faced with many of these costs if he or she becomes a defendant in a liability suit seeking substantial damages.

Damages. If the plaintiff wins the suit against the defendant, the court probably will require the defendant to pay the plaintiff money damages. Money damages awards may represent nominal damages, compensatory damages, and punitive damages.

Nominal Damages. If the plaintiff has shown that he or she was wronged by the defendant but actually suffered little or no financial loss as the result of the defendant's actions, the court may award what are called nominal damages. Nominal damages awards may be for as little as $1. For instance, if one neighbor slanders another, causing damage to the neighbor's reputation but no financial loss, a court might award nominal damages to the slandered neighbor.

Compensatory Damages. Compensatory damages are awarded to compensate the plaintiff for the injury or harm caused by the defendant. When compensatory damages are awarded for losses to property, the amount of the damages may include the cost to repair or replace the property, loss of income due to the property damage, and additional expenses that the plaintiff incurred because of the property damage.

Compensatory damages paid to the plaintiff because of bodily injury may consist of *special damages* and *general damages.* Special damages are amounts paid to compensate the plaintiff for direct expenses such as medical treatment, lost wages, and rehabilitation expenses required because of the bodily injury. General damages may be paid to compensate the plaintiff for things such as pain and suffering, physical disfigurement, and loss of consortium.

Punitive Damages. Punitive damages may be awarded if the court finds that the defendant's actions were particularly outrageous. As the name implies, punitive damages are intended to punish the defendant. Punitive damages also may be awarded to make an example of the defendant in the hope that others will not repeat his or her actions. Whether or not punitive damages effectively modify people's behavior is a matter of intense debate.[2]

HUMAN LOSS EXPOSURES

A *human loss exposure* is the possibility that a *human loss* could occur. Human losses happen directly to people, such as the losses caused by death, poor health, disability, and unemployment.

Human loss exposures are sometimes referred to as personal loss exposures because they directly affect people. However, the term personal loss exposures also is used to denote the full range of property, liability, and human loss exposures faced by individuals and families. Likewise, personal insurance—the subject of this text—refers to those insurance coverages designed to treat personal loss exposures. To avoid confusion, this text uses the term human loss exposures to describe losses that directly affect individuals.

Two types of consequences result from human losses. The first is purely personal in nature, such as the discomfort of an illness or injury and the grief experienced when there is a death in the family. Although insurance payments may help soften the blow of such consequences of human losses, remedying the purely personal effects of these losses is beyond the scope of the insurance mechanism. The second type of consequence of human losses is financial. These financial consequences include the cost of medical care and the loss of income that often results from a death in the family. The focus here will be on financial consequences of human losses.

Human loss exposures have the following elements:

- Human resources exposed to loss
- Perils that may cause human losses
- The financial consequences that may result

Human Resources

Each individual represents a *human resource,* a potential for making contributions toward his or her own well-being and that of a family unit or society as a whole. For the purpose of evaluating human loss exposures, the contributions made by human resources can be categorized as economic and noneconomic.

Economic Contribution—Earning Power. The major economic contribution made by human resources results from the *earning power* of individuals. As used in this context, earning power means the ability of an individual to use his or her physical and mental labor to produce income. An individual's earning power makes it possible for him or her to provide for personal needs, to support other family members, and to benefit society through programs funded by the individual's voluntary contributions and tax payments.

Noneconomic Contributions. Individuals also engage in many activities whose benefits cannot be measured in dollars. For example, when a parent volunteers to lead a child's scout troop, benefits are likely to be created for the parent, the child, and the children of others.

Losses to human resources may reduce their productive capacity or even bring it to an end. In large measure, the extent to which human resources are diminished as a result of loss depends on the peril that causes the loss.

Perils Causing Human Losses

Human resources may be affected by the perils of death, diminished physical or mental health, disability, and forced unemployment. Each peril, in its own way, diminishes human resources or precludes an individual from making the contributions of which he or she would otherwise be capable.

Death. An individual's death brings to an end his or her earning power and the ability to make noneconomic contributions. Individuals may leave financial or humanitarian legacies when they die, but additional future contributions are precluded by death. In this sense, the peril of death results in the destruction of human resources.

The term *premature death* often is used to describe the peril under consideration here. In an economic sense, death is premature if it occurs while an individual is making economic contributions. As a result, death that occurs during a person's normal working years is categorized as premature. Considering the noneconomic contributions that some individuals make late in their lives, death could be considered premature even if it occurs well into the retirement years. There is no hard and fast rule for defining premature death if noneconomic contributions are taken into account. In an insurance context, however, emphasis is placed on economic contributions in defining this peril.

Several hazards are likely to increase the possibility of premature death. If an individual is in poor general health or suffers from a life-threatening disease, the chance of death is increased. To some extent, these conditions may be beyond an individual's control. Other hazards, however, are not. An individual's choice of vocation and avocations can increase the likelihood of premature death. Certain occupations, such as construction work, put an individual at higher risk. Likewise, hobbies such as flying and scuba diving increase the chance of premature death. Personal habits, such as alcohol or drug abuse, are hazards that may lead to premature death.

Perils Causing Diminished Physical or Mental Capacity. Unlike death, perils that result in diminished physical or mental capacity usually do not destroy human resources. They impair the productive capacity of individuals, reducing their ability to make economic and noneconomic contributions to themselves and to others.

Illness. An illness is a sickness, disease, or condition that adversely affects the health of an individual. Illnesses may be mild or severe, resulting in corresponding degrees of loss to human resources. An individual may catch a cold and, with the exception of some personal discomfort, suffer no reduction in the ability to make economic or noneconomic contributions. At the other end of the scale, a severe illness may result in total incapacity.

An illness may affect a person's physical health, mental health, or both. Physical illness reduces the body's ability to function as it should, thereby diminishing a physical human resource. Mental illness reduces the mind's ability to function properly. Reduced mental capacity may lead to the inability to use one's mind in a productive way. Because the mind controls the body, mental illness also may lead to the diminishment of a physical human resource.

Several hazards are associated with the illness peril, including poor physical condition, smoking, and abuse of alcohol or drugs. Lack of exercise, obesity, and poor dietary practices are likely to result in poor physical condition, which may increase the likelihood that an individual will develop certain diseases or conditions of poor health.

Another potential hazard, one that may be beyond the control of the individual, is the environment in which he or she lives. Air pollution, water pollution, and noise pollution, to name just a few of the recognized environmental hazards, may contribute to a reduction in physical well-being. While individuals can make some choices regarding where they live and work, environmental hazards that threaten human resources appear to be more and more difficult to escape.

Bodily Injury. Bodily injury results from physical trauma, the injury of living tissue by an outside force. As with illness, the personal consequences of bodily injury may range from mild to severe, with corresponding effects on an individual's productive capacity.

Bodily injury may result from a force beyond the individual's control, such as a speeding auto that jumps the curb and strikes down a pedestrian. However, several hazards within the individual's control may contribute to bodily injuries. These include personal carelessness (morale hazard), choice of vocation and avocations, and the use of alcohol and drugs.

Disability. A serious illness or bodily injury may cause an individual to become disabled. Disability is the inability to perform one's occupational duties. Disability may range from partial to total. A partially disabled individual is likely to suffer a reduction in earning power. For the totally disabled individual, earning power ceases, at least for the duration of the disability. Disability also may be categorized as temporary or permanent. If a disability is temporary, the disabled individual's earning power is expected to return at the end of the disability. When a disability is permanent, an individual's earning power is reduced, or even ended, for the rest of his or her productive years.

Unemployment. The economic effect of unemployment is much like that of a total and temporary disability. An individual's earnings cease for an unknown period of time. However, the peril of unemployment is different from the perils of death and diminished health in that the physical well-being of the person is not directly affected. Nevertheless, the financial consequences of unemployment can be equally severe.

As used in this context, unemployment refers to involuntary unemployment of healthy individuals during their productive years. Involuntary unemployment may occur for a number of reasons. Poor overall economic conditions, declining profits of an individual employer, and the performance of a particular employee all may lead to unemployment.

Financial Consequences of Human Losses

Human losses have both direct and indirect consequences. In many situations, the indirect consequences of a human loss may be more severe than the direct consequences.

Direct Consequences. The most significant direct financial consequence of premature death is the cessation of an individual's earnings. In the absence of adequate life insurance, the death of a breadwinner can have devastating financial consequences for a family. In addition, death may be preceded by an illness or injury for which medical expenses must be paid. The family also will be faced with final expenses such as burial and estate settlement costs.

A serious illness or bodily injury from which an individual fully recovers can nevertheless result in physician and hospital bills in the tens of thousands of dollars. Even relatively minor illnesses or surgical procedures that require hospital care can cost several thousand dollars. The expense of treatment is the most significant direct financial consequence of these perils.

If illness or bodily injury results in disability, the individual suffers the additional direct consequence of loss of income. In the event of the permanent and total disability of a breadwinner, the direct financial consequences may be worse than those caused by death. Long-term medical costs will have to be paid while, at the same time, the breadwinner's income will have ceased.

Indirect Consequences. When a family's income stops, the money to pay for the family's ongoing expenses must come from some other source. Likewise, medical bills resulting from a serious illness or bodily injury are likely to be greater than the average family can pay out of its current income. The amount that cannot be paid out of current income must come from some other source.

In the absence of adequate insurance coverage, the family may call on several sources to pay for the direct financial consequences of human losses.

The use and possible depletion of some of these resources are the indirect financial consequences of human losses. Depending on the severity of a loss, a family may be able to pay for the loss costs by drawing on its liquid assets, such as those held in bank accounts, money market funds, or stocks and bonds. If the loss does not result in long-term cessation of a breadwinner's earning power, the family also may be able to borrow the funds needed to pay for the loss costs.

If the loss is severe and the breadwinner's future earning power is reduced or ceases, the family may be forced to liquidate other assets, including valuable personal belongings and even the family home. In addition, a spouse or older child may be forced to enter the labor market in an attempt to make up lost income.

Finally, if all of the family's financial resources are not sufficient to meet the burden caused by a loss, the family may become dependent on welfare payments to help meet its living expenses or medical costs. When this happens, the financial burden of the family's loss is transferred to other individuals whose taxes provide the funds used to make welfare payments.

INSURANCE FOR PERSONAL LOSS EXPOSURES

Protection against the financial consequences of personal losses can be provided through the various types of insurance introduced in this section. These types of insurance are the subjects of Chapters 2 through 12.

Property and Liability Insurance

Most individuals purchase property and liability insurance to cover their homes and autos. Homeowners (HO) policies provide a package of property and liability coverages tailored to meet the needs of most home owners, apartment renters, and condominium owners. (Auto insurance is discussed below.) An overview of five homeowners policies is presented here. The three most widely used homeowners policies are examined in more detail in Chapters 2, 3, and 4.

Types of Homeowners Policies. The HO forms introduced here are developed by the Insurance Services Office (ISO) for use by its member companies.[3] There are five HO forms currently in use throughout the country:

- HO 00 02 Broad Form (HO-2)
- HO 00 03 Special Form (HO-3)
- HO 00 04 Contents Broad Form (HO-4)
- HO 00 06 Unit-Owners Form (HO-6)
- HO 00 08 Modified Coverage Form (HO-8)

A sixth form (HO 00 01), which provides basic coverage for dwellings and personal property, is available in only a few states. Because all HO forms provide essentially the same liability coverage (discussed in Chapter 3), the following overview focuses on the differences in the property coverage provided by HO policies. Exhibit 1-1 presents a comparison of the property coverage provided by the various policies. Before the homeowners forms were revised in 1991, they

Exhibit 1-1
Comparison of 1991 Homeowners Forms

	HO 00 02 Broad Form	HO 00 03 Special Form	HO 00 04 Contents Broad Form	HO 00 06 Unit Owners Form	HO 00 08 Modified Coverage Form
Section I Coverages					
A Dwelling	$25,000 minimum	$25,000 minimum	Not applicable	$1,000 minimum on unit	$15,000 minimum
B Other structures	10% of A	10% of A	Not applicable	Not applicable (Included in Coverage A)	10% of A
C Personal property	50% of A	50% of A	$6,000 minimum 20% of C	$10,000 minimum 40% of C	50% of A
D Loss of use	20% of A	20% of A			10% of A
Covered perils	Fire or lightning Windstorm or hail Explosion Riot or civil commotion Aircraft Vehicles Smoke Vandalism or malicious mischief Theft Falling objects Weight of ice, snow or sleet Accidental discharge or overflow of water or steam Sudden and accidental tearing apart, cracking, burning or bulging of a steam or hot water heating system, an air conditioning or automatic fire protective sprinkler system, or an appliance for heating water Freezing Sudden and accidental damage from artificially generated electrical current Volcanic eruption	Dwelling and other structures covered against risks of direct physical loss to property except losses specifically excluded Personal property covered for loss by the same perils as HO 00 02 plus damage by glass or safety glazing material, which is part of a building, storm door, or storm window	Same perils as HO 00 02	Same perils as HO 00 02	Same perils as HO 00 02 (except theft coverage limited to $1,000 and only for theft on residence premises) Note: Building losses paid on basis of repair cost using common construction materials and methods

were known as HO-2, HO-3, and so on. For the sake of convenience, this text will continue to use these labels for the homeowners forms.

HO 00 02 Broad Form (HO-2). The HO-2, which provides coverage against loss from specified perils for both the dwelling and personal property of the insured, is the most basic HO form available in most states. One- or two-family dwellings occupied by their owners are eligible for coverage under this form.

HO 00 03 Special Form (HO-3). The HO-3 also provides coverage for one- or two-family dwellings that are owner-occupied. Unlike the other HO forms, the HO-3 provides coverage against risks of direct loss to real property except for those causes of loss that are specifically excluded. Personal property is covered against loss by specified perils.

HO 00 04 Contents Broad Form (HO-4). The HO-4 is designed for tenants of rented premises. Since the landlord or building owner normally provides insurance on the dwelling unit, this form does not include building coverage. It covers the tenant's personal property against loss from specified perils.

HO 00 06 Unit-Owners Form (HO-6). The HO-6 is designed to meet the unique requirements of condominium owners. There is no coverage on the condominium building because such coverage is normally purchased by the condominium association. The HO-6 covers loss from specified perils to the insured's personal property, as well as to alterations, appliances, fixtures, and improvements that are part of the building and contained within the insured's residence premises.

HO 00 08 Modified Coverage Form (HO-8). The HO-8 is designed to cover older homes, often in declining urban neighborhoods or in rural areas, whose replacement cost may greatly exceed the market value. Building losses under other HO policies are paid on the basis of replacement cost for like construction. Under the HO-8, building losses are paid on the basis of repair costs using common construction techniques and methods that will make the repairs functionally equivalent to the undamaged portion of the dwelling. However, the cost of repairs is usually much lower than the replacement cost for like construction. Thus, homeowners coverage is available to owners of older homes that otherwise would not qualify for coverage because of the wide difference between replacement cost and market value.

Other Property and Liability Coverage. Monoline policies, which provide coverage in a single line of insurance, include dwelling policies for property coverage and comprehensive personal liability insurance. These policies are discussed in Chapters 5 and 6. Coverage for certain types of property such as jewelry, furs, and cameras may be provided by endorsements to a homeowners policy or under separate contracts known as inland marine floater policies. This type of coverage is discussed in Chapter 6.

The personal auto policy is widely used to fulfill the insurance requirements of auto owners. This policy combines liability and medical payments coverages with physical damage protection for the vehicle itself. The personal auto policy and other auto coverages are the subjects of Chapters 7, 8, and 9.

Life Insurance

Life insurance provides protection against the financial consequences of premature death. With the increasing number of families in which both parents work, family financial planning should consider the economic loss in the event of the death of either spouse. A broad spectrum of life insurance contracts, to be examined in Chapter 10, has been developed to meet a family's life insurance needs. These contracts range from term life insurance, which provides basic life insurance protection, to universal life insurance, which includes both life insurance protection and savings/investment options for the insured.

Health Insurance

The most common type of medical expense insurance pays for both hospital expenses and physicians' fees. Medical expense insurance is often purchased on a group basis by an employer and is provided as an employee benefit. Medical expense coverage is also available under individual policies.

Disability income insurance provides a partial replacement of income that is lost when an insured is disabled as a result of an accident or illness. Medical expense insurance and disability income insurance are the topics of Chapter 11.

Government Insurance Plans

The most visible government insurance plan is social security. The formal name of the program is the Old Age, Survivors, Disability, and Health Insurance (OASDHI) program. Social security provides pension benefits to retired workers; survivor benefits to widows, widowers, and dependent children; and disability payments for workers who become totally disabled for a period of longer than six months.

The financial consequence of unemployment is mitigated to some degree by the unemployment compensation programs administered by each of the fifty states. These programs make modest payments to unemployed workers.

For property owners unable to find coverage in the standard insurance market, government-run FAIR (Fair Access to Insurance Requirements) plans provide access to insurance coverage for dwellings and their contents.

Flood insurance on many types of property is not available in the standard insurance market because of adverse selection. The federal government provides flood insurance at subsidized rates for both dwellings and commercial buildings.

These government insurance plans, as well as others that treat personal loss exposures, are discussed in Chapter 12.

SUMMARY

Personal loss exposures exist when personal resources are subject to perils that may adversely affect an individual's or family's financial condition in the event of a loss. The major categories of personal loss exposures are property loss exposures, liability loss exposures, and human loss exposures.

The elements of a property loss exposure are property that may be exposed to loss, perils that may cause a property loss, and the financial consequences that may result from such a loss. Property losses may affect real property, such as dwellings and other structures, and personal property, including a dwelling's contents. Other categories of personal property exposed to loss are high-value property, property with intrinsic value, business personal property, and mobile property, such as autos and watercraft. These several types of property are exposed to a variety of perils, many of which can be insured against. The financial consequences of property losses include reduction in the value of the property, as well as increased expenses and lost income that may result from such losses.

The elements of a liability loss exposure are resources that may be exposed to loss, the possibility that a claim for damages may be brought, and the financial consequences that may result from such a claim. Liability loss exposures put all of an individual's resources at risk of loss. These resources include property, which might have to be liquidated to pay for a liability loss, and future earnings, which might be attached to make a liability loss payment. When a claim for money damages is made against an individual for alleged injury or harm to another, a liability loss results. Under civil law, liability claims may be made on the basis of tort liability, contractual liability, and absolute liability. If a defendant is found to be responsible for injury or harm to a plaintiff, a court may order the defendant to pay nominal, compensatory, and/or punitive damages.

The elements of human loss exposures are human resources exposed to loss, perils that may cause human losses, and the financial consequences that may result from such losses. Each individual represents a human resource with the potential for making both economic and noneconomic contributions to himself or herself, to a family, and to society. The perils that may destroy or diminish human resources include death, poor health, disability, and unemployment. The possible direct financial consequences of human losses include the cessation of earning power, the final expenses associated with death, and the costs of medical treatment and rehabilitation that illness or injury may require. The possible indirect costs of human losses include the forced liquidation of assets, welfare costs, and changes in family roles and lifestyle.

Personal insurance coverages are designed to transfer the financial consequences of many personal loss exposures from individuals and families to insurers. Many families use homeowners policies to provide coverage for property and liability loss exposures that arise out of owning or renting a home. Monoline policies are also available to provide property or liability coverage for individuals or families.

The personal auto policy provides property and liability coverage for auto-related loss exposures. A variety of life and health insurance policies are available to provide coverage for human losses caused by death, poor health, and disability. Government insurance programs have also been developed to help individuals and families with the financial burdens created by certain kinds of losses.

Chapter Notes

1. The analysis of property and liability loss exposures is based, in part, on Barry D. Smith, James S. Trieschmann, and Eric A. Wiening, *Property and Liability Insurance Principles* (Malvern, PA: Insurance Institute of America, 1987), Chapters 2 and 3.
2. See J. J. Launie, "The Incidence and Burden of Punitive Damages," *Insurance Counsel Journal,* January 1986, pp. 46-51.
3. This section of the chapter is based on contracts copyrighted by the Insurance Services Office, New York.

CHAPTER 2

Homeowners Insurance

As discussed in Chapter 1, homeowners policies provide a package of property and liability coverages tailored to the needs of most home owners, apartment renters, and condominium owners. This chapter focuses on the homeowners policies developed by the Insurance Services Office (ISO), an advisory organization serving insurers throughout the United States. Some insurers may use similar policy forms developed by the American Association of Insurance Services (AAIS), an advisory organization similar to ISO. Still other insurers may develop their own policy forms.

HOMEOWNERS POLICIES

The ISO homeowners (HO) policies were revised in 1990 and have an edition date of 1991. The discussions of homeowners policies and endorsements in Chapters 2, 3, and 4 are based on the 1991 editions of these forms. Each HO form provides the insured with a combination of property and liability coverages. The property coverages of the various HO forms differ largely on the basis of the covered property and the covered causes of loss (perils). The liability coverages, however, are essentially the same under all of the HO forms. With few exceptions, the insured must purchase the complete package of coverages provided under a given HO policy. Endorsements can be used to provide additional coverages or to modify coverage.

The most widely used HO policy is the HO 00 03 Special Form, and it is the basis for much of the discussion in this chapter. This discussion will be easier to follow if it is read along with a sample policy. Two other widely used homeowners forms—HO 00 04 Contents Broad Form (for apartment renters) and HO 00 06 Unit-Owners Form (for owners of condominium units)—are discussed in Chapter 3. Before the HO forms were revised in 1990, these three policies were known as HO-3, HO-4, and HO-6, respectively. Those designations are used in this text.

All homeowners policies include the following components:

- Declarations
- Insuring agreement
- Definitions
- Section I
    Property coverages
    Perils insured against
    Exclusions
    Conditions
- Section II
    Liability coverages
    Exclusions
    Additional coverages
    Conditions
- Conditions applicable to both Section I and Section II

The declarations, insuring agreement, and definitions are discussed below as they apply to the HO-3 policy. Section I of the HO-3 is described later in this chapter. The remaining components of HO policies are discussed in Chapter 3.

Declarations

The first items on the declarations page usually are the policy number and the policy period. In most states, the policy period begins at 12:01 A.M. standard time at the insured location. The date coverage begins is known as the *inception date*. The name of the insurance company may also be included in this section of the declarations.

The next items on the declarations page are the name and mailing address of the insured. If the address of the residence to be insured is not the same as the insured's mailing address, the address of the insured residence is also included.

The coverages under Section I and Section II are listed, and a limit of liability is shown for each coverage. The amount of the premium also is included in this part of the declarations page, either as a single amount for all coverages or broken down to reflect the premium for each coverage.

The HO form under which coverage is provided is also indicated on the declarations page. The HO form number may be preprinted, or it may be filled in as part of the listing of forms and endorsements that are part of the policy. Endorsements are listed by number, and any change in premium resulting from an endorsement is shown in the same section of the declarations page.

Next, the deductible to be applied to property losses is listed. The standard deductible is $250. The amount of the deductible may be increased or decreased with a corresponding decrease or increase in premium. Homeowners deductibles are discussed in Chapter 4.

If the insured owns another residence for which Section II coverage is to be provided, the location of that residence must be shown. For instance, if an insured owns a vacation home, the insured's HO policy covering the primary residence can also provide liability protection for the vacation home. The insured can then purchase separate insurance covering only the property loss exposures arising out of ownership of the vacation home.

Finally, if the insured premises is mortgaged, the mortgagee will typically require the insured to have the mortgagee's name and address listed on the declarations page. This gives the mortgagee specific rights under the policy.

The Insuring Agreement

The insuring agreement, which applies to all coverages, states the following:

We will provide the insurance described in this policy in return for the premium and compliance with all applicable provisions of this policy.

A contract requires consideration from both parties. The insurer's consideration is its obligation to provide the specified insurance coverage for the policy period. The insured's consideration has two parts—the obligation to pay the policy premium and the obligation to comply with the policy conditions.

Definitions

When a contract is drawn up by one party and accepted by the other party, it is known as a *contract of adhesion.* Any ambiguities in a contract of adhesion are construed against the party that drew the contract. Since the homeowners policy is a contract of adhesion, it is necessary to clearly define the terms used in the contract.

The terms "you" and "your" are defined in the HO-3 as referring to the "named insured" shown in the declarations and the spouse if a resident of the same household. The terms "we," "us," and "our" refer to the insurer providing the coverage.

The term "residence premises" is also defined. It means the one-family dwelling, other structures, and grounds, or that part of any other building in which the insured resides and which is shown as the "residence premises" in the declarations. "Residence premises" also means a two-family dwelling where the insured resides in at least one of the family units and which is shown as the "residence premises" in the declarations.

Most of the other terms defined at the beginning of the HO policy refer to Section II—Liability and are discussed in Chapter 3.

PROPERTY COVERAGES

The HO-3 policy includes the following five types of property coverage:

- Coverage A—Dwelling
- Coverage B—Other Structures
- Coverage C—Personal Property
- Coverage D—Loss of Use
- Additional Coverages

The description of each type of coverage includes definitions and exclusions intended to clarify the intent of the coverage.

Coverages A and B

Coverage for the insured's real property, that is, the dwelling and other structures such as a detached garage, is provided under Coverages A and B.

Covered Property. Coverage A applies to the dwelling and attached structures on the residence premises. In addition, coverage is provided for building materials and supplies located on or next to the residence premises for use in construction, alteration, or repair of either the dwelling or other structures on the residence premises. Coverage A does not apply to land, including the land on which the dwelling is located.

Coverage B applies to *other structures* on the residence premises that are detached from the dwelling. The policy clarifies the distinction between attached and detached structures by stating that a structure connected to the dwelling only by a fence or utility line is considered to be detached. Once again, land is specifically excluded.

Other structures used in whole or part for business are excluded. Other structures rented to someone other than a tenant of the dwelling are also excluded unless such a structure is used solely as a private garage.

The homeowners policy uses the phrase *limit of liability* to identify the amount of insurance applicable to each of the coverages. The phrases *amount of insurance, amount of coverage,* and *coverage amount* are used in insurance practice and in this text as synonyms for limit of liability.

When an HO-3 is purchased, the insured chooses the Coverage A limit of liability based on the value of the covered dwelling. The Coverage B limit of liability is automatically set at 10 percent of the amount of insurance for Coverage A unless the insured purchases a higher amount of insurance. An insured whose residence premises contains a large detached garage, workshop, barn, guest house, or several smaller detached structures may need to increase the Coverage B limit of liability beyond the amount automatically provided.

While the covered perils are the same for Coverages A and B, the determination of which coverage applies to a garage or a shed is important. A policy with a $100,000 Coverage A limit of liability would automatically provide $10,000 of additional insurance for a detached garage or shed. If the same structure was attached to the insured's dwelling, it would be included in the $100,000 Coverage A limit of liability.

Covered Perils. The HO-3 insures against risks of direct loss to property described in Coverages A and B, but only if that loss is a physical loss to property. Coverage is further limited by the exclusions described below.

Exclusions. Some of the exclusions that limit the property coverages in Section I apply only to Coverages A and B. Other exclusions apply to all of the Section I coverages.

Exclusions Applying Only to Coverages A and B. The exclusions are the key to analyzing the perils insured against under Coverages A and B because direct physical loss to property is covered unless specifically excluded. The following exclusions apply only to Coverages A and B.

Collapse. Losses involving collapse are specifically excluded unless the cause of the collapse is described under the additional coverages provision. These additional coverages are discussed later.

Freezing. When the dwelling is vacant, unoccupied, or under construction, the insured must maintain heat in the building or shut off the water supply and drain the system and appliances of water. Otherwise, freezing of a plumbing, heating, air conditioning, or automatic fire protective system or of a household appliance is not covered. Damage caused by discharge, leakage, or overflow from within such a system or appliance also is excluded unless the preceding precautions have been taken.

Foundations, Retaining Walls, and Nonbuilding Structures. Loss by freezing, thawing, pressure, or weight of water or ice to fences, swimming pools, foundations, retaining walls, piers, wharves, or docks also is excluded. This exclusion applies whether or not the water or ice was driven by wind. Therefore, there is no coverage even if a loss to any of these structures was the result of a windstorm.

Dwelling Under Construction. Theft in or to a dwelling under construction is excluded. Theft of materials and supplies for use in the construction is also excluded until the dwelling is finished and occupied, although Coverage A applies to other types of loss to materials and supplies located on or next to the residence premises used for construction, repair, or alteration. The theft exposure is much greater during construction than it is after construction is completed and the property is occupied.

Vandalism and Malicious Mischief. There is no coverage for vandalism and malicious mischief if the dwelling has been vacant for more than thirty consecutive days immediately before the loss. A dwelling being constructed is not considered vacant.

There is a distinction between "vacant" and "unoccupied." A vacant dwelling is empty and unfurnished. An unoccupied dwelling is furnished, but the residents are not on the premises. Therefore, if an insured from Vermont spends January and February in Florida, the Vermont dwelling is unoccupied, but not vacant, while the insured is in Florida.

Risks of Direct Physical Loss Exclusion. Coverages A and B insure property against risks of direct physical loss that are not specifically excluded. Policies that provide such broad coverage generally contain an exclusion that lists specific causes of loss that are not insured. Thus, Coverages A and B do not insure losses caused by any of the following:

1. Wear and tear, marring, deterioration
2. Inherent vice, latent defect, mechanical breakdown
3. Smog, rust or other corrosion, mold, wet or dry rot
4. Smoke from agricultural smudging or industrial operations

5. Discharge, dispersal, seepage, migration, release, or escape of pollutants (unless caused by a peril covered under Coverage C)
6. Settling, shrinking, bulging, or expansion, including resultant cracking, of pavements, patios, foundations, walls, floors, roofs, or ceilings
7. Birds, vermin, rodents, or insects
8. Animals owned or kept by an insured

Pollutants in the fifth cause of loss is defined as follows:

> . . .any solid, liquid, gaseous or thermal irritant or contaminant, including smoke, vapor, soot, fumes, acids, alkalis, chemicals and waste. Waste includes materials to be recycled, reconditioned or reclaimed. . .

There is coverage, however, if any of the listed perils cause water damage (not otherwise excluded) from a plumbing, heating, air conditioning, or automatic fire protective sprinkler system or household appliance. This includes the cost of tearing out and replacing any part of a building in order to repair the system or appliance. There is *no* coverage for loss to the system or appliance from which the water escaped.

Concurrent Causation Exclusions. It sometimes happens that more than one peril is involved in a loss. In such situations, each peril may be called a *concurrent cause* of the loss, and insurance problems can arise if one of the perils is covered and another is excluded. The HO-3 and many other insurance policies that provide coverage for risks of direct physical loss contain provisions intended to resolve problems arising from losses involving concurrent causation. Thus, the HO-3 does not insure for loss to property described in Coverages A and B if the loss is caused by any of the following:

1. Weather conditions. This exclusion applies only to weather conditions that contribute to a loss that would otherwise be excluded. Therefore, damage caused solely by a windstorm, for example, would not be affected by this exclusion.
2. Acts or decisions of others. This exclusion denies coverage when loss results from the acts or decisions, including the failure to act or decide, of any person, group, organization, or governmental body. Inappropriate action or inaction by any of these entities could be considered negligence. The intent of this exclusion is to deny coverage when such negligence is a concurrent cause of loss along with an excluded peril.
3. Faulty, inadequate, or defective plans or actions. This exclusion eliminates coverage for any loss resulting from improper planning, zoning, development, surveying, siting, design, specifications, workmanship, repair, construction, renovation, remodeling, grading, soil compaction, materials, or maintenance of any property on or off the residence premises.

However, these exclusions do not apply to any *ensuing* loss to property if such loss is not excluded or excepted by some other policy provision.

Exclusions Applying to All Section I Coverages. The HO-3 contains eight general exclusions that apply to all of the coverages in Section I. Those exclusions are discussed below.

Ordinance or Law. Loss caused by enforcement of any ordinance or law regulating the construction, repair, or demolition of a building or other structure is not covered unless specifically provided under this policy. (Coverage can be "specifically provided" by adding the HO 04 77 endorsement, described in Chapter 4, which enables the insured to "buy back" this coverage.)

The following is an example of the application of this exclusion. An old dwelling, not meeting the current building code, is damaged. Because of the provisions of a building ordinance, repairs would have to include extensive modifications to the dwelling's wiring, plumbing, and foundation. The additional cost of these modifications is not covered because of the ordinance or law exclusion.

Earth Movement. There is no coverage for property damage from earthquake (including land shock waves associated with a volcanic eruption); landslide; mine subsidence; mudflow; and earth sinking, rising, or shifting. However, if direct loss by fire, explosion, or breakage of covered glass or safety glazing material ensues, coverage is provided *for the ensuing loss.* The earth movement exclusion does not apply to loss by theft, such as looting following an earthquake.

Water Damage. The water damage exclusion is often referred to as the flood exclusion, but, in fact, it also excludes other types of water damage to which dwellings and their contents are exposed. Water damage from the following is excluded:

1. Flood, surface water, waves, tidal water, overflow of a body of water, or spray from any of these, whether or not driven by wind
2. Water which backs up through sewers or drains or which overflows from a sump
3. Water below the surface of the ground, including water which exerts pressure on or seeps or leaks through a building, sidewalk, driveway, foundation, swimming pool, or other structure

However, direct loss by fire, explosion, or theft resulting from water damage is covered. For example, if a dwelling is flooded and the insured is evacuated, the flood damage would not be covered, but furnishings stolen from the dwelling by looters would be covered.

Power Failure. Loss caused by the failure of power or other service utility is excluded if the failure occurs off the residence premises. Therefore, if a hurricane knocked out the power from the local electric company and a freezer full of meat spoiled, there would be no coverage for the loss of the meat. If the power failure is caused by an insured peril on the residence premises, any resulting loss is covered. Therefore, if lightning strikes the dwelling and causes a power interruption, the consequent spoilage of food in a freezer would be covered.

Neglect. If the insured neglects to use all reasonable means to save and preserve property at and after the time of a loss, there is no coverage for any damage that results from the insured's neglect. This exclusion encourages the insured to take *reasonable* steps to save endangered property. The requirement that property must also be protected following the loss encourages the insured to exercise the same degree of care for insured property as he or she would if the property were not covered by insurance.

War. The war exclusion applies to war as well as to any of the following types of actions and any consequences of these actions:

- Undeclared war, civil war, insurrection, rebellion, or revolution
- Warlike acts by a military force or military personnel
- Destruction, seizure, or use for a military purpose

Discharge of a nuclear weapon is considered a warlike act even if such discharge is accidental. The war exclusion takes away some of the worldwide coverage for personal property ordinarily provided under Coverage C. Therefore, the loss would not be covered if the insured's luggage and its contents are damaged when rebellion breaks out in the foreign country the insured is visiting.

Nuclear Hazard. Loss caused directly or indirectly by nuclear hazard is excluded, but direct loss by fire resulting from the nuclear hazard is covered. This exclusion is unusual in that the actual nuclear hazard exclusion is part of the Section I—Conditions, discussed later in this chapter.

Intentional Loss. There is no coverage for any loss arising out of any act committed by or at the direction of an insured with the intent to cause a loss. Not only must the act be intentional but the loss must also be intended. This exclusion eliminates coverage for all insureds when an intentional loss is committed by or at the direction of any insured. For example, there would be no coverage available to the innocent spouse of an arsonist who burned down the family home.

Coverage C—Personal Property

Coverage C provides insurance for personal property of the insured. Special limits apply to some types of property, and some property is excluded from coverage. Coverage applies to direct physical loss caused by covered perils.

Covered Property. Coverage C provides worldwide coverage for personal property owned or used by an insured. At the request of the insured, coverage is extended to personal property owned by others while the property is on the part of the residence premises *occupied by an insured.* The requirement that the property be on the part of the residence premises occupied by an insured is designed to eliminate coverage for the personal property of a tenant.

At the request of the insured, personal property owned by a guest or a residence employee is covered while the property is in *any* residence occupied by an insured. The term "any residence" is broader than the "residence premises," but note that coverage under this section is limited to guests of the insured and residence employees.

If personal property is scheduled (described and listed separately) on another policy or on an endorsement such as the scheduled personal property endorsement, such scheduled property is not covered under Coverage C. For this reason, the subject matter of Coverage C is sometimes called *unscheduled personal property.* The overall limit of liability for Coverage C is 50 percent of the Coverage A amount. There is a limitation of 10 percent of the Coverage C limit for personal property *usually located* at a secondary residence. There is a minimum of $1,000 of coverage for such property.

Assume that John and Marsha Cabot, residents of Boston, have an HO-3 with a Coverage A limit of $200,000. The limit of liability under Coverage C would be $100,000 (50 percent × $200,000). The Cabots also own a summer cottage at Bar Harbor, Maine. The HO-3 on their Boston house would provide $10,000 (10 percent × $100,000) coverage for personal property usually located at the secondary residence at Bar Harbor. Furniture, appliances, and household items left year-round at Bar Harbor would be subject to the $10,000 limitation. If the Cabots regularly carried their television, video cassette recorder, and clothing back and forth from Boston to Bar Harbor, these items would not fall under the $10,000 limitation.

Property Subject to Special Limits of Liability. Eleven types of property are subject to special limits of liability under Coverage C of the HO-3. These limits do not increase the overall Coverage C limit of liability but represent sub-limits within the overall limit. The special limit for each category is the total limit for each loss for all property in that category.

The following are the special limits of liability:

1. $200 on money, bank notes, bullion, gold other than goldware, silver other than silverware, platinum, coins, and medals.
2. $1,000 on securities, accounts, deeds, evidences of debt, letters of credit, notes other than bank notes, manuscripts, personal records, passports, tickets, and stamps. This dollar restriction applies regardless of the medium on which the material exists. The cost to research, replace, or restore the information from the lost or damaged material is included in this special limit of liability.
3. $1,000 on watercraft, including their trailers, furnishings, equipment, and outboard engines or motors.
4. $1,000 on trailers not used with watercraft.
5. $1,000 for loss by theft of jewelry, watches, furs, and precious and semi-precious stones.
6. $2,000 for loss by theft of firearms.
7. $2,500 for loss by theft of silverware, silver-plated ware, goldware, gold-plated ware, and pewterware. This includes flatware, hollowware, tea sets, trays, and trophies made of or including silver, gold, or pewter.
8. $2,500 on property, on the residence premises, used at any time or in any manner for any business purpose.
9. $250 on property, away from the residence premises, used at any time or in any manner for any business purpose.
10. $1,000 for loss to adaptable electronic apparatus while it is in or upon a motor vehicle or other motorized land conveyance. Such adaptable electronic apparatus is equipped to operate by power from the electrical system of the vehicle while retaining its capability of being operated by other sources of power.
11. $1,000 for loss to adaptable electronic apparatus while it is (a) not in or

upon a motor vehicle or other motorized land conveyance; (b) away from the residence premises; and (c) used at any time or in any manner for any business purpose.

Property Excluded From Coverage. There are nine categories of property not covered under Coverage C of the HO-3. The categories are described in the following paragraphs.

There is no coverage for articles separately described and specifically insured in this or other insurance. Coverage C provides unscheduled or blanket coverage. If a particular item, a diamond ring for example, is scheduled on a personal articles floater endorsement, then it is excluded from blanket coverage under Coverage C. This applies if the scheduled coverage is provided by an endorsement to the HO policy or if it is provided under a separate policy, thus eliminating duplicate coverage and possible disputes about which coverage should be primary in the event of a loss.

Animals, birds, or fish are excluded from coverage. Household pets are difficult to value and even more difficult to insure. They are subject to loss from a variety of causes including theft, illness, and simply becoming lost. Property policies have traditionally excluded household pets from coverage.

There is no coverage for motor vehicles, all other motorized land conveyances, and their equipment and accessories. Also excluded is electronic apparatus that can be operated solely by power from the electrical system of a motor vehicle or motorized land conveyance. However, the exclusion applies to equipment, accessories, and electronic apparatus only while such property is in or upon the vehicle or conveyance. Coverage C does provide coverage for vehicles or conveyances not subject to motor vehicle registration, which are used to service an insured's residence or designed for assisting the handicapped. For example, a garden tractor or motorized wheelchair owned by the insured would be covered.

Aircraft and parts are also excluded. An aircraft is defined as any contrivance used or designed for flight except model or hobby aircraft not used or designed to carry people or cargo.

Property of roomers, boarders, and other tenants (except property of roomers and boarders related to an insured) is excluded. Any nonrelated tenant should have his or her own insurance. This exclusion is consistent with the description of property of others that the policy would cover at the insured's option.

There is no coverage for property in an apartment that is regularly rented or held for rental to others by an insured. This refers to property, such as furniture, owned by the insured and used to furnish a rental apartment. This exclusion does not apply to the landlord's furnishings, which are the subject of an additional coverage discussed later.

Property rented or held for rental to others off the residence premises is also excluded. This section makes it clear that property related to an insured's rental operations is excluded whether on or off the residence premises.

There is no coverage for business data such as that stored in books of account, drawings, or other paper records; or electronic data processing tapes, wires, records, disks, or other software media. Coverage is provided for the cost of blank recording or storage media and of prerecorded computer programs available on the retail market. Business records, including computer floppy disks, could be covered under a valuable papers and records policy or electronic data processing policy if they are to be insured at all. The HO-3 is not intended to provide coverage for a business exposure of this nature.

Credit cards and fund transfer cards are excluded except as provided in the additional coverages section described later.

Covered Perils. Insurance is provided under Coverage C for direct physical loss to *personal property* from the following sixteen named perils. Notice that the Section I exclusions described earlier apply to Coverage C.

Fire or Lightning. The fire insurance provided by an HO policy is one of the most important coverages for the typical home owner. Nevertheless, the homeowners policy—following the practice in property insurance forms that preceded it—does not define the term *fire*. Insurers rely instead on the definition of fire that has grown out of court cases relating to insurance coverage. The courts have generally held that fire means combustion or oxidation rapid enough to cause a flame or glow. In addition, the courts have held that insurance coverage applies only to "hostile fires"—fires that are not within their intended confines. A fire that remains within its intended confines, such as a fireplace, charcoal grill, or stove top, is termed a "friendly fire." No coverage is provided for damage caused by friendly fires. For example, no coverage would be provided for scorching of the finish on a chair that was set too close to a fireplace unless the chair itself caught fire. Likewise, there would be no coverage for fire damage to a pair of eyeglasses that melted after being accidentally dropped into a charcoal grill.

Lightning, although not specifically defined in the HO policy, is generally considered to be a discharge of atmospheric electricity.

Windstorm or Hail. The windstorm peril includes damage from violent winds, such as hurricanes and tornadoes. However, the coverage for loss due to windstorm or hail excludes loss to property located within a building caused by rain, snow, sleet, sand, or dust *unless* the direct force of the wind or hail created an opening in the roof or wall through which these elements could enter. Windblown rain entering through an open window or around the crevices of a poorly fitting one is not covered. Wind or hail damage to a boat and its equipment is covered only if the boat is located inside a fully enclosed building.

Explosion. Explosion is not defined in the policy. A loss to the contents of a dwelling caused by an explosion off the property such as an industrial explosion or blasting work would be covered. Other covered explosions include water hammer, bursting pipes, and sonic boom.

Riot or Civil Commotion. The term riot is defined by state laws. One state defines riot as a public activity involving three or more persons with a common purpose who carry out that purpose with a show of force. A civil commotion is generally considered to be a large or prolonged riot. Damage to personal property resulting from a riot or civil commotion is covered.

Aircraft. Damage from aircraft, including self-propelled missiles and spacecraft, is covered.

Vehicles. HO policies provide coverage for damage to the insured's property by any vehicle—even a vehicle owned by an insured. For instance, if a motorist lost control of a vehicle and crashed into the insured's patio furniture, the loss to the furniture would be covered under all forms of the HO policy. In addition, if the insured's son ran over a lawn mower while putting the family car into the garage, the loss to the lawn mower would be covered.

Smoke. Sudden and accidental damage from smoke is covered. An example of a covered loss is damage to carpets, drapes, and furniture caused by smoke suddenly discharged from a faulty fireplace or heater. Coverage is not provided for damage to personal property caused by smoke from agricultural smudging or industrial operations.

Vandalism or Malicious Mischief. These perils are not defined in the policy, but coverage is provided for willful or malicious damage to property caused by one or several persons without the tumult associated with a riot.

Theft. The theft peril includes attempted theft and loss of property from a known place when it is likely that the property has been stolen. For example, an insured checks in at an airline gate one hour before the flight departs, places some carry-on luggage in the passenger waiting area, and leaves to buy a cup of coffee from a nearby vending machine. Upon returning to the waiting area, the insured finds that the carry-on luggage has disappeared. If the airline personnel at the gate have no knowledge of what happened to the luggage, the most likely presumption is that it was stolen. This type of loss would be covered, and the actual cash value of the luggage and its contents—in excess of the policy deductible—would be paid to the insured.

The following types of theft losses are excluded:

1. Theft committed by an insured. For instance, if a resident child of the named insured steals the family silverware, the loss is not covered.
2. Theft in or to a building under construction, including construction materials and supplies, that occurs before the building is completed and occupied. This parallels the exclusion of theft to a dwelling under construction for Coverages A and B, making it clear that no coverage is provided for such stolen property—either as real or personal property.
3. Theft from any part of the residence premises rented to someone other than an insured. If an insured rents a furnished room to someone who is not a family member, the theft of furniture from that room would not be covered. However, if an insured rents a furnished room to a nephew who is attending a nearby college, theft of furniture from that room would be covered. The nephew would be an insured under the HO-3 since he is a relative residing in the named insured's household.
4. Theft of covered property from a secondary residence except while an insured is temporarily living there. Theft coverage is specifically excluded for such premises during periods of unoccupancy because of the increased likelihood of theft during such periods. If the secondary

residence is that of a student away at school, theft coverage is provided during brief periods of unoccupancy, such as holidays and semester breaks. No theft coverage is provided if the student has been away from school continuously for more than forty-five days prior to the loss.

5. Theft of any of the following items that occurs away from the residence premises:
   - Watercraft, including their furnishings and equipment
   - Outboard motors
   - Trailers
   - Campers

Falling Objects.   Damage caused by a falling object to personal property contained within a building is covered only if the roof or an outside wall of the building is first damaged by that falling object. For instance, it would be possible for a tree to fall against the exterior wall of a masonry home with sufficient force to knock a mirror off an interior wall and onto the floor without actually damaging the exterior wall. In such a case, the damage to the mirror would not be covered. If the exterior wall were damaged, loss to the mirror would be covered subject, of course, to the policy deductible.

Weight of Ice, Snow, or Sleet.   Coverage is provided for personal property within a home damaged by the weight of ice, snow, or sleet. Therefore, if the weight of snow collapsed the roof of a home, the resulting damage to the contents of the home would be covered.

Accidental Discharge or Overflow of Water or Steam.   The policy covers loss resulting from accidental discharge or overflow of water or steam from within a plumbing, heating, air conditioning, or automatic fire protective sprinkler system or from a household appliance. For example, if an automatic dishwasher malfunctions and floods the kitchen, water damage to the kitchen furniture would be covered. Coverage is not provided for the damage to the system or appliance from which the water or steam escaped. Any loss or damage from freezing is covered under the terms of the freezing peril (subsequently described).

Any loss on the residence premises caused by accidental discharge or overflow that occurs off the residence premises is excluded. For instance, if an insured lived in a townhouse or row home and the next-door neighbor's dishwasher malfunctioned, causing water to leak into the insured's home and damage its contents, Coverage C of the insured's HO policy would not pay for the loss. The insured could, however, seek payment from the neighbor. If the neighbor had an HO policy, that policy would respond under Section II—Liability.

As it applies to this peril, the term "plumbing system" does not include a sump, a sump pump, or related equipment. Therefore, if discharge from a sump pump damaged property stored in the insured's basement, there would be no coverage for the damaged property.

Sudden and Accidental Tearing Apart, Cracking, Burning, or Bulging of a Steam, Hot Water, Air Conditioning, or Automatic Fire Protective Sprinkler System, or Appliance for Heating Water.   Coverage for this peril includes damage to the object or system and the ensuing damage to personal property, such as might occur when a water heater suddenly explodes. Loss from freezing is excluded.

Freezing of a Plumbing, Heating, Air Conditioning, or Automatic Fire Protective Sprinkler System, or of a Household Appliance. Freezing of such systems can result in burst pipes, releasing water or other liquids that damage personal property. Coverage applies unless the dwelling is unoccupied and the insured has not taken reasonable care to maintain heat in the building or to shut off the water supply and drain the system and appliances of water.

Sudden and Accidental Damage From Artificially Generated Electrical Current. Most damage of this type is caused by power surges, which are sudden increases in the current in an electrical system. Damage to a tube, transistor, or similar electronic component is excluded. If a power surge caused an electric clothes dryer to burn out, the loss would be covered.

Volcanic Eruption. Loss caused by a volcanic eruption is covered except for loss caused by earthquake, land shock waves, or tremors. Property damage caused by volcanic explosion, volcanic ash, lava flow, or airborne shock waves would be covered.

Coverage D—Loss of Use

In the event of a loss under Coverage A, such as fire damage to the dwelling, the insured may lose the use of the dwelling because it is uninhabitable while repairs are being made. The act of a civil authority, such as an evacuation ordered because of a nearby fire, may also cause the insured to temporarily lose the use of the dwelling. Coverage D provides compensation to the insured in the event of such loss of use. Compensation for loss of use is determined in one of two ways, depending on the circumstances of the loss.

One method of determining payment is the insured's *additional living expense,* which is the insured's *necessary increase* in living expenses required to maintain the household's normal standard of living. For example, if a family were forced to move out of its home for two weeks, the additional living expense would typically include the costs of items such as motel rooms, restaurant meals, and laundry service, less the cost of food normally prepared at home and any reduction in utility bills during the period of repairs.

The second method of determining payment for loss of use is *fair rental value,* which is the amount of rent that could reasonably be charged for the premises, less any expenses that do not continue while the premises are not fit for habitation.

Loss of Use Resulting From Coverage A Losses. Payment for this type of loss is made for the shortest time required to repair or replace the damage to the dwelling. If the insured chooses to permanently relocate rather than move back into the dwelling, payment is made for the shortest time required to relocate. The basis on which the insured is compensated depends on the use of the premises at the time of loss.

Insured's Principal Place of Residence. Loss payment is made on the basis of additional living expense or fair rental value at the option of the insured.

Not the Principal Residence of the Insured. Loss payment is made on the basis of additional living expense. The insured does not have the option of payment on the basis of fair rental value.

Part of the Insured's Residence Premises Rented to Others. When loss of use occurs to part of the residence premises rented to or held for rental to others, loss payment is made on the basis of fair rental value.

Loss of Use Resulting From Action of a Civil Authority. To be covered, loss of use must result when a civil authority prohibits the insured from using the residence premises because of a peril insured against under the policy. Loss payment is made for no more than two weeks on the basis of additional living expense or fair rental value, at the option of the insured.

Additional Coverages

The following additional coverages are included in the HO-3 to provide protection, subject to certain limitations, in the event of specific perils and types of losses:

- Debris removal
- Reasonable repairs
- Trees, shrubs, and other plants
- Fire department service charge
- Property removed
- Credit card, fund transfer card, forgery, and counterfeit money
- Loss assessment
- Collapse
- Glass or safety glazing material
- Landlord's furnishings

Debris Removal. Coverage is provided for the reasonable expense incurred for removal of debris of covered property if the loss was caused by a covered peril. An example of a covered expense is the cost of removing debris from a house following a fire. Coverage is also provided for the removal of ash, dust, or particles from a volcanic eruption that has caused direct loss to a building or to property contained in a building.

The cost of debris removal is included in the limit of liability that applies to the damaged property. In the event that the loss for actual damage to the property plus debris removal exceeds the policy limit, an additional 5 percent of the Coverage A limit of liability is available for debris removal expense.

The insurer will pay up to $500 to remove fallen trees *that damage a covered structure* on the residence premises. Payment will be made for (1) the insured's tree(s) felled by windstorm or hail, (2) the insured's tree(s) felled by weight of ice, snow, or sleet, or (3) a neighbor's tree(s) felled by a peril that is covered under Coverage C. The $500 amount is the most that will be paid in any one loss regardless of the number of fallen trees.

Reasonable Repairs.   Coverage is provided for the reasonable cost incurred by the insured, following a loss from a peril insured against, for necessary measures to protect covered property from further damage. For example, if part of the roof of the insured's house is blown off during a tornado, coverage for reasonable repairs would pay for the purchase of plywood, tarps, and other material to protect household goods from rain and weather damage until permanent repairs could be made. If the protective measures taken by the insured involve repair to other damaged property, payment will be made for those measures only if they involve covered property damaged by a covered cause of loss.

Payment for reasonable repairs does not increase the applicable limit of liability. In addition, this coverage does not relieve the insured of duties following a loss that are imposed by the conditions applicable to Section I.

Trees, Shrubs, and Other Plants.   Coverage is provided for trees, shrubs, plants, or lawns on the residence premises for loss caused by fire or lightning, explosion, riot or civil commotion, aircraft, vehicles not owned or operated by a resident of the residence premises, vandalism or malicious mischief, and theft. Notice that coverage is not provided for windstorm damage. If a strong wind blows down a tree, the only coverage that is provided under the HO-3 is for the removal of the tree under the additional coverage for debris removal, and then only if the tree damages a covered structure.

The limit for this coverage is 5 percent of the Coverage A limit of liability, but no more than $500 of this limit will be paid for any one tree, shrub, or plant. This is additional insurance and is not included within any of the other coverage limits. Trees, shrubs, and other plants grown for business purposes are not covered.

Fire Department Service Charge.   Up to $500 of coverage is provided for fire department service charges incurred when the fire department is called to save or protect covered property from an insured peril. These service charges may be assumed by contract or agreement. Coverage is not provided if the property is located within the limits of the city, municipality, or protection district furnishing the fire department response. This is additional insurance with no deductible.

Property Removed.   Covered property is insured against direct loss from any cause while being removed from a premises endangered by an insured peril. This coverage extends for no more than thirty days while the property is removed. The coverage does not change the limit of liability that applies to the property being removed.

Credit Card, Fund Transfer Card, Forgery, and Counterfeit Money. Up to $500 of coverage is provided for the following:

- The legal obligation of an insured to pay because of the theft or unauthorized use of credit cards issued to or registered in an insured's name
- Loss resulting from theft or unauthorized use of a fund transfer card used for deposit, withdrawal, or transfer of funds issued to or registered in an insured's name

- Loss to an insured caused by forgery or alteration of any check or negotiable instrument
- Loss to an insured through acceptance in good faith of counterfeit United States or Canadian paper currency

Coverage is not provided for use of a credit card or fund transfer card by a resident of the insured's household or by a person entrusted with either type of card. Coverage is similarly not provided if the insured has not complied with all the terms and conditions under which the cards are issued.

When the limit of liability is being determined, all loss resulting from a series of acts committed by any one person is considered to be one loss. This coverage is additional insurance. No deductible applies to this coverage.

Loss Assessment. Up to $1,000 of coverage is provided for loss assessments by a corporation or association of property owners charged against the insured as owner or tenant of the residence premises. This coverage is only provided when the assessment is made as a result of direct loss to the property owned collectively by all members and the loss is caused by a peril insured under Coverage A. Damage resulting from earthquake or land shock waves or tremors associated with a volcanic eruption is excluded. Also excluded are loss assessments charged against the insured, or a corporation or association of property owners, by any governmental body.

For instance, suppose four families with adjoining lakeside properties decide to construct a pier at which to dock their boats. To do this, they form an association to build and maintain the pier. Sometime later, the pier is struck by lightning and burns to the waterline. Repairs to the pier cost $6,000, and each property owner is assessed 25 percent of the cost ($1,500) to repair the pier. For any property owner who had insured his or her lakeside property under an HO-3, the insured's HO-3 policy would provide $1,000 toward this loss.

Collapse. Coverage is provided for direct physical loss to covered property involving collapse of a building or part of a building caused only by one of the following:

1. Perils insured against in Coverage C
2. Hidden decay
3. Hidden insect or vermin damage
4. Weight of contents, equipment, animals, or people
5. Weight of rain which collects on a roof
6. Collapse during construction, remodeling or renovation due to the use of defective materials or methods

Loss to nonbuilding structures, underground pipes and structures, retaining walls and piers, wharves, and docks is not covered under items 2 through 6 above unless the loss is a direct result of the collapse of a building. Collapse does not include settling, cracking, shrinking, bulging, or expansion.

This coverage does not increase the limit of liability that applies to the damaged covered property.

Glass or Safety Glazing Material. Coverage is provided for (1) breakage of glass or safety glazing material that is part of a covered building, storm door, or storm window and (2) damage to covered property that is *caused by* such glass or safety glazing material. However, there is no coverage for loss on the residence premises if the dwelling has been vacant for more than 30 consecutive days immediately before the loss occurs.

If an ordinance or law requires broken glass to be replaced with safety glazing materials, the loss will be settled on that basis. Coverage for glass and safety glazing material does not increase the applicable limit of liability.

Landlord's Furnishings. Up to $2,500 will be paid for loss to appliances, carpeting, and other household furnishings in an apartment on the residence premises that the insured regularly rents or holds for rental to others. Coverage applies to losses caused by the perils insured against in Coverage C (discussed earlier) except that there is no coverage for theft. The $2,500 limit is the most that will be paid regardless of the number of items of landlord's furnishings involved in a loss.

CONDITIONS

The conditions applicable to Section I of the HO-3 policy primarily deal with the rights and duties of the insured and the insurer following a property loss. With few exceptions, the conditions apply to all of the Section I property coverages. The Section I property coverages also are subject to the Sections I and II—Conditions, which are discussed in Chapter 3. These conditions deal with matters such as the policy period, cancellation and nonrenewal, assignment, subrogation, and other matters that apply to both the property and liability coverages of the policy. The Section I conditions are examined in the balance of this chapter.

Insurable Interest and Limit of Liability

This condition states the basic insurance principle that any insured's loss recovery is limited to the extent of that insured's insurable interest. Further, if more than one person has an insurable interest in the property covered, the company will not be liable for more than the applicable limit of liability. The following example illustrates this provision.

John Cabot and his sister Henrietta own a half share each in a hunting lodge in New Hampshire. John and Henrietta have both insured the lodge for $80,000, its total insurable value, under separate HO-3 policies from different insurers. If there is a total loss, the most either of the two insurers will pay to John or Henrietta is $40,000, their respective insurable interests in the lodge.

Duties After Loss

If there is a loss to covered property, the insured must make certain that the following duties are performed.

Prompt Notice.   Prompt notice must be given to the insurer or its agent. The police must be notified of a theft loss. The issuer of a credit card or fund transfer card must be notified of loss, theft, or unauthorized use of one of these cards. This helps prevent fraudulent losses and limits the amount of loss.

Protect the Property.   The insured must protect the property from further damage, make reasonable and necessary repairs to protect the property, and keep an accurate record of repair expenses. Payment for these expenses comes from the additional coverage for reasonable repairs.

Prepare an Inventory.   The insured must prepare an inventory of damaged personal property showing the quantity, description, actual cash value, and amount of loss. The insured should be able to justify the figures in the inventory with bills, receipts, and related documents.

Show the Damaged Property.   As often as the insurer reasonably requires, the insured must show the damaged property and provide records and documents. The insured also must submit to questions under oath while not in the presence of any other insured—again, as often as the insurer reasonably requires.

File a Proof of Loss.   Within sixty days of the insurer's request, the insured must submit a signed, sworn proof of loss. This must include, to the best of the insured's knowledge and belief, the time and cause of loss, the interest of the insured and all others in the property including all liens on the property, other insurance covering the loss, and other relevant information. This helps the company to determine insurable interest, to investigate the loss, and to coordinate payment with any other insurance.

Loss Settlement

The provisions in this condition explain how losses to covered property will be settled. Losses to personal property, awnings, carpeting, household appliances, outdoor antennas and outdoor equipment attached or not attached to buildings, and nonbuilding structures are all settled on an actual cash value basis. Nonbuilding structures are those not designed for human occupancy, such as fences, concrete patios, and swimming pools. An endorsement may be added to the policy that changes the settlement basis for personal property to replacement cost. This endorsement is discussed in Chapter 4.

Losses to the dwelling and other structures are paid on the basis of replacement cost with no deduction for depreciation. Insurance on a replacement cost basis is one of the most important features of the homeowners policy. Because most losses are partial, people may be tempted to underinsure. The greater the value of the property, however, the greater the exposure to the insurer. Therefore, the homeowners policy contains a provision that reduces the loss payment if the insured does not carry coverage equal to at least 80 percent of the replacement cost of the *damaged structure.* Note that the 80 percent figure applies not only to the dwelling, but also to other covered structures. For example, assume that an insured's residence premises includes a detached garage. The

Coverage B limit on that garage must be equal to at least 80 percent of the replacement cost of the garage for replacement cost coverage to apply to a loss to the garage.

Determining whether a loss under a homeowners policy will be settled on a replacement cost basis is a relatively straightforward process. First, the following insurance-to-value fraction is used to determine whether the insured has coverage equal to at least 80 percent of the replacement cost of the damaged structure.

$$\text{Insurance-to-value fraction:} \quad \frac{\text{Amount of insurance carried}}{80\% \times \text{Replacement cost}}$$

If the value of the fraction equals 1 or more, the amount of the insurance carried is equal to or greater than 80 percent of the replacement cost of the structure. Therefore, a covered loss would be paid on a replacement cost basis.

For example, assume that an insured carries a homeowners policy with a Coverage A limit of $100,000 on a dwelling that has a replacement cost of $110,000. Using these dollar amounts in the insurance-to-value fraction yields the following result:

$$\frac{\$100,000}{80\% \times \$110,000} = \frac{100}{88} \text{ or } 1.14$$

Because the value of the fraction is greater than 1, in the event of a covered loss to the dwelling, the insured would receive settlement on a replacement cost basis.

Continuing with this illustration, assume that the same insured's residence premises also includes a detached garage with a replacement cost of $20,000. Under the HO-3, the Coverage B limit is 10 percent of the Coverage A limit, unless the insured purchases additional limits. Therefore, the insured's policy with $100,000 of coverage on the dwelling also provides $10,000 of coverage on the detached garage. Given this information, the insurance-to-value fraction yields the following result with regard to coverage on the garage:

$$\frac{\$10,000}{80\% \times \$20,000} = \frac{10}{16} \text{ or } 0.625$$

Because the value of the fraction is less than 1, the amount of insurance carried on the garage does not meet the policy's insurance-to-value requirements. Therefore, if a covered loss occurred to the garage, payment would *not* be made on a replacement cost basis.

When the amount of coverage carried does not meet the insurance-to-value requirements, the policy will pay the *larger* of the following two amounts:

1. The insurance-to-value fraction, multiplied by the replacement cost of the loss
2. The actual cash value of the loss, typically meaning replacement cost less depreciation

For example, assume that the roof of the insured's $20,000 detached garage was damaged by a hurricane. The calculations above show that the loss will not be settled on a replacement cost basis. However, both the replacement cost and the actual cash value of the damage to the roof are needed to determine the amount the insured will receive. Assume that the replacement cost of the damage to the roof is $1,000. However, because the roof is ten years old, the actual cash value of the loss is $500. The amount the insured will receive depends on which amount is greater: (1) the insurance-to-value fraction, multiplied by the $1,000 replacement cost or (2) the $500 actual cash value. (For purposes of illustration, the effect of the policy deductible has been ignored.) Calculating the amount payable under the first option yields the following:

$$\frac{\text{Amount of insurance carried}}{80\% \ \times \ \text{Replacement cost}} \times \text{Replacement cost of loss}$$

$$\frac{\$10,000}{80\% \ \times \ \$20,000} \times \$1,000 \ = \ \$625$$

Because $625 is greater than $500, the insured will receive $625 in settlement of the loss. If, however, the actual cash value of the damage was $900 because the garage roof had recently been replaced, the insured would receive a $900 settlement. The insured always receives the *larger* of the two amounts.

The same procedure applies to determining the amount payable on any covered building loss under a homeowners policy. For instance, assume that another insured has a homeowners policy with a $60,000 Coverage A limit on a house that has a replacement cost of $100,000. In the event of a covered loss that has a replacement cost of $20,000 and an actual cash value of $12,000, the amount of the settlement would be determined using the same steps followed above. Settlement based on replacement cost would be calculated as follows:

$$\frac{\$60,000}{80\% \ \times \ \$100,000} \times \$20,000 \ = \ \$15,000$$

Because $15,000 is greater than $12,000, the insured would receive $15,000 in settlement of the loss. If the actual cash value of the loss had been greater than $15,000, payment would have been made on an actual cash value basis.

When loss settlement is made on the basis of replacement cost, the insurer will pay no more than the actual cash value of the damage to a covered building or structure until repair or replacement is actually completed. However, if the cost to repair or replace is less than 5 percent of the amount of insurance on the building *and* less than $2,500, settlement will be made according to the replacement cost provisions regardless of whether repair or replacement is complete.

The insured may choose to have loss or damage to buildings paid on an actual cash value basis. However, if the insured changes his or her mind within 180 days after the loss, a claim may be made for any additional amount payable for replacement cost settlement.

Loss to a Pair or Set

This condition applies when there is a loss to one item in a pair or to part of a set of items. The loss of one item does not result in a total loss of the value of the pair or set. Therefore, the insurer may elect to (1) repair or replace any part to restore the pair or set to its value before the loss or (2) pay the difference between the actual cash value of the property before and after the loss.

Glass Replacement

This condition is an exception to the exclusion for loss caused by enforcement of ordinances or laws. For safety purposes, many communities require that broken glass in storm doors or windows be replaced by safety glazing material such as tempered glass or plastics. Use of such materials can prevent injury that occurs when ordinary glass shatters. To encourage safety, the insurer agrees that if a glass door (or other glass subject to such a law) must be replaced following a covered loss, the insurer will pay the additional cost to meet the requirements.

Appraisal

The *appraisal* provision outlines the procedure for settling disputes between the insurer and the insured if they cannot agree about the *amount* of the loss. The insurer and the insured each select a competent appraiser within twenty days of receiving a written request from the other. These appraisers then select an umpire. The two appraisers review the items in question and set an amount of loss for each item. If the appraisers do not agree on the value of an item, the umpire is asked for an opinion. Agreement of two of the three persons will set a value for the amount of the loss. The final document setting the value of the contested items is called an *appraisal award*. If an appraisal is necessary, each party pays the expenses of its own appraiser and shares equally the other expenses of the appraisal and the expenses of the umpire. The advantage of a condition setting forth a procedure within the insurance contract for determining the amount of the loss is to save legal expense in resolving differences of opinion on loss values.

Other Insurance

If a loss covered by a homeowners policy is also covered by another insurance policy, the homeowners policy will contribute to the loss settlement on a *pro rata* basis. Under pro rata loss sharing, each policy's share of the loss is determined by comparing the amount of the policy's coverage limits (for the type of coverage that applies to the loss) with the sum of the coverage limits of all of the policies that provide coverage. For purposes of illustration, assume that a loss qualifies for payment under Coverage C of two homeowners policies. The calculation of each insurer's pro rata share of the loss is a two-step process. First, the Coverage C limits of the two policies would be added to find the sum of the Coverage C limits. Second, the Coverage C limit of each policy would be divided by the sum of the Coverage C limits. The result of this calculation, for each policy, is the percentage of the loss that policy will pay.

For example, assume that a loss is covered under policies A and B with coverage limits of $10,000 and $40,000, respectively. If the amount of the loss settlement is $5,000, the pro rata share of each insurer would be calculated as follows:

$$\text{Sum of coverage limits} = \$10,000 + \$40,000 = \$50,000$$

$$\text{Insurer A's pro rata share} = \frac{\$10,000}{\$50,000} \times \$5,000 = \$1,000$$

$$\text{Insurer B's pro rata share} = \frac{\$40,000}{\$50,000} \times \$5,000 = \$4,000$$

Suit Against the Insurer

This condition sets a time of one year, or longer in some states, during which the insured may take legal action to settle a dispute with the insurer. It also requires the insured to comply with all other policy provisions before a legal action may be brought against the insurer. For instance, if an insured disputes the *amount* of a loss settlement offered by the insurer, the insured must follow the policy's appraisal provision before filing suit against the insurer. This requirement also applies to the other conditions and provisions of the policy, such as filing a proof of loss or preparing an inventory.

Additional Loss Settlement Conditions

Insurer's Option. This condition gives the insurer the right, after providing written notice to the insured, to repair or replace any part of the damaged property with like property. Thus, if John's stereo system, television, and VCR are stolen, the insurer may, by giving written notice, replace any of these items with comparable pieces of equipment rather than exact duplicates. Insurers are often able to purchase such items from replacement services at a cost lower than the insured would have to pay in the retail market. The result is that the insured is indemnified, and the insurer has met its contractual obligation, while reducing loss settlement costs.

Loss Payment. This condition indicates who will be paid and when payment will be made. It is, with regard to the Section I coverages, the insurer's promise. It states that payment will be made to the named insured unless the policy provides otherwise or unless someone else is legally entitled to receive payment, for instance, the "legal representative" of the insured following the insured's death. The loss settlement provisions are reinforced by the requirement that a proof of loss be filed by the insured. After the insured files the proof of loss, the insurer will pay within sixty days after reaching an agreement with the insured, receiving a final judgment (in a legal action), or following the filing of an appraisal award. In most cases, settlement is made well within the time specified.

Abandonment of Property. This condition prohibits the insured from claiming that property damaged in a covered loss is automatically owned by, and the responsibility of, the insurer. The insurer has the option of paying for a damaged item in full and then taking the item as salvage. Alternatively, the insurer may pay to have the item repaired. This condition makes clear that the decision is the insurer's and not the insured's.

Mortgage Clause. Most insured dwellings are purchased with a mortgage. In such cases, the name and address of the mortgagee (the lender) are shown on the policy declarations page. The mortgage clause provides that any loss payable under Coverage A or B will be paid to the insured and the mortgagee as their interests appear. In practice, insurers often draw a settlement check payable to both the insured and the mortgagee, and the proceeds of the check are used to pay for repairs necessitated by the loss. However, the mortgagee does have the right to demand a separate settlement to the extent of its interest in the damaged property.

The mortgagee also gains additional rights under the mortgage clause. First, the insurer promises to give the mortgagee ten days' notice of cancellation or nonrenewal of the policy. Second, in the event of an otherwise covered claim for which payment is denied to the insured—for instance, because the insured violated a policy provision—the insurer agrees to make payment to the mortgagee in spite of its denial to the insured. For example, if the insured intentionally sets fire to the dwelling, the mortgagee would be paid for the loss to the extent of its financial interest, up to the policy limits, even though the insured would receive no payment under the policy for an intentional loss. In consideration for this guarantee of payment, the mortgagee is required to do the following:

1. Notify the insurer of any change with respect to the insured property of which it is aware and that could affect the quality of the exposure
2. Pay any premium not paid by the insured if the insurer so requests
3. Follow the loss settlement provisions of the policy that otherwise would apply to the insured

No Benefit to Bailee. When an insured delivers property to a bailee, the bailee's receipt may state that if the insured has valid insurance on the property and there is a loss, the bailee need not pay the insured. The no benefit to bailee condition states that coverage under the homeowners policy is not intended to pay on behalf of or otherwise benefit a bailee who damages an insured's property. It gives the insurer the right to make a payment to the insured and then pursue a claim against the bailee.

Nuclear Hazard Clause. This clause explains the nuclear hazard exclusion applicable to Section I that was mentioned earlier in this chapter. "Nuclear hazard" is defined by this clause as follows:

> . . .any nuclear reaction, radiation, or radioactive contamination, all whether controlled or uncontrolled or however caused, or any consequence of any of these.

According to this clause, any loss caused by the nuclear hazard will not be considered loss caused by fire, explosion, or smoke. However, if direct loss by fire *results* from the nuclear hazard, that loss is covered.

Recovered Property. If either the insurer or the insured recovers stolen property for which a loss payment has already been made, that party is required to notify the other of the recovery. The insured then has the option of accepting the recovered property and returning the loss payment to the insurer or giving the property to the insurer and keeping the loss payment.

Volcanic Eruption Period. This condition states that all damage done by volcanic eruption within seventy-two hours is considered to have occurred as the result of a single eruption. Volcanoes often have multiple eruptions within a short period. Without this clause, the policy's full limits of liability would be available to cover each eruption as a separate loss.

SUMMARY

The insuring agreement in the HO-3 states that the insurer will provide the insurance described in the policy in return for the premium and the insured's compliance with all applicable provisions of the policy.

Definitions for the Section I coverages discussed in this chapter include "you" and "your," which refer to the named insured shown in the declarations and the spouse if a resident of the same household. "We," "us," and "our" refer to the insurer. "Residence premises" means the one-family dwelling, other structures, and grounds, or that part of any other building in which the insured resides, as shown in the declarations.

Coverage A of the HO-3 insures the dwelling and attached structures. It does not apply to land. Coverage B applies to other structures on the residence premises, such as a detached garage or shed. Coverages A and B are written on a risks of direct physical loss basis. Coverage C provides coverage for personal property not otherwise scheduled or insured. Limited coverage also applies to property usually located at a second residence. Coverage C provides protection against sixteen specified perils.

For people who own their homes and suffer a covered loss, Coverage D offers the choice between (1) additional living expense, that is, payment of additional expenses incurred to live elsewhere following a loss that makes the home uninhabitable, *or* (2) a payment of the fair rental value of that part of the premises where the insured resides, less noncontinuing expenses.

Additional coverages, subject to certain limitations, are for debris removal; reasonable repairs; trees, shrubs, and other plants; fire department service charge; property removed; credit card, fund transfer card, forgery, and counterfeit money; loss assessment; collapse; glass or safety glazing material; and landlord's furnishings.

Certain exclusions apply only to Coverages A and B. Most of the exclusions listed in Section I—Exclusions apply to all Section I coverages. Those exclusions deal with losses resulting from ordinance or law, earth movement, water damage, off-premises power failure, neglect, war, nuclear hazard, and intentional loss.

Section I concludes with the conditions that apply to the property coverages in the homeowners policy. These conditions spell out the insurer's limit of liability, the insured's duties after a property loss, and other provisions related to property loss settlements.

CHAPTER 3

Homeowners Insurance, Continued

Chapter 3 begins with a discussion of insurance for tenants and for owners of condominium units and cooperative apartments. The emphasis is on the HO 00 04 Contents Broad Form (HO-4) and the HO 00 06 Unit-Owners Form (HO-6). The property coverage provided by each of these policies is compared with the property coverage in the HO-3. The bulk of this chapter is devoted to Section II—Liability Coverages, which is the same in all of the homeowners policies. The discussion includes the liability coverages provided under Section II, as well as the exclusions, additional coverages, and conditions applicable to Section II. The chapter concludes with a discussion of the common policy conditions that apply to both Section I and Section II.

INSURANCE FOR TENANTS

Insurance for tenants represents an important market. The number of apartment dwellers is already large and is increasing because of a number of reasons. The high price of single-family homes has forced many younger people to postpone home ownership and to continue to rent apartments. In addition, there are older people who move to apartments from large single-family homes and workers of all ages who rent apartments in urban areas to avoid commuting.

Exposures

The three major types of loss exposures faced by tenants are loss to additions and alterations, loss to personal property, and legal liability.

Additions and Alterations. Property exposures for tenants include additions and alterations the tenants may have made in the dwelling itself. These additions and alterations may include new paneling or electrical fixtures that become part of the building and as such are real property. Such additions and alterations are sometimes referred to as "tenant's improvements and betterments."

Personal Property. Personal property owned by the tenant represents the most significant property exposure. Personal property includes such items as furniture, bedding, clothing, TVs, videocassette recorders, stereos, and record and tape collections. Such items often are referred to as "contents."

Legal Liability. Tenants have a premises liability exposure for people who enter their home. For instance, a guest may be injured after tripping over a loose carpet in an apartment and may seek damages on the basis of negligence liability. Apartment dwellers also have a liability exposure for injuries to other tenants and damage to property of other tenants or the owner of the apartment building. If an apartment dweller allows a bathtub to overflow, for instance, the water may damage the contents of apartments below and the apartment building itself, resulting in liability actions against the forgetful tenant. Finally, tenants face liability exposures that arise out of their off-premises activities, such as golf or hunting.

Tenants' Exposures

Many people who rent furnished apartments forgo the purchase of tenants insurance because they think they do not have a sufficient amount of personal property at risk to justify the expenditure. This perception is often altered when they are asked to make an inventory, including values, of their clothing, books, stereos, TVs, records, and tapes. Since much personal property is acquired piecemeal, most people do not realize the total value of their possessions. A couple living in a small furnished apartment may easily have more than $10,000 in clothing, stereos, books, and records.

Regardless of the amount of personal property involved, all apartment dwellers have liability exposures. The HO-4 policy can be used to cover these property and liability exposures.

HO-4 Contents Broad Form

The HO-4 policy is a combination of property and liability coverages designed for apartment renters and other tenants. Discussed below are HO-4 eligibility, a comparison of the HO-4 Section I to the HO-3 Section I, and HO-4 endorsements.

Eligibility. A tenant of either a single-family residence or an apartment is eligible for the HO-4. There is no limit on the number of units in the apartment building, although the number of units affects the rate.

The owner-occupant of a dwelling, cooperative unit, or apartment building that is not otherwise eligible for one of the other homeowners policies also may purchase an HO-4. For example, a person might own a five-unit apartment building, residing in one of the units and renting the other four. Such an occupancy would not be eligible for an HO-3, but the owner-occupant could purchase an HO-4 for his or her unit. Commercial coverages would be purchased to provide coverage for the property and liability exposures represented by the apartment building itself.

Comparison of Section I of the HO-4 and HO-3.   Since the HO-4 provides insurance for tenants, the policy does not include coverage for the dwelling and other structures provided by Coverages A and B of the HO-3. Such coverage is not needed in the HO-4 because the tenant does not have an insurable interest in the building.

The limit of liability for Coverage C—Personal Property in the HO-4 is the primary limit for property coverage. In the HO-3, the limit of liability for Coverage A determines the limits for the other property coverages. There is no other difference in Coverage C between the two policies.

Under the HO-4, the limit of liability for Coverage D—Loss of Use is 20 percent of the Coverage C limit, and coverage applies if a peril insured under Coverage C makes the residence uninhabitable. Under the HO-3, the limit of liability for Coverage D is 20 percent of the limit for Coverage A and applies to loss of use resulting from a peril covered by Coverage A. In all other respects, Coverage D is the same under both policies.

There are three differences in the additional coverages provided by the two policies. First, the limit in the HO-4 for trees, shrubs, and other plants is 10 percent of the Coverage C limit. The limit for such property in the HO-3 is 5 percent of the Coverage A limit.

Second, both policies will pay up to $1,000 for the insured's share of a loss assessment, but the HO-4 pays for loss assessment that results from a peril insured against under Coverage C, and the HO-3 pays if the loss assessment results from an insured peril under Coverage A. (Neither policy pays if the loss assessment results from earthquake or volcanic eruption.) Since Coverage A of the HO-3 insures against risks of direct loss that are not otherwise excluded, the coverage for loss assessment under the HO-3 is broader than that provided by the HO-4.

Third, the HO-4 covers building additions and alterations. Coverage is provided for building improvements or installations, made or acquired at the insured's expense, to that part of the residence premises used exclusively by the named insured. This coverage represents additional insurance and has a limit of liability equal to 10 percent of the Coverage C limit. There is no corresponding coverage in the HO-3, but the coverage for landlord's furnishings in the HO-3 is not provided by the HO-4.

Because the HO-4 does not cover the dwelling and other structures, the perils insured against, exclusions, and conditions are different in the two policies. The insured perils in the HO-4 apply only to Coverage C, but they are the same perils insured under Coverage C of the HO-3. The corresponding section in the HO-3 also lists the perils that are excluded with regard to Coverages A and B.

The HO-4 does not contain the concurrent causation exclusions that are in the HO-3. (These exclusions are discussed in Chapter 2.)

The loss settlement condition in the HO-4 states only that losses are settled on the basis of actual cash value at the time of loss, but the settlement cannot be more than the amount to repair or replace the property. The loss settlement condition in the HO-3 is much more complex because of the replacement cost coverage on the dwelling and other structures. The HO-4 also does not contain the mortgage clause included in the Section I conditions of the HO-3.

HO-4 Endorsements. Most of the endorsements discussed in Chapter 4 can be used with the HO-4. However, the two endorsements discussed below apply specifically to the loss exposures of tenants.

Building Additions and Alterations (HO 04 51). As an additional coverage, the HO-4 insures building additions and alterations that a tenant has installed. The limit of liability is 10 percent of the Coverage C limit, but a person who has made substantial alterations to a rented unit is likely to require a higher limit. The HO 04 51 endorsement increases the limit of liability for the insured's building additions and alterations, for an additional premium. To avoid ambiguity, the endorsement shows both the increase in the limit of liability and the total limit of liability.

Waterbed Liability. Many landlords require proof of liability insurance before completion of lease arrangements for a tenant with a waterbed. A number of insurers have filed waterbed liability endorsements for use with the HO-4 to meet this need. For an additional premium, the endorsement provides coverage for liability arising out of an insured's ownership or use of a waterbed on the residence premises.

INSURANCE FOR UNIT OWNERS

Many home owners do not reside in one- or two-family dwellings. A special form of homeowners insurance is available for owners of condominium units and cooperative apartments.

Condominiums and Cooperative Apartments

Condominium ownership has two distinguishing characteristics. First, each unit owner has individual ownership and the right to exclusive occupancy of his or her unit. The *unit* is commonly defined as the space between the walls, ceiling, and floor. This is called the "bare walls" definition of exclusive ownership. Sometimes the unit owner is also responsible for parts of the unit beyond the bare walls such as exterior glass or a lean-to porch. The unit owner's responsibilities are usually outlined in the condominium agreement and bylaws. As defined in the condominium agreement, the unit is an area of space. The unit owner may occupy, sell, lease, or will that space.

Second, each unit owner also has an undivided interest (with the other members of the condominium association) in the common areas of the property.

Common areas include the land, stairways, halls, parking and storage areas, and the heating and cooling system. Usually the condominium complex is managed by an association of unit owners.[1]

The owner of a cooperative apartment does not own the individual unit as is the case with a condominium. Instead, the owner has an ownership interest in the cooperative association or corporation that owns all of the units. As a consequence of that ownership, the cooperative apartment owner has a right to a perpetual lease to occupy a specific unit.[2]

Particularly in urban areas, both condominiums and cooperative apartments have become increasingly popular. Both young couples and older people prefer ownership of such units because of their convenient urban locations and because the owners do not have to perform their own maintenance.

Exposures

The three major loss exposures for unit owners are loss to real property, loss to personal property, and legal liability.

Real Property. Real property exposures for the unit owner include alterations, appliances, and fixtures and improvements that are part of the residence premises. The residence premises consists of that part of the complex occupied exclusively by the unit owner. This would include any patio, yard, or parking area adjacent to the unit owner's portion of the building occupied exclusively by the unit owner.

The real property exposure also includes the common areas of the property. This exposure is usually insured in a separate policy by the condominium or cooperative association.

Personal Property. The personal property exposures of the unit owner are similar to those of a tenant. The unit owner's personal property may include furniture, clothing, television and stereo equipment, books, records, compact discs, and tapes. Any appliances not considered part of the building structure would also constitute personal property. Carpets and rugs that are placed over finished flooring would be considered personal property, while wall-to-wall carpeting installed over a rough subfloor or concrete slab is generally considered part of the building.

Legal Liability. The liability exposures for the unit owner include all of those previously discussed for tenants. In addition, the unit owner's interest in the common areas carries with it a corresponding liability exposure for events that occur in or on those areas. This "common areas" liability exposure usually is covered in a separate policy obtained by the condominium association or the cooperative apartment ownership association or corporation. A loss assessment may also be collected from all unit owners to pay the damages.

HO-6 Unit-Owners Form

The HO-6 is designed to meet the unique insurance requirements of owners of condominium units and cooperative apartments. The property coverages provided are for the insured's dwelling, as well as for personal property and loss of use.

Eligibility for the HO-6. An owner-occupant of a residential condominium unit or a cooperative apartment is eligible for an HO-6 regardless of the number of units in the complex. Since the residence premises is defined as the unit where the insured resides, the unendorsed HO-6 cannot be used to insure a unit owned by the insured but rented or leased to others.

Comparison of Section I of the HO-6 and HO-3. The following paragraphs describe the differences in the property coverage provided by the HO-6 and the HO-3. The primary difference is the coverage provided for the insured's dwelling.

Coverage A—Dwelling. Coverage A of the HO-6 applies to the insured's real property. This coverage is provided on a named-perils basis and is separated into four categories. The first category includes the alterations, appliances, fixtures, and improvements that are part of the building contained within the residence premises. This usually includes built-in appliances and cabinets, electrical fixtures, interior partitions, and the like.

The second category relates to items of real property that pertain exclusively to the residence premises, including such items as exterior glass or trees and shrubs located in a patio that is part of the residence premises. In addition, although it is excess over the association's coverage, the coverage provided would apply to any part of the unit owner's portion of the building itself in the event that the association's limits proved to be inadequate.

The third category includes property that is the insurance responsibility of the unit owner under an agreement of a corporation or association of property owners. Insurance for this category of property provides coverage for any portion of the common areas of the building that the association agreement made the insurance responsibility of the unit owner.

The final category of property relates to structures owned solely by the insured at the location of the residence premises but that are not a part of the residence premises. An example would be a private garage that was not adjacent to the residence premises but located elsewhere in the condominium complex.

An additional difference between Coverage A of the HO-6 and the corresponding coverage in the HO-3 is that the HO-6 provides no coverage for building materials and supplies.

Coverage A of the HO-6 does not cover structures used in whole or in part for business or structures rented to others unless used solely as a private garage. A similar exclusion is found under Coverage B of the HO-3. This illustrates the fact that Coverage A of the HO-6 combines Coverages A and B of the HO-3. The HO-6 does not include a Coverage B.

The basic limit of liability under Coverage A of the HO-6 is $1,000. This can be increased if necessary. If the association policy is written on a "bare walls" basis, then Coverage A of the HO-6 would have to provide coverage for the entire interior of the unit, including all fixtures, built-in appliances and, in a multistory unit, the floors, stairs, and ceilings between the lowest floor and the highest ceiling in the unit. This is why it is important to review the condominium or cooperative association's coverage to determine if the basic limit for Coverage A of the HO-6 is adequate.

Coverage C—Personal Property. Coverage C provides the same coverage as the corresponding section of the HO-3. The difference is that the usual amount of Coverage C of the HO-3 is based upon the limit of liability for Coverage A, but in the HO-6 the insured selects the limit of liability for Coverage C.

Coverage D—Loss of Use. The limit of liability for Coverage D in the HO-6 is 40 percent of the Coverage C limit. Coverage is provided if a loss caused by an insured peril to covered property or to the building containing the property makes the residence premises not fit to live in.

Additional Coverages. The additional coverages in the HO-6 differ from those in the HO-3 in two ways. In the HO-6, the coverage for trees, shrubs, and other plants is 10 percent of the limit of liability for Coverage C. In the HO-3, the corresponding limit of liability is 5 percent of the Coverage A limit. In addition, the HO-6 does not include the coverage for landlord's furnishings provided by the HO-3.

Perils Insured Against. The covered perils in the HO-6 are virtually identical to the perils insured against under Coverage C of the HO-3. Therefore, the HO-6 covers loss to the insured's dwelling only if the loss is caused by the specified perils. Under the HO-3 the insured's dwelling is covered for risks of direct loss that are not otherwise excluded.

Exclusions. Because the HO-6 is written on a named-perils basis, the Section I exclusions do not contain the concurrent causation exclusions of the HO-3. In all other respects, the Section I exclusions of the two policies are virtually identical.

Conditions. The only difference between the HO-3 and HO-6 with respect to the Section I conditions is found in the loss settlement paragraphs. In the HO-6, real property under Coverage A is covered at the actual cost to repair or replace if the damage is repaired or replaced within a reasonable time. In the HO-3, replacement cost coverage is provided for buildings insured under Coverages A and B, subject to an 80 percent insurance to value requirement.

HO-6 Endorsements. Just as certain endorsements relate specifically to the exposures of tenants insured by the HO-4, there are endorsements to the HO-6 that further tailor the policy to meet the needs of unit owners. Five of these endorsements are discussed below.

Unit-Owners Coverage A Special Coverages (HO 17 32). This endorsement can be used to change Coverage A of the HO-6 to provide coverage for risks of direct loss. When this endorsement is used, the perils insured under Coverage A of the HO-6 become identical to those insured by the HO-3.

The HO 17 32 endorsement also adds the concurrent causation exclusions that are otherwise omitted under the HO-6. This reflects the fact that concurrent causation is a problem only when policies provide coverage for risks of direct loss.

Unit-Owners Rental to Others (HO 17 33). This endorsement provides property and liability coverage for the unit owner while the residence premises is regularly rented or held for rental to others. Theft coverage is provided for personal property at a rented condominium, but high-value items such as money, securities, jewelry, watches, and furs are excluded. The HO 17 33 endorsement also provides liability and medical payments coverage on behalf of the unit owner from occurrences at or arising from the residence premises when rented or held for rental to others.

Loss Assessment Coverage (HO 04 35). For an additional premium, the HO 04 35 endorsement increases the limit of liability for the additional coverages for loss assessment provided in Section I and Section II. For a further additional premium, the insured's share of covered loss assessment at additional locations can be covered. These additional locations must be listed on the face of the endorsement. Coverage for an assessment that results from a deductible in the insurance purchased by a corporation or association of property owners is limited to $1,000.

A review of the unit owner's deed, the condominium declarations (also known as the master deed), and the condominium association bylaws will define the common areas. It is for damage to these areas that the unit owner will be assessed in the event of a covered loss. By determining the current coverage carried by the association, the value of these areas, the possibility of damage to more than one of these areas in one loss, and the number of unit owners who will be assessed, the individual unit owner can determine if his or her exposure is greater than the $1,000 provided by the unendorsed HO-6. If the exposure is greater than $1,000, the HO 04 35 endorsement should be considered.

Loss Assessment Coverage for Earthquake (HO 04 36). This endorsement provides coverage for a loss assessment made against the unit owner by a corporation or association of property owners due to the peril of earthquake. Loss assessments charged against the unit owner or a corporation or association of property owners by any governmental body are not covered. Flood and tidal wave are also excluded. This coverage is subject to a percentage deductible based upon the limit of liability for the unit; the percentage is stated in the endorsement. The deductible amount will not be less than $250 in any one assessment.

Unit-Owners Coverage C, Special Coverage (HO 17 31). This endorsement changes the HO-6 to provide coverage for risks of direct loss to property insured under Coverage C, that is, the insured's personal property. The typical exclusions that apply to this type of coverage are listed in the endorsement (the exclusions are similar to those for Coverage A of the HO-3). Coverage is provided under the HO 17 31 endorsement with the understanding that the insured occupies the unit in which the covered property is located.

SECTION II—LIABILITY COVERAGES

Homeowners policies meet both the property and liability exposures of a wide range of insureds. The Section I coverages discussed up to this point provide protection against direct losses to property and the loss of use of that property. The next part of this chapter is devoted to Section II of the homeowners policy, which provides liability coverage for personal loss exposures. Section II is uniform among all of the homeowners policies.

Types of Losses Covered

Section II of the homeowners policies covers bodily injury and property damage for which the insured is legally liable. Coverage is also provided for medical expenses incurred because of bodily injury to others.

Coverage E—Personal Liability. Coverage E provides liability coverage if a claim is made or suit is brought against an insured because of bodily injury or property damage caused by a covered occurrence. Coverage E provides a basic limit of liability of $100,000 for damages, which may be increased for an additional premium. Damages include prejudgment interest awarded against the insured. Costs of investigating claims and defending against lawsuits are not included in the liability limits but are paid in addition to any payments made for damages.

The coverage statement for Coverage E incorporates many of the terms set forth in the definitions section of the policy. The term *bodily injury* means bodily harm, sickness, or disease including required care, loss of services, and death that may result. The term *property damage* is defined as physical injury to, destruction of, or loss of use of tangible property. This coverage is on an occurrence basis. *Occurrence* means an accident, including continuous or repeated exposure to substantially the same general harmful conditions, which results in bodily injury or property damage during the policy period.

Coverage E provides liability protection for the named insured and members of the named insured's household who are relatives. Other persons under the age of twenty-one who are in the care of a household member are also covered. With respect to animals or watercraft to which the policy applies, coverage is extended to any person or organization legally responsible for animals or watercraft that are owned by any household member. Similarly, with respect to any vehicle to which the policy applies, coverage is provided for any person employed by the named insured or a family member and to other persons using the vehicle on a covered location with the insured's consent.

An important part of Coverage E is premises liability coverage. The policy defines an insured location to include not only the residence premises, but other premises used by the insured as a residence, permanently or temporarily. The definition of an insured location also includes vacant land owned by the insured, cemetery plots, and any part of a premises occasionally rented to an insured for other than business purposes.

One example of an occurrence that might give rise to a premises liability claim would be a neighbor's child who ran into a closed sliding glass door at the insured's home and was injured. Other occurrences that might result in a premises liability claim could include a neighbor's child drowning in the insured's swimming pool or a passer-by being bitten by the insured's "friendly" dog.

In addition to the premises liability coverage, Coverage E provides liability protection for off-premises, nonbusiness activities of the insured. Off-premises occurrences include sport and hobby accidents. For example, while playing baseball with friends, the insured may injure another player by throwing the bat in the excitement of getting a hit.

Coverage E also provides defense for liability suits even if the suit is groundless, false, or fraudulent. The duty to defend on the part of the insurance company is broader than the duty to indemnify.[3] Therefore, if there is doubt about coverage, the insurer often will defend the case but reserve its right to withdraw from the defense if it determines that the occurrence is not covered.

The insurer may investigate and settle any claim or suit that it decides is appropriate without the permission of the insured. The insurer's duty to defend ends when the amount paid for damages resulting from the occurrence equals the limit of liability.

Coverage F—Medical Payments to Others. Coverage F will pay the necessary medical expenses that are incurred or medically ascertained within three years from the date of an accident causing bodily injury. Coverage applies to accidents that occur on the insured premises or as the result of an action by the insured at any location. The basic limit is $1,000 per person under Coverage F, but the insured may select a higher limit. By prompt payment of physicians' and hospital bills for an accident for which the insured might be responsible, troublesome litigation often can be avoided.

Coverage F is not intended to provide accident insurance for the named insured's family. Therefore, any insured under the policy is excluded from coverage.

Exclusions to Coverages E and F

The liability coverages in Section II provide broad protection for the insured. However, the exclusions in Section II limit or eliminate coverage for specified types of occurrences. Some of the exclusions apply to both Coverages E and F. Others apply only to Coverage E or Coverage F. The following exclusions are applicable to Coverages E and F:

- Expected or intended injury or damage
- Insured's business
- Premises rented or held for rental
- Professional services
- Noninsured locations
- Motor vehicles
- Watercraft
- Aircraft
- War
- Communicable disease
- Abuse or sexual molestation
- Controlled substances
- Home day care (excluded by endorsement in most states)

These exclusions are described in the following paragraphs. The exclusions relating to noninsured locations, motor vehicles, watercraft, and aircraft do not apply to bodily injury to a residence employee if the injury arises out of and in the course of employment by an insured.

Expected or Intended Injury or Damage. Bodily injury or property damage that is expected or intended by the insured is excluded. An example would be an insured breaking a window in a neighbor's house following an argument.

Insured's Business. Bodily injury or property damage arising out of or in connection with a business engaged in by an insured is excluded. The home-owners policy is intended to provide only personal liability coverage. Business activities must be covered under an appropriate commercial lines policy.

Premises Rented or Held for Rental. There is no coverage for liability arising out of the rental or holding for rental of any part of any premises by an insured. However, this exclusion does not apply to rental of an *insured* location:

1. On an occasional basis if used only as a residence
2. In part for use only as a residence unless more than two roomers or boarders are lodged in a single family unit
3. In part as an office, school, studio, or private garage

Professional Services. Liability arising out of the rendering of or failure to render professional services is excluded. Professional services would include, for example, the services of an insurance agent, physician, nurse, engineer, or architect.

Noninsured Locations. An insured location is defined in the definitions section as noted above. The policy excludes coverage for liability arising out of any premises owned, rented, or rented to others by an insured that is not an insured location as defined in the policy. Premises other than the residence premises that the insured uses as a residence must be shown in the declarations or acquired during the policy period in order to be considered an insured location. Therefore, it is important for the insured to list all owned and rented locations in the policy declarations.

Motor Vehicles. With a few exceptions, homeowners policies exclude coverage for liability arising out of an insured's use of a motor vehicle or motorized land conveyance, including trailers. The policy does not define "motor vehicle," but in most states the term is defined by law for motor vehicle registration purposes. Therefore, if a vehicle is subject to motor vehicle registration, it is considered to be a motor vehicle. Notice, however, that the exclusion is broader than motor vehicles and applies to any motorized land conveyance.

With regard to the vehicles described above, HO policies provide no coverage for liability arising out of their ownership, maintenance, use, loading or un-loading, or entrustment to another person. Also excluded is vicarious liability, whether or not statutorily imposed, for the actions of a child or minor with regard to such a vehicle. This exclusion applies to any vehicle an insured owns, operates, rents, or borrows. Liability arising out of the use or ownership of motor vehicles and motorized land conveyances is covered under the following circumstances:

1. A trailer while it is not being towed by or carried on a motorized land conveyance.
2. A motorized land conveyance designed for recreational use off public roads, not subject to motor vehicle registration, which is not owned by an insured. An example would be an unregistered snowmobile rented by an insured. Liability arising out of the use of a similar vehicle *owned* by an insured is only covered while on an insured location.
3. A motorized golf cart when used to play golf on a golf course.
4. A vehicle or conveyance not subject to motor vehicle registration that is used to service an insured's residence, designed for assisting the handicapped, or in dead storage on an insured location. An example of a covered vehicle for each category, respectively, would be a garden tractor, a motorized wheelchair, and an unlicensed antique car that the insured was rebuilding as a hobby. If the antique car was put into operation after it was rebuilt, however, homeowners liability coverage would be excluded.

This limited coverage applies to the named insured, resident relatives, and employees of the insured both on and off the insured's premises. Coverage for others using one of the above vehicles with the insured's permission applies only on the insured's premises.

Watercraft. The policy excludes certain defined watercraft. The exclusion applies to the ownership, maintenance, use, loading, or unloading of these watercraft. Similarly, the entrustment by an insured of such a watercraft to any person is excluded. The exclusion extends to vicarious liability, whether or not imposed by statute, for the actions of a child or minor using such watercraft. The watercraft exclusions do not apply while the watercraft is stored.

Excluded watercraft are boats that are designed to be propelled principally by engine power or electric motor, or sailing vessels, and that are owned by or rented to an insured. Therefore, the following types of watercraft are among those excluded:

1. Inboard or inboard-outdrive power boats owned by an insured
2. Boats with inboard or inboard-outdrive motor power of more than 50 horsepower that are rented to an insured
3. Boats powered by one or more outboard engines or motors of more than 25 total horsepower, provided the engines or motors are owned by an insured
4. Sailing vessels with or without auxiliary power that are 26 feet or more in length and are owned by or rented to an insured

With regard to the third type of watercraft listed above, there *is* liability coverage for newly acquired outboard engines or motors, provided they are reported to the insurer within the time frame required by the policy. There is also coverage if the insured acquires the outboard engines or motors during the policy period.

Aircraft. The ownership, maintenance, use, loading, and unloading of an aircraft is excluded. As with motor vehicles and watercraft, the aircraft exclusion extends to the entrustment of an aircraft by an insured to any person or vicarious liability, whether or not imposed by statute, for the actions of a child or minor using an aircraft. An aircraft is defined as any contrivance used or designed for flight, except model or hobby aircraft not used or designed to carry people or cargo. Therefore, damage caused by a radio controlled model airplane would be covered.

War. Homeowners policies exclude bodily injury or property damage caused directly or indirectly or as a consequence of war. The definition of war includes civil war, insurrection, rebellion, revolution, warlike act by a military force or military personnel, destruction or seizure, or use for a military purpose. Discharge of a nuclear weapon is deemed to be a warlike act, even if it is accidental, and is excluded.

Communicable Disease. Bodily injury or property damage that arises out of the transmission of a communicable disease by an insured is excluded. This exclusion responds to a series of court decisions that found coverage in the homeowners policy for the insured's liability for damages as the result of infecting another person with the herpes virus. Such coverage was never contemplated by homeowners actuaries when setting the rates for the policy, and this exclusion makes that intent clear.

Abuse or Sexual Molestation. Liability for bodily injury or property damage arising out of sexual molestation is excluded. Also excluded is liability resulting from corporal punishment and physical or mental abuse.

Controlled Substances. HO policies also exclude liability for bodily injury or property damage arising out of the use, sale, manufacture, delivery, transfer, or possession of a controlled substance by any person. Controlled substances include, but are not limited to, cocaine, marijuana, LSD, and all narcotic drugs. This exclusion *does not apply* to the legitimate use of prescription drugs by a person following the orders of a licensed physician.

Home Day Care. Coverage for a home day care business is limited under Section I and excluded under Section II. To emphasize that there is no coverage for liability arising out of a home day care business, most states require insurers to add the HO 04 96 endorsement to homeowners policies. This endorsement does not constitute a reduction of coverage but, instead, represents a clarification of certain exclusions pertaining to home day care business. The endorsement states that if an insured regularly provides home day care services to a person or persons other than insureds and receives monetary or other compensation for such services, that enterprise is a business. However, the rendering of home day care services by an insured to a relative of an insured is not considered a business.

The endorsement points out that since home day care conducted for compensation is a business, there is no liability coverage whatsoever because of the business exclusion discussed above. Further, the HO 04 96 endorsement highlights the Section I exclusion pertaining to other structures under Coverage B where the other structures are used in whole or in part for business. The endorsement also states that the Section I limits of $2,500 on business property on the residence premises and $250 off the residence premises also apply to the home day care business.

Exclusions to Coverage E

The exclusions to Coverage E—Personal Liability restrict or eliminate coverage provided for bodily injury or property damage. These exclusions apply to the following:

- Loss assessment
- Property owned by the insured
- Property in the care, custody, or control of the insured
- Bodily injury covered by compensation law
- Nuclear liability
- Bodily injury to an insured

The exclusions applicable to Coverage E are described in the following paragraphs.

Loss Assessment. Coverage E does not apply to liability imposed as the insured's share of any loss assessment charged against all members of an association, corporation, or community of property owners. Therefore, if a condominium association were found liable, coverage would have to be found on the association's own policy and not the homeowners policies of the individual members. An association of owners of single-family dwellings could be exposed to a similar liability situation with respect to their individual homeowners policies. Reimbursement of certain loss assessments is provided as an additional coverage, however, and is discussed below.

This exclusion also applies to liability under any contract or agreement. However, liability coverage is provided for written contracts that directly relate to the ownership, maintenance, or use of an insured location or where the liability of others is assumed by the insured prior to an occurrence. Such contractual agreements are often a part of lease agreements. This contractual coverage is subject to both the loss assessment exclusion above and all other policy exclusions. The following example describes one instance of liability of others assumed by the insured.

The insured has a contract with a painter for the painter to paint the insured's home. In the contract, the insured agrees that if the painter is sued for negligence and the negligent act arises out of the performance of the painter's duties in painting the insured's home, the insured will provide a defense and pay on behalf of the painter. While the painting is being done, a passerby is struck by a falling paint can and sues the painter. Under the contract, the insured must answer the complaint and provide a defense for the painter. If a judgment is found against the painter, the insured must pay. The insured's homeowners policy would provide coverage because the insured assumed the liability of the painter before the injury to the passerby occurred.

Property Owned by the Insured. Property owned by the insured is excluded from property damage liability coverage under Coverage E. Coverage for damage to the insured's property is provided under Section I.

Care, Custody, or Control. The care, custody, or control exclusion is found in virtually all liability policies. Damage to property rented to, occupied or used by, or in the care of the insured is excluded. This exclusion does not apply to property damage caused by fire, smoke, or explosion. Therefore, liability coverage would be provided for a tenant insured by an HO-4 who is found to be responsible for a fire that destroys the apartment building.

Bodily Injury Covered by Compensation Law. The policy excludes bodily injury to any person eligible to receive any benefits either voluntarily provided or required to be provided by the insured under a compensation law. This exclusion applies to benefits payable under workers compensation, nonoccupational disability, or occupational disease laws.

Nuclear Liability. Bodily injury or property damage for which an insured under the homeowners policy is also an insured under a nuclear energy liability policy is excluded. This exclusion also applies in the case where the insured would have been an insured under a nuclear energy liability policy but for the exhaustion of its limit of liability. A nuclear energy liability policy is one issued by American Nuclear Insurers, Mutual Atomic Energy Liability Underwriters, the Nuclear Insurance Association of Canada, or their successor organizations.

Bodily Injury to an Insured. There is no liability coverage for claims arising from bodily injury to an insured resident of the household. This exclusion applies to the named insured, related residents of the same household, and other persons in their care who are under the age of twenty-one.

Exclusions to Coverage F

Coverage for medical payments to others is restricted or eliminated by the following exclusions that apply only to Coverage F:

- Residence employee off-premises
- Bodily injury covered by compensation law
- Nuclear reaction, radiation, or contamination
- Other regular residents

Residence Employee Off-Premises. Medical payments coverage is not provided in the case of bodily injury that is suffered by a residence employee while off the insured location unless the injury arises out of or in the course of employment by an insured. This emphasizes the fact that certain exclusions to Coverages E and F (discussed earlier) do not apply to residence employees who suffer bodily injuries arising out of and in the course of employment for the insured.

The phrase "for the insured" is important. A part-time gardener who works one day a week for the insured might be injured in the course of ordinary employment while working at someone else's house. Coverage would not be provided under the insured's policy because the injury, while arising out of the course of employment, did not arise out of employment *for the insured.* If the injury occurred while the gardener was purchasing seed for the insured at a hardware store, then coverage would apply.

Bodily Injury Covered by Compensation Law.   This exclusion is broader than the corresponding exclusion applicable to Coverage E, which refers to benefits voluntarily provided or required to be provided *by the insured.* The Coverage F exclusion refers to benefits voluntarily provided or required to be provided under any workers compensation, nonoccupational disability, or occupational disease law. Therefore, the Coverage F exclusion applies to anyone coming under the coverage of such a law, regardless of who provides, or is required to provide, the coverage.

The Nuclear Exclusion.   Medical payments coverage does not apply to bodily injury arising from any nuclear reaction, radiation, or radioactive contamination. This exclusion applies whether the reaction, radiation, or contamination was controlled or uncontrolled and however it was caused. Any consequence of such an occurrence is also excluded.

Other Regular Residents.   Medical payments coverage is not provided for bodily injury to any person, other than a residence employee, regularly residing on any part of the insured location. This parallels the Coverage E exclusion that applies to members of the insured's household.

Additional Coverages

Section II of the HO policy also provides four additional coverages related to an insured's liability exposures. Any amounts paid under these additional coverages are in addition to the limits of liability shown on the declarations page for Coverages E and F. Subject to certain limitations, coverage is provided for the following:

- Claim expenses
- First aid expenses
- Damage to property of others
- Loss assessment

Claim Expenses.   Defense costs are considered claim expenses and include those expenses incurred by the insurer and costs taxed against an insured in any case the insurer defends. These defense costs can be considerable and include the expenses of claims adjusters, defense attorneys, investigators, and expert witnesses. These claim expenses represent additional coverage beyond the limit of liability and do not count against it. Therefore, there is no upper limit to the amount of claim expenses that might be paid under the policy.

Other claim expenses that are paid include the following:

1. Premiums on bonds required in a suit defended by the insurer, but not for bond amounts that are more than the limit of liability for Coverage E.
2. Up to $50 per day for expenses incurred by an insured at the insurer's request while assisting in the investigation or defense of a claim or suit.

The reasonable expenses include actual loss of earnings but not loss of other income.

3. Post-judgment interest prior to the time the insurer tenders or deposits in court that part of the judgment that does not exceed the applicable limit of liability.

First Aid Expenses. Coverage is provided to pay expenses for first aid to others incurred by an insured for bodily injury covered under the policy. This coverage does not extend to the named insured or any other insured. This additional coverage is separate from any medical payments made under Coverage F and has no limit stated in the policy.

Damage to Property of Others. Replacement cost coverage is provided in the amount of $500 per occurrence for property damage to the property of others caused by an insured. This coverage is excess insurance over any amount recoverable under Section I of the policy. Property damage to property owned by an insured is excluded from this coverage. This additional coverage also does not pay for property damage:

1. Caused intentionally by an insured who is thirteen years of age or older.
2. To property owned by or rented to a tenant of an insured or a household resident.
3. Arising out of a business engaged in by an insured.
4. Arising out of any act or omission in connection with a premises owned, rented, or controlled by an insured other than an insured location.
5. Arising out of the ownership, maintenance, or use of aircraft, watercraft, motor vehicles, or other motorized land conveyances. A motorized land conveyance designed for off-road recreational use that is not subject to motor vehicle registration and not owned by an insured is exempt from this exclusion and therefore would be covered.

Loss Assessment. The homeowners policy will pay up to $1,000 for the insured's share of any loss assessments charged by a corporation or association of property owners under certain conditions. The assessment must be made as a result of bodily injury or property damage to which Section II of the policy would apply or for liability for an act of a director, officer, or trustee acting in that capacity. The coverage for loss assessment resulting from acts of a director, officer, or trustee of the corporation or association of property owners is provided only if that director, officer, or trustee is elected by the members of the association or corporation and serves without pay.

This coverage is limited to loss assessments charged against the insured as owner or tenant of the residence premises. Loss assessments charged against the insured or a corporation or association of property owners by any governmental body are excluded. Regardless of the number of assessments, the $1,000 limit is the most that will be paid for loss arising out of one accident or one covered act of a director, officer, or trustee (an act involving more than one director, officer, or trustee is a single act). The loss assessment exclusion under Coverage E, discussed previously, does not apply to this coverage, nor does the condition that sets forth the policy period (discussed later).

The question might arise, "Why exclude the coverage under Coverage E and then add it back as an additional coverage?" When coverage is provided under Coverage E, defense cost coverage is provided as well. The intent of this section is for the association or corporation to provide its own defense. The policy provides for $1,000 toward any subsequent assessment.

Conditions

Coverage under Section II is subject to certain policy conditions. These conditions are listed below and described in the following paragraphs.

- Limit of liability
- Severability of insurance
- Duties after loss
- Duties of an injured person under Coverage F
- Payment of claim under Coverage F
- Suit against the insurer
- Bankruptcy of an insured
- Other insurance under Coverage E

Limit of Liability. The limit of liability for Coverage E for all damages resulting from any one occurrence is the amount shown in the declarations regardless of the number of insureds, claims made, or persons injured. For example, assume that an insured's errant golf shot hit the driver of a golf cart, causing the driver to lose control and hit a tree. As a result, the insured is liable for injuries to the driver and a passenger in the golf cart and for damage to the golf cart. The limit for each occurrence represents an absolute limit on the total amount of damages that will be paid for all claims resulting from the insured's errant golf shot. Damages payable are also restricted to the policy limit for a single occurrence, regardless of the number of insureds under the policy who are held liable. Therefore, if a husband and wife insured under an HO policy are each found liable for $75,000 in damages resulting from a covered occurrence and the Section II limit of liability is $100,000, the policy will pay only $100,000 of their combined $150,000 in damages. In both of the above examples, defense costs would be paid in addition to the limit of liability.

The limit under Coverage F for all medical expense for bodily injury to one person as the result of one accident is shown in the declarations. The basic limit is $1,000. Therefore, in the case of the two injured golfers, each would be eligible for separate $1,000 limits under Coverage F, while the occurrence would be subject to a single limit of $100,000 under Coverage E.

Severability of Insurance. Insurance in an HO policy applies separately to each insured. The concept of severability of insurance can be illustrated by a New Hampshire case in which the seventeen-year-old son of an insured allegedly assaulted another minor.[4] The parents of the injured child sued both the son and his parents, alleging that the parents, through their neglect, allowed the assault to occur. The insurer denied coverage for both the son and his parents, relying on the exclusion regarding "bodily injury...which is expected or intended by the insured." The court agreed that there would be no coverage for the son because coverage for intentional acts is excluded. However, the court found that there would be coverage for the parents because the suit alleging their negligence would not be affected by the exclusion that applied to their son. Because coverage under Section II applies separately to each insured, the insurer was required to respond to the suit against the parents, even though it did not respond on behalf of their son.

In some situations, both the named insured and another party for which the policy provides coverage may be sued for different actions or omissions that result in one occurrence. For example, an insured loaned a canoe to a local scout troop. The policy would provide liability coverage to the troop for damages arising out of its use of the insured's canoe. If a scout was injured while using the canoe, the scout could make a claim against the named insured, alleging poor maintenance of the canoe, and against the scout troop, alleging improper supervision of the use of the canoe. The insurer would respond on behalf of both the insured and the scout troop. However, the limits of liability would not be increased even though two separate insureds were involved.

Duties After Loss. In case of an accident or occurrence, the insured has certain duties. Not all of these duties will necessarily apply to a given occurrence. The insured's duties after a loss are as follows:

1. To give written notice to the insurer or its agent as soon as practical, setting forth the identity of the policy and name of the insured. The notice should also include reasonably available information on the time, place, and circumstances of the accident or occurrence and the names and addresses of any claimants and witnesses.

2. To promptly forward to the insurance company every notice, demand, summons, or other process relating to the accident or occurrence. Legal demands or notice of suit frequently have a time limit during which an answer may be entered. Failure to answer will result in a default judgment. Therefore, the claimant might prevail with a groundless suit.

3. To assist the insurance company, at its request, to make settlement and to enforce any right of contribution or indemnity against any person or organization who might be liable to an insured. The insured also must assist with the conduct of suits by attending hearings and trials, and by securing and giving evidence and obtaining the attendance of witnesses. This section asks the insured to cooperate vigorously in the defense of any suit, just as the insured would if there were no insurance available.

4. When claims are made for damage to property of others, the insured, at the insurer's request, must submit a sworn statement of loss within 60 days after the loss. If the damaged property is still in the insured's control, it must be shown to the insurer on request.

5. The insured must not voluntarily make payment, assume obligation, or incur expense other than for first aid to others at the time of bodily injury. Any other voluntary payment or assumption of liability on the part of the insured is at his or her own expense.

Duties of an Injured Person Under Coverage F. Under Coverage F, medical payments to others, the injured person or someone acting for that person must send the insurer a written proof of claim as soon as is practical. The insurer may require this proof of claim to be written under oath. The injured person must also authorize the insurer to obtain copies of medical reports and records. The final duty of the injured person is to submit to a physical exam by a doctor selected by the insurer when and as often as is reasonable.

Payment of Claim Under Coverage F.   When a claim is paid under Coverage F, medical payments to others, such payment does not constitute an admission of liability by an insured or the insurer. Medical payments claims are often paid in situations where the insured feels a moral obligation to a guest or other person on his or her premises although no legal liability exists. This provision points out that payment under Coverage F does not mean that the claimant can automatically collect under Coverage E.

Suit Against Insurer.   The first provision of this condition states that no legal action can be brought against the insurer unless there has been compliance with the policy provisions.

The second provision states that no one has the right to add the insurer as a party to any action against an insured. This means that a claimant or a co-defendant involved in a lawsuit against the insured cannot name the insurer as a party to that lawsuit. A jury might be swayed in its decision regarding the award of damages by knowing that an insurance company, rather than the individual defendant, was responsible for payment. Some states have enacted "direct action statutes," which take precedence over these contract provisions and allow the insurer to be named in a suit.

A third provision states that no action with respect to Coverage E can be brought against the insurer until the obligation of the insured has been determined by a final judgment or an agreement signed by the insurer. An action may be brought at that time to compel the insurer to pay.

Bankruptcy of an Insured.   Bankruptcy or insolvency of an insured does not relieve the insurer of its obligations under the policy. Recall that Section II coverages are designed to pay damages for which the insured is legally liable. An insured who is bankrupt is not likely to be able to pay damages for which he or she may be liable. As a matter of social policy, liability insurers have assumed the obligation of paying covered liability damages on behalf of the insured, even though, in the absence of insurance, the insured could not pay the damages because of personal bankruptcy.

Other Insurance—Coverage E.   Coverage E—Personal Liability is excess over any other valid and collectible primary insurance. This provision does not apply with respect to insurance specifically written as excess over the limits of liability provided by the HO policy. For example, assume that an insured carries the basic $100,000 Coverage E limit. An excess policy purchased by the insured for $1 million, excess of loss of $100,000, would be recognized as specifically written excess insurance. Excess personal liability policies are discussed in Chapter 6.

COMMON POLICY CONDITIONS

Certain conditions in the homeowners policies, referred to as the "common conditions," apply to both Section I and Section II. Like the Section I conditions examined in Chapter 2 and the Section II conditions discussed above, these common policy conditions outline the rights and responsibilities of the insured and the insurer. The common policy conditions are as follows:

- Policy period
- Concealment or fraud
- Liberalization clause
- Waiver or change of policy provisions
- Cancellation
- Nonrenewal
- Assignment
- Subrogation
- Death of named insured

These conditions are discussed in the following paragraphs.

Policy Period

Homeowners policies cover only losses that occur *during the policy period*. The Section II coverage is on an occurrence basis, meaning that the claim does not have to be filed during the policy period as long as the occurrence giving rise to the loss occurred during the policy period.

Concealment or Fraud

Coverage is not provided for an insured who has intentionally concealed any material fact or circumstance relevant to the insurance policy, either before or after a loss. Concealment or misrepresentation must be intentional and *material* in order for the insurer to void the policy. A fact or circumstance is considered to be material if it would have affected the insurer's underwriting of the policy had the insurer been aware of it.

The policy will also be void if any insured has made false statements or engaged in fraudulent conduct relating to the policy.

Liberalization Clause

If the insurance company adopts a revision that would broaden the coverage under the policy without additional premium, the broadened coverage will automatically apply to the policy on the date the revision is implemented in the insured's state. The implementation date must fall within sixty days prior to the inception of the policy or during the policy period. The liberalization clause does not apply to changes that are implemented because a subsequent edition of the policy has been introduced.

Waiver or Change of Policy Provisions

A waiver or change of any policy provision must be in writing by the insurer in order to be valid. A request by the insurer for an appraisal or examination does not waive any of the insurer's rights. For example, if an insurer requests to examine damaged property following a loss, the insurer's request does not waive its right to deny coverage if its investigation determines that the cause of the loss is not a covered peril.

Cancellation

The insured may cancel an HO policy at any time by returning it to the insurer or by informing the insurer in writing of the date the cancellation is to take effect. The insurer may cancel the policy only under certain conditions. If an HO policy is canceled, the premium for the period from the date of cancellation to the expiration date is refunded on a pro-rata basis, regardless of which party cancels.

The insurer may cancel the policy at any time for nonpayment of premium, provided the insured is given ten days' written notice. Also, during the first sixty days of the policy term, the insurer may cancel for any reason by providing ten days' written notice.

If the policy has been in effect for sixty days or more, including subsequent renewals, then the insurer may cancel only under two circumstances. It may cancel if there has been a material misrepresentation of fact which, if known to the insurer, would have caused it not to issue the policy. The insurer also may cancel if there has been a substantial change in the risk since the policy was issued. After the policy has been in effect for sixty days or more, thirty days' written notice of cancellation is required.

When the policy is written for a period of more than one year, the insurer may cancel for any reason at the anniversary date by providing thirty days' written notice. The effect would be the same as nonrenewal of a one-year policy.

Nonrenewal

The insurer may elect not to renew the policy for any reason. Nonrenewal requires thirty days' written notice. Proof of mailing is considered sufficient proof of notice for either cancellation or nonrenewal.

Assignment

Assignment of the policy to another person or persons is not valid without written consent of the insurer. This follows from the fact that an insurance policy is a personal contract between the insurer and the insured.

Subrogation

An insured may waive in writing, before a loss, all rights of recovery against any person. Such waivers are often found in property leases. If the insured's rights have not been waived in writing prior to a loss, the insurer may require an assignment of rights of recovery for a loss to the extent that payment is made by the insurer. For example, an insured suffers an $8,000 loss because of a fire that was the result of negligence on the part of the tenant in the next apartment. If the loss is paid under the insured's HO-4, the insurer would be subrogated to the insured's cause of action against the negligent tenant to the amount of $8,000. If the insured's total loss was $10,000, but there had only been $8,000 of insurance, the insured could keep the last $2,000 if the insurer was able to recover $10,000 from the negligent party.

The policy requires the insured to sign and deliver all related papers and to cooperate with the insurer if an assignment of subrogation rights is sought. Subrogation does not apply under Section II to medical payments to others or to damage to property of others.

Death of Named Insured

In the event of the death of the named insured or resident spouse, the legal representative of the deceased is insured, but only with respect to the premises and property of the deceased covered under the policy at the time of death. The policy does not extend to the deceased's entire estate, which might include property not insured under that particular homeowners policy.

This condition includes a revised definition of "insured." In the event of the death of the named insured or spouse, the new definition of insured includes any member of the named insured's household at the time of the insured's death, but only while that household member is a resident of the residence premises. With respect to property of the named insured, in the event of the named insured's death the definition of insured includes the person having proper temporary custody of the property until a qualified legal representative is appointed.

SUMMARY

Homeowners insurance for tenants focuses on three major types of loss exposures: loss to additions and alterations, loss to personal property, and legal liability. The HO-4 contents broad form was designed to meet these exposures. Unlike the HO-3, the HO-4 does not include Coverage A or Coverage B. Coverages C and D and the additional coverages are, with few exceptions, similar to those under the HO-3. Under the HO-4, however, the insured selects the amount of coverage to be provided under Coverage C, and other coverage limits are based on that amount. Liability coverages for tenants under the HO-4 are the same as in the HO-3.

The HO-6 unit-owners form is designed to meet the three major types of loss exposure for condominium owners: loss to real property, loss to personal property, and legal liability. Any owner-occupant of a residential condominium unit or a cooperative apartment is eligible for an HO-6. Coverage A of the HO-6 has a basic limit of $1,000, but higher additional limits may be purchased. The unit owner selects the limits for Coverage C; Coverage D is 40 percent of this limit. The additional coverages are similar to those under the HO-3 and HO-4.

Because the HO-6 is written on a named-perils basis, the concurrent causation exclusions are not a part of the Section I exclusions. The Section I conditions of the HO-6 are similar to those of the HO-3. Five endorsements are tailored for the HO-6: (1) unit-owners Coverage A special coverages; (2) unit-owners rental to others; (3) loss assessment coverage; (4) loss assessment coverage for earthquake; and (5) unit-owners Coverage C, special coverage.

Section II provides liability coverage and is uniform among all of the homeowners policies. Coverage E—Personal Liability provides liability coverage if a claim is made or suit is brought against an insured because of bodily injury or property damage caused by a covered occurrence.

Coverage F—Medical Payments to Others will pay the necessary medical expenses that are incurred or medically ascertained within three years from the date of an accident causing bodily injury to someone other than an insured. Coverage applies to accidents that occur on the insured premises or as the result of an action by the insured at any location.

The exclusions applicable to Section II limit or eliminate coverage for specified types of occurrences. Certain exclusions apply to both Coverages E and F; others apply only to Coverage E or Coverage F.

The Section II conditions include limit of liability, severability of insurance, duties after loss, duties of an injured person under Coverage F, payment of claim under Coverage F, suit against the insurer, bankruptcy of an insured, and other insurance under Coverage E.

The common conditions that apply to both Section I and Section II of HO policies include policy period, concealment or fraud, liberalization clause, waiver or change of policy conditions, cancellation, nonrenewal, assignment, subrogation, and death of the named insured.

Chapter Notes

1. *FC&S Bulletins,* Personal Lines Volume, Dwellings Hoc 1-4, and Glenn L. Wood, Claude C. Lilly III, Donald S. Malecki, Edward E. Graves, and Jerry S. Rosenbloom, *Personal Risk Management and Insurance,* 4th ed. (Vol. I, Malvern, PA: American Institute for Property and Liability Underwriters, 1989), p. 31.
2. *FC&S Bulletins,* p. Hoc-5.
3. *CNA Casualty of Ca. v. Seaboard Surety Co.,* Superior Ct No. 761572, CCA 1st Appellate District, Division Three, 86 Daily Journal DAR 285.
4. Pawtucket Mut. Ins. Co. v. Lebrecht, 104 N.H. 465, 190 A.2d 420 (1963), 2 A.L.R. 3rd 1229 (1965) cited in R.E. Keeton, *Cases and Materials on Basic Insurance Law,* 2nd ed. (St. Paul, MN: West Publishing Co., 1977), pp. 463-465.

CHAPTER 4

Homeowners Pricing and Endorsements

With the exception of comments on a few endorsements that apply to only HO-4 or HO-6 policies, the discussions of homeowners policies in the preceding two chapters have focused on the standard, unendorsed HO forms. In practice, however, homeowners policies generally contain a variety of endorsements. These endorsements may be added to respond to an insured's special needs, to meet an insurer's underwriting requirements, or to satisfy state insurance regulations. The effect of such endorsements is to modify the coverage provided under the standard, unendorsed form.

In many cases, adding an endorsement also changes the pricing of the policy. Different types of endorsements have different effects on homeowners pricing. Therefore, a complete understanding of homeowners endorsements requires a knowledge of homeowners pricing as well as homeowners coverage. This chapter explains homeowners pricing and examines homeowners endorsements and their effect on both the coverage and pricing of the homeowners policy.

HOMEOWNERS INSURANCE PRICING

The following discussion of the development of the homeowners premium focuses primarily on the HO-3 policy. The same pricing procedures apply to the HO-1, HO-2, and HO-8, which contain, with some variations, the complete package of homeowners policy coverages. The examples of homeowners pricing presented in this chapter are based on information provided in the homeowners manual prepared by the Insurance Services Office (ISO).[1] Insurers that have developed their own homeowners rating manuals generally follow similar pricing procedures. Although many of the principles and practices presented here also apply to HO-4 and HO-6 policies, the pricing for these forms is not examined in this text.

Indivisible Base Premium

The homeowners policy has an indivisible *base premium,* reflecting the fact that the policy consists of a preset package of coverages. The base premium is the amount charged for the standard package of coverages under a particular HO form without modifications. Once the key rating factors have been determined and the HO form and amount of coverage on the dwelling have been selected, the homeowners pricing procedure calculates a single base premium for the entire policy.

Primary Rating Factors

The primary rating factors that determine the premium for a homeowners policy are the territory in which the dwelling is located, the quality of public fire protection, and the dwelling's construction. While territory reflects both property and liability loss potential, the fire protection and construction rating factors reflect only property loss potential. This is indicative of the fact that homeowners insurance is priced primarily on the basis of expected property loss frequency and severity. Except for territorial differences, the homeowners premium includes what is in essence a "flat charge" for the liability coverages.

Territory. Each state is divided into rating territories. Differences in territories represent different levels of exposure to loss with respect to the property, theft, and liability coverages provided in the homeowners policy.

Frequently, urban and rural areas are separated into different territories. Urban areas are often characterized by higher crime levels and a greater willingness of residents to file lawsuits. On the other hand, rural areas are likely to have less fire protection than is provided in cities. Different geographic areas may also represent different exposure levels to other perils, such as windstorm. Rating territories are established on the basis of an analysis of historical data on insured losses.

Protection. This primary rating factor reflects the level of fire protection available for the insured dwelling. It takes into account only the public fire protection.

Public Protection Classes. The public fire protection available to home owners is provided by the local fire department. Municipal fire departments are graded on a scale from class 1 (best protection) to class 10 (least protection). Properties located in areas graded class 10 are referred to as unprotected. This rating system is contained in the *Fire Suppression Rating Schedule* published by ISO.[2]

Other Factors. Other factors considered in evaluating public fire protection for homeowners rating purposes are the distance of the dwelling to the nearest fire station and the distance to the nearest hydrant. These additional factors are considered in the event that two or more fire protection classifications are indicated for a municipality or township. For example, assume that protection classes 5 and 8 are shown for a given township. In this case the fire station and hydrant location relative to the insured property would be considered.

If the distance from the dwelling to the fire station is five road miles or less and a hydrant is located within 1,000 feet, the lower class would be used, 5 in this case. If the distance to the fire station is five road miles or less but the hydrant is more than 1,000 feet away, then the higher classification would be used, 8 in this case. If the distance to the fire station is more than five road miles, the property is considered unprotected, and class 10 is used.

Construction. The homeowners manual divides dwellings into four construction categories: frame, masonry veneer, masonry, and superior construction.[3]

Frame. Frame construction consists of exterior walls of wood or other combustible materials on combustible supports or framing studs. Stucco on wood and plaster on combustible supports are considered frame. Aluminum or plastic siding over frame is rated as frame but given a different coding for statistical purposes. Although frame construction is most susceptible to fire, it has excellent earthquake resistance characteristics and is widely used in earthquake-prone regions.

Masonry Veneer. A masonry veneer structure has exterior walls of combustible construction veneered with brick or stone. Masonry veneer is typically rated the same as masonry, although a different statistical code is used. Masonry veneer is more resistive than frame construction to fire, but it is extremely susceptible to earthquake damage.

Masonry. Masonry construction, also referred to as ordinary construction, consists of exterior walls constructed of masonry materials such as brick, stone, adobe, or similar materials, and the floors and roof are made of joisted combustible materials. Masonry construction is less susceptible to loss from fire than frame or masonry veneer.

Superior Construction. In most cases and because of cost considerations, superior construction is found in residential construction only in apartment houses and condominiums. The following three types of construction are rated as superior:

- *Noncombustible* construction, which is distinguished by exterior walls, floors, and roof constructed of and supported by metal or other noncombustible materials.
- *Masonry noncombustible* construction, which is distinguished by masonry exterior walls, and floors and roof of metal or other noncombustible materials.
- *Fire-resistive* construction, which is distinguished by exterior walls, floors, and roof constructed of masonry or other fire-resistive materials. In most cases these structures are built of reinforced concrete. Most high-rise buildings fall into this category.

Determining a Homeowners Policy Base Premium

The homeowners base premium is calculated using the *key premiums* and the *key factors* found in the homeowners manual. Exhibit 4-1 shows the key premiums for the HO-1, HO-2, and HO-3 developed by the IIA Insurance Company, a fictitious insurer. Exhibit 4-2 shows the key factors for the same policies. The key premium is chosen from the manual on the basis of the territory, public fire protection, construction, and policy form that apply to the covered dwelling.

Exhibit 4-1
Key Premiums for HO-1, HO-2, and HO-3

Key Premiums						
Territory	Prot. Class	Const.	Prem. G.P.#	HO-1 (1)	HO-2 (2)	HO-3 (3)
30	3	M (3)	1	128	135	150
		F (1)	2	134	142	158
31,32	1-8	M (3)	3	112	119	132
		F (1)	6	119	126	140
	9	M (3)	4	131	139	154
		F (1)	7	149	158	175
	10	M (3)	5	155	164	182
		F (1)	8	184	194	216
02	1-8	M (3)	9	105	111	123
		F (1)	12	111	117	130
	9	M (3)	10	122	130	144
		F (1)	13	139	147	163
	10	M (3)	11	144	152	169
		F (1)	14	172	182	202

The key factor is chosen from the manual on the basis of the Coverage A limit on the dwelling. The base premium is calculated by multiplying the key premium by the key factor.

Assume that the following information is available for pricing a specific homeowners policy:

- Territory—32
- Protection class—9
- Construction—Masonry
- Policy form—HO-3
- Coverage A amount—$100,000

The first step in determining the base premium is to select the appropriate key premium. Referring to Exhibit 4-1 and reading from left to right on the key premium display, for a dwelling located in territory 32, protection class 9, and of masonry construction, to be insured under an HO-3, leads to a key premium of $154.

The next step is to find the key factor in Exhibit 4-2 for a Coverage A amount of $100,000. Reading down the column of key factors, one finds a factor of 2.250 to the right of $100,000.

Exhibit 4-2
Key Factors for HO-1, HO-2, and HO-3

Key Factors			
Coverage A Amount	Factor	Coverage A Amount	Factor
$ 10,000	.520	$ 55,000	1.225
12,000	.552	60,000	1.320
14,000	.584	65,000	1.430
16,000	.616	70,000	1.540
18,000	.648	75,000	1.650
20,000	.680	80,000	1.770
22,000	.712	85,000	1.890
24,000	.744	90,000	2.010
26,000	.776	95,000	2.130
28,000	.808	100,000	2.250
30,000	.840	110,000	2.490
32,000	.872	120,000	2.730
34,000	.904	130,000	2.970
36,000	.936	140,000	3.210
38,000	.968	150,000	3.450
40,000	1.000	160,000	3.690
42,000	1.030	170,000	3.930
44,000	1.060	180,000	4.170
46,000	1.090	190,000	4.410
48,000	1.120	200,000	4.650
50,000	1.150		
		Each Add'l $ 10,000	.240

The final step in determining the base premium is to multiply the key premium amount by the key factor. The product is the base premium:

$$\text{Key premium} \times \text{Key factor} = \text{Base premium}$$
$$\$154 \times 2.250 = \$346.50$$

An insured purchasing this HO-3 policy with no modifications in coverage would be charged an annual premium of $347. The base premium is rounded to the nearest whole dollar prior to billing (or before any additional calculations required by modifications in coverage).

There are two situations in which the base premium calculation is slightly more involved than in this example. The first is when the Coverage A amount falls between the factors given in the key factor table, such as a Coverage A amount of $105,000. The second is when the Coverage A amount is higher than the highest key factor shown in the table. The methods of handling these situations are detailed in the homeowners manual.

Adjustments to the Base Premium

The base premium for a homeowners policy may need to be adjusted in some situations. Such an adjustment would be necessary when additional rating factors must be considered and when the insured increases or decreases the standard deductible.

Additional Rating Factors. Two additional rating factors that apply only under certain circumstances may require an adjustment of the base premium. An adjustment is required if the covered dwelling is of superior construction or if it is a townhouse or row house.

Superior Construction. Dwellings of superior construction—noncombustible, masonry noncombustible, or fire-resistive—earn a credit that is applied to the base premium. All other things being equal, if the dwelling described above was of superior construction and earned a 15 percent credit, the adjusted annual premium would be $347 \times 0.85 = $294.95 or $295 rounded to the nearest whole dollar.

Townhouse or Row House. These types of dwellings share one or more interior walls with neighboring dwellings. As a result, their exposure to loss from a fire that starts in a neighboring residence is greater than that faced by single homes, which are physically separated from each other. If a homeowners policy, other than an HO-4 or HO-6, is written to provide coverage on a townhouse or row house, the base premium may be increased to reflect the greater exposure to loss from fire that originates in an adjoining dwelling. The increase is accomplished by multiplying the base premium by a factor that is based on the total number of individual family units within the fire division containing the dwelling and the applicable fire protection class, as shown in Exhibit 4-3. In a group of townhouses in which the common walls are of adequate masonry construction from the basement to eighteen inches above the roof line, each townhouse would constitute a single fire division.[4] In such a case, no adjustment of the base premium would be required, since a factor of 1.00 applies. On the other hand, in a group of townhouses with no fire-resistive walls between the units, the whole group of townhouses would constitute a single fire division, and an adjustment to the base premium would be necessary.

An adjustment to the base premium for a townhouse is accomplished in the following manner. Assume that the townhouse is one of six single-family units within one fire division and that the fire protection class is 2. Referring to Exhibit 4-3, read down the left column to find the row that applies to six family units, which is the row designated 5-8. Next, choose the protection class that applies—in this case classes 1-8 since the actual protection class is 2. The factor shown for 5-8 family units in protection classes 1-8 is 1.25. If the base premium is $200, the adjusted base premium for a policy covering this townhouse would be $200 \times 1.25 = $250.

Exhibit 4-3

Townhouse or Row House Factors

Total No. of Individual Family Units Within the Fire Division	No. of Family Code	Protection Class	
		1 — 8	9 & Over
1 & 2	(1 & 3)	1.00	1.00
3 & 4	(2)	1.10	1.15
5 - 8	(4)	1.25	1.30
9 & Over	(4)	Refer to Company	

Exhibit 4-4

Increased Deductible Factors

HO-1, HO-2 HO-3, and HO-8 Coverage A Limit	Deductible Amount		
	$500	$1,000	$2,500
Up to $ 59,999	.91	.83	.75
$ 60,000 to 99,999	.93	.85	.75
100,000 to 200,000	.95	.88	.75
200,001 to 250,000	.95	.88	.85
Over $250,000 refer to Company	—	—	—

Increase or Decrease in Deductible. The standard deductible for homeowners property coverages is $250. At the insured's option, this deductible may be increased to $500, $1,000, or $2,500. The new base premium for these deductibles is calculated by multiplying the base premium by a factor determined by the Coverage A limit and the deductible amount. The increased deductible factors used by the IIA Insurance Company are shown in Exhibit 4-4. Notice that the factors are all less than 1.0, meaning that an increase in the deductible results in a decrease in the base premium.

The $250 deductible may also be decreased to $100. The base premium is multiplied by a factor of 1.15 to develop the premium for this lower deductible. The increase in premium is subject to a minimum and a maximum additional charge.

HOMEOWNERS ENDORSEMENTS

A variety of endorsements can be used to modify homeowners policies. Some of the more widely used endorsements are discussed in this section.

The Need for Endorsements

A homeowners policy may be endorsed to meet the needs of insureds, the underwriting requirements of insurers, or state insurance regulations.

Insured's Needs. Endorsements may be used to customize the standard coverage under a particular HO form according to the needs of an insured. Property and liability loss exposures vary considerably from one household to another and, therefore, so do their insurance requirements. Endorsements provide flexibility in meeting these individual needs.

Insurer's Underwriting Requirements. Homeowners policies provide a very broad range of coverages to the insured. An insurer may not be willing to extend this breadth of coverage, for instance, on a dwelling located in an area where homes regularly suffer windstorm damage. An endorsement excluding windstorm damage may be required by an insurer as a condition to providing coverage on a dwelling located in such an area.

State Regulatory Requirements. The laws of the various states often require that certain homeowners policy provisions be amended. A series of HO endorsements have been developed by ISO to reflect the various modifications required by individual states. These "special provisions" endorsements typically modify standard HO policy provisions in ways that are advantageous to insureds. Affected policy provisions often include one or more of the following areas: cancellation and nonrenewal, definitions such as "actual cash value" and "intentional loss," suit against the insurer, duties of the insured, loss payment, and valuation of property.

Effects of Endorsements

When homeowners endorsements are used, they affect the coverage provided by the basic policy and the premium charged for coverage.

Effect on Coverage. Endorsements can be used to change many aspects of coverage under a homeowners policy, including the following:

- Persons covered
- Property covered
- Perils covered
- Activities covered
- Limits of liability
- Insurance to value requirement
- Loss settlement valuation method
- Applicable exclusions

Exhibit 4-5

Inflation Guard Endorsement Factors

Amount of Annual Increase	Factor
4%	1.02
6	1.03
8	1.04
Each additional 4 % over 8 %	add .02

The endorsements may affect coverage only under Section I, only under Section II, or under both.

Effect on Premiums.   When the coverage provided by an HO policy is changed by endorsement, the premium charged for the policy is often affected. A change in premium may occur in one of three ways: (1) adjusting the base premium, (2) making an additional premium charge for an increase in coverage and adding this charge to the base premium, or (3) giving credit for a decrease or restriction in coverage and subtracting the credit from the base premium.

Endorsements Affecting Section I Coverages

Some of the endorsements in this group modify all of the Section I coverages. Others modify only one or two of the coverages.

All Section I Coverages.   Two of the homeowners endorsements affect all of the Section I coverages—the inflation guard endorsement and the earthquake endorsement.

Inflation Guard Endorsement (HO 04 46).   The inflation guard endorsement increases the limits of liability for Coverages A, B, C, and D. The endorsement permits the insured to select the percentage of annual increase, which applies pro rata throughout the policy year. For instance, if the insured selects an 8 percent annual increase, at the end of six months the limits would be increased 4 percent.

Adding the inflation guard endorsement requires an adjustment to the base premium. The pricing factor varies with the annual percentage increase in coverage selected (see Exhibit 4-5). As with other adjustments to the base premium, the base premium is multiplied by the appropriate pricing factor to determine the adjusted base premium.

Earthquake Endorsement (HO 04 54).   The earthquake endorsement adds back an excluded peril to the Section I coverages of the policy. This endorsement is priced by means of an addition to the base premium.

Earthquake coverage is always written with a deductible. In most areas, the deductible is 5 percent of the limit of liability for each applicable coverage section, subject to a $250 minimum.

The HO 04 54 endorsement excludes loss resulting directly or indirectly from flood of any nature or tidal wave, whether caused by or resulting from earthquake. Exterior masonry veneer may be either excluded or covered. If masonry veneer is covered, the entire structure is rated as masonry.

The earthquake endorsement rating process consists of four steps. First, the appropriate rate table is selected. These rate tables vary, based on the HO form used and the presence of endorsements modifying limits of liability. Second, the earthquake zone is determined from the rate table. Third, the rate per $1,000 of coverage is selected based on the construction class. Frame construction has the lowest rate and masonry the highest; superior or fire-resistive construction is given an intermediate rate. Finally, the selected rate is applied to the Coverage A amount for all forms except HO-4 and HO-6. With HO-4 and HO-6, the Coverage C limit is used as the rating basis. In either case, the selected rate is also applied to any increased limits and other coverage options the insured may have selected.

Coverages A and B. Four of the endorsements that affect only Coverages A and B are discussed below:

- Premises Alarm or Fire Protection System (HO 04 16)
- Ordinance or Law Coverage (HO 04 77)
- Other Structures—Increased Limits (HO 04 48)
- Special Loss Settlement (HO 04 56)

Premises Alarm or Fire Protection System (HO 04 16). In order to encourage loss control on the part of the insured, premium credits are given for premises alarm or fire protection systems, such as central station reporting burglar or fire alarms. The credit is applied by multiplying the base premium by the appropriate factor. With a 5 percent credit, for example, the factor would be 0.95. If the base premium is $100 and the factor is 0.95, $100 × 0.95 = $95 adjusted base premium.

The endorsement acknowledges the installation of an approved alarm or automatic sprinkler system on the residence premises for a premium credit. It also provides that the insured agrees to maintain this system in working order and to notify the insurer promptly of any change made to the system or if it is removed.

Ordinance or Law Coverage (HO 04 77). Older buildings often do not conform to modern building or zoning codes. If the building is damaged, any repairs or new construction would have to conform to the present zoning or building codes. The basic coverage in the homeowners policy provides for repair or replacement of "like kind and quality." If the present code requires more costly repairs, the insured has a potential gap in coverage. This gap can become quite substantial if the code requires demolition of the damaged dwelling. Many city ordinances require demolition of nonconforming buildings if they are damaged to 50 percent of their value.

Assume Mary's old nonconforming dwelling valued at $100,000 suffers a

$50,000 fire loss. The homeowners policy would pay for the $50,000 loss, but if the city ordinance requires that the building be demolished, Mary has suffered another $50,000 loss. This loss is not covered in the basic policy since it is due to the effect of the building ordinance, not the fire.

The ordinance or law coverage endorsement, HO 04 77, provides that for an additional premium, loss for damage by an insured peril to covered property or the building containing the covered property will be settled on the basis of any ordinance or law that regulates the construction, repair, or demolition of this property. This endorsement changes the policy by changing the loss settlement valuation method employed.

The pricing process for this endorsement requires three steps. First, the Coverage A amount used in calculating the base premium must be equal to *at least* 80 percent of the sum of the full replacement cost of the dwelling *plus* the amount of insurance required to cover the estimated demolition and increased construction costs. For example, if the replacement cost of the dwelling is $100,000 and estimated demolition and increased construction costs are $20,000, the Coverage A amount used in calculating the base premium must be *at least* $96,000, calculated as ($100,000 + $20,000) × 0.80. (To be fully covered in the event of a total loss, however, an insured should carry a Coverage A amount equal to 100 percent of the replacement cost of the dwelling *plus* demolition and increased construction costs.)

Second, the base premium is calculated in the normal manner, multiplying the key premium from the manual by the key factor that applies to the increased Coverage A limit as determined above.

Finally, the base premium calculated in the second step is multiplied by a factor of 1.10 to arrive at an adjusted base premium for the endorsement. This pricing procedure applies to the HO-1, HO-2, HO-3, and HO-8.

Other Structures—Increased Limits (HO 04 48). The limit of liability for Coverage B—Other Structures can be increased from 10 percent of Coverage A by the addition of this endorsement. The additional premium developed for this endorsement is $2 per $1,000 of insurance. Each structure on the residence premises for which increased limits are sought is listed on the HO 04 48 endorsement, and the limit of liability is shown. The limits of liability shown on the endorsement are in addition to the 10 percent of Coverage A provided in the basic policy.

Special Loss Settlement (HO 04 56). The standard homeowners policy provides loss settlement on a replacement cost basis if the Coverage A limit of liability represents at least 80 percent of replacement cost. With this endorsement, the requirement can be modified to 50, 60, or 70 percent of replacement value without affecting the loss settlement provisions. When HO 04 56 is used, the Coverage A limit of liability representing 50, 60, or 70 percent of replacement value is shown in the policy declarations.

The endorsement is typically used on a policy written to cover a home for which the replacement cost is substantially greater than its market value. Insurers are reluctant to issue replacement cost coverage on such dwellings because of the potential for moral hazard. By adding the HO 04 56 endorsement and purchasing a Coverage A limit in line with the dwelling's market value, an insured may obtain replacement cost coverage for small and medium-sized losses. For instance, if a dwelling had a replacement cost of $100,000 but a market value of only $60,000, the insured could purchase a homeowners policy with a $60,000 Coverage A limit, endorsed with an HO 04 56 to reduce the replacement cost requirement to 60 percent. In this way, the insured would have replacement cost coverage on dwelling losses up to $60,000 without the penalty for failing to insure to 80 percent of replacement value, and the insurer would avoid providing coverage in excess of the dwelling's market value.

The endorsement also provides for the settlement of losses to personal property, awnings, carpeting, household appliances, outdoor antennas, outdoor equipment (whether or not attached to buildings), and nonbuilding structures at actual cash value at the time of loss but not more than the amount required to repair or replace.

The pricing procedure for HO 04 56 requires an adjustment of the base premium. The base premium is increased by varying amounts depending on the percentage of replacement value selected. The net result is that the insured pays a higher base premium per $1,000 of coverage than would be the case if the standard 80 percent replacement cost coverage had been purchased.

Coverage C. The following are four of the endorsements that affect Coverage C—Personal Property:

- Coverage C Increased Special Limits of Liability (HO 04 65)
- Scheduled Personal Property (HO 04 61)
- Special Personal Property Coverage—Form HO 00 03 Only (HO 00 15)
- Personal Property Replacement Cost (HO 04 90)

Coverage C Increased Special Limits of Liability (HO 04 65). The blanket coverage on personal property under Coverage C has special limits of liability for particular types of property. For an increased premium, these special limits may be increased. The increases permitted are shown in Exhibit 4-6. A similar endorsement (HO 04 66) is used for HO-3 policies that include the HO 00 15 endorsement described below.

Scheduled Personal Property (HO 04 61). The scheduled personal property endorsement is used to provide coverage for risks of direct loss for certain special classes of scheduled property. This endorsement is actually an inland marine personal articles floater, which is discussed in detail in Chapter 6.

Scheduled coverage may be provided for jewelry, furs, cameras, musical instruments, silverware, golfer's equipment, fine arts, postage stamps, and rare and current coins. The rating for these coverages is based on standard inland marine rating procedures. A different rate per $100 of value applies to each category of property.

For scheduled musical instruments, coverage applies only to amateur musicians. The endorsement states that the insured agrees not to perform with the covered instrument(s) for pay unless the policy specifically provides for such performance. Coverage for professional musicians requires payment of a significantly higher premium.

Exhibit 4-6
Coverage C Increased Special Limits of Liability (HO 04 65)

Property	Basic Limit	Maximum Limit
Money, bank notes, bullion, gold other than goldware, silver other than silverware, platinum, coins, and medals	$200	$1,000
Securities, accounts, deeds, evidences of debt, letters of credit, notes other than bank notes, manuscripts, personal records, passports, tickets, and stamps	$1,000	$2,000
Jewelry, watches, furs, and precious and semiprecious stones for loss by theft	$1,000	$5,000 ($1,000 per item)
Firearms for loss by theft	$2,000	$6,000
Silverware, silver-plated ware, goldware, gold-plated ware, and pewterware for loss by theft	$2,500	$10,000
Adaptable electronic apparatus while in or upon a motor vehicle or other motorized land conveyance	$1,000	$5,000
Adaptable electronic apparatus, not in or upon a motor vehicle or other motorized land conveyance, away from the residence premises, and used for business	$1,000	$5,000

The endorsement provides only limited named-perils coverage for breakage of fine arts. Upon the payment of an additional premium, specific fine arts articles may be covered for breakage on a risks of direct loss basis.

The advantages of scheduled coverage under the HO 04 61 endorsement for these classes of special property are twofold. First, the scheduled coverage provides limits of liability of any amount required. The homeowners policy has limitations with respect to these types of property. Second, the endorsement provides coverage for risks of direct loss. If Marie dropped her expensive camera into the surf while photographing an ocean sunrise, the loss would not be covered under Coverage C of her homeowners policy. If the camera is scheduled on the HO 04 61 endorsement, the loss would be covered.

When writing these classes of property on the HO 04 61, certain types of underwriting information must always be provided. Each item should be carefully described and identified, including serial numbers where applicable. Appraisals should be obtained on jewelry, furs, and fine arts items, and the appraisals should be periodically updated. Expensive jewelry items should be photographed.

Special Personal Property Coverage (HO 00 15). This endorsement can be used only with the HO-3 policy. It changes Coverage C to provide coverage for risks of direct loss, rather than for the perils specified in the basic HO-3. The HO 00 15 endorsement may not be used if the HO 04 56 endorsement (described above) is attached to the policy. The price of the HO 00 15 endorsement is determined by multiplying the base premium by appropriate factors provided in the homeowners manual.

Personal Property Replacement Cost (HO 04 90). The homeowners policy covers personal property on an actual cash value basis. Therefore, if an insured's four-year-old television set is stolen, the loss payment will be reduced by a deduction for depreciation and will fall short of the amount required to replace the television with a new one.

The HO 04 90 endorsement changes the basis of loss settlement for personal property from actual cash value to replacement cost. The endorsement also extends replacement cost coverage to certain articles or classes of property if they are separately described and specifically insured in the policy. These types of property include jewelry, furs, cameras and related equipment, musical equipment, silverware, goldware, pewterware, and golfer's equipment. The endorsement states that the payment at the time of loss will be no more than the least of the following amounts:

1. Replacement cost at the time of loss without deduction for depreciation
2. The full cost of repair at the time of loss
3. The limit of liability that applies to Coverage C, if applicable
4. Any special limits of liability stated in the policy
5. The limit of liability that applies to any item separately described and specifically insured in the policy

When the replacement cost for the entire loss under the endorsement is more than $500, the insurer will pay no more than the actual cash value until the actual repair or replacement is complete. After repair or replacement is complete, the insured may, within 180 days of the date of loss, make claim for the difference between actual cash value and replacement cost. This clause enables the insurer to ascertain that the insured actually replaces the property before payment is made on a replacement cost basis. Since the insured receives new for old, and is to that extent better off after the loss, this provision is designed to reduce moral hazard.

The homeowners manual indicates a 15 percent increase in the base premium when the HO 04 90 endorsement is added to an HO-2 or HO-3. If the Coverage C limits are increased to 70 percent of Coverage A, as some insurers require when this endorsement is added, the additional premium for the increased limits is added to the base premium, which is then increased by 15 percent. Even if the increase in Coverage C limits is not required, an inventory of replacement values of contents by the insured will most often show a need to increase the Coverage C limits for complete protection in the event of a total loss.

When the HO 04 90 endorsement is added to either an HO-4 or HO-6, the base premium is increased by 35 percent. This larger increase factor reflects the fact that the majority of the property coverage in the HO-4 and HO-6 forms is on personal property.

Endorsements Affecting Section II Coverages

Various endorsements are available to extend the personal liability coverages of Section II. Many of these endorsements provide an opportunity to "buy back" coverage excluded in the basic homeowners contracts. The following are among the endorsements that affect Section II of a homeowners policy:

- Watercraft (HO 24 75)
- Snowmobile (HO 24 65)
- Business Pursuits (HO 24 71)
- Personal Injury (HO 24 82)
- Additional Residence Rented to Others (HO 04 70)

Watercraft (HO 24 75). This endorsement provides liability and medical payments coverage for certain watercraft. For an additional premium, Coverage E—Personal Liability and Coverage F—Medical Payments to Others are extended to bodily injury and property damage arising out of the ownership, maintenance, use, loading, or unloading of a watercraft described in the endorsement. Losses arising out of entrustment of the described watercraft are also covered. Further coverage is provided for vicarious liability, whether or not imposed by statute, for the actions of a child or minor using the described watercraft.

The endorsement provides for the listing of the horsepower and description of watercraft powered by outboard engines or motors of more than twenty-five total horsepower and other watercraft with inboard or inboard-outdrive power. Sailing vessels, with or without auxiliary power, that are twenty-six feet or more in length are described in a separate paragraph. The descriptions and other information about the watercraft are used both for underwriting purposes and for rating.

Watercraft other than sailing vessels are not covered while being operated in or practicing for a prearranged or organized race. With respect to watercraft with inboard or inboard-outdrive motor power and sailing vessels, coverage does not apply to bodily injury to any employee of an insured arising out of and in the course of employment by the insured if the employee's principal duties are in connection with the maintenance or use of the watercraft. Many large inboard motor vessels have a paid captain or deckhand who operates and maintains the vessel. An insured with such an employee would have to obtain separate coverage for the employee. With respect to the same type of watercraft, no coverage is provided if the watercraft is used to carry persons for a charge or is rented to others. Notice that the last two exclusions do not apply to watercraft with outboard motors.

The additional premium for the watercraft endorsement is based on the type of vessel, its length, and its speed. The premium ranges from a nominal amount for outboard motors over twenty-five horsepower but less than fifty horsepower to hundreds of dollars for inboard or inboard-outdrive motorboats twenty-six to forty feet in length with a speed of over thirty miles per hour.

In some areas of the country, watercraft are used only during part of the year and are stored or laid up and not in use the rest of the year. The part of the year during which watercraft are used is called the *navigational period.* Although coverage under the HO 24 75 endorsement must be written for the entire policy period, a pro-rata adjustment may be made in the premium for the endorsement to reflect the navigational period of each year.

Snowmobile Endorsement (HO 24 64). Coverage may be provided for liability arising from the operation of owned snowmobiles by adding the HO 24 64 endorsement to a homeowners policy. The premium charge is a minimum premium for each snowmobile for any period within a policy year.

Business Pursuits (HO 24 71). When this endorsement is used, Coverage E—Personal Liability and Coverage F—Medical Payments to Others apply to the business pursuits of the insured. The type of business is specified in the endorsement. When the insured is a teacher, liability for corporal punishment may be added for an additional charge.

There is no coverage for liability arising out of business pursuits of the insured in connection with a business or partnership that the insured owns or financially controls. Liability arising out of professional services of any nature other than teaching also is excluded, as is bodily injury to a fellow employee of the insured injured in the course of employment. When the insured is a member of the faculty or teaching staff of any school or college, there is no coverage for liability arising out of the use of draft or saddle animals, aircraft, motorized land conveyances, and watercraft when used for instructional purposes.

Personal Injury (HO 24 82). This endorsement may be used to add personal injury coverage to Coverage E—Personal Liability. Personal injury is defined in the endorsement as injury arising out of false arrest, detention or imprisonment, or malicious prosecution; libel, slander, or defamation of character; or invasion of privacy, wrongful eviction, or wrongful entry. The HO 24 82 endorsement contains a special set of exclusions pertaining to this coverage. These provisions exclude liability assumed by the insured under contract or agreement except for any indemnity obligation assumed by the insured under a written contract directly relating to the ownership, maintenance, or use of the premises.

Further exclusions apply to injury caused while violating a penal law or ordinance; injury directly or indirectly related to the employment of a person by the insured; injury arising out of a business engaged in by the insured; civic or public activities performed for pay by an insured; and injury to any insured.

Additional Residence Rented to Others (HO 24 70).   The definition of insured location under Coverage E—Personal Liability and Coverage F—Medical Payments to Others is broadened under the HO 24 70 endorsement to include an additional residence rented to others. The residence may not house more than four families. The endorsement provides for the listing of the location of this additional residence and an indication of the number of families that occupy it.

The premium charge for this coverage is an additional premium that varies by territory and by the number of families at the additional residence. This charge varies from a nominal amount for one family to over $200 for four families in some territories.

Endorsements Affecting Sections I and II

Certain endorsements affect both Section I and Section II of the homeowners policy. The following three endorsements that affect both the property and liability coverages are discussed below:

- Permitted Incidental Occupancies—Residence Premises (HO 04 42)
- Home Day Care Coverage (HO 04 97)
- Additional Insured—Residence Premises (HO 04 41)

Permitted Incidental Occupancies—Residence Premises (HO 04 42). If an insured owns a business conducted on the residence premises, property and liability loss exposures arising out of that business may be insured through the use of the HO 04 42 endorsement. The business constituting the incidental occupancy is listed in the endorsement, which also provides for indication of whether the business is conducted in the dwelling or in a separate structure. The location of the business on the residence premises affects the rating of the endorsement.

When the HO 04 42 endorsement is added to the policy, the $2,500 special limit of liability on business personal property applies only to business personal property *not* used in the covered business. Consequently, in the event of a loss, personal property that is used in the business insured under the endorsement is covered, along with the insured's other personal property, up to the limit of liability for Coverage C. The endorsement also provides that Coverages E and F shall apply to occurrences that arise out of the insured's incidental use of the premises for the business covered by the endorsement.

Home Day Care Coverage (HO 04 97). Home day care centers represent a special kind of incidental occupancy. In recent years, increased litigation involving home day care centers has made this exposure difficult to underwrite. As stated in Chapter 3, most states require that the HO 04 96 endorsement be attached to homeowners policies to emphasize that there is only limited coverage under Section I for business personal property and no coverage under Section II for liability arising out of a business conducted by the insured. Therefore, if coverage is to be provided for a home day care center operated as a business and conducted by the insured on the residence premises, the HO 04 97 endorsement must be used.

The number of persons receiving day care services is listed on the endorsement. As is the case with the incidental occupancies endorsement, information is required about the location of the day care center, that is, whether it is in the dwelling or in another structure on the residence premises. If another structure is involved, a limit of liability is indicated, and a rating charge per $1,000 of coverage is made.

In addition to stating a specific limit of liability for the structure (other than the dwelling) in which the day care business is conducted, the endorsement extends the Coverage C limit of liability to property used in the day care business. Therefore, the $2,500 limit for personal property on the residence premises used for a business purpose does not apply to the property used in the day care business.

When the HO 04 97 endorsement is used, coverage under Section II of the homeowners policy applies to bodily injury and property damage arising out of the day care business. However, there is no coverage for liability arising out of the use of draft or saddle animals, vehicles for use with those animals, aircraft, motorized land conveyances, and watercraft. Bodily injury to any employee of an insured, other than a residence employee, is also excluded.

The endorsement includes an annual aggregate limit of liability applying to both Coverages E and F. This limit applies regardless of the number of occurrences, insureds, claims made, or persons injured. A similar aggregate annual limit of liability applies under Coverage F for any one person. Therefore, the most that will be paid under Coverage F for medical expense payable for bodily injury to any one person is the dollar amount shown in the declarations for Coverage F. This does not increase the aggregate limit of liability.

Additional Insured—Residence Premises (HO 04 41). The insured under a homeowners policy is usually an owner-occupant. There are some other situations in which more than one person or entity may have an insurable interest in the dwelling. For example, Bob is a purchaser-occupant who has entered into a long-term installment contract for the purchase of a dwelling. However, title does not pass to Bob from Sally, the seller, until all the terms of the installment contract have been satisfied. Sally retains title until completion of the payments and in no way acts as a mortgagee. In this case, Bob could purchase a homeowners policy as named insured on the declarations page, and Sally could be covered as an additional insured by using the HO 04 41 endorsement. The endorsement would show not only Sally's name but also the extent of her insurable interest.

The protection provided for Sally as an additional insured under Bob's homeowners policy includes Coverages A and B, to the extent of Sally's interest in the dwelling and other structures, and Coverages E and F but only with respect to liability and medical payments arising out of the residence premises. Also, if Bob's homeowners policy were canceled or not renewed by the insurer, Sally would receive written notice from the insurer. Coverages C and D under Bob's homeowners policy would not apply to Sally. Additionally, coverage for bodily injury to an employee of the additional insured is specifically excluded.

The endorsement may also be used to cover the interests of the grantor of a life estate. Additionally, if a two-family dwelling is co-owned by two persons, each of whom has a distinct residence with a separate entrance, only one of the co-owners may be shown as the named insured under the homeowners policy that insures the dwelling. The interests of the co-owner not shown as the named insured may be partially protected by use of the HO 04 41 endorsement, but there would be no coverage for bodily injury to an employee of that co-owner.

SUMMARY

The homeowners policy has an indivisible base premium, reflecting the fact that it is a preset package of coverages. The base premium is derived from key rating factors and the amount of coverage selected. The key rating factors are territory, fire protection, and construction. Homeowners insurance is priced primarily on the basis of property loss frequency and severity.

The homeowners key premium is determined on the basis of the applicable territory, public fire protection, construction, and the particular form that is used. The key premium is multiplied by a key factor, based on the amount of coverage selected, to determine the base premium. Adjustments are made to the base premium for superior construction, when the dwelling is a row house or townhouse, and when the deductible is increased or decreased.

Endorsements may be added to a homeowners policy to meet the special needs of an insured, to meet insurer underwriting requirements, or to comply with state insurance regulations. Some endorsements require an adjustment of the base premium. Others impose an additional premium charge for an increase in coverage, which is added to the base premium. Likewise, for endorsements that restrict or decrease the coverage, a credit is deducted from the base premium.

Endorsements affecting all of the Section I coverages include the inflation guard endorsement and the earthquake endorsement. Endorsements affecting Coverages A and B include the premises alarm or fire protection system endorsement, the ordinance or law coverage endorsement, the other structures—increased limits endorsement, and the special loss settlement endorsement.

Coverage C can be modified in several ways by endorsements. The increased special limit of liability endorsement increases the limits for the blanket coverage that applies to certain classes of personal property. The scheduled personal property endorsement provides coverage for risks of direct physical loss on items in certain classes when they are listed with an appraised value. Both endorsements provide coverage above the policy sublimits for the classes or items of property covered. Insureds wishing coverage for risks of direct physical loss on all personal property can add the special personal property coverage endorsement, available only with the HO-3. Finally, the personal property replacement cost endorsement can be used to provide replacement cost coverage for personal property under Coverage C.

Several endorsements affecting Section II of the homeowners policy permit the insured to "buy back" coverage excluded in the unendorsed policy. For example, the watercraft endorsement adds back the coverage for listed watercraft that would otherwise be excluded because of the type or length of vessel. Another endorsement adds liability coverage for snowmobile owners. For an additional premium, Coverages E and F can be added for losses arising out of a business conducted by the insured. The personal injury endorsement adds coverage for liability arising from additional acts not covered in the unendorsed policy. The additional residence rented to others endorsement protects the insured from claims and lawsuits arising from the rental of an additional residence.

Endorsements affecting both Section I and Section II coverages include the permitted incidental occupancy—residence premises endorsement, the home day care coverage endorsement, and the additional insured—residence premises endorsement.

Chapter Notes

1. The explanation of the rating process is drawn from the Insurance Services Office *Homeowners Policy Program (1991 Edition) Manual.*
2. For a detailed analysis of fire protection see E. P. Hollingsworth and J. J. Launie, *Commercial Property and Multiple Lines Underwriting,* 2nd ed. (Malvern, PA: Insurance Institute of America, 1984), pp. 204-211.
3. Construction types are covered in Hollingsworth and Launie, pp. 131-170.
4. For a discussion of the concept of a fire division see Hollingsworth and Launie, pp. 8-9.

CHAPTER 5

Other Residential Insurance

The previous three chapters described the homeowners policies used by a large number of people to insure their real and personal property. This chapter discusses other types of residential insurance.

Owners of mobilehomes and farms can insure their residences under homeowners policies that include endorsements specifically designed for these types of residences. Other home owners may insure their residences under dwelling policies, which are monoline policies that provide property coverage similar in many ways to the property coverage in homeowners policies. In some instances, the owner of a residence may not be able to purchase homeowners insurance because the location of the residence does not meet underwriting requirements. The owners of such residences may be able to purchase property insurance through FAIR plans or beachfront plans, which are assigned risk plans for property that is difficult to insure in the standard insurance market.

The chapter concludes with a family residence insurance case. This case presents several loss situations and explains how homeowners policies and other types of residence insurance would apply to the losses.

HOMEOWNERS INSURANCE FOR MOBILEHOME OWNERS

As housing prices have increased in recent years, so have mobilehome sales. Mobilehomes are generally less expensive than conventional housing. The flexibility of mobilehomes also makes them useful when the housing requirement may not be permanent. Often, in "boom" towns when employment is temporarily increased due to the operation of an oil shale facility or surface mine, the workers purchase and set up mobilehomes. Mobilehomes also are used as summer or vacation homes.

Exposures

The owners of mobilehomes face the same exposures to loss as do owners of conventional homes. Therefore, a mobilehome owner may experience loss to the dwelling or another structure on the residence premises and the contents of either. There is also an exposure to liability loss because of bodily injury or damage to the property of others.

The Mobilehome and Other Structures. The mobilehome itself is personal property rather than real property. The essence of the mobilehome is its impermanence. In some areas of the country, a mobilehome is required to have wheels and axles attached even when set up. This is to emphasize the mobile nature of the structure and to differentiate it from a conventionally constructed dwelling. These differences are usually recognized in the manner in which the mobilehomes are taxed. Therefore, mobile homes are sometimes taxed as vehicles rather than structures.

When a mobilehome is set up, it may be surrounded by skirting that conceals the wheels and gives the appearance of a permanent structure. Patio covers are often attached to mobilehomes and sheds and similar outbuildings set up nearby. When they are set up, mobilehomes are subject to the same perils as any other structure. Exposures to the perils of fire, vandalism, and crime are roughly equivalent to those of a conventional dwelling. Mobilehomes are also susceptible to damage from windstorm and earthquake depending on how they are set up.

Mobilehomes generally do not remain on their tires. They are set up on blocks or piers and, in some cases, on masonry footings. Masonry footings provide a very stable foundation, but they are costly and therefore seldom used. When the mobilehome is set up, there are two major considerations with respect to the windstorm and earthquake perils. First, the piers or footings must be strong and stable enough to properly support the unit. The second consideration, tie-down, is important because a windstorm may either move a mobilehome sideways or lift it off the ground. An earthquake can subject the unit to sudden and severe upwards and sideways thrusts. Therefore, a properly set up mobilehome should not only have a strong and stable foundation, but it should also be tied down to anchors buried in the ground to prevent the unit from moving upwards or sideways.

Mobilehomes frequently suffer severe damage in hurricanes or tornadoes, often resulting in total loss of the units as well as loss of life of the occupants. Since mobilehome parks may be relegated to less desirable housing areas by zoning laws, they are often located in areas subject to flooding. Theoretically, the mobile nature of the mobilehome should make it possible to move a unit that is threatened by rising waters, but this is seldom practical. A residential mobilehome may be constructed of two or three modules. Each of these modules may be as large as ten feet by sixty feet. These units are mobile only in a technical sense. It usually takes many hours of specialized labor to prepare a unit for moving. Units on masonry foundations can take days to prepare.

When mobilehomes are moved from the sales lot to the set-up site, or from one site to another, they are subject to transportation perils such as upset, overturn, collapse of bridges, or sinking of ferries. The wall areas of long mobilehome modules create a large surface area exposed to the wind, increasing the likelihood of upset or overturn if high winds strike while they are being moved. The high cost of disassembly, transportation, and reassembly results in infrequent moves of mobilehomes after the initial set up.

Other Personal Property and Personal Liability. The contents of a mobilehome are similar to those in a conventional dwelling and are subject to the same perils. The mobilehome owner also is subject to the same liability perils as the owner of a conventional home. Consequently, there are corresponding similarities in coverage needs.

Mobilehome Coverage

Owners of mobilehomes have several options for insuring their dwellings. The American Association of Insurance Services (AAIS) and some specialty insurers have developed policies especially for mobilehomes. Insurers that use forms developed by the Insurance Services Office (ISO) provide coverage for mobilehomes by attaching a mobilehome endorsement, MH 04 01, to a homeowners policy. The following discussion is based on the ISO forms, specifically the MH 04 01 endorsement used with an HO-3 policy. According to ISO rules, the endorsement may also be used with an HO-2 policy; tenants of mobilehomes may use the HO-4 policy without modification.

Mobilehome Endorsement (MH 04 01). A mobilehome is eligible for coverage if it is designed for portability and year-round living. The mobilehome also may not be less than ten feet wide and forty feet long.

The mobilehome endorsement, the attached homeowners form, and the declarations page constitute the complete mobilehome policy. As with all homeowners policies, however, other endorsements may be attached to modify the coverage. The mobilehome endorsement states that the insurance is subject to all applicable provisions of the homeowners form except as revised by the endorsement. The differences between the HO-3 and the mobilehome policy are in the definition of "residence premises" and in some of the provisions that relate to coverage under Section I. Only the revisions in the mobilehome endorsement are discussed here.

Definitions. The definition of "residence premises" is changed to mean the mobilehome and other structures located on land owned or leased by the insured where the insured resides. This location must be shown as the residence premises in the declarations.

Coverage A—Dwelling. The dwelling coverage applies to a mobilehome used primarily as a private residence. Coverage applies to structures and utility tanks attached to the mobilehome. It also applies to floor coverings, appliances, dressers, cabinets, and similar items that are permanently installed. This provision recognizes the fact that standard features of most mobilehomes are built-in cabinets and appliances.

Coverage B—Other Structures. The limit of liability for Coverage B is 10 percent of the limit that applies to Coverage A. However, if that amount is less than $2,000, a minimum limit of $2,000 is provided.

Vacation Mobilehomes

Many mobilehomes are used in recreational areas as vacation homes. While some of these are set up in mobilehome parks, many are not. For instance, a mobilehome may be placed in the mountains or at the side of a lake or river.

The exposures faced by vacation mobilehomes are somewhat different from the exposures for mobilehomes used as ordinary year-round residences. Often vacation areas do not have full-time fire departments. Also, there may be no telephone in the mobilehome or no neighbors nearby to report a fire in the owner's absence. All of these factors contribute to the likelihood of increased loss severity if a fire does occur. Because many vacation mobilehome residences are located in heavily wooded areas, they are subject to unusually high fire hazards. This hazard can be reduced by the knowledgeable insured through use of clear spaces where brush and timber are removed for a distance around the mobilehome. Nevertheless, placing a mobilehome in a forest area increases potential loss frequency and probable severity.

Additional Coverages. The additional coverage for property removed provides up to $500 for reasonable expenses incurred by the insured for removal and return of the mobilehome if it is endangered by an insured peril. No deductible applies to this coverage.

Section I—Conditions. The condition regarding loss settlement does not include carpeting and appliances as property to be valued on the basis of actual cash value. These types of property are included in Coverage A and are covered for risks of direct loss.

The mobilehome endorsement applies to loss to a pair, set, or panels and will pay the reasonable cost of repairing or replacing damaged paneling to match the undamaged part as closely as possible. The insurer, however, does not guarantee the availability of matching panels and will not be liable for replacement of all paneling if a suitable match is not found.

Under the mortgage clause, the word "mortgagee" includes a trustee or lienholder. Mobile homes are not considered real property, and liens may take the form of chattel mortgages or trust certificates.

Other Mobilehome Endorsements. A mobilehome policy can be endorsed with many of the homeowners endorsements. The following four endorsements are unique to mobilehome coverage:

- Actual Cash Value (MH 04 02)
- Transportation/Permission to Move (MH 04 03)
- Mobilehome Lienholder's Single Interest (MH 04 04)
- Property Removed Increased Limit (MH 04 06)

Actual Cash Value—Mobilehome (MH 04 02). If coverage on an actual cash value basis is desired for the mobilehome, the MH 04 02 endorsement is used in addition to the MH 04 01. The MH 04 02 endorsement changes the loss settlement terms to an actual cash value basis. At the insurer's discretion, covered property losses may be settled in one of three ways. The insurer may pay the cost of repairing the damage, the cost of replacing the damaged property with similar property (but not necessarily from the same manufacturer), or it may pay the amount in money. If the amount is paid in money, the insurer will pay no more than the lowest of (1) the difference between actual cash value of the property before and after the loss, (2) the cost of repairing the damage, or (3) the cost of replacing the damaged property with similar property.

Transportation/Permission to Move (MH 04 03). The transportation/permission to move endorsement provides coverage for perils of transportation and at the new location anywhere in the United States or Canada for a period of thirty days from the effective date of the endorsement. The perils of transportation are collision, upset, and stranding or sinking (while the mobilehome is being transported on a licensed ferry line).

Mobilehome Lienholder's Single Interest (MH 04 04). The mobilehome lienholder's single interest endorsement provides coverage for the lienholder only. The first coverage is transportation coverage for the limited perils of collision and upset. This coverage is designed to cover a loss while the unit is being delivered. In addition, coverage is provided to the lienholder for loss due to the owner's conversion, embezzlement, or secretion of the mobilehome. Since the mobilehome can be moved, some lienholders require the mobilehome owner to purchase this endorsement to protect the lienholder's interest in the event of any of the covered losses.

Property Removed Increased Limit (MH 04 06). The mobilehome endorsement provides $500 in order to cover removal expenses for a mobilehome threatened by an insured peril. With a large, multi-unit mobilehome, removal costs alone may run over $2,000. To this would be added a roughly equivalent expense in setting the mobilehome back up after the threat from the insured peril had passed. For this reason, the property removed increased limit endorsement, MH 04 06, provides a means for the insured to purchase a sufficiently high removal limit to cover the expenses to take down, transport, and set the mobilehome up again.

HOMEOWNERS INSURANCE FOR FARM OWNERS

Farm owners may be eligible to insure the liability exposures from their farming operations under homeowners policies with the appropriate endorsements. These endorsements cover incidental farming operations on the residence premises or at another location, or larger farms operated away from the residence premises. The endorsements can be used only if farming is not the insured's primary occupation.

Incidental Farming Personal Liability (HO 24 72)

The incidental farming personal liability endorsement extends the personal liability and medical payments coverage in Section II to incidental farming operations conducted by the insured. If the farming is on the insured's residence premises, it must be incidental to the use of the premises as a dwelling, and the income derived from the farming operations may not be the insured's primary source of income. Coverage also applies if the residence premises is used for the sheltering and grazing of animals. Coverage is not available, however, if the residence premises is used for racing purposes.

If the incidental farming activities are at a separate location, that location must be specified in the endorsement. The permissible farming activities include the boarding or grazing of the insured's animals or use of the land as garden space. The income derived may not be the insured's primary source of income, and there is no coverage if the location is used for racing purposes.

Farmers Personal Liability (HO 24 73)

This endorsement is designed to cover the liability exposures arising out of a commercial farming operation conducted away from the insured's residence premises. The endorsement contains a supplemental declarations page, and some of the definitions applicable to Section II of the homeowners policy are modified to reflect that farming operations are covered. The Section II—Liability Coverages and Section II—Exclusions in the endorsement replace those in the homeowners policies. A new coverage (Coverage G) may be selected by the insured to cover animal collision, and additional conditions apply if farm employees are covered.

Declarations. The first portion of the HO 24 73 endorsement consists of a supplementary declarations page. The first part of the declarations sets forth all farm premises owned, rented, or operated by the insured. Each such premises is listed and designated as either operated by the insured or rented to others. An advance premium is charged for each of the farm premises indicated.

For farms owned and operated or rented and operated by the insured or the insured's employees, the total acreage of the initial farm premises is indicated. Any additional farm premises with buildings and a rate per premises are also listed.

For farms owned by the insured but rented to others, the declarations list all farm premises without buildings, each farm premises with buildings and the rate that applies per premises, and the total acreage of farms rented to others. An additional flat charge for all such farms is based on the total acreage.

Coverage under the endorsement assumes that no business other than farming is conducted on the insured location. Therefore, if any other businesses are conducted, they must be listed in the declarations.

The next section of the declarations applies to farm employees. The covered employees are separated into three categories based on the number of days per year they are employed. A different rate per employee in each category may be charged, or the premium may be based on a rate per $100 of payroll.

If coverage for animal collision (Coverage G) is desired, the number of animals to be covered should be indicated in the final section of the declarations. The Coverage G limit of liability is $400 per animal.

Definitions. The definition of "business" as it applies to coverage under the HO 24 73 endorsement does not include farming, and the definition of "insured location" is changed to include the farm premises. The endorsement also adds definitions of "farm employee," "farming," and "insured farm employee."

Coverages and Exclusions. Only Section II of the homeowners policies is changed by the HO 24 73 endorsement. Medical payments coverage is extended to insured farm employees and to persons who are injured by farm employees off the insured location in the course of employment by the insured. Under the endorsement, the exclusions for Coverages E and F apply to pollution liability and to bodily injury to farm employees.

Coverage G is provided only if a premium is paid for this coverage. Coverage G pays the amount shown in the declarations for loss by death of any cattle, horse, mule, donkey, swine, sheep, or goat owned by an insured. In order to be covered, death must have been the result of a *collision* between the animal and a vehicle not owned or operated by the insured or an employee, and the collision must occur while the animal is within a public highway and is not being transported. Therefore, if a farmer's cow were killed by a vehicle that entered the pasture, there would be no coverage.

Additional Conditions. If a premium is shown in the declarations for coverage of farm employees, the coverage is subject to additional conditions. The premium shown in the declarations is a deposit premium that will be applied to the earned premium due at the end of the policy period. The insured must keep records necessary for premium computation and must send copies to the insurer at the end of the policy period. The insurer also reserves the right to inspect the insured's operations and audit the insured's records and books.

OTHER COVERAGE FOR RESIDENCES

Coverage for residences is not always written on homeowners policies. Some residences are not eligible for homeowners coverage. In some cases, this is because the value of the dwelling is below the homeowners program minimum. In other cases, the residence may not be owner-occupied, or it may not be eligible because of underwriting reasons. For example, many residences in southern California are located in brush areas and subject to wind-driven brush fires. Few, if any, insurance companies write homeowners policies for homes in these areas. Most of these residences must find alternative coverage.

In other cases, the insured may not want the full range of homeowners coverages, preferring a monoline approach. A final reason for purchasing alternative coverages is cost. An individual may only be able to afford the minimum fire insurance required by the lending institution holding the mortgage on the dwelling. In this case, the homeowners package of coverages may appear to be too expensive.

The dwelling program is one of the alternatives to the homeowners policies. Other alternatives include FAIR plans and beachfront plans.

The Dwelling Program

The dwelling program provides property coverage for dwellings and their contents. The dwelling program includes three forms—DP 00 01, DP 00 02, and DP 00 03—which offer dwelling and contents coverage similar to that offered under Section I of the HO-1, HO-2, and HO-3, respectively. The policy structure and approach to property coverage is much like that found in the homeowners policies. The following discussion compares the monoline coverage in the dwelling forms with the coverage in the homeowners policies.

Insuring Agreement and Definitions. The format of the dwelling forms is similar to that of the homeowners policy. The insuring agreements are identical. The first major difference occurs in the definitions section. The dwelling forms only define "you" and "yours" (the named insured and the spouse if a resident of the same household) and "we," "us," and "our" (the insurance company). The remainder of the definitions in the homeowners policy pertain to the liability and medical payments coverages of Section II. Since the dwelling forms do not have liability or medical payments coverage, these definitions are unnecessary.

Coverages. The dwelling forms provide coverage for the insured's dwelling, other structures on the described location, the insured's personal property, and loss of use of the dwelling.

Coverage A—Dwelling. The dwelling forms refer to the "described location," while the homeowners policy refers to the "residence premises." When referring to the dwelling on the described location, the dwelling forms specify that it is used principally for dwelling purposes. The dwelling forms also specifically state that if not covered elsewhere in the policy, building equipment and outdoor equipment used for the service of and located on the described location is covered. The remainder of the Coverage A language is identical in the dwelling and homeowners forms.

Coverage B—Other Structures. There are some minor differences in wording between the dwelling and homeowners forms, but the coverage is essentially the same.

Coverage C—Personal Property. The coverage for personal property in the dwelling forms applies to personal property, usual to the occupancy of a dwelling, owned or used by the insured or resident family members, while the property is on the described location. This is a more restrictive description of the covered property than is in the homeowners policy, which covers personal property owned or used by an insured while it is anywhere in the world.

There are no special limits of liability in the dwelling forms with respect to any type of property, while the homeowners policy provides special limits of liability on many types of property excluded in the dwelling forms. For example, the dwelling forms exclude boats, other than rowboats and canoes, but the homeowners policy provides a limit of $1,000 on watercraft, including their furnishings, equipment, and outboard motors. The homeowners policy also has special limits on theft losses to jewelry, furs, firearms, silverware, and similar types of property. The unendorsed dwelling forms have no theft coverage, only coverage for damage done by burglars.

The Coverage C limit of liability in the dwelling forms is chosen by the insured. In the homeowners policy, the Coverage C limit of liability is a set percentage of Coverage A and can be increased at the insured's option. If an insured is a landlord, he or she can choose to purchase only Coverage A under the dwelling program. There is no such option with the homeowners policy. A tenant may choose to purchase only Coverage C under a dwelling form, thereby obtaining property coverage similar to that provided by an HO-4 policy.

Coverage D—Fair Rental Value and Coverage E—Additional Living Expense. Coverages D and E in the dwelling forms correspond to Coverage D—Loss of Use in the homeowners policy. The only distinction between the forms concerns fair rental value. The homeowners policy provides fair rental value coverage only if the residence premises where the loss occurred is the principal place of residence of the insured. The dwelling forms provide fair rental value coverage for that part of the described location that is rented to others or held for rental by the insured. There is no requirement that the dwelling be the principal place of residence of the insured.

Dwelling form DP 00 01 (the basic form) includes only Coverage D—Fair Rental Value. Coverage for additional living expense can be added by endorsement, for an additional premium.

Other Coverages. Many of the "other coverages" provided in the dwelling forms correspond to the "additional coverages" in the homeowners policy, but there are some differences. Loss assessment coverage, which is included automatically in the homeowners policy, can be added to the dwelling forms by endorsement, for an additional premium. The additional coverages in the homeowners policy for credit cards, fund transfer cards, forgery, and counterfeit money and for landlord's furnishings are not available in the dwelling program. The following paragraphs discuss the other coverages in the dwelling forms and compare them with the coverage provided in the homeowners policy.

Other Structures. The dwelling forms provide up to 10 percent of the Coverage A limit of liability for loss to other structures. Use of this coverage does not reduce the Coverage A limit of liability for the same loss. Similar coverage is provided in the homeowners policy under Coverage B.

Debris Removal. The debris removal coverage of the dwelling forms is included in the Coverage A limit of liability. The homeowners policy provides an additional 5 percent of the Coverage A limit for debris removal if required.

Improvements, Alterations, and Additions. The dwelling forms, like the HO-4 policy, provide 10 percent of the Coverage C limit of liability to cover a tenant's improvements, alterations, and additions. There is no comparable coverage in the other homeowners forms.

World-Wide Coverage. In the dwelling forms, up to 10 percent of the Coverage C limit of liability is provided for loss to the property covered under Coverage C, except rowboats and canoes, while anywhere in the world. The homeowners policy provides worldwide coverage for personal property owned or used by an insured, but a 10 percent limitation applies to property usually located at a secondary residence.

Rental Value and Additional Living Expense. Under the broad and special dwelling forms (DP 00 02 and DP 00 03, respectively), the insured may use up to 10 percent of the Coverage A limit of liability for loss of both fair rental value and additional living expense. Use of this coverage does not reduce the Coverage A limit of liability for the same loss. Under homeowners forms HO-2 and HO-3, the corresponding limit for loss of use is 20 percent of the Coverage A limit of liability.

The basic dwelling form, DP 00 01, provides up to 10 percent of the Coverage A limit of liability for loss of fair rental value only. Payment under this coverage reduces the Coverage A limit of liability by the amount paid for the same loss.

Reasonable Repairs. The dwelling forms and the homeowners policy provide coverage for the cost of reasonable repairs made solely to protect covered property from further damage. This coverage does not increase the limit of liability that applies to the covered property.

Property Removed. Covered property is protected if it is removed from a premises endangered by an insured peril under both the dwelling and homeowners forms. In both cases this coverage applies to direct loss from any cause for a period of thirty days (a limit of five days applies to the basic dwelling form).

Trees, Shrubs, and Other Plants. In the dwelling forms and the homeowners policy, the aggregate limit of liability that can be applied to trees, shrubs, plants, or lawns is 5 percent of the Coverage A limit. The limit for any one tree, plant, or shrub is $500. This coverage can be added by endorsement to dwelling form DP 00 01, the basic form.

Fire Department Service Charge. As in the homeowners policy, the dwelling forms will pay up to $500 for fire department service charges. Coverage is not provided if the property is located within the limits of the city, municipality, or protection district furnishing the fire department response. This coverage is additional insurance, and no deductible applies.

Collapse. The broad and special dwelling forms (DP 00 02 and DP 00 03) provide the same coverage for collapse that is provided in the homeowners policy. This coverage is not available in the basic dwelling form.

Glass or Safety Glazing Material. Dwelling forms DP 00 02 and DP 00 03 provide coverage for the breaking of glass or safety glazing material that is part of a building, storm door, or storm window; and for damage to covered property by such glass or safety glazing material. The coverage does not apply if the dwelling has been vacant for more than thirty days. Similar coverage is provided in the homeowners policy.

Perils Insured Against. The analysis in Chapter 2 of the perils insured against in the homeowners policies focused on the HO-3 form. The following examination of the perils insured against in the dwelling program is based on the dwelling special form, DP 00 03. (This form will be referred to as DP-3 in the following discussion). Forms DP 00 01 and DP 00 02 provide coverage against essentially the same perils covered by the HO-1 and HO-2 forms. To the extent that there are differences, the dwelling forms tend to provide narrower coverage. For instance, there is no theft coverage for personal property under any of the dwelling forms, although such coverage can be added by endorsement.

Coverages A and B. The DP-3, like the HO-3, insures against risks of direct loss to property under Coverages A and B. In each policy, the coverage for direct loss to real property is defined by the perils that are excluded. Those causes of loss that are not excluded are covered. The DP-3 form excludes coverage for theft of any property that is not part of a covered building or structure. It also excludes loss by wind, hail, ice, snow, or sleet to (1) outdoor radio and television antennas and aerials and (2) trees, shrubs, plants, or lawns. The other exclusions in the DP-3 are essentially the same as those in the HO-3.

Coverage C. Although the Coverage C perils under the DP-3 form are similar to the perils covered by the HO-3, there are some differences. Theft of personal property is not covered under the DP-3, but coverage is provided for damage to personal property caused by burglars, unless the dwelling has been vacant for more than thirty days. The DP-3 specifically excludes pilferage, theft, burglary, and larceny under the vandalism or malicious mischief peril.

The windstorm or hail coverage also differs slightly from the HO-3, in that the DP-3 specifically excludes windstorm or hail damage to canoes and rowboats and to plants, shrubs, and trees. The HO-3 does not cover windstorm or hail damage to trees, shrubs, and other plants, but it does cover such damage to watercraft and their trailers, furnishings, equipment, and outboard motors while inside a fully enclosed building.

Dwelling Policy Exclusions. The general exclusions under the DP-3 track very closely with the Section I exclusions in the HO-3. The difference is that the DP-3 exclusions for earth movement and water damage also apply to loss by theft.

Dwelling Policy Conditions. The DP-3 form contains a single section of conditions. These same conditions are found in the HO-3 policy. However, some conditions are applicable only to Section I while others are applicable to both Sections I and II. The dwelling policy does not contain the references to loss by theft and to credit card or fund transfer card coverage that are in the homeowners policy.

Coverage for Liability and Theft Losses. The dwelling forms do not provide coverage for liability or for theft losses. Such coverage is available, however, through a personal liability supplement and theft endorsements.

Personal Liability Supplement.   Liability coverage may be written in conjunction with the dwelling policy or independently as a separate policy through the Personal Liability Supplement. The personal liability form DL 24 01 provides basic personal liability coverage (Coverage L) and medical payments to others coverage (Coverage M). These coverages are very similar in format and language to Coverages E and F in Section II of the homeowners policy.

The definitions in the Personal Liability Supplement (DL) differ from the homeowners policy only in regard to the "residence premises." The definition of "residence premises" in the DL form includes a one- to four-family dwelling. The corresponding language in the homeowners policy refers to one- or two-family dwellings.

Coverage L—Personal Liability and Coverage M—Medical Payments to Others of the DL form are identical to Coverages E and F of the homeowners policy. Similarly, the exclusions and additional coverages in the DL form are virtually the same as those applicable to Section II of the homeowners policy. The only difference is that the additional coverage for loss assessment in the homeowners policy is not provided in the DL form. As with the dwelling forms, the conditions contained in the DL form are a combination of the Section II conditions and the conditions applicable to Sections I and II in the homeowners policy.

Residential Theft Coverage.   An insured may choose between two endorsements to the dwelling forms to provide theft coverage similar to that provided in the homeowners policy. Broad theft coverage is provided by endorsement DP 04 72, which is for use with policies covering owner-occupied dwellings. This endorsement provides coverage against the perils of theft, including attempted theft, and vandalism or malicious mischief as a result of theft or attempted theft. Off-premises coverage is available only if the insured purchases on-premises coverage. The endorsement includes special limits of liability that are identical to the limits included in the homeowners policy, except that there are no special limits of liability for property used for business purposes or for adaptable electronic apparatus. Other types of property not covered by the endorsement are the same as those not covered in the dwelling forms.

Limited theft coverage for dwellings that are not owner-occupied is available through endorsement DP 04 73. This endorsement is similar to the broad theft coverage endorsement. However, the limited theft coverage endorsement excludes from coverage certain items of personal property that are subject to special limits under the broad theft coverage endorsement. The DP 04 73 endorsement also excludes coverage for loss caused by a tenant of the described location or by employees or members of the household.

FAIR Plans

FAIR (Fair Access to Insurance Requirements) plans were set up in response to the urban riots of the 1960s. At that time, property insurance was difficult to obtain in the "congested urban core" areas of many major cities.

The FAIR plan program is an assigned risk property program. In order to be eligible for FAIR plan coverage, the insured must have the property inspected. Only property that meets the inspection criteria will be insured in the program.

When the program was drawn up, the concern was that well kept properties with inner city locations would be prevented from obtaining coverage by virtue of their location. The program directs that the inspection of the property must concentrate on that property alone and ignore any "environmental perils." The environmental perils that the program designers had in mind were primarily those found in run-down, crime-ridden urban slums. Others noticed that brush hazards found in wealthy, tree-studded suburban areas might also be considered "environmental hazards." The current California FAIR plan, for example, contains both inner city properties and suburban homes located in hazardous brush areas.

Many FAIR plans do not provide the package of homeowners coverages, but such coverage is available in some states. In most states, however, only coverage for fire and a limited number of other perils is provided by the FAIR plan. Often when an expensive suburban home is written in the FAIR plan, other coverages are provided by means of a difference in conditions policy written outside of the FAIR plan. Such a policy can provide coverage for risks of direct loss, while excluding fire and the other perils covered under the FAIR plan policy. Since it is the fire peril that is the major concern in these cases, the difference in conditions policy can be written in the private market.

Beachfront Plans

Beachfront plans are part of an assigned risk property insurance program that is somewhat similar to the FAIR plan. The origins of the plans differ in that the beachfront plans were set up in response to heavy windstorm losses rather than urban riots.

Beachfront property in many parts of the country is exposed to heavy windstorm losses during hurricanes and lesser windstorms. Much of this property also is vulnerable to damage from high waves. The beachfront plans provide coverage for fire and windstorm losses. Losses from high waves are generally excluded.

FAMILY RESIDENCE INSURANCE CASE

This case has been developed to illustrate how the homeowners policy and other residential insurance would apply to various loss situations.

The Family Situation

John and Marsha Cabot own a home at 2626 Vernon Street in the Back Bay section of Boston, Massachusetts. It is a single-family home with three bedrooms and two baths. The mortgage on this dwelling is held by Bank and Trust Company.

John Cabot has an office in the home where he runs an investment advisory business as a sideline. His in-home office is the only location of that business, which John operates as a sole proprietorship. Marsha Cabot is an amateur nature photographer and has several expensive cameras and lenses. With the exception of John's business property and Marsha's photography equipment, they own no other remarkable personal property.

The Cabots also have a summer cottage at 125 Shorecliff Drive, Bar Harbor, Maine. This cottage has two bedrooms and two baths. A two-car detached garage also is located on the premises. The Cabots have no mortgage on this property.

Family Residence Coverages

John and Marsha Cabot have purchased an HO-3 policy with a $200,000 Coverage A limit on their Vernon Street home. This $200,000 of coverage is approximately equal to the replacement cost of the dwelling. The declarations page of the Cabot's homeowners policy is shown in Exhibit 5-1.

The Cabots have added several endorsements to their HO-3 policy to meet their needs. Since John has an office in the home, which is a permitted incidental occupancy, endorsement HO 04 42 has been added to the policy. In order to keep the policy's property coverages current with inflation, the Cabots purchased inflation guard coverage under an HO 04 46 endorsement. Marsha's camera collection is listed as scheduled property on the scheduled personal property endorsement, HO 04 61. The first page of this three-page endorsement is shown in Exhibit 5-2. The Cabots have added the personal property replacement cost endorsement, HO 04 90, to their policy. Because of this endorsement, the Cabots' insurer requires that they carry a Coverage C limit of $140,000, which equals 70 percent of the Coverage A limit. The Cabots have three smoke alarms in the house for which they receive a premium credit. The premises alarm or fire protection system endorsement, HO 04 16, was added to the policy to reflect the presence of alarms. Bank and Trust Company has its interest in the Cabots' dwelling protected by being listed as the mortgagee on the declarations page of the Cabots' policy.

The Cabots have purchased a DP-3 policy to cover their summer cottage in Bar Harbor, Maine. The dwelling is covered for $50,000, which is its approximate replacement cost. The garage is covered for $6,000, which is the limit chosen by the Cabots. They have also purchased $15,000 of DP-3 contents coverage on the furnishings and other items usually left at the cottage. A $100 deductible applies to all covered losses.

Homeowners Loss Situations

Section I Coverages.   The following situations apply to the property coverages of the HO-3 and DP-3 policies. Each loss is a separate occurrence.

Loss.   John and Marsha Cabot suffered a loss to the kitchen of their Boston home as a result of a smoky grease fire started by food cooking on their stove. The woodwork and ceiling were stained by the heavy smoke, and built-in kitchen cabinets were damaged. The Cabots reported the loss and were asked by their insurer to get three estimates from contractors. The estimates ranged from

Exhibit 5-1

Homeowners Policy Declarations Page

HOMEOWNERS POLICY
Declarations applicable to all policy forms

Policy Number   0000006 7/8
Policy Period: 12:01 a.m. Standard time   **From:** Jan 20, 1991   **To:** Jan 20, 1992
         at the residence premises

Named Insured and mailing address

> John and Marsha Cabot
> 2626 Vernon Street
> Back Bay
> Boston, Massachusetts 02555

The residence premises covered by this policy is located at the above address unless otherwise stated:

Coverage is provided where a premium or limit of liability is shown for the coverage.

SECTION I COVERAGES	Limit of Liability	Premium ●
A. Dwelling	$200,000	$484.00
B. Other structures	20,000	Incl.
C. Personal Property	140,000	Incl.
D. Loss of use	40,000	Incl.
SECTION II COVERAGES		
E. Personal liability: each occurrence	100,000	Incl.
F. Medical payments to others: each person	1,000	Incl.

Total premium for endorsements listed below

	Policy Total	**$484.00**

Forms and endorsements made part of this policy:

Number	Edition Date	Title	Premium
HO 00 03	04/91	Special Form	Incl.
HO 04 42	04/91	Permitted Incidental Occupancies	Incl.
HO 04 46	04/91	Inflation Guard	Incl.
HO 04 61	04/91	Scheduled Personal Property	Incl.
HO 04 16	04/91	Premises Alarm System	Incl.
HO 04 90	04/91	Personal Prop. Replacement Cost	Incl.

[Special State Provisions: South Carolina: Valuation Clause (Cov. A) $
                        Minnesota Insurable Value (Cov. A) $
                        New York: Coinsurance Clause Applies ___Yes   ___No]

DEDUCTIBLE - SECTION I: $ 250.00
In case of a loss under Section I, we cover only that part of the loss over the deductible stated.

Section II: Other insured locations:
> 125 Shorecliff Drive
> Bar Harbor, Maine

[Mortgagee/Lienholder (Name and address)]
> Bank and Trust Co.
> 12555 Beacon Street
> Boston, Massachusetts 02555

Countersignature of agent/date   **Signature/title - company officer**

Ed. 04/91

Exhibit 5-2
Scheduled Personal Property Endorsement

HO 04 61 04 91

THIS ENDORSEMENT CHANGES THE POLICY. PLEASE READ IT CAREFULLY.

SCHEDULED PERSONAL PROPERTY ENDORSEMENT

For an additional premium, we cover the classes of personal property indicated by an amount of insurance. This coverage is subject to the DEFINITIONS, SECTION I - CONDITIONS, SECTIONS I AND II - CONDITIONS and all provisions of this endorsement. The Section I deductible as shown on the Declarations does not apply to this coverage.

	Class of Personal Property	Amount of Insurance	Premium
1.	**Jewelry,** as scheduled	$* 0	$* 0
2.	**Furs** and garments trimmed with fur or consisting principally of fur, as listed.	0	0
3.	**Cameras,** projection machines, films and related articles of equipment, as listed	$2,430	$42
4.	**Musical instruments** and related articles of equipment, as listed. You agree not to perform with these instruments for pay unless specifically provided under this policy.	0	0
5.	**Silverware,** silver-plated ware, goldware, gold-plated ware and pewterware, but excluding pens, pencils, flasks, smoking implements or jewelry.	0	0
6.	**Golfer's equipment** meaning golf clubs, golf clothing and golf equipment	0	0
7.a.	**Fine Arts,** as scheduled. This premium is based on your statement that the property insured is located at the following address. at	Total Fine Arts Amount $ 0	0
7.b.	at For an additional premium, paragraph 5.b. under Perils Insured Against is deleted only for the articles marked with a double asterisk (**) in the schedule below.	Amount of 7.b. only $ 0	0
8.	**Postage Stamps**	0	0
9.	**Rare and Current Coins**	0	0

SCHEDULE*

	Article	Description	Amount of Insurance
1.	Nikon ER-2 Camera Body ID# 2205743		$340
2.	Nikon FA Camera body ID# 12344321		480
3.	Nikon Reflex 500 mm lens kit ID# 185158		500
4.	Nikon 35-200 mm F3.5 lens & case ID# L-200451		600
5.	Nikon macro lens 55 mm F1.4 & case ID# 474817		200
6.	Slik 7160 Pro Tripod & case		200
7.	Kiwi camera bag		110
		Total	$2,430

THE AMOUNTS SHOWN FOR EACH ITEM IN THE SCHEDULE ARE LIMITED BY CONDITION 2. LOSS SETTLEMENT ON PAGE 3 OF THIS ENDORSEMENT.

*Entries may be left blank if shown elsewhere in this policy for this coverage.

HO 04 61 04 91   Copyright, Insurance Services Office, Inc., 1990   **Page 1 of 3**

$3,850 to $4,425 to clean and repaint the kitchen and to repair and replace the damaged cabinets. The contents of the kitchen were also damaged. The Cabots can replace the damaged small appliances, cookware, and utensils for $625.

Comment. Because the Cabots carry insurance to value, the repairs to the kitchen will be paid under Coverage A with no deduction for depreciation. The adjuster for their insurance company accepted the estimate of $3,850 for the Coverage A loss. The Coverage C loss of $625 was also found to be in order. Thus, if replacement is made, the Cabots' recovery will be as follows:

Coverage A	$3,850
Coverage C	625
Less deductible	(250)
Total payment	$4,225

Assume that the Cabots had carried Coverage A limits of only $100,000 at the time of the above loss. What amount would the Cabots receive for the loss to the dwelling? The insurance-to-value fraction yields:

$$\frac{\text{Insurance carried}}{80\% \times \text{Replacement cost}}$$

$$\frac{\$100,000}{80\% \times \$200,000} = \frac{5}{8} \text{ or } 0.625$$

Because the insurance-to-value fraction equals less than 1.0, the Cabots would not receive replacement cost coverage on the loss to the dwelling. The Cabots would receive the greater of the following amounts: (1) the insurance-to-value fraction, multiplied by the replacement cost of the loss less the deductible, or (2) the actual cash value of the loss less the deductible.

If the Cabots and the adjuster agreed that the actual cash value of the loss was $3,300, what settlement would the Cabots receive? To answer this question, the following calculation of the settlement using the insurance-to-value fraction is required:

$$\frac{\$100,000}{80\% \times \$200,000} \times (\$3,850 - \$250) = \frac{5}{8} \times \$3,600 = \$2,250$$

Loss settlement on an actual cash value basis would be $3,300 − $250, or $3,050. Because $3,050 is greater than $2,250, the Cabots' loss would be settled on an actual cash value basis for $3,050.

Loss. The sewer backed up at the Cabots' Boston home, and water overflowed from the drains. The overflow in their first-floor powder room damaged the contents of their linen closet and vanity. In addition, it cost $475 for cleanup in their home.

Comment. Damage caused by water backing up through sewers and drains is excluded under Coverage A and is not a peril insured against under Coverage C. Therefore, there would be no coverage for damage to the dwelling or its contents.

Loss. Due to a malfunction of the water heater, steam sprayed into the laundry room of the Cabots' Boston home, causing irreparable damage to $350 worth of their clothing. It cost $50 to replace a defective part in the water heater.

Comment. Under Coverage C, damage to personal property caused by the accidental discharge of steam from within a plumbing system is covered. The Cabots will receive the replacement cost of the clothing, because of the personal property replacement cost coverage (HO 04 90) endorsement, less the $250 deductible. Under Coverage A, coverage for this type of accidental discharge excludes damage to the system or appliance from which the water or steam escaped. Therefore, there will be no payment for the cost to repair the water heater.

Loss. A five-story apartment building near the Cabots' Boston home was severely damaged by fire. The fire department ordered the Cabots and several of their neighbors to evacuate their homes because the fire threatened to spread to homes near the apartment building. The Cabots were not allowed to return to their home for three days after the fire because the fire department feared that the fire-gutted apartment building might collapse. The Cabots incurred the following additional living expenses during this period:

1. $375 for three nights' lodging at a motel
2. $270 for three days' meals in restaurants

The cost of groceries for the Cabots averages $35 per day when they eat at home.

Comment. Coverage D—Loss of Use provides coverage for additional living expenses if a civil authority prohibits the insured from use of the residence premises as the result of direct damage to a neighboring premises by a peril insured against under the homeowners policy. The Cabots' $375 motel bill and their additional expenses for meals therefore qualify for payment under Coverage D. The Cabots' additional expense for food is the $270 cost of meals in restaurants, less the $105 that they would have spent for food eaten at home, which comes to $165. The Cabots' recovery will be as follows:

Motel bill	$375
Additional cost of meals	165
Less deductible	(250)
Total payment	$290

Coverage D also applies when an insured peril causes direct damage to the *insured's residence* that results in additional living expenses. When determining the loss settlement in such a case, it may be necessary to consider other increased expenses, such as laundry, transportation, and telephone. However, the insured's usual expenses for such items, as well as any decrease in the cost of utilities or other expenses, would be considered in determining the total amount of the additional living expense.

Loss. When the Cabots returned to Boston from Bar Harbor one Sunday night, they found that the rear door of their home had been broken open and that several items had been stolen. The Cabots' losses are as follows:

Item	Replacement Cost or Value
Jewelry	$1,495
Cash	250
Video cassette recorder	350
Nikon FA camera body	525
Nikon 500mm lens	475
Replacement of rear door and trim	300

The Cabots reported the loss to their insurer and the police, as required in the HO-3 loss settlement conditions. An adjuster visited the Cabots' home, photographed the rear door, and obtained copies of receipts and other supporting evidence for the Cabots' personal property claims.

Comment. Theft is a covered peril under Coverage C of the homeowners policy and under the scheduled personal property endorsement. The Cabots will receive settlement under these coverages for the loss of their personal property. Damage done by burglars is not excluded under Coverage A; therefore, the Cabots' loss settlement will include the cost of repairs to the rear door. Each item of the loss settlement is described below.

Jewelry. The Cabots' $1,495 jewelry loss is $495 greater than the $1,000 HO-3 sublimit on jewelry. In addition, their HO-3 contains a $250 deductible to be applied to the total theft loss. These two limits on recovery are applied in the following way. First, the $250 deductible is applied to the total jewelry loss of $1,495, leaving an insured jewelry loss of $1,245. Next, the sublimit of $1,000 is applied to the loss, resulting in a payment of $1,000 for the jewelry loss. Because the deductible has been satisfied by this portion of the loss, no deductible applies to the balance of the loss.

As a general rule, if policy sublimits reduce the insured's recovery by an amount equal to or more than the policy deductible, the deductible is satisfied by that reduction in loss payment. The jewelry loss is used here to illustrate this point, but the principle applies whenever a sublimit reduces the loss payment to the insured. If the application of sublimits reduces the loss payment by less than the full amount of the deductible, the balance of the deductible amount would still apply to the total loss.

Cash. The HO-3 contains a $200 sublimit on cash, which is the amount the Cabots will receive for this loss.

Video Cassette Recorder. The HO-3 provides the insurer with the option of making loss settlement by replacing damaged or stolen property. Insurers frequently use replacement services from which they can purchase appliances at a lower cost than the insured would have to pay in the retail market. The Cabots' insurer may replace their stolen VCR with a comparable new model or pay its replacement cost.

Camera Body. The replacement cost of the stolen camera is greater than the amount shown on the Cabots' scheduled personal property (HO 04 61) endorsement. Therefore, the insurer's payment will be limited to the amount of insurance shown, which is $480.

500mm Lens. The replacement cost of the lens is less than the amount of insurance shown on the Cabots' HO 04 61 endorsement. Therefore, the insurer will pay this lesser amount of $475 or replace the lens.

Damage to the Dwelling. The full $300 cost of repairing the damage done by the burglars breaking into the dwelling will be paid under Coverage A, since the Cabots carry Coverage A limits that meet the HO-3 insurance-to-value requirements.

Additional Comments. The personal property replacement cost endorsement, HO 04 90, provides that if the entire loss is more than $500, the insurer will pay no more than the actual cash value of covered personal property until the actual repair or replacement of an item is complete. If the Cabots should decide not to replace any of the stolen items, payment for any item not replaced would be made on an actual cash value basis because their total personal property loss exceeds $500.

If any of the stolen items are recovered and returned to the Cabots or their insurer after the loss settlement, the party to whom the items are returned must notify the other. The Cabots would then have the option of accepting the recovered items and returning the loss payment to the insurer or allowing the insurer to keep the items as salvage and retaining the loss payment already made.

Loss. During a severe winter storm, several feet of snow accumulated on the roof of the detached garage at the Cabots' Bar Harbor property. The garage roof caved in under the weight of the snow, causing some structural damage to the garage walls. At the time of the loss, the replacement cost of the garage was $8,000. Based on estimates from three contractors and considering the age of the roofing material destroyed, the Cabots and their insurer's adjuster agreed on the following values of the loss: (1) a replacement cost value of $3,300 and (2) an actual cash value of $2,800.

Comment. Damage to the garage is covered for risks of direct loss under Coverage B of the Cabots' DP-3 policy. Because damage to the garage caused by the accumulation of snow is not excluded, this cause of loss is covered. The DP-3 policy provides replacement cost coverage on other structures if the amount of coverage carried equals at least 80 percent of the replacement cost of the structure. However, the coverage carried by the Cabots does not meet this requirement. Therefore, the insurance-to-value fraction must be applied to the replacement cost of the loss to determine the amount payable if settlement is made on this basis. The calculation, which includes the $100 policy deductible, is as follows:

$$\frac{\$6,000}{80\% \times \$8,000} \times (\$3,300 - \$100) = \frac{15}{16} \times \$3,200 = \$3,000$$

The Cabots will receive $3,000 in payment for the loss because this is greater than the $2,700 settlement amount on an actual cash value basis ($2,800 less the $100 deductible).

Section II Coverages. The following situations apply to the liability and medical payments coverages of the HO-3 policy. Each loss is a separate occurrence.

Loss. The Cabots went to Vermont on a weekend ski trip. As John was skiing down a steep slope, he collided with another skier who had stopped to adjust the bindings on his skis. The other skier, Bruce, was hospitalized with a broken hip as a result of the accident. Bruce brought suit against John seeking $100,000 in damages for medical expenses, lost wages, and pain and suffering.

Comment. Coverage E of the homeowners policy provides coverage for liability arising out of accidental bodily injury caused by the insured. Because the Coverage E limit of the Cabots' homeowners policy is $100,000, the insurer will pay court awarded damages or a negotiated settlement for this loss up to the $100,000 policy limit. In addition, the insurer will pay the costs associated with investigating the claim, negotiating a settlement, or defending the case if it goes to court.

Loss. John and Marsha entertained their friends, Darby and Joan, at their Boston home one weekend. Joan tripped while walking up the stairs and hurt her ankle. Marsha and Joan went to the emergency room of a local hospital, where the doctor determined that Joan had sprained her ankle and had suffered no broken bones. The cost of the emergency room visit and the follow-up care by Joan's doctor amounted to $375.

Comment. Coverage F of the homeowners policy provides for the payment of necessary medical expenses that arise out of bodily injury to a guest in the insured's home. Coverage is provided without regard to negligence or fault on the part of the insured up to the policy limit purchased. The Cabots' Coverage F limit is $1,000 and Joan's medical expenses will be paid in full under the Cabots' homeowners policy.

Assume that Joan sustained this injury at the Cabots' Bar Harbor cottage. Would either the Cabots' DP-3 or HO-3 policy respond?

The DP-3 policy provides property coverage only and, therefore, would not respond to this loss. However, the Cabots had requested their insurer to include their Bar Harbor cottage as an "other insured location" for Section II coverage under their HO-3 policy, as shown on the HO-3 declarations page in Exhibit 5-1. Therefore, Coverage F, as well as Coverage E, apply to losses occurring at either the Cabots' Boston home or their Bar Harbor cottage. Joan's medical expenses would have been paid in full if the loss had occurred at the Cabots' vacation cottage.

Loss. John trimmed several trees and bushes at the Cabots' Boston home one weekend. He borrowed a gas-powered chipper from a neighbor to turn the cuttings into mulch for the garden. John accidentally dropped a rock into the machine, breaking some if its blades. Repair costs for the machine were $175.

Comment. The HO-3 provides up to $500 of coverage for accidental property damage to the property of others. In this case, the adjuster would confirm that the repair costs were reasonable and pay the full bill or reimburse John or the neighbor for payments made. The payments under this additional coverage are made whether or not the Cabots are legally liable for the loss.

Loss. As Sandy, one of John's investment clients, was leaving the Cabots' home on a winter evening, she slipped on ice and snow that had been allowed to accumulate on the front steps. Sandy suffered a broken wrist. Her medical expenses were $1,500. Sandy sought payment from John for these medical expenses.

Comment. Sandy's injury arose out of John's use of the Cabots' residence for business purposes. Coverage for liability damages and medical expenses arising out of this bodily injury is available to the Cabots only because they added the permitted incidental occupancies endorsement (HO 04 42) to their HO-3 policy. Sandy's medical expenses exceed the Cabots' Coverage F medical payments limit of $1,000. However, because of the circumstances of the injury, it is possible that the Cabots could be held legally liable for the cost of Sandy's medical expenses, as well as other damages should she choose to bring suit against them. The insurer will respond under Coverage E of the HO-3 policy and pay Sandy's $1,500 of medical expenses.

Loss. Sam, a client of John's investment advisory service, asked John whether he should sell 1,000 shares of a particular stock or hold onto it in the hope that the price would go higher. John recommended that Sam sell the stock immediately, which Sam did. In the two weeks after Sam sold the stock its price increased $10 per share. Sam sued John alleging that John's bad advice had resulted in a $10,000 loss for Sam.

Comment. Any liability on John's part for Sam's loss arises out of John's rendering of professional investment advisory services. Liability arising out of the rendering of *professional services* is excluded under the HO-3 policy, and the permitted incidental occupancies endorsement does not provide this coverage. The insurance company would provide no coverage for this liability claim under the Cabots' HO-3 policy.

SUMMARY

Mobilehomes not less than ten feet wide and forty feet long may be insured under an HO-2 or HO-3 policy by adding the mobilehome endorsement. Although mobilehomes are considered to be personal property, they are subject to the same perils as permanent structures. In addition, when they are moved, mobilehomes are subject to the transportation perils of upset, overturn, stranding, and sinking.

When the mobilehome endorsement is added, the homeowners policy Coverage A specifically includes permanently installed floor coverings, appliances, dressers, and cabinets as part of the structure. Under the mobilehome endorsement, losses to carpets and appliances are settled on a replacement cost basis, rather than at actual cash value. The pair-and-set clause is modified to provide for matching or replacing the mobilehome's paneling in the event of loss. The wording of the mortgage clause is changed to protect the interests of trustees or lienholders, because mobilehomes are financed by secured loans rather than mortgages.

The homeowners policy can be endorsed in one of two ways to provide needed additional coverages for a family involved in farming. If the farming activities are relatively minor and do not constitute the full-time employment of the insured, the incidental farming personal liability endorsement can be attached to a homeowners policy. This brief endorsement extends the Section II coverage to include incidental farming activities conducted either on the residence premises or at a separate location.

A family that farms on a commercial basis has the option of obtaining another endorsement, farmers personal liability, to provide coverage for liability arising out of the farming operations. All premises farmed, both owned and rented, must be listed in the endorsement. Employees must also be listed. Coverages E and F are extended to include those farming operations listed in the declarations, and coverage for animal collision, Coverage G, may be added at the insured's option for an additional premium. Certain exclusions are replaced to reflect the farming exposures.

Some residences are not eligible for homeowners coverages. Other residence owners or tenants may prefer to purchase monoline policies to meet their particular needs. Cost may also be a consideration in purchasing monoline coverage. The dwelling program is designed to meet these needs. The dwelling program includes the DP 00 01, which provides limited named perils coverage; the DP 00 02, which is similar in coverage to Section I of the HO-2; and the DP 00 03, which is similar to Section I of the HO-3. Liability coverage and coverage for theft losses can be obtained through a personal liability supplement and theft endorsements.

CHAPTER 6

Other Personal Property and Liability Insurance

This chapter continues the discussion of personal property and liability insurance with an examination of other types of insurance that provide significant protection to some individuals and families—inland marine, watercraft, and personal umbrella insurance.

Inland marine insurance is designed to cover property that is frequently moved from one location to another, such as jewelry, furs, cameras, clothes and luggage, sports equipment, musical instruments, and so on. These kinds of property can be insured by an appropriate inland marine form, such as the personal articles floater.

Millions of Americans own or operate boats for recreational uses. This chapter discusses the loss exposures associated with boats and the major contracts for insuring pleasure boats, such as outboard motor and boat insurance, watercraft package policies, and personal yacht insurance.

Claims or judgments arising out of personal liability exposures associated with the home, automobiles, boats, recreational vehicles, sports, and other personal activities can reach catastrophic levels. Catastrophic, in this context, means a settlement or judgment so large that it would impair the insured's standard of living. The personal umbrella policy, designed to meet the problem of a catastrophic liability claim or judgment, is also examined in this chapter.

INLAND MARINE FLOATERS

Because of various exclusions and limitations on coverage under a homeowners policy, owners of valuable personal property often require broader and more comprehensive coverage than that provided by a homeowners policy. This protection often can be obtained through an appropriate inland marine insurance policy.

117

Meaning of Inland Marine Insurance

Inland marine insurance covers property transported from one place to another; goods in transit (except over oceans); and bridges, tunnels, television broadcasting towers, and other means of transportation and communication. Inland marine insurance also includes various floater policies that insure personal property. A floater policy provides coverage that "floats," or moves along with the covered property as it changes location, rather than providing coverage only at a fixed location.

Inland marine insurance developed out of ocean marine insurance in the 1920s. Marine insurers traditionally wrote much of the early insurance on transportation loss exposures. Fire and casualty insurers were limited in their ability to compete because fire and casualty lines had to be written separately, and rates and forms were subject to state regulation. Marine insurers, in contrast, wrote property and casualty lines in one contract and had considerable experience with broad "all-risks" contracts on movable property. They were not bound by rate regulation and could design special contracts to meet particular needs.

As the marine business developed, conflicts arose between marine insurers and fire insurers. To resolve the conflict, the Nation-Wide Marine Definition was developed in 1933 to define the property that marine insurers could cover. The definition was revised in 1953 and again in 1976. At present, the following types of property can be insured by marine insurers: imports, exports, domestic shipments, means of transportation and communication, personal property floater risks, and commercial property floater risks.

Characteristics of Inland Marine Floaters

Although there are no "standard" inland marine floater policies, all share four general characteristics:

1. *The coverage can be tailored to the specific type of property to be insured.* For example, the personal articles floater provides coverage for nine optional classes of personal property including jewelry, cameras, and musical instruments. The insured can select coverage for the class or classes of property needed. It is also possible to write the coverage separately, such as with a jewelry floater, a camera floater, or a musical instruments floater.

2. *The insured can select the appropriate policy limits.* The homeowners policy has limitations on coverage of certain types of valuable personal property. Higher limits are available under a floater policy. In addition, when the value of certain types of personal property (such as fine arts) is combined with unscheduled personal property under the homeowners policy, the combined total amount may exceed the policy limits on personal property. Again, higher limits can be obtained with a floater policy.

3. *The floaters provide extensive coverage with respect to the perils covered.* Floaters are typically written on a "risks of direct physical loss" (or "all-risks") basis. The floater covers all direct physical loss to the

covered property except for certain losses that are commonly excluded (discussed below).

4. *Most floaters cover the described property anywhere in the world.* However, fine arts are generally covered only in the United States and Canada.

Floater Policy Provisions

The following provisions commonly appear in inland marine floater policies.[1] Each floater policy also contains other conditions and exclusions that apply specifically to the coverage provided.

Insuring Agreement. Most floater policies insure covered property on an "all-risks" basis. All direct physical losses are covered except those losses specifically excluded. The following causes of loss are typically excluded:

- Wear and tear, deterioration, or inherent vice
- Insects or vermin
- Mechanical or electrical breakdown or failure
- Repairing, adjusting, servicing, or maintaining the property (except for fire or explosion)

General Conditions. Numerous conditions appear in an inland marine floater covering personal property. Notice their similarities to those in Section I of the homeowners policy as discussed in Chapter 2. The most important conditions include the following.

Loss Settlement. With certain exceptions such as fine arts, the amount paid for a covered loss is the *lowest* of the following four amounts:

1. The actual cash value at the time of loss or damage
2. The amount for which the insured could reasonably be expected to have the property repaired to its condition immediately prior to the loss
3. The amount for which the insured could reasonably be expected to replace the property with property substantially identical to the article lost or damaged
4. The amount of insurance stated in the policy

Item 3 should be explained. Much of the property insured in a floater policy can be purchased by the insurer at a discounted price. Thus, the insurer may offer to replace the lost or damaged property rather than make a cash settlement. If the replacement offer is rejected by the insured, the insurer's cash settlement is limited to the amount for which the insured could reasonably be expected to replace the item. This amount is the insurer's discounted price since the insured can reasonably be expected to replace the item at that price.

Loss to a Pair, Set, or Parts. In the event of loss of or damage to an item in a pair or set, such as the loss of one earring, the amount paid is not based on a total loss. Instead, the insurer may either (1) repair or replace any part to restore the pair or set to its value before the loss or (2) pay the difference between the actual cash value of the property before and after the loss.

Loss Clause.   Under this provision, the amount of insurance is not reduced except for the total loss of a scheduled article. If the insurance is reduced because of a total loss of a scheduled article, the unearned premium is refunded, or the insured can apply it to the premium due if the scheduled article is replaced.

Claim Against Others.   This provision is similar to a subrogation clause. If a loss occurs, and the insurer believes it can recover the loss payment from the person or parties responsible, the loss payment to the insured is considered a loan to be repaid out of any recovery from others. The insured is expected to cooperate with the company in its attempt to recover from others responsible for the loss. However, if the recovery attempt is unsuccessful, the insured is not required to repay the loss settlement "loan."

Insurance Not to Benefit Others.   Under this provision, no other person or organization that has custody of the property and is paid for services can benefit from the insurance on the property. This provision prevents a third party who caused the loss from denying liability for payment because the property is insured; thus, the insurer's right of subrogation against the negligent party is retained.

Other Insurance.   If at the time of loss there is other insurance that applies to the property in the absence of this policy, the insurance provided by the floater policy is considered excess insurance over the other insurance.

General Exclusions.   The general exclusions of war and nuclear reaction or radiation appear in all floater policies. In addition to the general exclusions, there are special exclusions that apply to the specific type of property that is insured. These special exclusions are subsequently examined when the different floater policies are analyzed.

Personal Articles Floater

The personal articles floater (PAF) insures nine optional classes of personal property against risks of direct physical loss.[2] That is, all direct physical losses to the described property are covered except those losses specifically excluded. Coverage is worldwide with the exception of fine arts. The following nine classes of personal property can be insured:

1. Jewelry
2. Furs
3. Cameras
4. Musical instruments
5. Silverware
6. Golfer's equipment
7. Fine arts
8. Postage stamps
9. Rare and current coins

Certain classes of newly acquired property (jewelry, furs, cameras, and musical instruments) are automatically covered for thirty days if insurance is already written on that class of property. The amount of insurance on newly acquired property is limited to 25 percent of the amount of insurance for that class of property or $10,000, whichever is lower. The property must be reported to the company within thirty days after acquisition to continue the coverage, and an additional premium must be paid from the date of acquisition.

Jewelry. Personal jewelry is covered anywhere in the world. Each item of jewelry must be scheduled and a specific amount of insurance shown for it. Insurance on jewelry is carefully underwritten because of moral hazard. Original bills of sale or a signed appraisal may be required before the jewelry is insured. The insured must also have satisfactory financial resources and must not be in the habit of losing or misplacing articles.

Furs. The PAF can be used to insure personal furs, items consisting principally of fur, garments trimmed with fur, fur rugs, and imitation fur. Each item must be separately listed and a specific amount of insurance shown for it. As with jewelry, insurance on furs is carefully underwritten because of moral hazard.

Cameras. The PAF can also be used to insure most photographic equipment, including cameras, projection machines, portable sound and recording equipment used with motion picture cameras and projectors, films, binoculars, and telescopes. Each item must be described and valued. However, miscellaneous smaller items, such as carrying cases, filters, and holders, can be written on a blanket basis without scheduling each item if the total value of the blanketed items is not more than 10 percent of the total amount of insurance on cameras.

Musical Instruments. Musical instruments, instrument cases, sound and amplifying equipment, and similar equipment can be insured under the PAF. However, musical instruments played for pay during the policy period are not covered unless an endorsement is added and a higher premium paid. Thus, a professional musician must pay a higher premium for coverage.

Silverware. Silverware and goldware can also be insured under the PAF. However, pens, pencils, flasks, smoking implements, or jewelry cannot be insured as silverware. These kinds of property can be insured as jewelry.

Golfer's Equipment. Golf equipment (including golf clothes) can be insured under the PAF. Other clothing contained in a locker while the insured is playing golf is also covered. Golf balls, however, are covered for loss only by fire and by burglary if there are visible marks of forcible entry into the building, room, or locker.

Fine Arts. Fine arts include private collections of paintings, antique furniture, rare books, rare glass, bric-a-brac, and manuscripts. *Fine arts are insured on a valued basis.* Thus, if a valuable painting is stolen, the amount of insurance stated in the schedule for that item is the amount paid.

Newly acquired fine arts are automatically insured for ninety days, However, the insured is required to notify the company of the acquisition within ninety days and pay an additional premium. The limit on such property is 25 percent of the total insurance.

Fine arts coverage is subject to three major exclusions:

1. Damage caused by repairing, restoration, or retouching is excluded.
2. Breakage of art glass windows, glassware, statuary, marble, bric-a-brac, porcelains, and similar fragile articles is also excluded. However, the exclusion does not apply if the breakage is caused by fire, lightning, explosion, aircraft, collision, windstorm, earthquake, flood, malicious damage or theft, and derailment or overturn of a conveyance.
3. Loss to property on exhibition at fairgrounds or at national or international expositions is excluded unless the premises are covered by the policy.

Stamp and Coin Collections. Valuable stamp and coin collections can also be insured under the PAF. The stamps and coins can be insured on either a scheduled or blanket basis. If the items are valuable, the property should be *scheduled* so that each item is listed and insured. If the property is insured on a *blanket basis*, each item is not separately described, and the insurance applies to the entire collection.

Loss Settlement. In the case of loss to a *scheduled* item, the amount paid is the lowest of the following amounts: (1) actual cash value, (2) the amount for which the property could reasonably be expected to be *repaired*, (3) the amount for which the property could reasonably be expected to be *replaced*, or (4) the amount of insurance.

If the stamps or coins are covered on a blanket basis, the amount paid is the *cash market value* at the time of loss. However, there is a $1,000 maximum limit on any unscheduled coin collection and a $250 maximum limit on any single stamp, coin, or individual article, or any single pair, block, series, sheet, cover, frame, or card.

Another limit also applies if the stamps or coins are insured on a blanket basis, and it has the effect of a 100 percent coinsurance clause. The insurance company is not liable for a greater proportion of any loss than the amount of insurance on blanket property bears to the cash market value at the time of loss. For example, assume that Jack has a coin collection insured on a blanket basis for $500. Assume that one coin worth $50 is stolen. At the time of the theft, the collection has a current market value of $1,000. Jack's maximum recovery is $25, as indicated by the following calculation:

$$\frac{\$500 \text{ (amount of insurance on blanket property)}}{\$1,000 \text{ (cash market value at time of loss)}} \times \$50 \text{ loss} = \$25$$

If Jack had purchased $1,000 of insurance, the loss would have been paid in full.

Exclusions. The following exclusions apply specifically to stamp and coin collections:

- Damage from fading, creasing, denting, scratching, tearing, or thinning
- Transfer of colors, inherent defect, dampness, extremes of temperature, or depreciation

- Damage from being handled or worked on
- Mysterious disappearance unless the item is scheduled or specifically insured, or is mounted in a volume and the page to which it is attached is also lost
- Loss to property in the custody of transportation companies
- Shipments by mail other than by registered mail
- Theft from any unattended automobile unless shipped as registered mail
- Loss to property not part of a stamp or coin collection

Notice that these exclusions relate to losses that are not chance losses and losses that are the responsibility of other organizations, such as transportation companies.

Personal Property Floater

The personal property floater (PPF) provides extensive coverage on unscheduled personal property that is owned or used by the insured and is normally kept at the insured's residence. The PPF also provides worldwide coverage on the same property when it is temporarily away from the residence. The property is insured on a risks of direct physical loss ("all-risks") basis.

Unscheduled Personal Property.   The PPF can be used to insure thirteen classes of unscheduled personal property; a separate amount of insurance applies to each of the following classes:[3]

1. Silverware, goldware, and pewterware
2. Clothing
3. Rugs and draperies
4. Musical instruments and electronic equipment
5. Paintings and other art objects
6. China and glassware
7. Cameras and photographic equipment
8. Guns and other sports equipment
9. Major appliances
10. Bedding and linens
11. Furniture
12. All other personal property, and professional books and equipment while in the residence
13. Building additions and alterations

The total amount of insurance in each category is the maximum limit of recovery for any single loss to property in that category. The total amount for the thirteen categories is the total policy limit. A $100 deductible applies to each loss. A higher deductible of $250 or $500 is also available with a reduction in premium.

Newly Acquired Property.   Newly acquired property is automatically covered up to 10 percent of the total amount of insurance or $2,500, whichever is lower. The insurance on newly acquired property can be applied to any of the thirteen classes. However, the total amount of insurance is not increased.

When Should Personal Property Be Scheduled?*

An unendorsed homeowners policy covers unscheduled personal property on a named-perils basis. However, some people own valuable personal property that should be scheduled and specifically insured under a floater policy. It is generally agreed that, in addition to *high-value* property such as diamond rings, other jewelry, and fur coats, the following types of personal property may be appropriate for scheduled coverage:

1. *Unique objects.* This includes works of art, rare antiques, paintings, and collections of unusual property, such as a valuable stamp or rare coin collection. The value of the property should be established in advance to avoid the problem of proving its value after the loss occurs.
2. *Portable property.* Certain types of portable property such as cameras and camera equipment, musical instruments, or sports equipment can be scheduled and specifically insured under a floater policy.
3. *Fragile articles.* Certain fragile articles with high value could be scheduled and specifically insured, such as glassware, statuary, scientific instruments, typewriters, or home computers.
4. *Business or professional equipment.* The homeowners policy provides only limited coverage for business or professional equipment. Business or professional property is covered only for a maximum of $2,500 on the residence premises and $250 away from the residence premises. Business and professional property can be more adequately insured by scheduling the property with a stated amount of insurance shown for it.

*Adapted from *Fire, Casualty, & Surety Bulletins*, Management and Sales Volume, Surveys Section, pp. Apc 3-4.

In addition, property located in a newly acquired principal residence is also covered for thirty days from the time the property is moved there. However, the coverage is subject to the amount of insurance for each of the classes of covered property.

Property Not Covered. The PPF does *not* cover the following types of personal property:

- Animals, fish or birds
- Boats, aircraft, trailers, and campers

- Motor vehicles (including motorcycles and motorized bicycles) designed for transportation or recreational use
- Equipment and furnishings for the above vehicles unless they are removed from the vehicle and are at the insured's residence (however, chairs for invalids and similar conveyances are covered)
- Owned property pertaining to a business, profession, or occupation (however, professional books, instruments, and equipment are covered while in the insured's residence)
- Property normally kept elsewhere than at the insured's residence throughout the year

In addition, the PPF has specific limits on certain types of property. There is a $100 limit on money and numismatic property; a $500 limit on securities, notes, stamps, passports, tickets, and similar property; and a $500 limit on jewelry, watches, and furs.

Exclusions. The PPF excludes certain types of losses. Losses caused by the following are specifically excluded:

- Animals owned or kept by an insured
- Insects or vermin
- Marring and scratching of property, or breakage of eyeglasses, glassware, and other fragile articles (but not if the loss is caused by fire, lightning, theft, vandalism or malicious mischief, and several other causes of loss specifically named in the policy)
- Mechanical or structural breakdown (except by fire)
- Wear and tear, deterioration, or inherent vice
- Dampness or extreme changes of temperature (except if caused by rain, snow, sleet, hail, or bursting of pipes or apparatus)
- Any work on covered property (other than jewelry, watches, and furs)
- Acts or decisions of any person, group, organization, or governmental body
- Types of water damage excluded elsewhere in the policy

Comparison with the HO-3 Policy. The major differences between the PPF and the HO-3 are illustrated in Exhibit 6-1.

Personal Effects Floater

The personal effects floater (PEF) is designed for tourists who want coverage on their personal effects. The PEF provides "all-risks" coverage on the personal property of tourists and travelers anywhere in the world, but only while the covered property is away from the residence premises.[4] Coverage applies to the named insured and his or her spouse and any unmarried children who permanently reside with the named insured.

Coverage of Personal Effects. Personal effects refers to personal property normally worn or carried by an individual. The PEF is designed to

Exhibit 6-1

Personal Property Floater and HO-3 Policy Compared

Personal Property Floater	HO-3 Policy
1. Risks of direct physical loss coverage on unscheduled personal property	1. Named-perils coverage on unscheduled personal property
2. Thirteen categories of property, with a specific limit of insurance for each category	2. No such provision
3. Exclusion of property located at other than the insured's residence throughout the year	3. No such exclusion
4. $500 aggregate limit on watches, jewelry, and furs	4. $1,000 aggregate limit
5. $100 limit on money	5. $200 limit
6. $500 limit on securities, evidences of debt, valuable papers, passports, tickets, and stamp collections	6. $1,000 limit

cover the insured's personal effects, such as luggage, clothes, cameras, and sports equipment while the insured is traveling or on vacation.

Property Not Covered. The PEF excludes coverage for certain types of property even though the article may be carried or used by travelers. The following property is excluded:

- Automobiles, motorcycles, bicycles, boats, and other conveyances and their accessories
- Accounts, bills, currency, deeds, evidences of debt, and letters of credit
- Passports, documents, money, notes, securities, and transportation or other tickets
- Household furniture and animals
- Automobile equipment, salesperson's samples, and physicians' and surgeons' equipment
- Contact lenses and artificial teeth or limbs
- Merchandise for sale or exhibition, theatrical property, and property specifically insured

In addition to the requirement that the property must be used or worn by the insured, the article must *belong* to the insured. Therefore, if the insured rents

Caution Needed In Scheduling Personal Property*

Standard homeowners policies exclude personal property that is separately described and specifically insured by any other insurance. Thus, the amount of insurance under a floater policy must be sufficient to pay for losses to covered property *in full*, since the exclusion rules out any contribution by the homeowners policy. In addition, unscheduled personal property under the homeowners policy may be insured on a *replacement cost* basis by adding the HO 04 90 endorsement. Replacement cost insurance on personal property that is scheduled and specifically insured generally is available only under the HO 04 61 scheduled personal property endorsement when the underlying homeowners policy also is endorsed to provide replacement cost coverage. Consequently, the advantage of risks of direct loss coverage under the personal property floaters must be carefully weighed against the possibility of being underinsured at the time of loss. Thus, it is important for the insured to review frequently the amounts and types of insurance on scheduled items.

*Adapted from *Fire, Casualty, & Surety Bulletins*, Management and Sales Volume, Inland Marine Section, p. Pro 2.

or borrows property (other than from another insured), the coverage does not apply.

"All-Risks" Coverage. Personal effects are covered on an "all-risks" basis. Therefore, all direct physical losses are covered except for certain losses that are specifically excluded. The following losses are excluded:

- Damage to personal effects from wear and tear, gradual deterioration, insects, vermin, inherent vice, or any damage while the property is being worked on
- Breakage of brittle articles unless caused by a thief, fire, or accident to a conveyance

Other Exclusions. In addition to the preceding exclusions, the PEF also imposes the following exclusions and limitations on coverage:

- Personal effects are not covered while on the named insured's residence premises.
- Property in storage is not covered. However, there is coverage of the property at points and places en route during travel. For example, if the insured stores luggage in a locker at the airport or train station while on a sightseeing tour, the exclusion does not apply.

- Personal effects in the custody of students while at school are not covered except for loss by fire.

Limitations on Certain Personal Effects. Jewelry, watches, and furs are subject to certain special limits. Coverage on any single article is limited to 10 percent of the total amount of insurance with a maximum of $100. For example, if a thief breaks into an insured's hotel room and steals an expensive fur coat, the maximum amount payable is $100 (assuming $1,000 or more of insurance is in effect).

Finally, theft of personal effects from an unattended automobile is also excluded. There would be coverage, however, if the automobile is locked and there are visible marks of forcible entry. The amount paid is limited to a maximum of 10 percent of the total amount of insurance or $250, whichever is lower.

Comparison with the HO-3 Policy. With the major exception of "all-risks" coverage, the PEF provides more limited coverage for unscheduled personal property than does the HO-3 policy. The major differences between the PEF and HO-3 policy are illustrated in Exhibit 6-2.

INSURANCE ON WATERCRAFT

Recreational watercraft can range from small dinghies, rowboats, and canoes to outboard and inboard motorboats, sailboats, speedboats, and large and expensive houseboats and yachts. This section briefly examines the loss exposures from the ownership and operation of watercraft and the major insurance contracts for insuring these exposures.[5]

Hull and Trailer Loss Exposures

Watercraft and related equipment, furnishings, and trailers are exposed to a wide variety of physical damage and theft losses as indicated by the following examples:

- A speedboat collides with another boat.
- A heavy wind causes a sailboat to overturn.
- A houseboat is stranded on a sandbar.
- A severe storm causes a boat to sink.
- An outboard motor accidentally falls into a lake.
- A boat trailer is stolen while a boat is out on a lake.
- An explosion causes serious damage to a boat.

Physical Damage Coverage Under the Homeowners Policy. There is only limited coverage of watercraft and trailers for physical damage and theft losses under Section I of the homeowners policy. The major limitations on coverage are as follows:

1. Coverage on watercraft including trailers, furnishings, equipment, and furnishings is limited to a maximum of $1,000.

Exhibit 6-2
Personal Effects Floater and HO-3 Policy Compared

Personal Effects Floater	HO-3 Policy
1. "All-risks" coverage	1. Named-perils coverage
2. Coverage only while personal effects are off the residence premises	2. Coverage both on and off residence premises
3. Only personal effects covered (narrower)	3. Unscheduled personal property covered (broader)
4. No coverage for borrowed property (except from another insured)	4. Coverage for borrowed personal property
5. Limit of 10 percent of amount of insurance up to $100 on any single article	5. $1,000 limit on jewelry, watches, furs
6. No coverage on money	6. $200 limit
7. No coverage on passports, tickets, securities, valuable papers	7. $1,000 limit
8. No coverage on property of students while at school (except for fire)	8. Covered

2. Theft of watercraft, trailers, furnishings, equipment, and outboard motors away from the residence premises is specifically excluded.
3. Direct loss to watercraft, trailers, furnishings, equipment, and outboard motors from *windstorm or hail* is covered only if the property is inside a fully enclosed building.
4. Watercraft and other boating property are covered only for a limited number of named perils. Risks of direct loss ("all-risks") coverage is not provided.

Because of these exclusions and limitations, boat owners may wish to insure their boats under other insurance contracts that provide more comprehensive protection against a direct physical damage or theft loss.

Physical Damage Coverage Under the Personal Auto Policy. The personal auto policy (PAP) does not cover any physical damage loss to boats since the auto policy is not designed to cover this type of property. However, a boat trailer can be insured for physical damage loss under a personal auto policy if the trailer is described in the declarations.

Liability Loss Exposures

Owners and operators of watercraft also face a wide variety of liability loss exposures as indicated by the following examples:

- A boat collides with a dock, causing substantial property damage.
- A boat collides with another boat, and several occupants are seriously injured.
- A speedboat swamps another boat causing it to overturn.
- A water skier is injured because of excessive speed.
- A boat runs into and severely injures several swimmers.
- A boat operator fails to provide a small child with a life preserver, and the child falls overboard and drowns.

As discussed in Chapter 3, personal liability insurance under Section II of the homeowners policy covers certain watercraft loss exposures. However, because of the various exclusions and limitations under the homeowners policy, many boat owners want more adequate protection. Insurers have developed special contracts for boat owners, which include outboard motor and boat insurance, special watercraft package policies, and personal yacht insurance.

Outboard Motor and Boat Insurance

Outboard motor and boat insurance is designed for the owners of motorboats who have adequate liability insurance but want broader physical damage coverage on the boat. This coverage can be provided by an inland marine floater. Although the floaters are not standard, they contain certain common features.

Covered Property.   The insured can select the property to be insured. The floater can be written to cover the hull, motor or motors, boat equipment and accessories, and boat carrier or trailer. The insurance is written on an actual cash value basis and may contain a deductible of $25, $50, $100, or more.

Covered Perils.   The floater can be written to cover named perils or risks of direct loss ("all-risks" coverage). Most floaters currently are written on an "all-risks" basis and cover all direct physical losses except those losses that are specifically excluded.

The coverage does not include liability insurance for bodily injury, loss of life, or illness. It is assumed that the insured has adequate personal liability insurance to cover third-party bodily injury claims. The floater, however, may provide *collision damage liability insurance* that protects the insured from a claim for property damage from the owner of another boat if the insured's boat collides with another boat while afloat.

Exclusions.   The exclusions in outboard motor and boat insurance contracts vary according to the insurer. The following are some common exclusions:

- *General risks of direct loss.* There is no coverage for loss or damage from wear and tear, gradual deterioration, vermin and marine life, rust and corrosion, inherent vice, latent defect, mechanical breakdown, and extremes of temperature.

- *Repair or service.* Loss or damage from refinishing, renovating, or repair is not covered. The person repairing the boat or equipment should be held responsible for the damage.
- *Business pursuits.* There is no coverage if the boat is used as a public or livery conveyance for carrying passengers for compensation; if the boat or insured property is rented to others; or if the covered property is being operated in any official race or speed contest. The policy is meant to cover the boat for pleasure purposes and not for business purposes, which require substantially higher premiums.

Watercraft Package Policies

Many insurers have developed a special *boat owners package policy* that combines physical damage, liability, and medical payments insurance in one policy. Although boat owners package policies are not uniform, they contain certain common features.

Physical Damage Coverage. Most boat owners package policies are written on an "all-risks" basis. Under the physical damage insuring agreement, the insurer agrees to pay for a direct physical loss to covered property. All losses are covered except those specifically excluded. The physical damage insurance covers the boat, equipment, accessories, motor, and trailer. Therefore, there is coverage if the boat collides with another boat, is damaged from heavy winds, or is stolen.

Liability Coverage. The boat owners package policy also includes liability insurance that covers the insured for bodily injury and property damage liability arising from the ownership or operation of the boat. For example, if the operator accidentally damages another boat or injures some swimmers, protection is provided under this coverage.

Medical Payments Coverage. This coverage is similar to the medical expense coverage in an automobile insurance contract. Medical payments coverage pays the necessary medical expenses incurred or medically ascertained within one to three years from the date of a watercraft accident that causes bodily injury to a covered person. For the purposes of medical payments coverage, a covered person is defined as the insured or a family member, or any person while occupying the covered watercraft. Medical expenses are the reasonable charges for medical, surgical, x-ray, dental, ambulance, hospital, professional nursing, and funeral services as well as prosthetic devices. For example, if occupants of a covered boat are injured in a collision with another boat, the medical expenses are paid up to the medical payments limits of the policy. Some policies also cover the medical expenses of water skiers who are injured, or coverage can be obtained by an endorsement to the policy.

Other Coverages. Other coverages that may be found in a boat owners package policy include the *cost of removing a wrecked or sunken vessel* following a loss; *life salvage,* which is compensation to other people who act to save human life because of an accident on the water; and *uninsured boaters coverage.*

Exclusions. With respect to physical damage coverage, the following exclusions are commonly found in a boat owners package policy:

- "All-risks" exclusions for wear and tear, inherent vice, latent defect, mechanical breakdown, war, and nuclear hazard
- Damage caused by any repair or restoration process (except for fire)
- Carrying persons or property for a fee or renting covered property to others
- Using the covered property (except sailboats) in any official race or speed test
- Infidelity of persons to whom the covered property is entrusted (except carriers for hire)
- Portable electronic, photographic, or water sports equipment, or fishing gear (thus cameras, fuel, portable radios, and sports equipment generally are not covered)

With respect to liability and medical expense coverages, the following exclusions are commonly found:

- Intentional injury or damage
- Renting the watercraft to others or carrying persons or property for a fee
- Using watercraft (except sailboats in some policies) in any official race or speed test
- Losses covered by workers compensation or similar law or by a nuclear energy liability policy
- Contractual liability
- Injury to an employee if the employee's work involves operation or maintenance of the watercraft.

Personal Yacht Insurance

Personal yacht insurance is a form of ocean marine insurance for larger boats such as yachts, inboard motorboats, cabin cruisers, and sailboats more than twenty-six feet in length. Personal yacht insurance provides the coverages described below.

Hull Insurance. Hull insurance refers to physical damage insurance on the boat. The coverage applies to the boat, sails, tackle, machinery, furniture, and other equipment. The insurance can be written on a named-perils basis or an "all-risks" basis. A deductible usually applies to all physical damage losses.

Protection and Indemnity (P&I) Insurance. This coverage is a form of marine liability insurance. The owner of the boat is covered for bodily injury and property damage liability on an indemnity basis. For example, if the boat owner negligently crashes into a marina and injures several persons, the loss to the dock and any bodily injury claims would be covered under protection and indemnity insurance.

Uninsured Boaters Coverage

Many boat owner package policies include an optional coverage for uninsured boats. Uninsured boaters coverage is similar to the uninsured motorists coverage in an automobile policy. The company agrees to pay the damages that a covered person is legally entitled to recover from an uninsured boat owner or operator because of bodily injury the covered person sustained in a boating accident. However, the uninsured boat owner's or operator's liability for the damage must arise out of the ownership, maintenance, or use of a watercraft. For example, if an uninsured boat operator negligently strikes another boat and causes bodily injury to a covered person, the injured person could collect from his or her insurer.

The uninsured boaters coverage has several exclusions. Bodily injuries from the following are excluded:

- While occupying or when struck by any watercraft owned by the insured or by any family member not insured under the policy
- If the bodily injury claim is settled without the insurer's consent
- While occupying a covered watercraft when it is being used to carry persons or property for a fee or is rented to others
- Using or occupying a watercraft without a reasonable belief that the person is entitled to do so

If there is disagreement about whether a covered person is legally entitled to recover damages from the uninsured boat owner or operator, or on the amount of damages, the coverage has an *arbitration provision*. Each party selects an arbitrator. The two arbitrators then select a third arbitrator or, if they cannot agree within thirty days, a judge in a court of law appoints the arbitrator. A decision by any two of the three parties is binding on all.

Optional Coverages.   Several optional coverages can be added to the personal yacht policy:

- Medical payments insurance for covered persons
- Possible liability of the insured to maritime workers injured in the course of employment who are covered under the United States Longshore and Harbor Workers Compensation Act
- Boat trailer insurance

- Land transportation insurance that extends the insurance to cover the insured vessel while being transported by land conveyance
- Water skiing clause that provides liability protection if the boat is used for water skiing

Warranties.   Personal yacht insurance contains several warranties or promises. If a warranty is violated, higher premiums may be required, or the coverages do not apply, depending on the warranty. The major warranties are as follows:

- *Private pleasure warranty.* The insured warrants that the vessel will be used only for private pleasure purposes and will not be hired or chartered unless the insurance company approves.
- *Seaworthiness warranty.* The insured warrants that the vessel is in a seaworthy condition.
- *Navigational limits.* The vessel will be used only in the territorial waters described in the declarations.
- *Lay-up warranty.* The insured warrants when the vessel will not be in operation during certain periods, such as the winter months.

PERSONAL UMBRELLA LIABILITY INSURANCE

Lawsuits arising from personal liability can reach catastrophic levels. A liability judgment may exceed the liability limits of insurance policies carried by the insured, such as a homeowners policy or a personal auto policy. After these liability limits are exhausted, the insured may be forced to pay a substantial amount out of personal assets. Thus, protection is needed against a catastrophic lawsuit. Physicians, surgeons, dentists, attorneys, corporate executives, and other professionals typically need this type of protection.

It is a mistake, however, to assume that only professionals need protection against catastrophic lawsuits. Faced with the increasing frequency and severity of liability lawsuits and the increased complexities of modern living, most people require this protection. A catastrophic lawsuit can easily result from common situations such as a chain-reaction collision on a congested expressway, injury to swimmers or boaters in a boating accident, or defamation of character. Personal umbrella liability insurance addresses these kinds of exposures.

Nature of Personal Umbrella Insurance

The *personal umbrella policy* is designed to provide coverage in the event of a catastrophic claim, lawsuit, or judgment.[6] The amount of insurance purchased typically ranges from $1 million to $10 million. The policy covers the entire family, and coverage is worldwide. The personal umbrella policy typically covers catastrophic liability loss exposures associated with the home, automobiles, boats and recreational vehicles, sports, and other personal activities.

The personal umbrella policy is not a standard contract but varies depending on the insurer. However, personal umbrella policies have several common features:

- The umbrella policy provides excess coverage over basic underlying policies, such as the homeowners and personal auto policies.
- Coverage is broad and applies to some loss exposures not covered by the underlying contracts.
- A self-insured retention must be met for certain losses covered by the umbrella policy but not covered by any underlying insurance.

Excess Liability Insurance. The personal umbrella policy provides excess liability insurance over any underlying insurance that may apply. The umbrella policy pays only after the limits of the underlying policies are exhausted.

The personal umbrella policy requires the insured to carry certain minimum amounts of liability insurance on the basic underlying contracts. Typical required amounts are $250,000 per person and $500,000 per occurrence for bodily injury liability and $50,000 for property damage liability under the automobile policy, or a combined single limit of at least $300,000. Personal liability insurance limits of at least $100,000 must also be carried under a homeowners policy. Insureds with a watercraft liability exposure may be required to carry $500,000 of single limit underlying coverage. If the insured fails to maintain the required amounts of underlying liability insurance, the umbrella insurer pays only that amount it would have been required to pay if the underlying policies had been in force. The relationship between umbrella coverage, underlying policies, and uninsured exposures is shown in Exhibit 6-3.

Broad Coverage. The personal umbrella policy provides broad coverage with respect to personal loss exposures. In addition to excess liability insurance, the personal umbrella policy typically broadens the liability coverage provided by the underlying contracts. The personal umbrella policy also covers certain losses that are not covered by the underlying contracts after a self-insured retention or deductible is met. These losses include personal injury claims such as libel, slander, defamation of character, false arrest, false imprisonment, and humiliation. Examples of claims paid by umbrella liability insurers include the following:[7]

- During a race, the mast on a rented boat broke and seriously injured a crew member. Primary coverage was not available to the insured.
- The insured slandered two police officers. Protection was provided by the personal umbrella policy.
- The insured borrowed a tractor and damaged it. The personal umbrella policy covered the loss after a self-insured retention was met.
- The insured rented a car in France and was involved in a serious accident. The personal umbrella policy responded to the loss since only limited underlying coverage was available.
- The insured's son rented a motorcycle and was involved in a serious accident. Since the underlying automobile and homeowners contracts did not cover the ensuing third-party claim, the personal umbrella policy covered the loss.

Exhibit 6-3
Personal Umbrella Policy

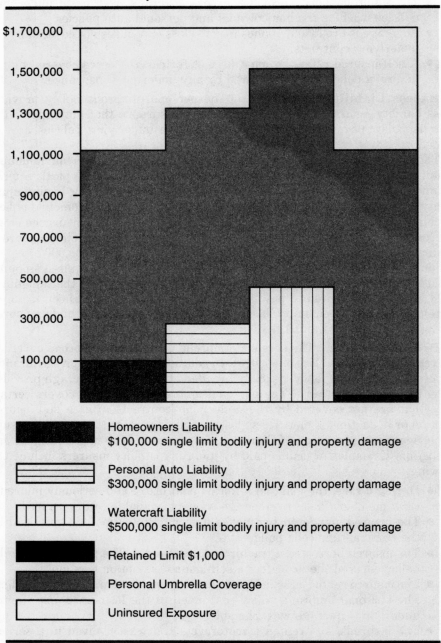

	Homeowners Liability $100,000 single limit bodily injury and property damage
	Personal Auto Liability $300,000 single limit bodily injury and property damage
	Watercraft Liability $500,000 single limit bodily injury and property damage
	Retained Limit $1,000
	Personal Umbrella Coverage
	Uninsured Exposure

Self-Insured Retention. If the loss is covered by the umbrella policy but not by any underlying insurance, a *self-insured retention* or deductible must be satisfied. Most personal umbrella policies require a self-insured retention of at least $250 per occurrence, but it can be as high as $10,000.

Personal Umbrella Coverages

The insuring agreement of the umbrella policy typically states that coverage is provided on an excess basis for personal injury liability and property damage liability.

Personal Injury Liability. The personal umbrella policy covers the insured's liability for personal injury. *Personal injury* is broadly defined to include bodily injury, sickness, disease, disability, shock, mental anguish, and mental injury. The definition also includes false arrest and imprisonment, wrongful entry or eviction, malicious prosecution or humiliation, libel, slander, defamation of character or invasion of privacy, and assault and battery not intentionally committed or directed by a covered person.

Property Damage Liability. Property damage liability is also covered. *Property damage* is defined as physical injury to tangible property and includes loss of use of the property.

The umbrella insurer agrees to pay losses for personal injury or property damage for which the insured is legally liable and which exceed the retained limit. The retained limit is either (1) the total of the applicable limits of all required underlying contracts and any other insurance available to a covered person or (2) the self-insured retention if the loss is not covered by the underlying insurance.

Defense Costs. In addition to the policy limits, the personal umbrella policy typically pays the legal defense costs that are not payable by the underlying contracts. Defense costs include payment of attorney fees, premiums on appeal bonds, court costs, interest on the judgment, and other legal costs. As noted above, these costs are in addition to the liability limits.

However, some personal umbrella policies include the cost of defending the insured as part of the total loss. In the event of a catastrophic judgment, it is possible that the insured may have to absorb part of the loss, as in the following example.

The insured has a personal umbrella policy with a limit of $1 million and personal liability insurance with a limit of $100,000 under a homeowners policy. The insured incurs a liability judgment in the amount of $1.1 million. The homeowners policy pays $100,000 of the total claim and the legal costs of defending the insured. In defending the insured for the remaining $1 million of the claim, the personal umbrella insurer incurs legal costs of $25,000. Since defense costs are included in the total loss, the umbrella insurer pays a maximum of $1 million, which includes $975,000 of the judgment and $25,000 for defense costs. The insured must pay the remaining $25,000 since the umbrella limits are now exhausted. Under an umbrella policy that pays defense costs in addition to the policy limits, the insured would not have to absorb any of the loss.

Finally, most umbrella policies provide and pay the defense costs of a covered loss if the loss is not covered by any underlying insurance. The amount paid is in addition to the policy limits.

Exclusions

Although the personal umbrella policy provides broad coverage, certain exclusions are usually present. The following exclusions are typical:[8]

1. *Workers compensation.* Any obligation for which the insured is legally liable under a workers compensation, disability benefits, or similar law is not covered.
2. *Fellow employee.* Some personal umbrella contracts exclude coverage for any insured (other than the named insured) who injures a fellow employee in the course of employment arising out of the use of an automobile, watercraft, or aircraft. The intent is to have the loss covered by workers compensation insurance.
3. *Care, custody, or control.* All personal umbrella contracts exclude damage to property a covered person owns. In addition, most contracts also exclude damage to nonowned aircraft in the insured's possession, and some umbrella policies also exclude damage to nonowned watercraft in the insured's possession. However, most personal umbrella policies cover damage to property rented to, used by, or in the care of an insured (except aircraft and watercraft).
4. *Nuclear energy.* All personal umbrella policies contain a nuclear energy exclusion.
5. *Intentional acts.* An act committed or directed by a covered person with intent to cause personal injury or property damage is not covered.
6. *Aircraft.* Most personal umbrella policies exclude all liability arising out of the ownership, maintenance, use, loading, or unloading of aircraft.
7. *Watercraft.* The personal umbrella policy covers smaller boats that normally are covered by the insured's underlying homeowners policy. However, the policy generally excludes coverage for larger watercraft such as inboard or inboard-outdrive watercraft exceeding fifty horsepower, outboard motorboats with more than twenty-five horsepower, and sailing vessels more than twenty-six feet in length.
8. *Business activity.* Most personal umbrella policies exclude liability arising out of business activity or business property. However, the exclusion does not apply to the use of a private passenger automobile by the named insured or member of the insured's family.
9. *Professional liability.* Personal umbrella policies typically exclude professional liability. A professional liability policy is needed to insure this exposure.
10. *Officers and directors.* Personal umbrella policies typically exclude liability coverage for an act or failure to act as an officer, trustee, or director of a corporation or association. The exclusion does not apply to officers and directors of a nonprofit corporation or association.

11. *Recreational vehicles.* Some personal umbrella policies exclude liability arising out of the ownership, maintenance, or use of recreational vehicles such as golf carts and snowmobiles. However, in those policies that contain this exclusion, there is usually excess liability protection if the insured carries underlying insurance at least equal to the minimum requirements.

Loss Payment Examples

Several examples can illustrate how loss payments are made by the personal umbrella policy. Assume that Fred has a $1 million personal umbrella policy with a $250 self-insured retention. He also has automobile liability coverage with a single limit of $300,000 and personal liability coverage under the homeowners policy with a limit of $100,000. Assume that Fred seriously injures another motorist in an accident and must pay a $750,000 judgment. The underlying automobile policy pays the first $300,000, and the personal umbrella policy pays the remaining $450,000 since the underlying limits of $300,000 per person are exhausted.

If Fred's dog bites and mauls a neighbor's child and Fred incurs a judgment of $200,000, the homeowners policy would pay $100,000, and the umbrella policy would pay the remaining $100,000.

Finally, assume that Fred is sued by his ex-wife for defamation of character and must pay damages of $25,000. There is no underlying coverage because the homeowners policy does not provide personal injury liability coverage. Fred must pay the retention of $250, and the umbrella policy will pay $24,750.

SUMMARY

Inland marine insurance was developed to make coverage available for movable property. In personal lines insurance, coverage for valuable movable personal property is provided by inland marine floater policies. Floaters can be tailored to the type of property to be covered. The insured often can set the appropriate policy limits. A wide variety of perils can be protected against, often on an "all-risks" basis. Many floaters have worldwide territorial limits.

Floaters that can be used to insure personal property include the personal articles floater, the personal property floater, and the personal effects floater. Provisions common to floater policies include coverage for risks of direct physical loss subject to exclusions, settlement provisions permitting replacement by the insurer, pair-and-set clauses, subrogation clauses, and other-insurance clauses.

The coverage chosen by a watercraft owner depends on the property and liability loss exposures envisioned, and the size and type of watercraft. Homeowners coverage (as discussed in Chapters 2 and 3) includes limited coverage for certain watercraft exposures. Auto policies also provide limited coverage for boat trailers. Policies offering more adequate protection for a greater variety of boats are available.

Outboard motor and boat insurance, an inland marine floater, provides physical damage coverage for outboard motors and motorboats. For larger boats, a boat owners package policy combines physical damage, liability, and medical payments coverage. The physical damage coverage includes damage to the boat, its equipment, and accessories. Liability coverage for bodily injury and property damage is included in the boat owners package policy, as are medical payments and uninsured boaters coverage.

The owner of a yacht, inboard motorboat, cabin cruiser, or large sailboat may wish to have personal yacht insurance. Such policies include hull insurance for physical damage coverage on the boat, its contents, and accessories, and protection and indemnity insurance for bodily injury and property damage liability coverage.

An additional loss exposure facing a family or individual is the possibility that the amount to be paid as the result of a lawsuit will be above the limits or outside of the coverage of the homeowners and auto policies. Personal umbrella policies can be obtained to provide protection against excess liability and certain loss exposures not covered by underlying policies.

A typical personal umbrella policy provides coverage for personal injury and property damage. Personal injury is broader than bodily injury and includes, for example, sickness, disease, anguish, and the personal injury perils such as libel, slander, false imprisonment, and invasion of privacy. Any payment is in excess of the insured's retained limit or underlying coverage. Defense costs also are covered, sometimes in addition to the liability limits or, occasionally, as a part of the total loss. While the coverage is broad, all forms include certain exclusions such as nuclear energy, professional liability, and officers and directors liability.

Chapter Notes

1. This section is based on Insurance Services Office, *Inland Marine Floater Policy— Personal Lines* (IPL 01 01), 1977; *Fire, Casualty & Surety Bulletins*, Personal Lines Volume, Misc. Personal Section, pp. Af1-Af6; and Glenn L. Wood, Claude C. Lilly III, Donald S. Malecki, Edward E. Graves, and Jerry S. Rosenbloom, *Personal Risk Management and Insurance*, 4th ed., vol. I (Malvern, PA: American Institute for Property and Liability Underwriters, 1989), pp. 282-286.
2. The discussion of the personal articles floater is based on Insurance Services Office, *Personal Articles Floater* (IPA 06 01), April 1983; *Fire, Casualty & Surety Bulletins*, Personal Lines Volume, Misc. Personal Section, pp. Afc1-Afc10; and Wood *et al.*, pp. 286-295.
3. The discussion of the major characteristics of the personal property floater is based on Insurance Services Office, *Personal Property Floater* (IPF 17 01), 3rd ed., June 1987 and *Fire, Casualty & Surety Bulletins*, Personal Lines Volume, Misc. Personal Section, pp. Pep1-Pep8.
4. The discussion of the personal effects floater is based on *Fire, Casualty, & Surety Bulletins*, Personal Lines Volume, Misc. Personal Section, pp. Pet 1-Pet 4 and Insurance Services Office, *Personal Effects Floater*.
5. Insurance on watercraft is based on Wood *et al.*, pp. 295-302; *Policy Form & Manual Analyses*, Property Insurance Volume (Indianapolis, IN: The Rough Notes Company), pp. 152.9-152.9.1; and Section II of the Homeowners 3 Special Form, Insurance Services Office, April 1991.
6. This section is based on the Personal Umbrella Policy in *1989 Policy Kit for Students of Insurance* (Schaumburg, IL: Alliance of American Insurers, 1989), pp. 54-56 and Wood *et al.*, pp. 302-312.
7. *Policy Form & Manual Analyses*, Casualty Insurance Volume (Indianapolis, IN: The Rough Notes Company, 1987), p. 272.11-1.
8. Wood *et al.*, pp. 307-312.

CHAPTER 7

Personal Auto Policy

In one recent year, there were about 34 million automobile accidents in the United States. More than 5 million injuries resulted from these accidents and nearly 49,000 persons were killed. Automobile accidents can cause great financial and economic insecurity to individuals and families. Legal liability arising out of the negligent operation of an automobile can reach catastrophic levels. Medical expenses, pain and suffering, loss of earned income, the unexpected death of a close family member, and damage to or loss of an expensive automobile can have serious financial impact on the individual and his or her family.

This chapter begins the study of automobile insurance. The discussion is limited to the personal auto policy (PAP), which is widely used throughout the United States to cover personal loss exposures arising out of the ownership or operation of an automobile.[1]

OVERVIEW OF THE PERSONAL AUTO POLICY (PAP)

The PAP was first introduced in several states by the Insurance Services Office in 1977. The PAP is designed to be easy to read and understand. Highly technical terms have been eliminated, and simple definitions and short sentences are used throughout the policy. The result is that the insured should be able to understand the basic provisions of this important contract without too much difficulty.

The PAP has been revised several times since it was first introduced. The following discussion is based on the 1989 edition of the PAP.

Eligible Vehicles

The PAP is designed to insure only certain types of motor vehicles. The vehicles must be *owned*, or leased for a minimum of six months, by an individual or by a husband and wife residing in the same household. An eligible vehicle is a four-wheel vehicle that is owned by the insured or is leased for at least six continuous months. Thus, a private passenger automobile, station wagon, or jeep owned by the insured is eligible for coverage.

A pickup or van also can be insured if the vehicle has a gross vehicle weight of less than 10,000 pounds and is not used to deliver or transport goods and materials. However, coverage is provided if such use of a pickup or van is (1) incidental to the insured's business of installing, maintaining, or repairing furnishings or equipment, or (2) for farming or ranching.

A private passenger automobile owned by two or more resident relatives (such as father and son) or by two or more nonrelated individuals residing together can also be insured under the PAP by adding a miscellaneous type vehicle endorsement (PP 03 23) to the policy. This endorsement is discussed in Chapter 8.

Finally, the PAP can be used to insure motorcycles, golf carts, snowmobiles, and similar vehicles by adding an appropriate endorsement to the policy. These special endorsements are discussed in Chapter 8.

Summary of Coverages

The PAP consists of a declarations page, an agreement and definitions page, and six separate parts. The six parts are as follows:

- Part A—Liability Coverage
- Part B—Medical Payments Coverage
- Part C—Uninsured Motorists Coverage
- Part D—Coverage for Damage to Your Auto
- Part E—Duties After an Accident or Loss
- Part F—General Provisions

Part A provides liability coverage that protects an insured against a suit or claim arising out of the negligent operation of an automobile. Part B provides medical expense coverage that pays reasonable and necessary medical expenses incurred by an insured because of bodily injury caused by an automobile accident. Part C provides protection if an insured is injured by an uninsured motorist, a hit-and-run driver, or a driver whose insurer is insolvent. Part D provides physical damage insurance on a covered auto. Part E outlines the duties imposed on an insured after an accident or loss. Finally, Part F contains certain general provisions, such as cancellation and termination of the policy. Only Parts A, B, and C are examined this chapter. The remaining parts are discussed in Chapter 8.

In addition to the preceding coverages, other optional coverages can be added to the policy, such as towing and labor costs coverage. These optional coverages also are discussed in Chapter 8.

Declarations

The *declarations page* provides information about the insured, a description of the insured automobile(s), a schedule of coverages, and other important details. The following information is typically provided.

Named Insured. The declarations page states the named insured and the named insured's mailing address. The named insured can be a single individual, husband and wife, or other parties.

Policy Period. The period of protection starts at 12:01 A.M. standard time on the date the policy becomes effective and ends at 12:01 A.M. standard time on the date the policy expires. The period of protection is usually six months or one year.

Description of Insured Automobiles. The declarations page describes the automobiles or trailers that are insured. This description includes the age of the automobile, model and body type, trade name, vehicle identification number, annual mileage, use of the automobile, date of purchase, and other information. Two or more automobiles may be described on the declarations page. A multiple-car discount is generally available if all vehicles are insured in the same company.

Premium Amount. The premium for each coverage and the total premium amount are shown.

Limits of Liability. Liability limits for bodily injury and property damage are shown. The amount of insurance can be shown as a single limit per accident, or as separate limits that apply to bodily injury and property damage.

Schedule of Coverages. The various coverages and the amount of insurance for each coverage are shown. Part A shows the limits of liability and premiums for liability insurance, Part B indicates the amount of medical payments coverage for each person, Part C shows the amount of uninsured motorists coverage, and Part D indicates whether there is coverage for damage to the insured's auto. If physical damage coverage applies, the deductible amounts for collision loss and other than a collision loss are indicated.

Lienholder. The vehicle may be financed through a bank, savings and loan association, credit union, or other financial institution, which holds a lien on the vehicle until the loan is paid off. In such a case, the name of the lienholder is usually stated on the declarations page.

Garage Location. Unless otherwise stated, the described automobile is assumed to be principally garaged at the mailing address stated on the declarations page.

Cancellation by Another Insurer. If the insured has been previously canceled by another insurer, this information may also be shown on the declarations page.

Rating Information. The rating class in which the vehicle is placed and any applicable credits and discounts are shown. Premiums can be reduced by a multiple-car discount, driver training, good student discount, bumper discount, accident prevention course, passive restraint discount, anti-theft device discount, and other discounts and credits.

Applicable Endorsements. The declarations page also indicates any endorsements that are attached to the policy. For example, a high-risk teenage driver may be excluded from coverage under his or her parents' policy by a driver exclusion endorsement.

Signatures. The signatures of authorized legal representatives of the insurer are shown at the bottom of the declarations page.

Agreement and Definitions

The first page of the personal auto policy contains the insuring agreement and definitions of several terms used throughout the policy.

Agreement. The policy begins with a brief general agreement that serves as an introduction to the policy and states that the insurer's obligations under the policy are dependent upon the payment of premiums by the insured.

Definitions. A series of important definitions apply to the entire contract. The definitions are written in simple, easily understood language. The following words and phrases are defined in this section:

1. *You and your.* The words "you" and "your" refer to the named insured shown on the declarations page and also to the spouse of the named insured if he or she is a resident of the same household.
2. *We, us, and our.* The words "we," "us," and "our" refer to the insurance company that is providing the insurance under the contract.
3. *Private passenger auto.* This definition clarifies that, for purposes of the policy, a private passenger auto that is leased is deemed to be an owned automobile if it is *leased* under a written agreement for a continuous period of at least six months. Thus, a private passenger sedan that is rented under a six-month leasing agreement would be considered an *owned* automobile under the PAP.
4. *Bodily injury.* Bodily injury is defined as bodily harm, sickness, or disease, including death that results.
5. *Business.* Business includes a trade, a profession, or an occupation.
6. *Family member.* A family member is a person who is related to the named insured or spouse by blood, marriage, or adoption and resides in the named insured's household. This definition also includes a ward or a foster child.
7. *Occupying.* Occupying is defined as in, upon, getting in, on, out, or off a motor vehicle. This definition has relevance for Part B—Medical Payments Coverage and Part C—Uninsured Motorists Coverage.
8. *Property damage.* Property damage is physical injury to or destruction of tangible property. It also includes loss of use of tangible property that is not physically injured.
9. *Trailer.* A trailer is defined as a vehicle designed to be pulled by a private passenger auto, pickup, or van. A trailer also is a farm wagon or farm implement while towed by such a vehicle.
10. *Your covered auto.* An extremely important definition applies to the vehicles that are covered under the PAP. The four classes of vehicles

considered to be covered vehicles are listed below and described in the text that follows.

- Any vehicle shown in the declarations
- A newly acquired vehicle
- A trailer owned by the insured
- A temporary substitute auto or trailer

A covered auto is *any vehicle listed in the declarations.* As noted, covered vehicles include a private passenger automobile, station wagon, jeep, pickup truck, or van owned by the named insured. A private passenger automobile leased for at least six months is also considered a covered auto.

A *newly acquired vehicle* is also considered to be a covered auto. Coverage is automatically provided from the date the insured becomes the owner. Therefore, if the insured purchases a new car, the car is automatically covered when the insured drives it away from the car dealer's lot. However, the coverage continues only if the insured asks the insurance company to insure the vehicle within thirty days after it is acquired. An additional premium must be paid for the newly acquired vehicle. If the newly acquired vehicle is a pickup or van, the automatic coverage provision applies only if no other insurance policy provides coverage for that vehicle.

If the new vehicle the insured acquires *replaces* one shown in the declarations, it automatically has the same coverage as the vehicle it replaced. However, the insured must report the replacement vehicle to the insurer within thirty days if the insured wishes to add or continue physical damage insurance (Part D—Coverage for Damage to Your Auto) on the replacement vehicle. For example, assume that the insured has collision insurance on a 1985 car that is traded in for a 1991 car. The insured has thirty days to notify the insurance company to continue the collision insurance on the new car. If the insured forgets to notify the company and six weeks later is involved in an accident, the physical damage loss to the new car is not covered.

If the newly acquired vehicle is an *additional vehicle*, it has the broadest coverage provided for any vehicle listed in the declarations. For example, if two cars are listed in the declarations, one with collision coverage and the other without, an additional vehicle purchased by the insured would be insured for a collision loss.

A *trailer owned by the named insured* also is a covered auto. As noted earlier, a trailer is a vehicle designed to be pulled by a private passenger auto, pickup, or van. It also is a farm wagon or farm implement while towed by such vehicles.

A *temporary substitute vehicle* is also a covered auto under the PAP. A temporary substitute vehicle is a nonowned auto or trailer that the insured is using because of the breakdown, repair, servicing, loss, or destruction of a covered vehicle. However, temporary substitute vehicles are not within the definition of covered auto as that definition applies to Part D—Coverage for Damage to Your Auto. (With respect to physical damage coverage, temporary substitute vehicles are considered nonowned vehicles, as discussed in Chapter 8.)

PART A—LIABILITY COVERAGE

In terms of the protection it provides for the insured, the liability coverage is the most important coverage in the PAP. It provides protection against legal liability arising out of the ownership or operation of an automobile.

Insuring Agreement

In the insuring agreement, the company agrees to pay damages for bodily injury or property damage for which the insured is legally responsible because of an automobile accident. The liability limit is written as a *single limit* that applies to both bodily injury and property damage liability. For example, a single limit of $300,000 could apply to both bodily injury and property damage liability. The policy also can be written with *split limits* in which the amounts of insurance for bodily injury and property damage are stated separately. For example, split limits of $100,000/$300,000/$50,000 mean that the insured has bodily injury liability limits of $100,000 per person and $300,000 for each accident, and a limit of $50,000 for property damage liability.

The damages paid also include any prejudgment interest awarded against the insured. The laws of many states now allow plaintiffs (injured persons) to receive interest on a judgment from the time a suit is entered to the time the judgment is handed down. Prejudgment interest is considered to be part of the award for damages and is subject to the policy limit of liability. For example, assume an insured is legally liable for a $30,000 judgment and $3,000 of prejudgment interest. If the policy has adequate limits, the liability payment is $33,000.

In addition to the payment of damages for which an insured is legally liable, the insurer also agrees to defend the insured and pay all legal defense costs. The defense costs are *in addition* to the policy limits. However, the insurer's duty to settle or defend the claim ends when the limit of liability has been exhausted. Thus, once the policy limits (including prejudgment interest) are paid, the insurer has no further obligation to settle or defend the claim. The insurer also has no obligation to defend any claim that is not covered under the policy. For example, if an insured intentionally causes bodily injury or property damage and is sued, the company has no obligation to defend the insured. The PAP specifically excludes intentionally caused bodily injury or property damage.

Insured Persons

The following four groups are insured for liability coverage under the PAP:

- The named insured and any family member
- Any person using the named insured's covered auto
- Any person or organization, but only for legal liability arising out of an insured person's use of a covered auto on behalf of that person or organization
- Any person or organization legally responsible for the named insured's

Structured Settlements in Automobile Liability Insurance

Awards for damages resulting from bodily injury liability claims are increasingly being paid as structured settlements. Unlike a one-time cash payment for damages, a *structured settlement* consists of periodic and guaranteed payments over a specified time period. The automobile insurer purchases an annuity from a life insurer that pays periodic and guaranteed payments to the injured accident victim. For example, in one case, an injured plaintiff aged twenty-five received a lifetime income of $400 monthly with twenty years of guaranteed payments and a $250,000 retirement benefit at age sixty. The annuity provides total guaranteed payments of $346,000 to the injured person. However, the cost of the annuity to the automobile insurer was less than $60,000.

Structured settlements have advantages to both injured victims and automobile insurers. The injured person receives the periodic annuity payments income-tax free; the accident victim is protected against squandering a large lump sum payment; and the payments are guaranteed, which provides protection against an unprofitable investment. Automobile insurers also benefit because claim costs can be reduced, and cash reserves are protected. Also, by offering a flexible and attractive benefit, insurers can often reach a settlement agreement more quickly with an injured person, and costly court expenses and delays are avoided.

or family members' use of any automobile or trailer (other than a covered auto or one owned by that person or organization)

The named insured and family members are insured for liability coverage. The named insured also includes the spouse of the named insured if he or she is a resident of the same household. Family members are also covered. As noted, family members are persons related to the named insured by blood, marriage, or adoption who reside in the same household, as well as a ward or a foster child. While children are temporarily away from home, such as when attending college, they are still covered under their parents' policy.

Any person using the named insured's covered auto also is covered, provided that person has a reasonable belief that permission exists to use the covered auto. For example, assume that Mary has allowed her roommate to drive her car several times during the past month. If Mary is not around and the roommate drives Mary's car believing that Mary would have granted permission, the roommate is covered under Mary's policy.

Any person or organization legally responsible for the acts of a covered person while using a covered auto is also covered. For example, assume that Bob's employer asks him to drive to the post office to pick up a package. While driving his covered auto on company business, Bob negligently injures another person. If Bob's employer is sued because of his negligence, the employer is also covered under Bob's PAP.

Finally, *any person or organization legally responsible for the named insured's or family members' use of any automobile or trailer* (other than a covered auto or one owned by that person or organization) is also covered. Using the previous example, if Bob borrows the car of a fellow employee to go to the post office and negligently injures another motorist, Bob's employer is covered under Bob's PAP if the firm is sued because of his negligence. However, the PAP does not extend coverage to the employer if Bob were to use an automobile *owned* by the employer. Thus, if Bob drives to the post office in a company car, the employer is not covered under Bob's PAP.

Supplementary Payments

The following supplementary payments are paid *in addition* to the liability limits and legal defense costs:

- Bail bonds
- Premiums on appeal bonds and bonds to release attachments
- Interest accruing after a judgment
- Loss of earnings
- Other reasonable expenses

Premiums on a *bail bond* can be paid up to $250 because of an accident that results in bodily injury or property damage. However, there must be an accident. Bail bond premiums are not paid for speeding tickets.

Premiums on *appeal bonds and bonds to release an attachment of property* in a lawsuit defended by the insured are also paid as a supplementary payment. If interest accrues after a judgment, the *accrued interest* is also paid as an additional payment. (However, prejudgment interest is part of the liability limits.)

The insurer also pays up to $50 daily for an insured's *loss of earnings* (but not other income) because of attendance at a hearing or trial at the insurer's request.

Finally, *other reasonable expenses* incurred at the insurer's request are also paid. For example, an insured may incur travel and transportation expenses in testifying at a trial at the insurer's request. These expenses are paid as a supplementary payment.

Liability Coverage Exclusions

A lengthy list of exclusions applies to the liability coverage under the PAP. The major exclusions are summarized in the following paragraphs.

Intentional Injury.   Bodily injury or property damage intentionally caused is specifically excluded. For example, if a teenager, who is angry because he lost his job, deliberately and repeatedly rams the vehicle in front of him on a crowded expressway, the intentional property damage to the other motorist's car would not be covered under the teenager's PAP.

Property Owned or Transported. Liability coverage does not apply to property damage to property owned or being transported by that person. For example, if Alice's suitcase and clothes are damaged in an automobile accident while she is on vacation, the loss is not covered under the PAP. (However, a homeowners policy would cover the loss.)

Property Rented, Used, or in the Care of the Insured. Property damage to property rented to, used by, or in the care of the insured is not covered under the PAP. For example, if Tom rents skis that are damaged in an automobile accident, damage to the skis is not covered. The exclusion, however, does not apply to damage to a residence or private garage. Thus, if Tom rented a vacation house and carelessly backed his car into the side of the house, the property damage claim by the landlord would be covered.

Bodily Injury to an Employee of a Covered Person. The liability coverage also excludes bodily injury to an employee of a covered person who is injured during the course of employment. The intent is that compensation for the employee's injury should be provided under a workers compensation law. One exception, however, is that a domestic employee injured in the course of employment is covered if workers compensation benefits are not required or available.

Public or Livery Conveyance. Liability insurance does not apply to a vehicle while it is being used as a public or livery conveyance to carry people or property for a fee. For example, if the city taxicab drivers are on strike and Harry decides to capitalize on the situation by transporting persons in his car for a fee, Harry's liability coverage does not apply to this activity. The exclusion does not apply to share-the-expense car pools.

Garage Business Exclusion. Liability insurance does not apply to any person while employed or engaged in the business of selling, repairing, servicing, storing, or parking vehicles designed for use mainly on public highways. This includes road testing and delivery. For example, if an automobile mechanic has an accident while road testing a customer's car, the mechanic's PAP liability coverage does not apply. Likewise, if a parking lot attendant accidentally injures someone while parking cars, the loss is not covered under the attendant's PAP. The intent is to exclude a loss exposure that should be covered under the employer's liability policy, such as a garage policy.

The preceding exclusion does not apply to the operation, ownership, or use of a covered auto by the named insured, family member, or any partner, agent, or employee of the named insured or family member. For example, referring to the previous illustration, if an auto mechanic drove his covered auto to a parts shop to pick up a part for his employer and he injured someone on the way, the mechanic's PAP liability insurance would cover the loss.

Other Business Use. Liability coverage does not apply to any vehicle

Liability Coverage and Car Pools

PAP rates are not designed to cover the increased exposure to the insurer if a covered auto is used as a public taxi or livery conveyance for hire by the general public. For this reason, the PAP excludes legal liability arising out of ownership or operation of a vehicle while it is being used as a public or livery conveyance to carry persons or property for a fee. However, share-the-expense car pools are an exception. Thus, if Barbara picks up several persons and transports them to work in an organized car pool, and automobile expenses are shared, the liability coverage still applies. Likewise, if Barbara and several friends go on a vacation in her car and she is reimbursed for car expenses, her liability coverage is still in force.

maintained or used in any business other than farming or ranching. This exclusion is similar to the preceding garage exclusion except that it applies to all other business use, with certain exceptions. The intent is to exclude liability coverage for commercial vehicles and trucks used in a business. For example, if an insured drives a city bus or operates a large cement truck, the insured's PAP liability coverage does not apply.

The above exclusion does not apply to the maintenance or use of a private passenger auto (owned or nonowned), a pickup or van owned by the insured, or a trailer while it is being used with a covered vehicle. For example, if Fred drives his covered auto on company business, the liability coverage is in force.

Using a Vehicle Without Reasonable Belief of Permission. If a person uses a vehicle without a reasonable belief that he or she is entitled to do so, the liability insurance does not apply. Thus, a thief who steals an insured's car and injures someone is not covered under the insured's PAP.

Nuclear Energy Liability Losses. Liability of insureds who are covered under special nuclear energy liability contracts is also excluded under the personal auto policy.

Motorized Vehicles With Fewer Than Four Wheels. Liability arising out of the ownership, maintenance, or use of any motorized vehicle having fewer than four wheels is specifically excluded. Thus, motorcycles, mopeds, motorscooters, and similar vehicles are excluded under the policy. However, these vehicles can be insured by adding a miscellaneous type vehicle endorsement to the PAP. This endorsement is discussed in Chapter 8.

Vehicle Furnished or Available for Regular Use. Any vehicle other than a covered auto that is owned by, furnished, or made available for the named insured's regular use is also excluded. An insured can occasionally drive another person's automobile and still have coverage under his or her policy. *However, if the nonowned automobile is driven regularly or is furnished or made available for the insured's regular use, the insured's liability coverage does not apply.* The key point is not how frequently one drives someone else's automobile but whether it is furnished or available for regular use.

The intent of this exclusion is to limit the insurance company's exposure. Otherwise, the insured could insure one vehicle and pay premiums for only one vehicle even though several cars are also being driven on a regular basis. Thus, without this exclusion, the exposure to the insurance company could be substantially increased.

Vehicle Furnished or Available for Regular Use of Any Family Member. A similar exclusion applies to a vehicle (other than the covered auto) that is owned by any family member or is furnished or made available for the regular use of any family member. However, the exclusion does not apply to the named insured and spouse while maintaining or occupying such a vehicle. Therefore, if the father *occasionally* drives a car owned by another household member, such as the son, the liability insurance under the father's PAP would cover him while driving the son's car.

Limit of Liability

The PAP also states that regardless of the number of insureds involved in an accident, the limit of liability for the policy will not be increased. The most any claimant can recover for one accident is the limit stated in the declarations. For example, if Betty were doing an errand for the Red Cross in her personal automobile and caused an accident, the claimants could sue both Betty and the Red Cross, since she was acting on its behalf. Betty's insurer would handle the claim and answer a lawsuit on behalf of both Betty and the Red Cross. However, the insurer would not pay more than Betty's limit of liability even though it is responding on behalf of two parties.

Out-of-State Coverage

The PAP also contains a provision that applies when an automobile accident occurs in a state other than the one in which the covered auto is principally garaged. If the accident occurs in a state that has a financial responsibility law or similar law that requires higher liability limits than the limits shown in the declarations, the PAP automatically provides the higher required limits.

In addition, if the state has a compulsory insurance law or similar law that requires a nonresident to maintain insurance whenever the nonresident uses a vehicle in that state, the PAP provides the required minimum amounts and types of coverage. Thus, this provision ensures compliance with an out-of-state no-fault law and the payment of required benefits. A driver not insured for no-fault benefits in his or her home state would have no-fault insurance in a state that requires it. No-fault automobile insurance is discussed in Chapter 9.

Compliance With Financial Responsibility Laws

Many states have financial responsibility laws that require proof of financial responsibility after an accident occurs (see Chapter 9). When the PAP policy is used to demonstrate proof of financial responsibility, the PAP policy will comply with the law to the extent required. Thus, if the financial responsibility law is changed, the PAP is adjusted to comply with the law.

Other Insurance

The PAP also has a provision that applies when more than one automobile policy covers a liability claim. If there is other applicable liability insurance that applies to an *owned vehicle,* the insurer pays only its pro rata share of the loss. The insurer's share is the proportion that its limit of liability bears to the total of all applicable limits. However, if the liability insurance applies to a *nonowned vehicle,* the PAP coverage is excess over any other collectible insurance. These rules are illustrated by the following two examples.

- *Example 1.* Joseph negligently injures another motorist and must pay damages of $60,000. If two automobile liability policies cover an *owned vehicle,* each company pays its pro rata share. Assume Joseph is insured for $100,000 in Company A and also has coverage of $50,000 in Company B. Each company pays as follows:

$$\text{Company A} \quad \frac{\$100,000}{\$150,000} \times \$60,000 = \$40,000$$

$$\text{Company B} \quad \frac{\$50,000}{\$150,000} \times \$60,000 = \$20,000$$

- *Example 2.* Ken borrows Patti's car with her permission. Ken has a $100,000 liability limit and Patti has a $50,000 limit. Ken negligently injures another motorist and must pay a judgment of $75,000. Patti's insurance is primary and Ken's is excess. Each company pays as follows:

Patti's insurer (primary)	$50,000
Ken's insurer (excess)	$25,000

PART B—MEDICAL PAYMENTS COVERAGE

Medical payments coverage is an accident benefit that can be optionally added to the PAP. This benefit pays the medical expenses up to certain specified limits of insureds who are injured in an automobile accident.

Insuring Agreement

The insurer will pay all reasonable and necessary medical and funeral expenses incurred by an insured because of bodily injury caused by an accident. The company will pay only those expenses incurred within three years from the date of the accident. The types of expenses paid include those incurred for medical, surgical, x-ray, dental, and funeral services. Medical payments coverage typically ranges from $1,000 to $10,000 per person and applies to each insured person who is injured in an automobile accident.

Medical payments coverage applies without regard to fault. Thus, if an insured and other occupants of the car are injured in an automobile accident caused by the insured, medical payments benefits will be paid for the insured and the injured occupants of the insured's covered auto.

Insured Persons

Two groups of persons are considered insured persons for medical payments coverage. They are (1) the named insured and family members, and (2) any other person while occupying a covered auto.

The *named insured and family members* are covered for their medical expenses if they are injured while occupying a motor vehicle or are injured as pedestrians when struck by a motor vehicle designed for use mainly on public roads. As indicated above, occupying is broadly defined to mean in, upon, getting in, on, out, or off of a motor vehicle. Examples of covered losses include payment of medical expenses if the named insured is injured in an automobile accident, if a child's hand is injured when the insured's car door slams on it, and if a guest of the insured breaks a leg while getting out of the insured's vehicle.

If the named insured or any family member is struck by a motor vehicle or trailer while walking as a pedestrian, his or her medical expenses are also paid. However, because the injury must be caused by a vehicle designed for use mainly on public roads, if an insured is struck by a farm tractor, for example, medical payments coverage does not apply since the tractor is not designed for use mainly on public roads.

Any other person while occupying a covered auto is also insured. Therefore, medical expenses of other passengers in the car are covered if the vehicle is a covered auto. For example, if Mary owns her car and is the named insured, all passengers in her car are covered for their medical expenses under her policy. However, if Mary is operating a *nonowned vehicle*, other persons in the car (other than family members) are not covered under Mary's medical payments coverage. The intent of this restriction is to have other persons in the nonowned vehicle who are not family members seek protection under their own contracts or under the medical expense coverage that applies to the nonowned vehicle.

Medical Payments Exclusions

Numerous exclusions also apply to medical payments coverage. These exclusions are summarized in the following paragraphs.

Vehicles With Fewer Than Four Wheels. Medical expenses for bodily injury sustained while occupying a motorized vehicle with fewer than four wheels are excluded. For example, if an insured is injured while operating a motorcycle, the medical payments coverage does not apply.

Public or Livery Conveyance. Medical payments coverage does not apply if a covered auto is being used as a public or livery conveyance to carry people or property for a fee. The exclusion does not apply to share-the-expense car pools.

Vehicle Used as a Residence or Premises. If the injury occurs while the vehicle is used as a residence or premises, medical payments coverage does not apply. For example, if an insured owns and occupies a house trailer and uses it as a residence, the medical payments coverage of the PAP does not apply to injuries arising out of the use of this vehicle.

Injury During the Course of Employment. If the injury occurs during the course of employment and workers compensation benefits are available, medical payments coverage does not apply. For example, if an insured is injured while driving his or her car on company business and workers compensation benefits are available, the medical payments coverage of the PAP does not apply.

Vehicle Furnished or Available for Regular Use. Medical payments coverage does not apply to an injury sustained by an insured while occupying or when struck by any vehicle (other than a covered auto) that is owned by the insured or is furnished or available for his or her regular use. The intent is to exclude medical payments coverage on an owned or regularly used vehicle that is not described in the policy and for which no premium is paid.

Vehicle Furnished or Available for Regular Use of Any Family Member. A similar exclusion also applies to any vehicle (other than a covered auto) that is owned by or is furnished or available for the regular use of any family member. However, there is an important exception. The exclusion does not apply to the named insured and spouse. For example, assume that a son living at home owns a car that is separately insured. If the parents are injured while occupying the son's car, their medical expenses are covered only under their personal auto policy.

Using a Vehicle Without Reasonable Belief of Permission. If a person sustains an injury while using a vehicle without a reasonable belief that he or she is entitled to do so, medical payments coverage does not apply. For example, if a thief steals a car and is injured in an automobile accident, the medical payments coverage under the auto owner's PAP does not apply.

Vehicle Used in the Business or Occupation of an Insured. Medical payments coverage does not apply to bodily injury sustained by a person while occupying a vehicle used in the business or occupation of an insured. The intent is to exclude medical payments coverage for nonowned trucks and commercial vehicles used in the business or occupation of an insured. However, the exclusion does not apply to a private passenger automobile, an owned pickup or van, or a trailer while used with the preceding vehicles.

Bodily Injury From Nuclear Weapons or War. Injury from the discharge of a nuclear weapon (even if accidental) or from war, insurrection, rebellion, or revolution is also excluded.

Nuclear Radiation Exclusion. Bodily injury caused by nuclear reaction, radiation, or radioactive contamination is also excluded. For example, if an insured were driving a covered auto near a public utility plant when a nuclear meltdown occurred, the radiation exposure would not be covered.

Limit of Liability

The limit of liability for medical payments coverage is stated in the declarations. This limit is the maximum amount that will be paid to *each injured person* in a single accident regardless of the number of injured persons, claims made, vehicles or premiums shown, or vehicles involved in the auto accident. The intent is to prevent an insured person from "stacking" or "pyramiding" medical payments under a policy that covers more than one car.

In addition, the amount paid for medical expenses is *reduced* by any amounts paid for the same medical expense under Part A—Liability Coverage or Part C—Uninsured Motorists Coverage. The intent of this provision is to avoid a double payment for the same medical expenses. For example, assume Janice has $5,000 of medical payments coverage, and she is injured by an uninsured motorist. Janice's medical bills are $5,000. Without this provision, Janice could collect $10,000—$5,000 under the medical payments coverage and $5,000 under the uninsured motorists coverage. However, if the amount paid under the uninsured motorists coverage is $5,000, nothing is paid to Janice under the medical payments coverage.

Finally, no payment is made for medical expenses unless the injured person agrees in writing that any such payment shall be applied toward any settlement or judgment that the person receives under the liability or uninsured motorists coverages.

Other Insurance

If other automobile medical payments insurance applies to a *covered auto,* the company pays its pro rata share based on the proportion that its limit of liability bears to the total of applicable limits.

With respect to a *nonowned vehicle,* however, medical payments coverage is *excess* over any other collectible automobile insurance that provides payment for medical or funeral expenses. For example, assume that Mary is driving her own car and picks up Patti for lunch. Mary loses control of the car and hits a tree. Mary has $2,000 of medical payments coverage under her PAP, and Patti has $5,000. If Patti's medical expenses are $3,000, Mary's insurer pays $2,000 as primary insurance and Patti's insurer pays the remaining $1,000 as excess insurance.

PART C—UNINSURED MOTORISTS COVERAGE

The *uninsured motorists coverage* is designed to meet the problem of bodily injury caused by an uninsured motorist. The uninsured motorists coverage pays for the bodily injury of a covered person who is injured by an uninsured motorist, a hit-and-run driver, or by a driver whose insurer is insolvent.

Insuring Agreement

The insurer agrees to pay compensatory damages that the insured person is legally entitled to recover from the owner or operator of an uninsured motor vehicle because of bodily injury caused by an accident. For example, if an uninsured driver fails to stop at a red light and injures an insured, the uninsured motorists coverage would pay for the insured's bodily injury up to the limits of the policy.

Many states also include property damage as part of the uninsured motorists coverage. In such states, the property damage is subject to a deductible, such as $200 or $300.

The coverage for bodily injury and property damage applies only if the uninsured motorist is legally responsible for the accident. Although a covered person is not required to sue the uninsured driver, legal liability must be established. The insurer will not pay for the bodily injury if the uninsured driver is not legally responsible for the injury.

Insureds. Three groups are considered insureds under the uninsured motorists coverage: (1) the named insured and family members, (2) any other person occupying a covered auto, and (3) any person legally entitled to recover damages. The *named insured and family members* are covered if injured by an uninsured motorist while occupying a covered auto or nonowned auto. They are also covered as pedestrians if they are injured by a hit-and-run motorist.

Any other person who is injured while occupying a covered auto is also covered. The coverage applies only if the individual is occupying a covered auto. Thus, passengers in an insured's car have protection against injuries caused by an uninsured motorist. However, other persons in a nonowned auto operated by the named insured or family member generally are not covered, since they are insured under their own uninsured motorists coverage or have protection under the coverage on the nonowned auto.

Finally, *any person legally entitled to recover damages* is insured. An individual may not be physically involved in the accident but may be entitled to recover damages from the person or organization legally responsible for the bodily injury to the insured person. For example, if an insured were killed by an uninsured motorist, a surviving spouse could still collect damages under the uninsured motorists coverage.

Uninsured Vehicles. The uninsured motorists coverage clearly specifies the types of vehicles that are considered uninsured vehicles. An uninsured vehicle is a land motor vehicle or trailer of any type that meets one of the following criteria:

1. No bodily injury liability insurance policy or bond applies at the time of the accident.
2. A bodily injury liability policy or bond is in force, but the limit for bodily injury liability is less than the minimum amount required by the financial

responsibility law in the state where the named insured's covered auto is principally garaged.

3. The vehicle is a hit-and-run vehicle whose operator or owner cannot be identified and hits (a) the named insured or any family member, (b) a vehicle that the named insured or family member is occupying, or (c) the named insured's covered auto.

4. A bodily injury liability policy or bond applies at the time of the accident, but the insurance or bonding company (a) denies coverage or (b) is or becomes insolvent. For example, if Tom has a valid claim against a negligent motorist whose liability insurer becomes insolvent before the claim is paid, Tom can still collect under the uninsured motorists coverage of his PAP.

Certain vehicles, however, are not considered to be uninsured motor vehicles. If an insured were injured by one of these vehicles, uninsured motorists coverage would not apply. The definition of uninsured motor vehicle does not include the following types of vehicles or equipment:

1. Owned by or furnished or available for the regular use of the named insured or any family member
2. Owned or operated by a self-insurer under any applicable motor vehicle law, except a self-insurer that is or becomes insolvent
3. Owned by a governmental unit or agency
4. Operated on rails or crawler treads
5. Designed mainly for use off public roads while not on a public road
6. Located for use as a residence or premises

Uninsured Motorists Exclusions

The uninsured motorists coverage also has several general exclusions. The following is a summary of these exclusions.

1. *No uninsured motorists coverage on vehicle.* There is no coverage for bodily injury sustained by any person who occupies or is struck by a motor vehicle or trailer owned by the named insured or a family member if that vehicle does not have uninsured motorists coverage under the policy.

2. *Settling the claim without insurer's consent.* The uninsured motorists coverage does not apply if a bodily injury claim is settled without the insurer's consent. The purpose of this exclusion is to protect the insurer's interest in the claim.

3. *Public or livery conveyance.* If a person is injured while occupying a covered auto when it is being used as a public or livery conveyance to carry persons or property for a fee, the uninsured motorists coverage does not apply. The exclusion does not apply to a share-the-expense car pool, however.

4. *Using a vehicle without reasonable belief of permission.* The coverage

does not apply to any person who uses a vehicle without a reasonable belief that the person is entitled to do so.

5. *Cannot benefit workers compensation insurer.* The uninsured motorists coverage cannot directly or indirectly benefit any insurer or self-insurer under a workers compensation law or disability benefits law. In some states, if an employee is injured and workers compensation benefits are paid, the workers compensation insurer has a legal right of subrogation against a third party to recover the amounts paid. Thus, the workers compensation insurer could sue the uninsured driver or attempt to make a claim as a derivative insured under the injured employee's uninsured motorists coverage. This exclusion prevents the workers compensation insurer from benefiting in such a way through the uninsured motorists coverage.

6. *Punitive damages not paid.* The PAP excludes payment for punitive or exemplary damages under the uninsured motorists coverage. Therefore, only compensatory damages are paid under this coverage.

Limit of Liability

The minimum amount of uninsured motorists coverage available under the PAP is equal to the amount required by the financial responsibility or compulsory insurance law of the state in which the named insured's covered auto is principally garaged. This amount is typically $25,000 per person, but higher amounts can be purchased by payment of an additional premium.

The limit of liability for uninsured motorists coverage is shown in the declarations and is the maximum amount that will be paid for all damages resulting from any one accident. That amount is the most that will be paid regardless of the number of insured persons, claims made, vehicles or premiums shown in the declarations, or vehicles involved in the accident. This provision prevents the "stacking" of uninsured motorists payments under a policy that covers more than one car owned by the named insured. For example, assume the insured owns three cars that are covered by a PAP with an uninsured motorists limit of $25,000. If the insured is injured by an uninsured motorist, the most the insured can recover is $25,000, not $75,000.

The amount paid under the uninsured motorists coverage may be reduced in certain situations. Amounts payable are reduced by all sums paid (1) by the person or organization legally responsible for the accident or (2) under a workers compensation or disability benefits law. In addition, any payment made under the uninsured motorists coverage reduces the amount recoverable for the same damages under the liability coverage of the PAP.

Other Insurance

If other uninsured motorists insurance applies to the loss, the PAP pays only its pro rata share of the loss, which is the proportion that its limit of liability bears to the total of all applicable limits.

With respect to a *nonowned vehicle*, however, the uninsured motorists coverage is *excess* over any other collectible insurance. For example, assume that Lou has $25,000 of uninsured motorists coverage under her PAP. She is injured by an uninsured motorist while riding in Gayle's car. Gayle also has $25,000 of uninsured motorists coverage. If Lou has $35,000 of bodily injuries, Gayle's insurer pays the first $25,000 as primary insurer, and Lou's insurer pays the remaining $10,000 as excess insurance.

Arbitration

If the insurer and insured cannot agree as to whether the insured is entitled to recover damages or on the amount of damages, the dispute can be settled by arbitration. Under this provision, either party can make a written demand for arbitration. Each party selects an arbitrator, and the two arbitrators select a third arbitrator. If the two arbitrators cannot agree on a third arbitrator within thirty days, either party can request that the selection be made by a judge of a court having jurisdiction. Each party pays the expenses it incurs, and both parties share the expenses of the third arbitrator.

A decision agreed to by two of the three arbitrators is binding as to (1) whether the insured is legally entitled to recover damages and (2) the amount of damages. However, this decision is binding only if the amount of damages does not exceed the minimum limit for bodily injury specified by the state's financial responsibility law. If the amount of damages exceeds that limit, either party can demand the right to a trial within sixty days of the arbitrators' decision. If this demand is not made within the time limit, the amount of damages agreed to by the arbitrators is binding on all parties.

SUMMARY

The personal auto policy (PAP) consists of a declarations page, an insuring agreement, definitions, and six separate parts. To be eligible for coverage under the personal auto policy, the vehicle to be insured must be owned, or leased for at least six months, by an individual or by a husband and wife residing together. It must be a four-wheel vehicle, not rented to others, and not used as a public or livery conveyance.

The PAP declarations page identifies the named insured, his or her address, and the location at which the vehicle is garaged. It also describes the covered vehicle(s) and lists the premiums, the limits of liability, endorsements, and other information. The definitions clarify the terms enclosed in quotation marks in the policy. Four classes of vehicles are covered by the personal auto policy: (1) the vehicle(s) shown in the declarations, (2) a newly acquired vehicle, (3) a trailer owned by the insured, and (4) a temporary substitute vehicle or trailer.

Part A—Liability Coverage of the PAP pays damages for bodily injury or property damage for which the insured is legally responsible because of an auto accident. The policy has a combined single limit. Therefore, the policy's limit of liability is available to pay for any combination of bodily injury and property damage for which the insured is legally liable. The insurer also agrees to defend the insured and pay all legal defense costs, in addition to the policy limits, until the limits are exhausted by settlement or payment of a judgment.

Four groups of persons are insured under the PAP liability coverage: the named insured and family members; persons using the named insured's covered auto with permission; a person or organization held responsible for liability arising out of an insured's use of a covered auto on behalf of that person or organization; and a person or organization legally responsible for the named insured and family members' use of any auto or trailer other than a covered auto or one owned by that person or organization.

Excluded from liability coverage are intentional injury, damage to the insured's own property, nonowned property in the care of the insured, bodily injury to an employee of the insured, bodily injury or property damage when the vehicle is being used as a public or livery conveyance, and claims arising out of the use of the auto by someone in the garage business. Other business uses of the auto are also excluded, with certain exceptions. A person using the auto without reasonable belief that he or she is entitled to do so is not protected under the PAP liability coverage. Other exclusions relate to nuclear energy liability losses, motorized vehicles with fewer than four wheels, vehicles made available for the insured's regular use, and vehicles owned by or furnished or available for the regular use of any family member.

Part B—Medical Payments Coverage pays medical expenses, up to specified limits, of insured persons who are injured in an auto accident. The medical expenses must be incurred within three years of the date of the accident. The insureds under this part of the policy are the named insured and family members, as well as any other person while occupying a covered auto. A number of the exclusions mentioned above also apply to the medical payments coverage.

Part C—Uninsured Motorists Coverage pays for bodily injury to an insured who is injured by an uninsured motorist, a hit-and-run driver, or a driver whose insurer becomes insolvent. Many states also include property damage as part of the uninsured motorists coverage. The minimum amount of uninsured motorists coverage is equal to the amount of the state's financial responsibility or compulsory insurance law. The named insured, family members, and any other person occupying a covered auto are insured under the uninsured motorists coverage. Vehicles considered to be uninsured and not uninsured are described in the policy.

Chapter Note

1. The material in this chapter is based on the 1989 edition of the Personal Auto Policy (copyrighted) drafted by the Insurance Services Office; George E. Rejda, *Principles of Insurance*, 3rd ed. (Glenview, IL: Scott, Foresman and Company, 1989), Chapter 11; *Fire, Casualty & Surety Bulletins*, Personal Lines Volume, Personal Auto Section; and Glen L. Wood, Claude C. Lilly III, Donald S. Malecki, Edward E. Graves, and Jerry S. Rosenbloom, *Personal Risk Management and Insurance*, 4th ed. (Malvern, PA: American Institute for Property and Liability Underwriters, 1989), Chapter 2.

CHAPTER 8

Personal Auto Policy, Continued

This chapter continues the discussion of the personal auto policy (PAP) by examining the remaining coverages and provisions, including damage to a covered auto (Part D), duties after an accident or loss (Part E), and the general provisions (Part F) that apply to all coverages. The chapter also examines some common endorsements that can be added to the PAP to broaden the various coverages. The chapter concludes by analyzing a typical case situation to see how the various coverages and endorsements fit together.

The discussions of the PAP and endorsements in this chapter are based on the 1989 editions of these forms drafted by the Insurance Services Office.[1]

PART D—COVERAGE FOR DAMAGE TO YOUR AUTO

Part D of the personal auto policy provides physical damage insurance for the damage or theft of a covered auto. Coverage under Part D also applies to nonowned autos, including temporary substitute vehicles.

Insuring Agreement

In the insuring agreement, the insurer agrees to pay for any direct and accidental loss to a covered auto or to any nonowned auto, including its equipment, minus any applicable deductible shown on the declarations page. Two coverage options are available. A covered auto can be insured for (1) collision loss and (2) loss caused by other than collision. Collision losses are covered only if the declarations page indicates that collision coverage is in effect. Likewise, coverage for other than collision losses is effective only if the declarations page indicates that other than collision coverage is provided for that auto. If the insured elects to purchase both coverages, the premium for each coverage is shown separately on the declarations page.

Collision Loss. Collision is defined as the upset of a covered auto or a nonowned auto or their impact with another vehicle or object. The following are examples of collision losses:

- An auto is hit by another vehicle.
- An auto runs into a telephone pole.
- A driver loses control of an auto, causing it to turn over (upset) and land in a ditch.
- An owner parks an auto and goes shopping; when the owner returns, the rear fender of the auto is dented.
- A driver opens the auto door in a parking lot, and the door is damaged when it hits a vehicle parked alongside.

Collision losses are paid regardless of fault. For example, if Frank is responsible for an accident, his insurer will pay for any physical damage to his car, minus any deductible that applies. If another driver causes damage to Frank's car, Frank can collect either from the other driver (or the driver's insurer) or from his own insurer. If Frank collects from his own insurer, the insurer has the right to recover payment from the driver who caused the accident.

Other Than Collision Loss. The PAP makes a distinction between a collision loss and an other than collision loss. This distinction is important because many motorists wish to purchase only the less expensive coverage for other than collision losses and do not desire collision insurance on the car. In addition, coverage for loss caused by other than collision is frequently purchased with no deductible, or the deductible may be lower than the deductible that applies to a collision loss.

Certain losses are considered to be caused by other than collision. Under Part D, loss caused by any of the following is considered other than collision:

- Missiles or falling objects
- Fire
- Theft or larceny
- Explosion or earthquake
- Windstorm
- Hail, water, or flood
- Malicious mischief or vandalism
- Riot or civil commotion
- Contact with a bird or animal
- Breakage of glass

Such losses are self-explanatory, but two important points should be stressed. First, colliding with a bird or animal is not a collision loss. Thus, if Anna hits a bird, deer, or cow with her car, any physical damage to her car is considered to be an other than collision loss. Second, if glass breakage is caused by a collision, the insured can elect to have it considered as a collision loss. This distinction is important because otherwise the insured would have to satisfy two deductibles if the car suffers glass breakage and other physical damage in the same collision (assuming both coverages are elected). By electing to treat the glass breakage as part of the collision loss, only one deductible has to be satisfied.

Nonowned Auto. As noted, the Part D coverages also apply to a non-owned auto. A nonowned auto is any private passenger auto, pickup, van, or trailer that is not owned by or furnished or made available for the regular use of the named insured or any family member while such a vehicle is in the custody of or being operated by the named insured or any family member. Therefore, if Lois borrows a car that belongs to her friend, any physical damage coverage that applies to Lois's covered auto also applies to the borrowed vehicle.

The physical damage coverages apply only if the nonowned auto is not furnished or made available for the regular use of the named insured or any family member. An insured can drive a borrowed automobile occasionally, and physical damage insurance will cover the borrowed vehicle. However, if the vehicle is driven on a regular basis or is furnished or made available for regular use, the insured's coverage does not apply. For example, if an employer furnishes an insured with a company car, or the car is made available for regular use in a carpool, the Part D coverages of the insured's PAP do not apply. The key point is not how frequently the insured drives a nonowned auto, but whether the nonowned auto is furnished or made available for the insured's regular use.

The definition of a nonowned auto also includes any auto or trailer that is being used as a temporary substitute for a covered auto that is out of normal use because of its breakdown, repair, servicing, loss, or destruction. For example, if Jim's car is in the shop for repairs and he is furnished a loaner car, his physical damage insurance also applies to the loaner car.

If there is a loss to a nonowned auto, the PAP provides the broadest coverage applicable to any covered auto shown in the declarations. For example, assume that Oscar owns two cars that are insured by his PAP. One car has coverage for both collision and other than collision losses, while the second car has coverage only for other than collision losses. If Oscar borrows his neighbor's car, the borrowed car is covered for both collision and other than collision losses.

Deductible. A flat deductible of $100, $200, $250, or some higher amount typically applies to each covered collision loss. In addition, a deductible usually applies to other than collision losses. The deductible for other than collision losses, however, is generally lower in amount than the collision deductible.

A deductible is used for Part D in order to (1) reduce small claims, (2) hold down premiums, and (3) encourage the insured to be more careful in protecting his or her car from damage or theft by requiring the insured to share all losses.

Transportation Expenses

Part D also provides a supplementary payment that applies in the event of the total theft of a covered auto or a nonowned auto. The coverage applies only if it is indicated in the declarations that other than collision coverage is in effect. If a *covered auto* is stolen, the insurance company will pay up to $15 a day, to a maximum of $450, for transportation expenses the insured may incur. If a *nonowned auto* is stolen, the insurer will pay loss of use expenses for which the insured becomes legally responsible, subject to the $15 a day and $450 maximum limit. Coverage applies only to the transportation or loss of use expenses incurred during the period beginning forty-eight hours after the theft and ending when the auto is returned to use or payment is made for its loss.

Such expenses may be incurred to rent a car or to pay train, bus, or taxi fares. No deductible is applied to payments made for transportation or loss of use expenses. For example, assume that Harry's car is stolen and is returned to him by the police seven days later. If Harry rented a car for those seven days at a cost of $30 a day, his insurer would pay him $15 a day for five days, or a total of $75 (no payment is made for the forty-eight hours immediately following the theft).

Exclusions

Twelve exclusions apply to the Part D coverages. These exclusions are summarized in the following paragraphs.

Public or Livery Conveyance. The physical damage insurance does not apply if the vehicle is used as a public or livery conveyance to carry persons or property for a fee. The exclusion does not apply to a share-the-expense car pool. For example, if Ken uses his covered auto as a taxi on the weekends, any physical damage loss to the auto while it is being used as a taxi is not covered under Part D of Ken's PAP.

Wear and Tear, Freezing, and Mechanical and Electrical Breakdown. Loss due and confined to wear and tear, freezing, mechanical or electrical breakdown or failure, or road damage to tires is excluded. The intent is to exclude regular maintenance expenses. However, the exclusion does not apply if the damage results from the total theft of a covered auto or nonowned auto. For example, if the wiring harness in Bill's covered auto fused due to a short circuit, the cost of replacing the wiring harness would not be covered. However, if the wiring harness fused because a thief had damaged it while hot-wiring and stealing the car, the cost of replacing the wiring harness would be covered.

Radioactive Contamination or War. Loss due to radioactive contamination, discharge of a nuclear weapon, insurrection, rebellion, or revolution is excluded. For example, if a covered auto is damaged from radioactive contamination because of a nuclear meltdown in a public utility plant, the damage is excluded.

Electronic Equipment. The PAP excludes a wide variety of automobile electronic equipment and their accessories. Loss to electronic equipment designed for the reproduction of sound is excluded. Such equipment includes, but is not limited to, radios, stereos, tape decks, and compact disc players. The exclusion does not apply if the equipment and accessories are permanently installed in a covered auto or nonowned auto. For example, if a permanently installed tape deck is stolen from a covered auto, the theft of the tape deck would be covered.

The policy also excludes loss to any other electronic equipment that receives or transmits audio, visual, or data signals. Such equipment includes citizens band radios, telephones, two-way mobile radios, scanning monitor receivers, television monitor receivers, video cassette recorders, audio cassette recorders, and personal computers. An endorsement can be added to cover loss to such equipment for an additional premium.

Finally, loss to tapes, records, discs, or other media or accessories used with previously described electronic equipment is also excluded. For example, the theft of stereo tapes from an insured's car is not covered even if the car is locked. However, coverage can be obtained by an endorsement to the policy.

There are two major exceptions to the previous exclusions. First, as stated, equipment and accessories designed for the reproduction of sound are covered if the equipment is permanently installed in the auto. Second, electronic equipment that is necessary for the normal operation of the auto or the monitoring of the auto's systems would also be covered.

Government Destruction or Confiscation. The PAP also excludes coverage for loss to a covered auto or nonowned auto due to destruction or confiscation by governmental or civil authorities because the named insured or a family member has engaged in illegal activities. For example, loss resulting from confiscation of a drug dealer's van by a federal drug agency would not be covered. The policy also excludes loss due to failure to comply with Environmental Protection Agency or Department of Transportation standards. The exclusion for government destruction or confiscation does not apply to the interests of any loss payees in the covered auto.

Camper Body or Trailer Not Shown in the Declarations. Loss to an owned camper or trailer not shown in the declarations is excluded. However, the exclusion does not apply to a newly acquired camper body or trailer acquired during the policy period if the insurer is asked to insure it within thirty days after the insured becomes the owner.

Nonowned Auto Used Without a Reasonable Belief of Permission. There is no coverage for loss to a nonowned auto when it is used by the insured or a family member without a reasonable belief of being entitled to do so.

Awnings or Cabanas. Loss to awnings, cabanas, or equipment designed to create additional living facilities is excluded.

Radar Detection Equipment. Loss to equipment designed for the detection or location of radar is excluded. Therefore, damage to a "fuzz buster" or other radar detection device in the insured's auto is not covered. The exclusion is justified, since these devices are designed to circumvent federal or state speed laws; some states have enacted legislation banning these devices; and it is questionable whether radar-detection devices should be considered as auto equipment, since such devices are not normal to the use of the auto.[2]

Customized Equipment. It has become popular to equip and customize pickups and vans with special equipment so that the vehicle has living quarters and can be occupied as a mobile home. However, the Part D coverages exclude loss of any custom furnishings or equipment in or on any pickup or van. Custom furnishings and equipment include but are not limited to the following:

● Special carpeting and insulation, furniture, or bars
● Facilities for cooking and sleeping
● Height-extending roofs
● Custom murals, paintings, or other decals or graphics

It is possible, however, to add a special endorsement that covers the excluded equipment and facilities by payment of an additional premium. This endorsement is discussed later in the chapter.

Nonowned Auto Used in the Automobile Business. Also excluded under Part D is loss to a nonowned auto maintained or used in the business of selling, repairing, servicing, storing, or parking of vehicles designed for use on public highways, including road testing and delivery. For example, if Ross is employed as an automobile mechanic and damages a customer's car while road-testing it, the physical damage loss to the car is not covered under Ross's PAP. This is a commercial loss exposure that should be insured by the repair shop's garage liability policy.

Nonowned Pickups and Vans Used in Any Other Business. The final exclusion applies to physical damage coverage for nonowned pickups and vans that are used in any business not described in the previous exclusion (Exclusion 11). This exclusion (Exclusion 12) does not apply to the maintenance or use of any nonowned private passenger auto or trailer. For example, if Larry borrows his friend's pickup truck for use in a landscaping business, Larry's physical damage coverages do not apply to the borrowed pickup truck. This is a business exposure that should be insured under a commercial policy covering the landscaping business.

Limit of Liability

The insurer's limit of liability for a physical damage loss to a covered automobile is the lower of (1) the actual cash value of the damaged or stolen property or (2) the amount necessary to repair or replace the property. In determining actual cash value, an adjustment is made for depreciation and physical condition of the damaged property. If the vehicle has only a partial loss (such as a damaged grill and fender), the cost of repairing the vehicle is usually the amount that is paid, less any applicable deductible. However, if the physical damage to the vehicle is extensive and the cost of repairs exceeds the vehicle's actual cash value, the car may be declared a total loss. In such cases, the amount paid by the insurer is limited to the actual cash value of the damaged vehicle, less any applicable deductible.

The maximum amount paid for a physical damage loss to a *nonowned trailer* is $500. For example, if an insured rents a trailer to move his or her personal property to another house or apartment and the trailer is damaged in an accident, the most that will be paid under the insured's PAP is $500.

Payment of Loss

The insurer has the option of paying for the loss in money or repairing or replacing the damaged or stolen property. If a covered auto is stolen, the insurer pays the cost of returning the stolen car or its equipment to the insured and also pays for any damage resulting from the theft. However, the insurer has the right to keep all or part of the stolen property at an agreed or appraised value.

Other Sources of Recovery

If the insured drives a nonowned auto that is damaged in an accident or stolen, other sources of recovery may be available to cover the loss. For example, the owner of the vehicle may be a rental car company that self-insures its vehicles; a travel or accident policy may provide coverage if the vehicle is damaged; or a credit card company may automatically cover damage to a rental car rented with the credit card. In such cases where other sources of recovery are available to cover the loss, the insurer pays only its share of the loss, which is the proportion that its limit of liability bears to the total of all applicable limits.

However, any physical damage insurance provided by the insurer to a nonowned auto is excess over any other collectible source of recovery. Other sources of recovery include coverage provided by the owner of the "nonowned auto," any other applicable physical damage insurance, and any other source of recovery that applies to the loss. For example, if Andy borrows a car and damages it, the owner's physical damage insurance applies first, and Andy's insurance is excess, subject to his deductible. If the owner's collision deductible is $200 and Andy's collision deductible is $100, and the damage is $1,000, the owner's policy pays $800 ($1,000 − $200), and Andy's policy pays $100 ($200 − $100). The remaining $100 would have to be paid either by Andy or by the owner of the car. In effect, if the owner's collision deductible is *larger* than Andy's deductible, Andy's insurer will pay the difference between the two deductibles.

Appraisal

In some cases, the named insured and insurer cannot agree on the amount of the loss. This is especially true if the insured claims that the car is above average and in "mint condition" and has a value that exceeds the value listed in the various publications of car prices. In the event of a disagreement on the amount of loss, either party may demand an appraisal of the loss. Each party selects a competent appraiser. The two appraisers then select an umpire. If the appraisers cannot agree on the actual cash value and the amount of loss, any differences are submitted to the umpire. A decision by any two is binding on all. Each party pays its chosen appraiser and shares equally the expenses of the appraisal and the umpire. If the insurer agrees to an appraisal, it does not waive any of its rights under the policy.

PART E—DUTIES AFTER AN ACCIDENT OR LOSS

Part E of the PAP outlines a number of duties the insured must perform after an accident or loss. The insurer has no obligation to provide coverage unless there is full compliance with these duties. Additional duties are also imposed if the insured is seeking protection under Part C—Uninsured Motorists Coverage or Part D—Coverage for Damage to Your Auto.

General Duties

The following general duties must be met after an accident or loss in order to have protection under the policy:

1. *Prompt notice.* The insurer must be promptly notified of how, when, and where the accident or loss occurred. The notice should also include the names and addresses of any injured persons and witnesses.
2. *Cooperation with the insurer.* The insured must cooperate with the insurer in the investigation, settlement, or defense of any claim or suit.
3. *Submission of legal papers to insurer.* The insured must promptly submit to the insurer copies of any notices or legal papers received in connection with the accident or loss.
4. *Physical examination and examination under oath.* The insured must agree to submit to a physical examination at the insurer's expense. In addition, the insured must agree to an examination under oath if required by the insurer.
5. *Authorization of medical records.* The insured must authorize the insurer to obtain medical reports and other pertinent records.
6. *Proof of loss.* The insured must submit a proof of loss when required by the insurer.

Additional Duties for Uninsured Motorists Coverage

In addition to the general duties, a person seeking benefits under Part C—Uninsured Motorists Coverage must perform the following two additional duties:

1. *Notify the police.* The insured must notify the police if a hit-and-run driver is involved. This is required to reduce fraudulent claims. If the police are notified, the accident is subject to police investigation, thereby reducing fraudulent claims.
2. *Submission of legal papers.* If the insured sues the uninsured motorist, a copy of the legal papers must be sent to the insurance company.

Additional Duties for Physical Damage Coverage

Three additional duties are required if the insured is seeking benefits under Part D—Coverage for Damage to Your Auto, as follows:

1. *Prevent further loss.* The insured must take reasonable steps after a loss to protect a covered auto or nonowned auto and its equipment from further loss. The insurer will pay the reasonable expenses incurred to protect the vehicle from further damage. For example, the insurer will pay the cost of having a wrecker transport the damaged car to another location for safekeeping.
2. *Notify the police of a stolen auto.* If a covered auto or nonowned auto is stolen, the insured must promptly notify the police of the theft. Prompt

notification significantly increases the possibility of recovering the stolen vehicle.

3. *Inspection and appraisal.* The insured must permit the insurer to inspect and appraise the damaged property before its repair or disposal. Some insurers have drive-in claim centers where damaged but drivable vehicles may be appraised. For more severely damaged cars, appraisers see the car at the insured's home or at the garage or body shop where the car is located. For small losses, the insurer sometimes waives its right to inspect and appraise the damaged auto and allows the insured to submit two or three repair estimates that serve as the basis for the loss settlement.

PART F—GENERAL PROVISIONS

Part F—General Provisions is the final part of the PAP. It presents general provisions and conditions that apply to the entire policy.

Bankruptcy of Insured

The insurer is not relieved of any obligations under the policy even if the insured declares bankruptcy or becomes insolvent. For example, if the insured is sued for an amount exceeding the policy limits and declares bankruptcy to escape payment of the judgment, the insurer is still required to pay that part of the judgment covered by insurance.

Changes in the Policy

The policy contains all the agreements between the named insured and the insurer. The terms of the policy cannot be changed except by an endorsement issued by the insurer. If the change requires a premium adjustment, the adjustment is made in accordance with the manual rules of the insurer. Changes during the policy term that can result in a premium increase or decrease include changes in (1) the number, type, or use of insured vehicles; (2) the operators of insured vehicles; (3) the place of principal garaging of insured vehicles; and (4) the coverage, deductibles, or limits of liability.

If a change is made that broadens the coverage without an additional premium, the change automatically applies to the policy on the date the revision is effective in the named insured's state. However, this provision does not apply to changes that are implemented in a general program revision either by a subsequent edition of the policy or by an amendatory endorsement.

Fraud

The PAP also contains a specific provision dealing with fraud. There is no coverage for any insured who makes fraudulent statements or engages in fraudulent conduct in connection with any accident or loss for which a claim is made. For example, if a car owner deliberately abandons a covered auto and reports the car as stolen, the insurer will not provide coverage for the claim.

Legal Action Against the Insurer

Because of a dispute, an insured may wish to bring legal action against the insurer. However, the PAP states that no legal action can be brought against the insurer until the insured has fully complied with all of the policy terms. In addition, under Part A—Liability Coverage, no legal action can be brought against the company unless the insurer agrees in writing that the insured has an obligation to pay damages, or the amount of that obligation has been finally determined by a judgment after a trial. Finally, no person or organization has any right under the policy to involve the insurer in any action to determine the liability of an insured.

Insurer's Right to Recover Payment

This provision is essentially a subrogation clause. If the insurer makes a loss payment to a person who has a right to recover damages from a negligent third party, the insurer has a legal right of subrogation against that party. The covered person must do whatever is necessary to enable the insurer to exercise its subrogation rights. In addition, the person to whom the loss payment is made is not allowed to do anything after the loss that would prejudice the insurer's right of subrogation.

This provision, however, does not apply to any person who is using a covered auto with a reasonable belief that he or she is entitled to do so. For example, if Karen borrows Patti's car with her permission and damages the car in a collision, Patti's collision coverage will pay for the damage to the car. Patti's insurer will not subrogate against Karen according to the terms of this provision.

Finally, if the person to whom a loss payment is made recovers damages from another party, that person is required to hold the proceeds of the recovery in trust for the insurer and must reimburse the insurer to the extent of its loss payment.

Policy Period and Territory

The PAP applies only to accidents and losses that occur within the policy period and within the policy territory. The *policy period* is stated in the declarations and is usually a six-month or one-year period. In some high risk specialty insurers, the policy period can be as short as one month.

The *policy territory* includes the United States, its territories and possessions, Puerto Rico, and Canada. The policy also applies to a covered auto while being transported between the ports of the United States, Puerto Rico, or Canada. Insureds are not covered anywhere outside of the policy territory. For example, if an insured drives his or her car into Mexico, the insured must have valid liability insurance from a Mexican insurer. A motorist from the United States who has not purchased valid insurance from a Mexican insurer and is involved in an accident can be detained in jail, have his or her car impounded, and be subject to other penalties.

Termination

The PAP also contains a provision that applies to termination of the policy by either the insured or insurer. The termination provision consists of four parts:

- Cancellation
- Nonrenewal
- Automatic termination
- Other termination provisions

Cancellation. The named insured can cancel any time during the policy period by returning the policy to the insurer or by giving advance written notice of the date the cancellation is to become effective.

The insurer also has the right of cancellation. If the policy has been in force for less than sixty days and is not a renewal or continuation policy, the insurer can cancel by mailing a cancellation notice to the named insured. If the cancellation is for nonpayment of premiums, the named insured must be given at least ten days' notice; at least twenty days' notice must be given in all other cases. Thus, the insurer has sixty days to investigate and determine whether a new applicant meets the insurer's underwriting standards.

After the policy is in force for sixty days, or if it is a renewal or continuation policy, the insurer can cancel for only three reasons: (1) the premium has not been paid, (2) the driver's license of an insured has been suspended or revoked during the policy period (or since the last anniversary of the original effective date if the policy is for other than one year), or (3) the policy has been obtained by a material misrepresentation. For example, if an insured knowingly provides false information to the insurer regarding a poor driving record, the insurer has the right to cancel that person's coverage after this information is discovered.

Nonrenewal. Rather than cancel, the insurer may decide not to renew the policy. If the insurer decides not to renew, the named insured must be given at least twenty days' notice before expiration of the policy period. If the policy period is other than one year, the insurer has the right not to renew only at the anniversary of the policy's original effective date. Thus, a policy written for only six months will not be subject to nonrenewal by the insurer more than once a year.

Automatic Termination. The automatic termination provision becomes effective once the insurer decides to renew the policy. Under this provision, if the named insured does not accept the insurer's offer to renew, the policy automatically terminates at the end of the current policy period. Failure to pay the renewal premium means that the named insured has not accepted the insurer's offer to renew the policy. Thus, once the named insured is billed for another period, the premium must be paid, or the policy automatically terminates on its expiration date. However, some insurers provide a short period of time for an insured to pay an overdue premium.

Finally, if the named insured obtains other insurance on a covered auto, the PAP automatically terminates on that auto on the effective date of the other insurance.

Other Termination Provisions. Several additional termination provisions are stated in the policy:

1. Many states place additional restrictions on the company's right to cancel or renew. If state law requires a longer notice period, requires a special form or procedure for giving notice, or modifies any termination provision, the PAP is automatically adjusted to conform to those requirements.
2. The insurer may choose to deliver the cancellation notice rather than mail it. However, proof of mailing of any cancellation notice is considered sufficient proof of notice.
3. If the policy is canceled, the named insured may be entitled to a premium refund. Any premium refund is computed according to the insurer's manual rules. Making or offering to make the refund is not a condition of cancellation.
4. The effective date of cancellation stated in the cancellation notice becomes the end of the policy period.

Transfer of Insured's Interest in the Policy

This provision is essentially an assignment clause. The named insured's rights and duties under the policy cannot be assigned to another party without the insurer's written consent. However, if the named insured dies, the coverage is automatically continued to the end of the policy period for both the surviving spouse (if a resident of the same household at the time of death) and the legal representative of the deceased person.

Two or More Auto Policies

If two or more auto policies issued by the same insurer apply to the same accident, the insurer's maximum limit of liability is the highest applicable limit of liability under any one policy. For example, if Ben has two cars insured with the same insurer and has an accident while driving a nonowned auto, the most the insurer will pay under both policies is the highest limit of liability under either of the policies. The intent of this provision is to prevent the stacking or pyramiding of policy limits when two or more cars are insured by the same insurer.

ENDORSEMENTS TO THE PERSONAL AUTO POLICY

Because of various exclusions and limitations, the PAP may not completely meet the automobile insurance needs of some people. Several additional coverages are available by an appropriate endorsement to the PAP.[3] The PAP endorsements are identified by ten letters and digits. The first two are PP for the personal automobile policy. The next four digits are the endorsement number. The last four digits indicate the month and year the version of that endorsement was introduced. Because new versions of endorsements are frequently introduced, only the first six characters will be used here.

Endorsements Affecting Multiple Coverages

Certain endorsements affect more than one coverage under the PAP:

- Miscellaneous type vehicle endorsement (PP 03 23)
- Snowmobile endorsement (PP 03 20)
- Named nonowner coverage (PP 03 22)
- Extended nonowned coverage (PP 03 06)
- Mexico coverage (PP 03 21)

These endorsements are described in the following paragraphs.

Miscellaneous Type Vehicle Endorsement. Many people own motor homes, motorcycles, recreational vehicles, and other vehicles that are ineligible for coverage under an unendorsed PAP. To meet the special needs of these vehicle owners, the *miscellaneous type vehicle endorsement* can be added, which provides coverage for a motor home, motorcycle or similar type of vehicle, all-terrain vehicle, dune buggy, or golf cart. One exception is a snowmobile, which requires a separate endorsement to the PAP. The miscellaneous type vehicle endorsement can be used to provide the same coverages found in the PAP, including liability, medical payments, uninsured motorists, collision, and other than collision loss. Each insured vehicle is listed in a schedule, which states the applicable coverages, premiums, and limits of liability.

The miscellaneous type vehicle endorsement can also be used to insure a private passenger auto owned jointly by two or more relatives, other than husband and wife, or by resident individuals. Resident individuals are persons who are living together but are not related.

A *passenger hazard exclusion* also can be activated as part of the miscellaneous type vehicle endorsement. It excludes liability for bodily injury to any person while occupying the covered vehicle. For example, if a passenger on a motorcycle is thrown off the vehicle and is injured, the PAP liability coverage of the motorcycle owner does not apply. When the exclusion is activated, the insured pays a lower premium.

Finally, under the miscellaneous type vehicle endorsement, the amount paid for physical damage losses is limited to the lowest of (1) the stated amount shown in the schedule or declarations, (2) the actual cash value of the stolen or damaged property, or (3) the amount necessary to repair or replace the property (less any deductible). In determining the actual cash value, an adjustment is made for depreciation and physical condition of the damaged vehicle.

Snowmobile Endorsement. Snowmobiles can be insured by adding the *snowmobile endorsement* to the PAP. A snowmobile is defined as a land motor vehicle propelled solely by wheels, crawler-type treads, belts, or similar mechanical devices and designed for use mainly off public roads on snow or ice. A vehicle propelled by airplane type propellers or fans is not considered to be a snowmobile.

Available coverages include liability, medical payments, uninsured motorists, collision loss, and other than collision loss. Each covered snowmobile is listed in a schedule that states the applicable coverages, premiums, and limits of liability.

The named insured and family members are covered for liability insurance while using *any snowmobile*. For example, if Jacques's snowmobile injures another person, the loss is covered. However, other persons are covered only while using an *owned snowmobile* (or temporary substitute) and are not covered while using a snowmobile rented or leased by the named insured. For example, Jacques owns a snowmobile that he occasionally lends to his friend, Gaston. If Gaston is operating Jacques's snowmobile and someone is injured through his carelessness, the liability portion of Jacques's PAP with the snowmobile endorsement would provide coverage. If Jacques borrows a snowmobile and lends it to Gaston and someone is injured through Gaston's negligence, Jacques's PAP would not provide coverage to Gaston. An exception would be if the snowmobile was a temporary substitute vehicle.

The liability coverage has several exclusions and modifications:

- Coverage does not apply if the snowmobile is used in any business.
- The exclusion of vehicles with fewer than four wheels does not apply.
- Coverage is excluded for any person or organization, other than the named insured, while renting or leasing a snowmobile.
- Coverage does not apply when the snowmobile is used in a racing or speed contest or in practice for the race.
- A passenger hazard exclusion can be activated, which excludes liability for bodily injury to any person while occupying or being towed by the snowmobile. For example, if a passenger in a covered snowmobile is injured and the insured is sued, the coverage does not apply. Likewise, if the insured is towing a skier with the snowmobile, liability coverage does not apply.

Named Nonowner Coverage Endorsement. The *named nonowner coverage endorsement* provides coverage for someone who does not own an automobile. Some people do not own cars because they live in large cities and rely on public transportation; they may not be able to afford expensive parking and garage fees; or they prefer not to drive in congested areas. However, a person who does not own a car may drive another person's car or may rent a car to go on a trip or vacation. Liability loss exposures arising out of the use of a nonowned auto can be insured by adding named nonowner coverage to the PAP.

The endorsement provides liability, medical payments, and uninsured motorists coverage for a named individual. *Coverage is provided only for the person named in the endorsement.* Unlike an unendorsed PAP, the spouse and other resident family members are not automatically covered. A spouse, family members, or other individuals also must be named in the endorsement to have coverage.

Liability insurance under the policy is excess over any other applicable liability insurance on the nonowned auto. The endorsement provides important protection to the named insured who is driving a nonowned auto with inadequate liability limits or perhaps with no insurance at all.

Finally, if the named insured buys a car, he or she has insurance on the car for up to thirty days. Coverage automatically terminates when the named insured purchases insurance on the newly acquired car.

Extended Nonowned Coverage Endorsement. The PAP excludes liability and medical payments coverage for vehicles furnished or made available for the regular use of the named insured and family members. The PAP also excludes the use of a nonowned vehicle (other than a nonowned private passenger auto) for business purposes. These exclusions can be eliminated by adding the *extended nonowned coverage endorsement* to the PAP. The coverage applies only to the individual(s) named in the endorsement. The liability coverage provided by the endorsement is excess over any other applicable insurance on the nonowned vehicle. There is also a provision for broadening medical payments coverage as well.

When the endorsement is added to the PAP, several loss exposures excluded under the PAP are now covered:

1. *A nonowned car furnished or made available for the regular use of the named individual is now covered.* For example, an individual may be furnished with a company car; have regular access to a car in a carpool; or regularly drive a state car on government business. These loss exposures are now covered.

2. *A nonowned vehicle used in business is now covered, except vehicles used in the auto business.* (However, business use of a nonowned private passenger auto is automatically covered by an unendorsed PAP.) For example, if Terry drives a truck for her employer, she has coverage under her policy while driving the nonowned truck.

3. *Use of a nonowned vehicle as a public or livery conveyance is now covered.* For example, a taxicab driver has coverage under his or her policy while driving a company taxicab. The liability coverage is excess over any other applicable insurance on the taxi.

4. *The named individual also has protection against a fellow-employee suit arising out of a work-related accident.* For example, Rudy may be driving a company truck, and a fellow employee in the truck is injured when he is involved in an accident with another motorist. If Rudy is sued by the injured employee, the loss is covered.

Mexico Coverage. The PAP does not cover driving in Mexico. However, the *Mexico coverage endorsement* can be added to the PAP to extend PAP benefits to a covered person who is involved in an accident in Mexico within twenty-five miles of the United States border on a trip of ten days or less.

The endorsement is effective only if primary liability coverage is purchased from a licensed Mexican insurer. The liability insurance provided by the endorsement is excess over the Mexican insurance and any other valid and collectible insurance. The Mexican insurance can be purchased from a licensed agent at the border. This method can be used by insureds who decide to travel into Mexico on the spur of the moment. However, if an insurance company is a member of a foreign insurance association, liability coverage that meets the Republic of Mexico requirements may be added to an existing policy issued by an American insurer. This method has the advantage of securing protection prior to the trip.

Mexican authorities recommend that the liability limits carried should be at least $25,000/$50,000 for bodily injury liability and $8,000 for property damage. The major advantage of the endorsement is that it provides additional liability insurance on an excess basis beyond that provided by the Mexican policy.

Underinsured Motorists Coverage

The *underinsured motorists coverage endorsement* (PP 03 11) can be added to the PAP to supplement the uninsured motorists coverage. Underinsured motorists coverage is important in those situations where a negligent driver has liability limits that are insufficient to pay the insured's damages. That is, the underinsured motorists coverage applies when the negligent driver has liability insurance at the time of the accident, but *the limits carried are less than the limits provided by the underinsured motorists coverage.* For example, assume that Patricia has underinsured motorists coverage in the amount of $100,000/ $300,000 and is injured by a negligent driver who has minimum bodily injury liability limits of $25,000/$50,000, which satisfies the state's financial responsibility law requirement. If Patricia's actual damages are $75,000, she would recover a maximum of $25,000 from the negligent driver's insurer, since that is the applicable limit of liability. She would receive an additional $50,000 from her insurer under the underinsured motorists coverage.

The underinsured motorists coverage should not be confused with the uninsured motorists coverage. The two coverages are mutually exclusive and do not overlap or duplicate each other. An insured can collect under one coverage or the other depending on the situation, but not under both. As previously stated, the uninsured motorists coverage applies when the bodily injury is caused by an uninsured motorist, a hit-and-run driver, or a driver whose insurer is insolvent. In contrast, the underinsured motorists coverage applies only when the other driver has liability insurance at the time of the accident, but the liability limits carried are less than the limits provided by the underinsured motorists coverage.

In all cases, the most the insured can receive from underinsured motorists coverage is the limit for the coverage. That is, the limit of liability for the underinsured motorists coverage is reduced by any amount recoverable from the underinsured motorist. This provision varies from state to state, however.

Finally, the underinsured motorists coverage can be written only if certain conditions are satisfied:

- The insured must carry increased limits for the underinsured motorists coverage that are higher than the limits required by the state's financial responsibility law.

- Both the uninsured and underinsured motorists coverages must be written for the same amount.
- The underinsured motorists coverage must apply to all automobiles covered under the personal auto policy.

Physical Damage Endorsements

Part D—Coverage for Damage to Your Auto can also be broadened by adding certain endorsements to the PAP. Some of the more widely used physical damage endorsements are discussed in this section.

Extended Transportation Expenses Coverage. When a covered auto or nonowned auto is damaged, the insured may be inconvenienced and may also incur sizable expenses in renting a car until the auto is repaired. This indirect loss exposure can be covered by adding the *extended transportation expenses coverage endorsement* (PP 03 02) to the PAP. Under this endorsement, if a covered auto or nonowned auto is withdrawn from use for more than twenty-four hours because of a collision loss or any loss covered under Part D (except loss by total theft), the insurer will pay up to $15 daily to a maximum of $450 for transportation expenses incurred by the named insured, or for any loss of use expenses for which the named insured is legally liable because of loss to a nonowned auto. No deductible is applied to this payment. However, the endorsement does not apply when there is total theft of a covered auto or nonowned auto since such coverage is provided under transportation expenses in Part D of the policy.

The effect of this endorsement is to broaden the transportation expenses coverage. As stated, the total theft of a covered auto or nonowned auto is covered under the PAP when the insured purchases coverage for other than collision losses. The extended transportation expenses endorsement extends the coverage to include collision losses and other losses.

Towing and Labor Costs Coverage. A car may break down or fail to start, and a repair truck may have to be called for assistance. Under the *towing and labor costs coverage endorsement* (PP 03 03), the insurer pays for towing and labor costs each time a *covered auto* or *nonowned auto* is disabled, up to some stated amount such as $25, $50, or $75. For example, if your car will not start because of a dead battery in cold weather and a repair truck is called, the labor and towing costs are covered up to the stated limits. The cost of labor, however, is covered only when it is performed at the place of disablement. Labor costs for work done at a service station or garage are not covered.

If a nonowned auto is disabled, the insurer provides the broadest towing and labor costs coverage that applies to any covered auto shown in the schedule or declarations.

Electronic Equipment and Tapes. As noted, the PAP excludes a wide variety of electronic equipment, as well as tapes, records, discs, and other media. Coverage for such equipment can be obtained by adding the *coverage for audio,* *visual, and data electronic equipment and tapes, records, discs, and other media endorsement* (PP 03 13) to the PAP.

Under this endorsement, the insurer will pay, without any deductible, for direct and accidental loss to electronic equipment that receives audio, visual, or data signals and is not designed solely for the reproduction of sound. The electronic equipment must be permanently installed in a covered auto at the time of loss for the coverage to apply. Thus, the endorsement can be used to insure a citizens band radio, car telephone, video cassette recorder (VCR), television receiver, personal computer, and similar electronic equipment.

In addition, the insurer will pay, without any deductible, for direct and accidental loss to (1) any accessories used with electronic equipment permanently installed in a covered auto and not designed solely for the reproduction of sound and (2) tapes, records, discs, or other media owned by the named insured or family member that is in a covered auto at the time of loss. It should be noted that the endorsement can be used to insure only tapes, records, discs, and other media if coverage of the electronic equipment is not desired.

The maximum amount paid for the total of all losses to electronic equipment and accessories is (1) the stated amount shown in the schedule or declarations, (2) the actual cash value of the stolen or damaged property, or (3) the amount necessary to repair or replace the property. However, the maximum amount paid for the total of all losses to tapes, records, discs, or other media is the lowest of (1) $200, (2) the actual cash value of the stolen or damaged property, or (3) the amount necessary to repair or replace the property.

Stated Amount. Some people own expensive antique cars or cars with expensive equipment that results in a higher than normal value for the vehicle. To establish the car's value when the policy is first written, a stated amount of insurance can be inserted in the policy. This can be done by adding a *stated amount endorsement* (PP 03 08) to the PAP. Under this endorsement, each vehicle is described and a stated amount of insurance applies to collision loss and other than collision loss. The stated amount endorsement, however, does not create a valued policy. The insurer's maximum limit of liability for a covered loss is limited to the *lowest* of (1) the stated amount shown in the schedule or in the declarations, (2) the actual cash value of the stolen or damaged property, or (3) the amount necessary to repair or replace the property. For example, if the stated amount is *less than* the actual cash value at the time of loss, or the amount necessary to repair or replace the property, the stated amount is used as the basis of the loss settlement. The amount paid is reduced by any applicable deductible shown in the schedule or declarations. However, if the stated amount *exceeds* the actual cash value or the amount necessary to repair or replace the property, the lower of these latter two figures is the amount paid (less any deductible).

Finally, in determining the actual cash value at the time of loss, an adjustment is made for depreciation and physical condition of the damaged or stolen property.

Covered Property Coverage. Under the *covered property coverage endorsement* (PP 03 07), the insurer agrees to pay for direct and accidental loss to covered property while it is in or attached to the auto shown in the schedule or declarations. Covered property is defined as awnings, cabanas, or equipment designed to create additional living facilities. However, losses to business or office equipment and articles that are sales samples or used in exhibitions are specifically excluded.

The insurer's limit of liability is the lowest of (1) the stated amount shown in the schedule or declarations, (2) the actual cash value of the stolen or damaged property, or (3) the amount necessary to repair or replace the property. In determining the actual cash value, an adjustment is made for depreciation and physical condition of the damaged or stolen property. Finally, the amount paid is reduced by the applicable deductible shown in the schedule or declarations.

Customizing Equipment. The Part D coverages specifically exclude custom furnishings and equipment in or upon a pickup or van. This exclusion can be deleted by adding the *customizing equipment coverage (stated amount insurance) endorsement* (PP 03 18) to the PAP. Under this endorsement, the insurer agrees to pay for direct and accidental loss to customized furnishings or equipment, which include the following:

- Special carpeting and insulation, furniture, or bars
- Facilities for cooking and sleeping
- Height-extending roofs
- Custom murals, paintings, or other decals or graphics

For example, a grease fire in a van that causes considerable damage to a built-in stove would be covered by this endorsement.

The customizing equipment endorsement, however, does not apply to the following types of property that are specifically excluded:

- Electronic equipment that is necessary for the normal operation of the auto or monitoring of the auto's operating systems
- Electronic equipment that is both an integral part of the same unit housing any sound reproducing equipment designed solely for the reproduction of sound and is permanently installed in the opening of the dash or console of a covered auto
- Camper body or trailer

The amount paid for a loss to custom equipment is the lowest of (1) the stated amount shown in the schedule or in the declarations, (2) the actual cash value of the stolen or damaged property, or (3) the amount necessary to repair or replace the property. In determining the actual cash value at the time of loss, an adjustment is made for depreciation and physical condition of the damaged or stolen property. The amount paid for a loss is reduced by any applicable deductible. However, the deductible applies only once if both the vehicle and customized equipment are damaged. For example, if a van is upset, causing both body damage and damage to sleeping and cooking facilities, only one deductible has to be satisfied.

PERSONAL AUTO POLICY CASE

The loss situations presented in this case illustrate the coverage provided by the personal auto policy. The examples include covered losses and losses that would be excluded. Relevant endorsements are discussed where applicable.

Family Auto Situation

Bob and Marie Gordon are both employed. Bob is a supervisor for a large automobile repair firm. Marie is a social worker for the state welfare department. Bob and Marie have two children. Karen, aged twenty, is attending college 200 miles from home. Ken, aged sixteen, lives at home and attends high school. The Gordons own four vehicles. Marie is the principal driver of a one-year-old sedan, which she uses to drive to and from work. The car is also driven occasionally on state business. Bob is the principal driver of a three-year-old customized van, which he uses to drive to and from work. The van is also used by the family for fishing, camping, and outdoor recreation. Karen is the principal driver of a four-year-old sedan, which she uses at college and to travel home on holidays and weekends. Ken is the principal driver of a six-year-old compact car, which he drives to and from school. All vehicles are legally titled in the names of Robert and Marie Gordon.

Personal Auto Policy Coverages

A copy of the Gordons' declarations page is shown in Exhibit 8-1. No-fault auto insurance does not apply in the Gordons' state. Endorsement PP 03 03 is the towing and labor costs coverage, and endorsement PP 03 11 is the underinsured motorists coverage with limits of $100,000 for each accident.

Loss Situations

The following loss situations involve the various types of coverage provided by the Gordons' personal auto policy. Not all of these losses are covered by their PAP; the comments about each loss explain the coverage that applies or why the loss is not covered.

Liability Coverage. The following loss situations apply primarily to the liability coverage (Part A) under the PAP. Each loss is a separate occurrence.

Loss. Bob is involved in an accident with another motorist who claims that Bob did not have the right of way. Damage to the other driver's car is $5,000. The other motorist also sues Bob for $100,000 and is awarded damages for bodily injury in the amount of $50,000. The court also awards $2,500 as prejudgment interest. Legal defense costs incurred by Bob's insurer are $25,000.

Comment. The property damage claim of $5,000, the bodily injury claim of $50,000, and prejudgment interest of $2,500 are paid by Bob's insurer under the liability section of the PAP. The legal defense costs of $25,000 are paid in addition to the amount that Bob is legally required to pay.

Exhibit 8-1
Personal Auto Policy Declarations Page

PERSONAL AUTO POLICY | DECLARATIONS

Policy Number   AC 794014049

1 Named Insured and mailing address	2 Policy period	
Robert and Marie Gordon Two Mill Road Anytown, Anystate 07920	From 7/1/91 To 7/1/92 12:01 a.m. standard time	The premium stated in the Declarations is the initial premium for this policy. On each renewal, continuation or anniversary of the effective date of this policy the premium shall be computed by us in accordance with our manual then in use.

The Auto(s) or Trailer(s) described in this policy is principally garaged at the above address unless otherwise stated:

Agent/Broker

Anytown Agency

Insured's occupation   Supervisor, Speedy Motors

3 Description of auto(s) or trailer(s)

Auto	Year	Trade name	Model	Body type	Vehicle identification number	Actual cost when purchased	Purchased Mo. Yr.	New or used
1	90	Chev.	Caprice	Sdn	C12345678910	17,500	9/90	New
2	88	Ford	Van	Van	F10987654321	19,250	4/88	New
3	87	Plym.	Reliant	Sdn	P43411098765	11,900	7/87	New
4	85	AMC	Eagle	Sdn	A48316758461	4,000	11/89	Used

Auto	Driven to or from work yes/no | mi. one way	Car pool	Use	Annual mileage	Sym-bol	Inspection	Classification	Territory liability | phy. dam.	Credits (see below)
				Rating information, not used in the PAP Case, would appear here.					

4 Coverages, Limits of liability, and Premiums.   Coverage is provided only where a premium or limit of liability is shown for the coverage.

Auto	A–Liability—in thousands	B–Medical payments each person	C–Uninsured motorists in thousands	D–Damage to your auto Actual cash value minus deductible 1-Collision loss 2-Other than collision loss		Towing and labor per disablement
	$ 300	$5,000	$100	$250	$100	$ 25

Auto	Cov. A	Cov. B	Cov. C	Cov. D-1	Cov. D-2	Towing	Supp. Cov.*	Auto Total
	$ $ $ $	Premium information, not used in the PAP Case, would appear here. Coverages A,B,C, D-1, Towing, and Underinsured Motorists on all autos.						

*Any supplementary coverage premium stated above is for the endorsements indicated here:

Auto	Endorsement no.	Premium $	Auto	Endorsement no.	Premium $	Auto	Endorsement no.	Premium $	Total premium
									$

Endorsements made part of this policy at time of issue:

PP 03 03 04 86, PP 03 11 12 89

Loss payee

Anytown Bank, Anytown, Anystate 07920

Countersigned at   Anytown, Anystate

Countersignature of licensed resident agent

Premium credits
(not all credits available in every state)

1 Two or more cars
2 Driver training
3 Compact car
4 Good grades saving
5 Good student
6 Bumper discount
7 Accident prevention course
A Passive restraint discount
B Anti-theft device discount

AK 3004 36M 7-82-3

Loss. Bob is confronted by an irate customer who claims that the brakes of his car are not repaired properly. The mechanic who repaired the brakes states that the brakes are fine. To determine who is correct, Bob decides to road-test the customer's car. While Bob is road-testing the car, the brakes fail, and Bob hits another motorist. The motorist is seriously injured, and Bob is personally sued for $200,000. Damage to the customer's car is $4,000. Bob also has medical expenses of $3,000 resulting from the collision.

Comment. The bodily injury incurred by the injured motorist and the property damage to the customer's car are clearly excluded under the liability section of the PAP, since Bob was using the customer's car in the automobile or garage business. The medical expenses incurred by Bob are excluded under medical payments coverage, since the injury occurred during the course of employment and benefits are required and available to Bob under the state's workers compensation law. The excluded liability losses are commercial loss exposures that would be covered under a commercial garage liability policy. Bob's injury is covered by the firm's workers compensation insurance.

Loss. Ken, Bob and Marie's son, was driving his girlfriend's car. After a football game, they went to a party, where Ken drank several cans of beer. After the party, he was involved in an accident with another motorist who became permanently disabled from the accident. The police arrested Ken and charged him with driving while intoxicated. He was required to post a bail bond of $2,500. Ken is later convicted of driving while intoxicated. The injured motorist is awarded a judgment against Ken in the amount of $500,000. The liability limit on the girlfriend's car is $25,000.

Comment. Ken's girlfriend's PAP is primary and pays the first $25,000 of the judgment. The girlfriend's policy will also pay up to $250 for the cost of the bail bond. The Gordons' PAP pays only $300,000 as excess insurance, since that is the applicable limit of liability. If Bob and Marie were insured under a personal umbrella policy, the remaining $175,000 of the judgment would have been paid by the umbrella insurer. As a result of the driving while intoxicated conviction, Ken will most likely be excluded from future coverage under his parents' policy.

Loss. Marie is attending a professional meeting in a large city. She rents a car at the airport. While driving to her hotel, she is involved in an accident with another motorist when she suddenly changes lanes without signaling. The other driver is seriously injured and is later awarded a judgment of $250,000. The rental agency carries liability limits of $100,000 on the rental car.

Comment. The loss is covered under the nonowned auto coverage of the Gordons' PAP. The first $100,000 of the judgment, however, is paid by the rental agency's insurer as primary insurance. The Gordons' PAP pays the remaining $150,000 as excess insurance.

Collision and Other Than Collision Losses. This section deals with the distinction between collision losses and other than collision losses.

Loss. When Karen returned to her car after a class, the rear bumper had been damaged by another driver who left no name or phone number. Damage to Karen's car cost $400 to repair.

Comment. This is a common collision loss. In this case, Karen will receive $150 for the loss, since there is a $250 deductible. If the driver who caused the damage had left his or her name, Karen may have been able to collect the full $400 from the negligent driver's insurer. In this case, Karen or her parents must absorb the PAP deductible.

Loss. While Karen is driving home over the weekend, her car collides with a deer crossing an interstate highway. The accident caused $300 damage to the car's front fender.

Comment. Hitting a bird or animal is considered to be an other than collision loss. In this case, the PAP pays only $200, since a $100 deductible must be met.

Loss. Bob and Marie purchase a new pickup truck. Three weeks after the vehicle is purchased, the pickup is damaged when Bob backs the vehicle into a tree. Damage to the truck is $1,500. When the accident occurred, Bob had not yet notified his automobile insurer that the pickup had been purchased.

Comment. This is a covered collision loss. Bob has thirty days to notify and ask the insurance company to insure the vehicle for a collision loss. The collision coverage applies to the loss, and the amount paid is $1,250.

Loss. Because a state car was not available, Marie used her own car to visit a client in a high-crime area of the city. Hub caps valued at $200 were stolen while the car was parked. The thief also broke a window to get inside the car. The cost of replacing the glass is $150. The following property was also stolen from the car: (1) a car radio valued at $200, (2) stereo tapes valued at $100, and (3) a camera valued at $150.

Comment. A private passenger automobile can be used in the business or occupation of the insured, and PAP coverage applies. The theft of the hub caps and car radio and breakage of glass are therefore covered as an other than collision loss. The amount paid is $450. The theft of the stereo tapes is not covered, since loss to stereo tapes is specifically excluded. The tapes can be covered by adding an endorsement for *coverage for audio, visual, and data electronic equipment and tapes, records, discs, and other media* to the PAP. The camera theft is not covered under the PAP, since the PAP does not cover personal property.

Loss. While on vacation, Bob turned the van too sharply on a hairpin curve in the mountains, and the van overturned. The cost to repair the van is $3,500. A built-in range and furniture were also damaged in the accident. The cost of replacing the special equipment is $2,500.

Comment. This is a collision loss. The amount paid for damage to the van is $3,250. However, damage to the built-in range and furniture is specifically excluded under Part D. Customized equipment, however, can be insured by adding the *customizing equipment coverage (stated amount insurance) endorsement* to the PAP.

Nonowned Auto. The following loss situations apply primarily to non-owned auto coverage.

Loss. Bob borrows a pickup from a friend to haul some wood. The pickup is stolen while in Bob's possession. The actual cash value of the stolen pickup is $1,500. The owner of the pickup does not have any physical damage coverage on the vehicle.

Comment. The physical damage (Part D) coverages also apply to a non-owned auto. As noted, a nonowned auto is a private passenger auto, pickup, van, or trailer not owned by or furnished or made available for the regular use of the named insured or a family member. If Bob drives the pickup only on an occasional basis, his PAP coverage applies. The loss is an other than collision loss, and the amount paid is $1,400.

Loss. Ken has a job as a parking lot attendant during the summer. He accidentally backed a customer's car into another parked car. Both cars are damaged. The damage to the car that Ken is driving is $500. Damage to the parked car is $650.

Comment. Although Ken is driving a nonowned auto, the PAP excludes loss to a nonowned auto when it is used in the automobile or garage business. The loss, therefore, is not covered.

Loss. Karen borrows her roommate's car with permission. She is involved in an accident in which she is at fault. The cost of repairing the roommate's car is $1,500. The roommate has a $100 deductible for both collision and other than collision losses.

Comment. The PAP coverages on Karen's car apply to the borrowed vehicle. As long as Karen does not drive her roommate's car on a regular basis, the Gordons' PAP coverages apply. However, insurance on the car being driven is primary, and the Gordons' insurance is excess. The roommate's collision insurance, therefore, pays $1,400 for the physical damage loss to the car. The remaining $100 is submitted to the Gordons' insurer as excess insurance. However, because that policy has a $250 deductible, the insurer pays nothing.

Vehicles Regularly Furnished or Made Available. This section applies to loss situations involving vehicles that are furnished or made available for the regular use of the named insured or a family member.

Loss. Marie drives a state car daily to visit her clients. She is involved in an accident with another motorist, who is seriously injured. Investigation of the accident reveals that Marie's negligent driving caused the accident. The bodily injury to the other motorist is $50,000. The damage to the motorist's car is $3,000.

Comment. The entire loss is excluded. Although the PAP covers the named insured or family members while driving a nonowned auto on an occasional basis, the coverage does not apply to a vehicle furnished or made available for the regular use of the insured. Since Marie drives a state car on a daily basis, her PAP coverage does not apply. This important loss exposure can be covered by adding *extended nonowned coverage* to the PAP and naming Marie in the endorsement, which covers nonowned vehicles driven on a regular basis.

Loss. Karen obtains a summer job as a salesperson. She is furnished with a company car. While driving the company car on company business, she is involved in an accident with another motorist. The motorist claims that Karen caused the accident. The motorist suffers injuries with a value of $10,000. The cost of repairing the company car is $2,500.

Comment. The loss is excluded, since the company car is furnished and made available for Karen's use on a regular basis. The regular use of the company car can be covered by adding *extended nonowned coverage* to the PAP in which Karen is specifically named as an insured.

Loss. Ken's car is being repaired in the automobile repair shop. He borrows a friend's car and uses it until his car is repaired. While driving the vehicle, Ken is involved in an accident with a motorist who claims that Ken did not have the right of way. Investigation of the accident reveals that Ken is at fault. The injured motorist sues Ken for $15,000.

Comment. Since Ken's car is being repaired, the borrowed vehicle is considered a temporary substitute vehicle. Therefore, all PAP coverages on Ken's car apply to the temporary substitute vehicle. The injured motorist's suit is a covered liability loss. However, any insurance on the borrowed car is primary, and Ken's insurance is excess.

Other Loss Situations. The following section discusses some miscellaneous loss situations.

Loss. Karen's car will not start. A wrecker tows the car to a service station where a defective water pump is replaced. Towing charges are $40. The cost of replacing the water pump is $150.

Comment. The towing charges are covered for only $25, since this is the applicable limit of liability. The cost of replacing the water pump is not covered because only labor performed at the scene of the disablement is covered.

Loss. While Bob is walking across the street, he is struck by a driver who runs a red light. The driver has no liability insurance. Bob's claim for bodily injuries totals $35,000.

Comment. Bob's $35,000 claim for bodily injury will be paid in full under the uninsured motorists coverage. The underinsured motorists coverage does not apply in this case, since Bob was injured by an uninsured driver.

Loss. While driving home from work, Marie is seriously injured by a drunk driver who was driving in the wrong direction on a one-way street. Marie's claim for bodily injuries is valued at $45,000. Marie's sedan, valued at $12,500, is totally destroyed. The negligent driver carries liability insurance in the amount of $15,000/$30,000/$10,000, which satisfies the state's minimum financial responsibility law.

Comment. The underinsured motorists coverage is relevant here. Marie will collect $15,000 for her injuries from the other driver's insurance company, since that is the maximum limit of liability per person. Marie's PAP insurer will pay $30,000, the difference between the $15,000 collected from the other driver's insurer and the total value of her injuries. The physical damage loss of $12,500 to Marie's car exceeds the other driver's $10,000 property damage limits. The negligent driver's insurer will pay its $10,000 limit; Marie's insurer will pay the remainder of the loss.

SUMMARY

Under Part D—Coverage for Damage to Your Auto of the personal auto policy, the insurer agrees to pay for direct and accidental loss to a covered auto or nonowned auto, less the deductible that applies to this coverage. The auto can be insured for collision loss, for other than collision loss, or for both. Limited coverage is also provided for transportation expenses in the event that a covered auto is stolen.

If a nonowned automobile is being operated by an insured, the insured's coverage is available to pay losses in excess of any physical damage coverage carried by the owner of that auto. If a nonowned auto replaces a covered auto that is out of use because of a breakdown, loss, or destruction, it is considered a temporary substitute vehicle, and Part D coverage also applies to it.

A lengthy list of exclusions applies to Part D of the PAP. Physical damage coverage is excluded when the vehicle is being used as a public or livery conveyance or is damaged from wear and tear, freezing, mechanical and electrical breakdown, radioactive contamination, or war. Equipment designed for the reproduction of sound is excluded unless the equipment is permanently installed in the auto. Stereo tapes, records, and discs are also excluded, as well as certain electronic equipment, including citizens band radios, telephones, television receivers, video cassette recorders, and similar equipment. Also excluded are loss to the vehicle due to confiscation by a governmental authority because of illegal activities; camper bodies and trailers not shown in the declarations; damage to nonowned vehicles used without permission; loss to awnings and cabanas; loss to radar detection equipment; loss to customized furnishings or equipment in a van or pickup; nonowned vehicles used in the automobile business; and nonowned pickup trucks and vans used in any other business.

The insurer's liability for physical damage losses is the lower of the actual cash value of the property or the amount necessary to repair or replace it. If the cost of repairs exceeds the auto's value, the auto may be declared a total loss. Provisions dealing with loss payment, other sources of recovery, and appraisal are also included in Part D.

Part E—Duties After an Accident or Loss lists six general duties of the insured under the personal auto policy: give prompt notice to the insurer, cooperate with the insurer, submit legal papers to the insurer, submit to a physical examination or an examination under oath, authorize the release of medical records, and submit a proof of loss. If benefits are sought under the uninsured motorists coverage, the insured also must notify the police of the accident and submit to the insurer any legal papers involved in a suit against the uninsured motorist. An insured seeking payment under the auto physical damage coverage is required to prevent further damage to the vehicle, notify the police if the auto has been stolen, and permit the insurer or its agents to inspect and appraise the damaged auto before its repair.

The final part of the personal auto policy, Part F—General Provisions, contains provisions and conditions that apply to the entire policy. They include bankruptcy of the insured, changes in the policy, fraud, legal action against the insurer, the insurer's right to recover payment, and policy period and territory. The termination provision has four sections: cancellation, nonrenewal, automatic termination, and other termination provisions. Additional general provisions concern transfer of the insured's interest in the policy and the liability of the insurer if there are two or more auto policies issued by the *same* insurer applying to any one accident.

The coverage of the personal auto policy can be changed by endorsement. Several endorsements affect all coverages: the miscellaneous type vehicle endorsement, the snowmobile endorsement, the named nonowner coverage endorsement, the extended nonowner coverage endorsement, and the Mexico coverage endorsement.

The underinsured motorists coverage endorsement supplements the uninsured motorists coverage in the policy. This endorsement provides coverage when a negligent driver injuring the named insured or family members has liability insurance limits that are insufficient to pay damages arising out of the auto accident.

Several endorsements affect only the physical damage coverage. Some of these involve coverage for certain electronic equipment, tapes, records, and discs. Other endorsements affecting PAP physical damage coverage include the extended transportation expenses coverage endorsement, towing and labor costs coverage, and the stated amount endorsement.

Chapter Notes

1. The material in this chapter is based on material derived from the following sources: *Personal Auto Policy*, Insurance Services Office, 1989 edition, and the 1989 PAP endorsements drafted by the Insurance Services Office; *Fire, Casualty & Surety Bulletins*, Personal Lines Volume, Personal Auto Section; George E. Rejda, *Principles of Insurance*, 3rd ed. (Glenview, IL: Scott, Foresman and Company, 1989), Chapter 11; and Glen L. Wood, Claude C. Lilly III, Donald S. Malecki, Edward E. Graves, and Jerry S. Rosenbloom, *Personal Risk Management and Insurance*, 4th ed., vol. I (Malvern, PA: American Institute for Property and Liability Underwriters, 1989), Chapter 2.
2. *Explanatory Memorandum*, Insurance Services Office, 1985, p. 6.
3. This section is based on specimen PAP endorsements copyrighted by the Insurance Services Office, 1989.

CHAPTER 9

Automobile Insurance and Society

In this chapter, the discussion of automobile insurance continues with an examination of several important problems. First, millions of motorists are injured or disabled each year in automobile accidents, and thousands of persons are killed. The high cost of medical expenses, pain and suffering, the unexpected death of a family member, and damage to or loss of an automobile can have a profound financial impact on the family.

In addition, society must deal with the problem of compensating innocent automobile accident victims for their bodily injuries or property damage caused by negligent drivers. The various methods for compensating automobile accident victims include the tort liability system, financial responsibility laws, compulsory insurance laws, unsatisfied judgment funds, uninsured motorists coverage, and underinsured motorists coverage.

Critics of the present reparations system for compensating auto accident victims argue that the system is slow, expensive, inequitable, and should be replaced by a new system. No-fault automobile insurance laws are examined as an alternative technique for compensating accident victims.

Automobile insurers also have the problem of providing automobile insurance to irresponsible drivers, such as high-risk drivers, drunk drivers, and persons who habitually violate traffic laws. This chapter examines the various methods for providing automobile insurance to irresponsible drivers, which include automobile insurance plans, joint underwriting associations, reinsurance facilities, and automobile insurance from specialty insurers.

The chapter concludes by examining the underwriting and rating of personal automobile insurance. The factors that determine the cost of automobile insurance are treated in some depth.

NATURE OF THE AUTOMOBILE INSURANCE PROBLEM

Millions of Americans drive automobiles. In recognition of rising medical, legal, and automobile repair costs, most drivers have purchased automobile insurance contracts that provide considerable protection against the financial consequences of automobile accidents. Automobile insurers, however, have experienced serious underwriting problems in their efforts to insure the driving population. These factors and others comprise the automobile insurance problem, which is described in this section.

In general, the automobile insurance problem consists of the following components:

- High frequency of automobile accidents
- High costs of automobile accidents
- Substantial underwriting losses
- Irresponsible drivers
- Availability and affordability of automobile insurance

High Frequency of Automobile Accidents

American motorists are smashing into each other at an alarming rate. In 1988, motorists were involved in 34 million motor vehicle accidents. About 6 million injuries resulted from these accidents, and about 49,000 persons were killed. Although the majority of accidents occur in urban locations, drivers in rural areas are more likely to be killed. In 1988, 64 percent of the fatal accidents occurred in rural areas.[1]

Most fatal accidents are due to two major causes: (1) improper driving and (2) alcohol. One study showed that 62 percent of the fatal accidents in 1987 involved improper driving, such as speeding, right of way violations, driving to the left of center, and other careless acts. In addition, it is estimated that drinking drivers are involved in 50 to 55 percent of all fatal accidents.[2]

High Costs of Automobile Accidents

The economic costs of motor vehicle accidents are staggering. In 1988, motor vehicle accidents resulted in an economic loss of an estimated $89 billion, which was nearly 5 percent higher than the 1986 estimate of $85 billion.[3] The economic loss includes the cost of property damage, medical costs, lost productivity, emergency services, legal and court costs, public assistance programs, and insurance administrative expenses.

The costs of automobile insurance claim settlements and court awards have also increased sharply in recent years. From 1979 through 1988, the average paid bodily injury claim arising from private passenger cars increased from $3,559 to $8,736, or 145 percent. During the same period, the average paid property damage liability claim arising from private passenger cars increased from $715 to $1,535, or about 115 percent. At the same time, the cost of living increased only 63 percent, which indicates that automobile accident claim costs have increased more rapidly than the rate of inflation.[4] This more rapid increase in automobile accident costs has been largely attributed to sharp increases in medical costs, automobile repair costs, and legal costs.

Substantial Underwriting Losses

Substantial underwriting losses experienced by automobile insurers are another part of the overall problem. Major automobile insurers have experienced such losses in many states; business has been only marginally profitable in several other states. Overall, the automobile liability insurance business experienced underwriting losses during each year from 1979 through 1988.[5]

Because of substantial underwriting losses, most automobile insurers have increased premiums and tightened their underwriting standards. As a result, some motorists have considerable difficulty in obtaining the necessary coverages from insurers in the voluntary standard markets.

Irresponsible Drivers

Irresponsible drivers are another part of the overall automobile insurance problem. Irresponsible drivers can generally be classified into three groups: (1) uninsured drivers, (2) drunk drivers, and (3) high-risk drivers. These categories are not mutually exclusive since an individual driver may be part of all three groups.

Uninsured Drivers. The proportion of uninsured drivers varies by state, and up-to-date accurate statistics are not available. However, an earlier study by the General Accounting Office indicated that the proportion of uninsured drivers in 1976 ranged from fewer than 1 percent in certain states to as high as 32 percent in others.[6] The problem is that some uninsured drivers cause accidents that injure other persons and cannot pay for the injuries or property damage they have caused. Society then has the problem of protecting and compensating innocent accident victims who are injured by uninsured drivers.

Drunk Drivers. There is widespread drug and alcohol abuse in the United States, and drinking drivers are estimated to be involved in about half of all fatal automobile accidents. Drinking drivers are also responsible for a disproportionate number of nonfatal automobile accidents.

Society is cracking down hard on drunk drivers. One federal law requires the states to increase their legal drinking age to twenty-one or lose federal highway funds. Also, the states have tightened their drunk-driving laws, have increased the penalties for first-time offenders, such as mandatory jail time, and have passed laws holding tavern owners and hosts legally liable for accidents caused by drunk customers and guests. Other groups such as Mothers Against Drunk Drivers (MADD) are highly visible and are aggressively pushing for effective measures to remove drunk drivers from the roads.

High-Risk Drivers. High-risk drivers are motorists who habitually violate traffic laws, who are involved in a disproportionate number of traffic accidents, or who are convicted of certain offenses, such as reckless driving, driving on a suspended license, or driving under the influence of drugs or alcohol. It is extremely difficult for private insurers to insure these individuals because of the catastrophic potential of a claim if the high-risk driver should kill or seriously injure another person.

Availability and Affordability of Automobile Insurance

A final part of the problem is that some groups are unable to purchase automobile insurance contracts at affordable premiums in the voluntary standard markets. Because of substantial underwriting losses, potential catastrophic liability judgments, and adverse selection, automobile insurers restrict the sale of automobile insurance to certain groups, or they make the coverages available only at substantially higher premiums.

The undesirable groups include the high-risk drivers and drunk drivers discussed earlier. Also, younger drivers, especially unmarried male drivers, are generally considered undesirable as insureds by most companies. In 1988, drivers under age twenty-five comprised about 19 percent of all drivers in the United States but accounted for 32 percent of all accidents and 31 percent of the fatal accidents. Drivers who were ages twenty through twenty-four had the highest overall accident rate (37 per 100 drivers) and the highest fatal accident rate (68 per 100,000 drivers).[7]

Both automobile insurers and society have enacted insurance plans that make automobile coverages available to the high-risk groups. These special plans include automobile insurance plans, joint underwriting associations, reinsurance facilities, and a special state fund in Maryland. The major features of these plans are examined later in this chapter.

AUTOMOBILE INSURANCE AND THE LAW: COMPENSATION OF ACCIDENT VICTIMS

Under the United States legal system, persons who are injured or incur property damage because of the negligence of the owner or operator of an automobile are entitled to compensation and damages. Both automobile insurers and society have had to deal with the problem of designing efficient compensation systems that would indemnify automobile accident victims in a fair and equitable manner. Also, as stated earlier, society has the problem of protecting innocent accident victims injured by motorists who drive without insurance and cannot pay for the injuries they have caused.

Methods of compensating accident victims include the following:[8]

- Tort liability system based on fault
- Financial responsibility laws
- Compulsory insurance laws
- Unsatisfied judgment funds
- Uninsured motorists coverage
- Underinsured motorists coverage

Each of these methods is described in this section.

Tort Liability System Based on Fault

The tort liability system based on fault is the traditional method for compensating injured automobile accident victims in the United States. A tort is a legal

Types of Comparative Negligence Laws*

There are four types of comparative negligence laws: (1) pure, (2) 49 percent rule, (3) 50 percent rule, and (4) slight and gross.

Under a *pure* comparative negligence law, the person bringing suit (the plaintiff) is entitled to damages regardless of the amount of his or her fault. For example, Bob, who is 80 percent at fault, is entitled to proceed against Mary, who is 20 percent at fault. Bob's recovery would be limited to a maximum of 20 percent of his actual damages. Mary's recovery is limited to 80 percent of her damages.

Under the *49 percent rule* (also called the Georgia plan), the plaintiff is entitled to recover only if his or her negligence is *less* than the negligence of the defendant. This means the plaintiff can recover from the other party only if he or she is 49 percent or less at fault.

Under the *50 percent rule* (also called the New Hampshire plan), the plaintiff can recover if his or her negligence does not exceed the negligence of the defendant. This means the plaintiff can recover if he or she is not more than 50 percent at fault. Unlike the 49 percent rule, the 50 percent rule allows each party to recover damages when both parties are equally at fault. Each party's recovery would be limited to 50 percent of the actual damages.

Finally, two states have comparative negligence laws based on *slight and gross negligence*. Under these laws, the plaintiff is entitled to recover only if his or her negligence is slight and the negligence of the defendant (the person being sued) is gross.

Pure comparative negligence laws are in existence in Alaska, California, Florida, Illinois, Iowa, Kentucky, Louisiana, Michigan, Mississippi, Missouri, New Mexico, New York, Rhode Island, and Washington. The 49 percent rule is followed in Arkansas, Colorado, Georgia, Idaho, Kansas, Maine, North Dakota, Utah, West Virginia, and Wyoming. The 50 percent rule is followed in Connecticut, Delaware, Hawaii, Indiana, Massachusetts, Minnesota, Montana, Nevada, New Hampshire, New Jersey, Ohio, Oklahoma, Oregon, Pennsylvania, Texas, Vermont, and Wisconsin. Comparative negligence is based on slight and gross negligence in Nebraska and South Dakota.

*Adaptation of "Comparative Negligence" from *FC&S Bulletins*, Management Sales Volume, Public Liability section, 1985, pp. C1-C4.

wrong for which the law allows a remedy in the form of money damages. *Negligence* is a tort, or legal wrong, that has great relevance for the owners or operators of automobiles. Negligence is the failure to exercise the standard of care required by law to protect others from harm. The laws in all states require the owners or operators of automobiles to exercise a high degree of care to protect others from harm while operating the automobile. Thus, if someone operates an automobile in a negligent manner that results in property damage or bodily injury to another person, that person can be held legally liable for the damages incurred by the injured person.

Before an injured automobile accident victim can collect damages, he or she must prove negligence and establish fault on the part of the other driver. A small number of states, however, have *contributory negligence laws* that make it difficult for an accident victim to collect damages. Under a contributory negligence law, if a person contributes in any way to his or her own injury, that person cannot recover damages. Thus, if one driver is 20 percent responsible for the accident, and the other driver is 80 percent at fault, the first driver cannot collect any damages.

Because of the harshness of the contributory negligence doctrine, most states have enacted some type of *comparative* negligence law that allows injured persons to recover damages even though they have contributed to the accident. Under a comparative negligence law, if both the injured person and the other driver are negligent, the financial burden of the injury is shared by both parties according to their respective degrees of fault. For example, under one type of comparative negligence law, if an insured is 20 percent responsible for the accident, and the other driver is 80 percent responsible, the insured can collect for his or her injury, but the damages awarded would be reduced 20 percent. Although comparative negligence laws vary among the states, they have a common element in that negligence on the part of the plaintiff does not necessarily bar a recovery for damages.

The dollar amount of the damages awarded to an injured accident victim depends on several factors. There are three types of damages that may be awarded:

1. *Special damages.* Special damages are paid for losses that can be determined and documented, such as medical expenses, past and future lost wages, funeral expenses, and property damage.
2. *General damages.* General damages are paid for losses that cannot be specifically measured and itemized, such as compensation for pain and suffering, loss of use of an arm or leg, loss of vision, or disfigurement.
3. *Punitive damages.* Punitive damages are awarded to punish people and organizations who through particularly malicious or outrageous actions cause bodily injury and property damage. Punitive damages are payments above the special and general damages and are designed to prevent the person causing the injury from repeating the same offense. To make sure that the damages are truly punitive to the person committing the offense, some states do not allow insurers to pay awards for punitive damages.[9]

The tort liability system based on fault has been under heavy attack in recent years. Critics argue that this system operates in a perverse and inequitable manner and contains numerous defects. They feel a new system for compensating automobile accident victims is needed, such as no-fault automobile insurance. No-fault automobile insurance laws are discussed later in this chapter.

Financial Responsibility Laws

Many states have enacted *financial responsibility laws* that require motorists to provide proof of financial responsibility equal to certain minimum amounts. Motorists typically are required to provide proof of financial responsibility under the following circumstances:

- After the occurrence of an automobile accident involving bodily injury or property damage exceeding a certain dollar amount
- When there is a conviction for certain offenses, such as drunk driving, reckless driving, or losing a license because of continued violation of laws
- If there is a failure to pay a judgment that results from an automobile accident

If proof of financial responsibility is not provided, both the driver's license and vehicle registration are suspended.

Types of Laws. With respect to accidents, there are two basic types of financial responsibility laws: (1) security-type laws and (2) security and proof laws.

Security-Type Laws. Under a security-type law, a motorist involved in an accident involving bodily injury or property damage over a certain amount must provide proof of financial responsibility at least equal to certain minimum amounts. Proof of financial responsibility is normally provided by having automobile liability insurance at least equal to certain minimum limits, such as $25/$50/$25 (see Exhibit 9-1). Other acceptable proofs of financial responsibility are posting a bond that guarantees financial responsibility, depositing money or securities equal to the required amounts, or valid self-insurance. As noted earlier, if the motorist cannot provide proof of financial responsibility *after* the accident occurs, both the driver's license and vehicle registration are suspended.

Security and Proof Laws. Under this type of law, the motorist must provide proof of financial responsibility arising out of current accidents and for future accidents. States generally require proof of future financial responsibility for three years after the accident, conviction, or judgment.

Defects in Financial Responsibility Laws. Although financial responsibility laws provide some protection against irresponsible motorists, critics point out the following defects:

1. *Most financial responsibility laws only become effective after the accident, conviction, or judgment.* Thus, accident victims may not be compensated for their injuries if some negligent drivers are unable to pay for a judgment.
2. *Financial responsibility laws do not guarantee payment to all accident victims.* Accident victims may not be compensated if they are

Exhibit 9-1
Automobile Financial Responsibility/Compulsory Limits

State	Liability Limits*	State	Liability Limits*
Alabama	20/40/10	Montana	25/50/5
Alaska	50/100/25	Nebraska	25/50/25
Arizona	15/30/10	Nevada	15/30/10
Arkansas	25/50/15	New Hampshire	25/50/25
California	15/30/5	New Jersey	15/30/5
Colorado	25/50/15	New Mexico	25/50/10
Connecticut	20/40/10	New York	10/20/5[2]
Delaware	15/30/10	North Carolina	25/50/10
District of Columbia	25/50/10	North Dakota	25/50/25
Florida	10/20/5	Ohio	12.5/25/7.5
Georgia	15/30/10	Oklahoma	10/20/10
Hawaii	35/15/10	Oregon	25/50/10
Idaho	25/50/15	Pennsylvania	15/30/5
Illinois	20/40/15[1]	Rhode Island	25/50/25
Indiana	25/50/10	South Carolina	15/30/5
Iowa	20/40/15	South Dakota	25/50/25
Kansas	25/50/10	Tennessee	20/50/10[1]
Kentucky	25/50/10	Texas	20/40/15
Louisiana	10/20/10	Utah	20/40/10
Maine	20/40/10	Vermont	20/40/10
Maryland	20/40/10	Virginia	25/50/20
Massachusetts	10/20/5	Washington	25/50/10
Michigan	20/40/10	West Virginia	20/40/10
Minnesota	30/60/10	Wisconsin	25/50/10
Mississippi	10/20/5	Wyoming	25/50/20
Missouri	25/50/10		

CANADA**			
Province	**Liability Limits**	**Province**	**Liability Limits**
Alberta	$200,000	Nova Scotia	$200,000
British Columbia	200,000	Ontario	200,000
Manitoba	200,000	Prince Edward Island	200,000
New Brunswick	200,000	Quebec	50,000
Newfoundland	200,000	Saskatchewan	200,000
Northwest Territories	200,000	Yukon	200,000

*The first two figures refer to bodily injury liability limits and the third figure to property damage liability. For example, 10/20/5 means coverage up to $20,000 for all persons injured in an accident, subject to a limit of $10,000 for one individual, and $5,000 coverage for property damage.
**In all Canadian provinces except Quebec, the amount of liability insurance shown is available to settle either bodily injury or property damage claims—or both. When a claim involving both bodily injury and property damage reaches this "inclusive" limit, payment for property damage is limited to $20,000 in British Columbia, Manitoba, New Brunswick and Newfoundland, and to $10,000 in the other provinces and territories having "inclusive" limits. Quebec has a complete no-fault system for bodily injury claims, scaled down for non-residents in proportion to their degree of fault. The $50,000 limit relates to liability for damage to property in Quebec and to liability for bodily injury and property damage outside Quebec.

[1] Effective January 1, 1990.   [2] 50/100 if injury results in death.

Based on data from *1990 Property/Casualty Insurance Facts* (New York: Insurance Information Institute, 1990), pp, 102-103.

injured by uninsured drivers, by hit-and-run drivers, by drivers of stolen cars, or by someone whose license has been suspended.

3. *Injured persons may not be fully indemnified for their injuries.* Most financial responsibility laws require only minimum amounts of liability insurance, which may not fully compensate the injured person.

4. *There may be considerable delay in the legal system in compensating the accident victim.* The delay can result in considerable financial hardship for some automobile accident victims.

Compulsory Insurance Laws

The majority of states have enacted *compulsory insurance laws* that must be met to drive legally in the state. A compulsory insurance law requires the owners or operators of automobiles to carry automobile liability insurance at least equal to certain minimum limits before the vehicle can be licensed or registered. Alternatively, the motorist can post a bond or deposit cash or securities that guarantee financial responsibility in the event of an accident.

Compulsory insurance laws are generally considered superior to financial responsibility laws since the motorist must provide proof of financial responsibility *before* the accident occurs. Critics of compulsory insurance laws, however, argue that compulsory insurance laws have serious defects. They include the following:

1. *Compulsory insurance laws may not reduce the number of uninsured motorists.* Some drivers may not license their vehicles because the insurance is too costly. Others may let the coverage lapse after the vehicle is licensed.

2. *Compulsory insurance laws do not guarantee payment to all accident victims.* For example, persons may be injured by (a) hit-and-run drivers, (b) drivers whose insurance has lapsed, (c) out-of-state drivers, (d) drivers of stolen cars, and (e) fraudulently registered vehicles.

3. *Compulsory insurance laws provide incomplete protection.* The required minimum amount of insurance may not meet the full needs of accident victims.

4. *Insurers argue that compulsory laws restrict their freedom to select profitable insureds.* In addition, insurers argue that needed rate increases may be denied, which results in underwriting losses.

5. *Compulsory insurance laws do nothing to prevent or reduce the number of automobile accidents,* which is the heart of the problem.

Unsatisfied Judgment Funds

Five states (New Jersey, Maryland, Michigan, North Dakota, and New York) have *unsatisfied judgment funds* that compensate accident victims who have exhausted all other means of payment. These funds have several common characteristics. First, the injured person must obtain a judgment against the negligent driver and show that the judgment cannot be collected. Thus, there must be an unsatisfied judgment against the negligent driver.

Second, the maximum amount paid is generally limited to the state's financial responsibility law requirement. In addition, most funds reduce the amount paid by any amount collected from other collateral sources of recovery, such as payments from a workers compensation law or from insurance.

Third, the negligent driver is not relieved of legal liability when the unsatisfied judgment fund makes a payment to the insured person. The negligent driver must repay the fund or lose his or her driver's license until the fund is reimbursed for the payments made.

Finally, several methods are used to finance the benefits paid. Funds can be obtained by charging each motorist a fee, by assessing the uninsured drivers in the state, and by assessing insurers based on the amount of liability insurance premiums written in the state.

Unsatisfied judgment funds have advantages and disadvantages. The major advantages are as follows:

1. Injured accident victims have some protection against irresponsible motorists.
2. Some drivers who are uninsured are kept off the road until the unsatisfied judgment fund is repaid.

The following are disadvantages of unsatisfied judgment funds:

1. Financing is inequitable since insured motorists within the state are charged a fee.
2. Amounts repaid into the funds by uninsured motorists are relatively small.
3. Administration of the funds is often cumbersome and slow. As noted earlier, the injured person must show that a judgment cannot be collected.
4. The funds have experienced serious financial problems in recent years.

Uninsured Motorists Coverage

The *uninsured motorists coverage* is another approach for compensating automobile accident victims. As noted in Chapter 7, the insurer agrees to pay the accident victim who has a bodily injury that is caused by an uninsured motorist, by a hit-and-run driver, or by a driver whose insurer is insolvent.

The uninsured motorists coverage appears to be working reasonably well as a technique for providing some protection against an uninsured driver. The majority of states require that all automobile liability insurance contracts contain the uninsured motorists coverage unless the insured voluntarily waives the coverage in writing. Thus, most motorists have some protection against uninsured drivers. In addition, the uninsured motorists coverage is relatively inexpensive in many states.

The uninsured motorists coverage, however, has several defects as a technique for compensating injured automobile accident victims:

1. *Unless the insured has purchased higher limits, the maximum paid for a bodily injury is limited to the state's financial responsibility or compulsory insurance law requirement.* Thus, an injured person may not be fully compensated for his or her economic loss.
2. *Before the injured person can collect under the uninsured motorists coverage, he or she must establish that the uninsured motorist is legally liable for the accident.* This may be difficult to establish in some cases and expensive if an attorney must be hired. Because of possible disputes concerning whether a covered person is entitled to collect or what the amount of damages is, an arbitration provision is included in the coverage.
3. *Property damage is excluded in most states.* Thus, if a negligent uninsured motorist runs a red light and damages another car, the owner of the damaged car would collect nothing for the property damage loss under the uninsured motorists coverage.

Underinsured Motorists Coverage

The *underinsured motorists coverage* can be added to an automobile insurance policy to provide more complete protection. The underinsured motorists coverage applies when the negligent driver has liability insurance at the time of the accident, but the limits carried are less than the limits provided by the underinsured motorists coverage. For example, assume that Tony has underinsured motorists coverage in the amount of $100,000 and is injured by a negligent driver who has bodily injury liability limits of $25,000/$50,000, which satisfies the state's financial responsibility law requirement. If Tony's actual damages are $75,000, he would recover a maximum of $25,000 from the negligent driver's insurer since that is the applicable limit of liability. He would receive an additional $50,000 from his own insurer from the underinsured motorists coverage.

The underinsured motorists coverage should not be confused with the uninsured motorists coverage. They do not overlap or duplicate each other. An insured can collect under one coverage or the other, depending on the situation, but not both. As stated earlier, the uninsured motorists coverage applies when the bodily injury is caused by an uninsured motorist, by a hit-and-run driver, or by a driver whose insurer is insolvent. In contrast, the underinsured motorists coverage applies only when the other driver has liability insurance, but the liability limits carried by the negligent driver are less than the limits provided by the insured's underinsured motorists coverage.

Finally, the underinsured motorists coverage can be written only if certain conditions are satisfied:

- The insured must carry increased limits for the uninsured motorists coverage that are higher than the limits required by the state's financial responsibility law.
- Both the uninsured and underinsured motorists coverages must be written for the same amount.
- The underinsured motorists coverage must apply to all automobiles covered under the policy.

NO-FAULT AUTOMOBILE INSURANCE

No-fault automobile insurance is another approach for compensating automobile accident victims. In 1990, twenty-six states had some type of no-fault automobile insurance law in operation.[10]

Meaning of No-Fault Insurance

No-fault insurance means that in the event of an automobile accident, each party collects from his or her own insurer regardless of fault. It is not necessary to establish fault and prove negligence in order to collect.

In addition, a true no-fault law places some restrictions on the right to sue the negligent driver who caused the accident. If a claim is below a certain *monetary threshold* (such as $1,000), an injured motorist would collect for the injury from his or her own insurer. If the loss exceeds the threshold amount, the injured person has the right to sue the negligent driver who caused the accident. A small number of states with no-fault laws use a *verbal threshold* rather than a monetary threshold. A verbal threshold means a lawsuit for damages is allowed only in serious accidents, such as those involving death, disfigurement, or dismemberment. Persons with less serious injuries cannot sue at all but must collect from their own insurers.

Types of No-Fault Laws

Three types of no-fault laws have been proposed or enacted in the various states: (1) pure no-fault laws, (2) add-on plans, and (3) modified no-fault laws. These types of laws are described below.

Pure No-Fault Laws. Under a pure no-fault law, the injured person cannot sue at all for damages regardless of the severity of the injury. In effect, the tort liability system for bodily injury would be abolished since the injured person cannot sue for damages. Instead, the injured person would collect certain no-fault benefits (discussed later) from his or her own insurer. No state has enacted a pure no-fault law at this time.

Add-On Plans. Add-on plans pay certain benefits to injured automobile victims without regard to fault, but the injured person retains the right to sue the negligent person who caused the accident. This explains the name "add-on." The law adds benefits but takes nothing away. Add-on plans are generally not regarded as true no-fault laws since the injured person retains the right to sue. As noted earlier, a true no-fault law must place some restriction on the right to sue for damages.

Modified No-Fault Laws. Under a modified no-fault law, injured persons are permitted to sue only if the claim exceeds the monetary or verbal threshold. If the claim is below the threshold, the injured person would collect certain benefits from his or her own insurer. Thus, modified no-fault laws partially restrict the right to sue but do not completely eliminate it.

Characteristics of No-Fault Laws

Twenty-six states, Puerto Rico, and the District of Columbia have enacted some type of no-fault law. Although the no-fault laws vary widely with respect to details, certain characteristics are common to all laws.

No-Fault Benefits. No-fault benefits are provided by adding an endorsement to an automobile insurance policy. The endorsement typically is called *personal injury protection (PIP)* and describes the no-fault benefits that are paid. No-fault benefits are limited to the injured person's actual *economic loss,* which includes the payment of medical expenses, a percentage of lost wages, and certain other expenses. The injured person can sue for *noneconomic loss factors* that are not measurable in dollars (such as pain and suffering, inconvenience, and mental anguish) only when the monetary threshold limit is exceeded or the verbal threshold is met.

The following no-fault benefits are typically provided:

1. *Medical expenses.* Medical expenses are paid up to some maximum limit. However, the laws in Michigan and New Jersey provide for unlimited medical expenses. *Rehabilitation expenses* incurred by the accident victim are paid in addition to the medical expenses.

2. *Loss of earnings.* A proportion of the insured person's lost earnings is also paid. There is usually a maximum limit in terms of amount and time. For example, an injured accident victim may receive a maximum benefit equal to 80 percent of the lost wages up to $1,000 monthly for three years.

3. *Expenses for essential services.* Benefits are paid for the expenses incurred for certain essential services that are ordinarily performed by the injured person, such as housework, house repairs, and lawn mowing. For example, New York pays up to $25 daily for a maximum of one year for essential services that the injured person cannot perform.

4. *Funeral expenses.* Benefits for funeral expenses are paid up to some limit. In some states, the funeral benefit is part of the medical expenses limit. In other states, payment for funeral expenses is a separate benefit.

5. *Survivors' loss benefits.* Benefits can be paid to certain survivors to compensate them for the death of a covered automobile accident victim. The benefits paid are periodic income payments that partially compensate the survivors for the death of a covered person.

Some states require that higher *optional no-fault benefits* should be made available to persons who want benefits above the prescribed minimums. In addition, some states also require companies to provide higher *optional deductibles* that can be used to reduce or eliminate certain no-fault benefits.

Right to Sue. The right to sue depends on the type of no-fault law. A minority of states currently have add-on plans. In these states, there is no restriction on the right to sue.

The majority of states with no-fault laws have enacted modified no-fault laws. As noted earlier, if the bodily injury is below the monetary threshold or does not meet the verbal threshold, the injured person is not allowed to sue for damages but would receive no-fault benefits from his or her own insurer. If the injury exceeds the threshold, the injured person has the option of continuing to receive the no-fault benefits or to sue for damages under the tort liability system. No-fault laws typically allow the insurer to subrogate against the negligent motorist's insurer to the extent that no-fault benefits are paid, or they allow the insurer to be reimbursed for the no-fault benefits paid if there is a tort liability recovery from a third party.

Two states (New Jersey and Pennsylvania) have recently enacted legislation that allows the following options: (1) coverage under the state's no-fault law with a verbal threshold and lower rates, or (2) retention of the right to sue for any auto-related injury with higher rates. If the no-fault option is elected, an injured motorist would not be allowed to sue unless the injury appeared on the list of injuries described in the verbal threshold; rates are lower if this option is elected. If the second option is elected, an injured motorist could sue for any auto-related injury, but higher rates are charged.

Exclusion of Property Damage.   No-fault laws apply only to bodily injury and not to property damage. Thus, if a person's property is damaged by a negligent motorist, that person has the right to sue for damages. Property damage generally is excluded from no-fault laws for several reasons:

- Property damage is relatively small and is usually confined to vehicles.
- The amount of damage can be determined without great difficulty.
- Responsibility for damage to vehicles can usually be settled quickly by insurers when the parties involved have collision insurance.

Thus, the states have not found it necessary to extend no-fault coverage to property damage. One exception is Michigan. The Michigan no-fault law includes mandatory property protection insurance, which pays up to $1 million for damage to property of others (except vehicles) resulting from an accident that occurs in Michigan. Under the Michigan law, motor vehicle owners are generally prohibited from suing other drivers for damage to their vehicles. However, drivers can be sued if they are liable for damage of less than $400 to another person's vehicle.

Evaluation of No-Fault Laws

This section presents arguments that favor no-fault automobile insurance laws as well as arguments that oppose such laws. The section also includes an evaluation of the effectiveness of no-fault laws.

Arguments for No-Fault Laws.   It is argued that no-fault laws are necessary because of serious defects in the present tort liability system, which is based on fault and the proving of negligence. Since automobile liability insurance is based on fault, critics point out the following defects in that system that no-fault laws are designed to correct.

1. *Difficult to determine fault.* Automobile accidents occur suddenly and

unexpectedly, and it is often difficult to determine who is actually at fault. In addition, the problem of determining fault is aggravated when both drivers contribute to the accident. It is argued that under a no-fault law, it is not necessary to determine fault in most accidents, and each party collects no-fault benefits from his or her own insurer.

2. *Inequities in claim payments.* It is argued that the present tort liability system is marred by inequities in claim payments. Under the present system, small claims may be overpaid, while serious claims may be underpaid. A Department of Transportation study showed that for a group of smaller claims of $500 or less, the actual settlement was four and one-half times the actual economic loss. In contrast, for automobile victims with an economic loss of $25,000 or more, only about one-third of the economic loss was recovered.[11]

3. *Limited scope of present reparations system.* It is also argued that many injured persons do not collect under the present system. The Department of Transportation study showed that only 45 percent of the seriously injured or the beneficiaries of those killed benefited from the tort liability system. One out of ten accident victims received no compensation from any source.

4. *Large proportion of premium dollar used for legal costs.* It is also argued that under the tort liability system, a large proportion of the premium dollars is used to pay attorneys, claim investigators, and other costs of fixing blame. The Department of Transportation study showed that for each dollar of liability insurance premiums collected, $.23 was used to pay defense attorneys, plaintiffs' attorneys, claim investigators, and other claim costs. Only $.44 was paid to automobile accident victims.

5. *Delay in payments.* The Department of Transportation study found that only about half of the claims were settled in six months or less. Persons who were seriously injured or their survivors had to wait an average of sixteen months for final payment from automobile liability insurance.

Arguments Against No-Fault Laws. Supporters of the present tort liability system, however, present persuasive arguments against no-fault laws.

1. *Defects of the present tort liability system are exaggerated.* It is argued that the present system is working reasonably well since most automobile claims are settled out of court.

2. *Claims of premium savings and greater efficiency are overstated.* It is argued that assertions of premium savings and greater efficiency under no-fault laws are exaggerated and unreliable. Under some federal no-fault proposals, automobile premiums would go up and not down.

3. *Safe drivers may be penalized.* It is argued that the rating system used would inequitably allocate the accident costs to the drivers who are not responsible for the accidents. Thus, their premiums may go up as a result.

4. *There is no payment for pain and suffering.* No-fault benefits do not include any payment for pain and suffering. Attorneys representing

injured automobile accident victims argue that the dollar amount of medical expenses and lost wages does not always represent the true economic loss to the victim since pain and suffering should also be considered.

5. *Court delays are not universal.* It is argued that court delays and clogged courts are not universal, but exist only in certain metropolitan areas. Thus, it is argued that court delay should be viewed as a separate problem and should be attacked as such rather than used as an argument for a no-fault law.

6. *Present system only needs reform.* Supporters of the present tort liability system argue that the system only needs to be reformed and not replaced with a no-fault law. This could be done by increasing the number of courts and judges, limiting contingency fees of attorneys, using arbitration panels rather than the courts in settling claims, and initiating other reforms.

Results of No-Fault Laws. Although problems have arisen with the no-fault laws enacted in some states, research studies indicate that properly designed no-fault laws are working reasonably well. The All Industry Research Advisory Committee (AIRAC) analyzed some 46,000 claims that were closed in 1987 to determine the effectiveness of no-fault laws. The AIRAC study compared claim costs in states that operated under the traditional tort liability system with claim costs in states that have enacted no-fault laws. The major conclusions are summarized as follows:[12]

1. *There is less incentive to exaggerate injuries in no-fault states.* Data show that tort states provide an incentive to exaggerate injuries in order to obtain a higher award for pain and suffering. No-fault states provide no such incentive.

2. *The percentage of total compensation paid to claimants for medical bills and lost wages is higher in no-fault states.* The AIRAC study showed that 78 percent of all payments in no-fault states is used to pay medical bills and lost wages. The remainder is paid for pain and suffering. In contrast, only 46 percent of the dollars received by accident victims in tort states is used to pay medical bills or to replace lost income; more than half of the total payments in tort states went for pain and suffering.

3. *Accident victims are paid more quickly in no-fault states.* In no-fault states, 72 percent of the accident victims with medical bills and lost wages in excess of $2,500 received their first payment within 90 days; the corresponding figure for the tort states is only 10 percent.

4. *No-fault tends to compensate more people.* In no-fault states, 16 percent of the claimants were individuals who were involved in accidents in which no other car was involved; the corresponding figure in the tort states was only 3 percent.

5. *No-fault states with verbal thresholds or with high monetary thresholds can be effective in holding down claim costs.* The AIRAC study compared insurance costs under no-fault with an estimate of what the

insurance costs would have been if the tort liability system had not been replaced. The study showed that Michigan and New York with verbal thresholds realized cost savings of 30 percent or more under their no-fault plans. The study also showed that states with monetary thresholds of $1,000 or more realized greater cost savings than the add-on states or states with thresholds under $1,000.

Some no-fault laws, however, have serious defects. One major defect is the low-dollar threshold in many states. Critics argue that the low-dollar thresholds on medical expenses in many states are too low to discourage lawsuits and that as a result, a large number of minor cases end up in the courts. To reduce the number of bodily injury claims in states with weak no-fault laws, critics recommend higher monetary thresholds or the enactment of a verbal threshold. As noted earlier, a verbal threshold means that a lawsuit for damages is permitted only in serious cases, such as death, disfigurement, or dismemberment. A properly worded verbal threshold has considerable potential for holding down bodily injury claim costs.

AUTOMOBILE INSURANCE FOR HIGH-RISK DRIVERS: THE SHARED MARKET

High-risk drivers frequently have difficulty obtaining automobile insurance in the standard markets. These drivers can obtain automobile insurance in the *shared market* (also called the residual market). The shared market refers to plans in which automobile insurers participate to make coverage available to drivers who cannot obtain coverage in the standard markets.

Several plans are specifically designed for high-risk drivers:[13]

- Automobile insurance plan
- Joint underwriting association (JUA)
- Reinsurance facility
- Maryland Automobile Insurance Fund
- Specialty insurers

These shared market plans are described below.

Automobile Insurance Plan

Most states have an *automobile insurance plan* (formerly called an assigned risk plan) for high-risk drivers who cannot obtain automobile insurance in the standard markets. Under this arrangement, all automobile insurers doing business in the state are assigned their proportionate share of high-risk drivers based on the total volume of automobile business written in the state. For example, if one insurer writes 5 percent of the automobile business in the state, it would be assigned 5 percent of the high-risk drivers.

Although automobile insurance plans vary from state to state, they have several common characteristics. First, persons applying for insurance must show they have been unable to obtain liability insurance within sixty days of the application.

Second, the amount of liability insurance that can be obtained is at least equal to the state's financial responsibility or compulsory insurance requirement, such as $25/$50/$25. Most plans make available higher limits on an optional basis. Most plans also make available medical payments coverage and physical damage insurance.

Third, certain persons may be ineligible for coverage. For example, persons convicted of a felony within the preceding thirty-six months, persons engaged in illegal activities such as drugs and gambling, and persons who are habitual violators of state and local laws may be ineligible for coverage.

In addition, the premiums paid are substantially higher than the premiums paid in the standard markets. High-risks drivers are rated on the basis of their driving records and are charged accordingly.

Also, drivers do not have a choice of insurers. As noted earlier, automobile insurers in the state are assigned their proportionate share of high-risk drivers based on the total volume of automobile business written in the state.

Finally, an insurer is not required to insure a high-risk driver for more than three years. The automobile insurance can be canceled under certain conditions, such as obtaining the insurance through fraud or misrepresentation or for non-payment of premiums.

Automobile plans have advantages and disadvantages. The major advantage is that high-risk drivers have at least one source of obtaining liability insurance to meet the state's financial responsibility or compulsory insurance requirement. The major disadvantages are as follows:

1. *Substantial underwriting losses.* Despite substantially higher premiums, the automobile insurance plans have experienced heavy underwriting losses. The result is that good drivers in the voluntary standard markets are heavily subsidizing high-risk drivers who are insured in automobile insurance plans.
2. *Uninsured high-risk drivers.* High premiums may force many high-risk drivers to go uninsured, which defeats the basic purpose of automobile insurance plans.
3. *Lack of choice of companies.* Drivers are not permitted to select their own company, which restricts freedom of choice.
4. *Clean risks.* Some drivers with clean driving records and no driving convictions are arbitrarily placed in automobile insurance plans. This can happen when poor loss experience or inadequate rates force insurers to stop providing coverage in a given territory.

Joint Underwriting Association

A small number of states have established *joint underwriting associations* that make automobile insurance available to high-risk drivers. A joint underwriting association (JUA) is an association of automobile insurers in which high-risk automobile business is placed in a common pool, and each company doing business in the state pays its proportionate share of pool losses and expenses.

Under this arrangement, the JUA dictates the auto insurance forms to be used by high-risk motorists and sets the rates. A limited number of companies are designated as *servicing insurers* to service the high-risk business. Agents and brokers are assigned to particular servicing insurers, which provide them with a market for placing high-risk business. The servicing insurer receives the application, issues the policy, collects the premiums, pays claims, and provides other necessary services. All automobile insurers in the state pay their proportionate share of underwriting losses and expenses based on the company's share of voluntary automobile insurance written in the state.

Supporters of JUAs maintain that they have certain advantages over automobile insurance plans:

1. *Less stigma to high-risk drivers.* Proponents claim the stigma associated with a shared market plan is less under a JUA than under an automobile insurance plan.
2. *Fairer method of paying losses.* It is argued that a JUA is a fairer method of paying losses since companies are proportionately sharing dollar losses rather than the number of drivers.
3. *Gives producers another company.* It is argued that this arrangement gives producers another company (JUA) in their portfolio of companies in which to place high-risk business.

Reinsurance Facility

A small number of states have enacted laws to establish a special *reinsurance facility* for high-risk drivers. Under this arrangement, the insurer underwrites the application for insurance, issues the policy, and receives the premiums. However, if an applicant for automobile insurance is considered a high-risk driver, the insurer has the option of placing the driver in the reinsurance facility. Any underwriting losses in the reinsurance facility are then shared by all automobile insurers doing business in the state. Although the high-risk driver is in the reinsurance facility, the original insurer pays any claims and continues to service the policy. However, as noted earlier, underwriting losses in the reinsurance facility are shared by all automobile insurers doing business in the state.

A reinsurance facility has several advantages as a shared market plan for high-risk drivers. They include the following:[14]

1. *High-risk drivers are not aware of transfer to a reinsurance facility.* Thus, the stigma of being placed in an assigned risk plan for poor drivers is avoided.
2. *Rate discrimination is reduced.* The original insurer writing the high-risk driver applies the same rates and classification plan to all of its policyowners.
3. *Coverage discrimination is reduced.* Insurers use the same policy forms and endorsements that are generally required and desired by customers in the same class.

4. *Delays in service and service deficiencies are reduced.* Agents are able to provide the same services to all policyowners, including high-risk drivers.

The major disadvantage of reinsurance facilities is that they have experienced substantial underwriting losses in recent years. As a result, good drivers in the standard markets are heavily subsidizing the high-risk drivers in reinsurance facilities.

Maryland Automobile Insurance Fund

A special state fund can be used to provide automobile insurance to high-risk drivers. Maryland is the only state that has such a fund. The Maryland Automobile Insurance Fund was established in 1973 for the specific purpose of providing automobile insurance to state motorists who could not obtain automobile insurance in the voluntary markets. The state fund limits the insurance to applicants who can provide evidence that their insurance had been canceled by one insurer or that their application was rejected by two insurers. The fund makes available liability insurance, personal injury protection, uninsured motorists coverage, and physical damage insurance. Any agent in the state can bind coverage in the state fund. However, all claims are adjusted by personnel employed by the state fund.

The financial results have been dismal since the fund's inception, and substantial underwriting losses have been incurred. State law requires private insurers in the state to subsidize any losses incurred by the state fund by charging the losses back to the policyowners. The result is that good drivers in the voluntary standard markets are heavily subsidizing the high-risk drivers in the state fund.

Specialty Insurers

In addition to the four shared market plans discussed above, high-risk drivers may be able to obtain automobile insurance from certain private insurers who specialize in insuring motorists with poor driving records. These specialty companies typically insure drivers who have been canceled or refused insurance, drunk drivers, teenage drivers, and other high-risk drivers.

Automobile insurance contracts from specialty insurers on high-risk drivers generally have several common features.[15] First, the premiums charged are substantially higher than the premiums charged in the standard markets. It is not uncommon for high-risk drivers to pay three or four times (or even higher) the premiums charged in the standard markets. The actual premium paid is based on the individual's driving record. The higher the number of traffic violations and chargeable accidents, the higher the premium that must be paid.

Second, the amount of liability insurance that can be obtained from specialty insurers is at least equal to the state's financial responsibility or compulsory insurance law. However, many specialty insurers offer higher limits on an optional basis.

Third, because high-risk drivers have a greater probability of being involved in another accident, medical payments coverage may be limited, and collision insurance may be available only with a higher deductible. For example, the collision deductible may be $250 or higher.

Finally, many insurers have safe driver incentive plans to encourage high-risk drivers to drive in a responsible manner. Under these plans, premiums are periodically reduced if the high-risk driver has no chargeable offenses; however, the high-risk driver is surcharged and must pay higher premiums if another chargeable accident or traffic violation occurs during the policy period.

UNDERWRITING AND RATING PERSONAL AUTO INSURANCE

Automobile insurers are in business to make a profit. Accomplishing this objective requires effective underwriting and appropriate rating. *Underwriting* refers to the selection and classification of profitable insureds. Applicants for automobile insurance are accepted or rejected based on the company's underwriting policy. If the applicant for automobile insurance is accepted, he or she is placed in the proper underwriting class and charged an appropriate rate for that class. *Class rating*, commonly used in private passenger automobile insurance, means placing individuals with similar characteristics in the same underwriting class and charging each person the same rate. The premiums collected from the class as a whole should be sufficient to pay all claims and expenses, and to yield a profit to the company during the policy period.

Competition Among Insurers

There often is intense price competition among automobile insurers. Competition is an extremely important factor in determining the number of underwriting classes that an insurer has. If a group of better-than-average drivers can be identified, they can be assigned to a new underwriting class and charged a lower rate, thereby improving the insurer's competitive position in the market.

Conversely, if a group of below-average drivers can be identified, they can be removed from their present classification, placed in a new class, and charged a higher rate. This will enable an insurer to reduce rates for the remaining drivers in the former class, which should also improve the insurer's competitive position.[16] To the extent that insurers are able to compete in this manner, the effect is reduced rates for better-than-average drivers and increased rates for below-average or substandard drivers. As a result, policyowners receive more equitable treatment since the good drivers pay less for their protection, and the poorer drivers pay more.

Rate Regulation

Automobile insurers, however, do not have unlimited freedom to charge any price they desire for the coverages they provide. Insurers are constrained by rating laws that require the rates to meet certain statutory standards. In general, rates are required by law to be adequate, reasonable (not excessive), and not unfairly discriminatory. With the exception of Illinois, all states have rating laws that affect the pricing of automobile insurance. The rating laws can generally be classified into the following categories:[17]

- Prior approval laws
- File-and-use laws
- Open competition laws
- Mandatory state or bureau rates

Prior Approval Laws. The majority of states have some type of prior approval law. Under a prior approval law, the rates must be approved by the state insurance department before they can be used. Prior approval laws have been criticized by insurers because there is often considerable delay in obtaining a rate increase, the rate increase may be inadequate, and the statistical data required by the state insurance department may not be readily available.

File-and-Use Laws. Under a file-and-use law, the rates have to be filed with the state insurance department, but they can be used immediately. The state insurance department has the authority to disapprove the rates if they cannot be justified or if they violate state law. A file-and-use law overcomes the problems of delay associated with prior approval laws.

Open Competition Laws. This type of rating law is the most liberal. Under an open competition law (also called a no-filing law), rates do not have to be filed with the state insurance department, and insurers can charge rates based on their own experience and market conditions. This type of law is based on the assumption that price competition in the marketplace will keep rates reasonable and competitive. Thus, market prices based on competition rather than the discretionary acts of regulatory authorities determine the price and availability of insurance. However, insurers may be required to furnish rate schedules and supporting statistical data to regulatory officials. Also, the state insurance department has the authority to monitor competition and disapprove the rates based on the standards of market share and workable competition.

Mandatory Rates. Under this type of law, rates are set by some state agency or rating bureau, and all licensed insurers are required to use these rates. In Texas and Massachusetts, automobile insurance rates are determined by the state agency, and all companies doing business in the state must use the rates. Texas, however, allows certain rate deviations. In North Carolina, a rating bureau determines the automobile insurance rates. Again, all insurers are required by law to use these rates, and rate deviations are allowed.

Selection of Insureds

As noted earlier, the basic objective of automobile underwriting is to select profitable insureds. The goal of profitable business, however, often conflicts with the public's right to buy insurance.

For most drivers, automobile insurance is viewed as an absolute necessity for two reasons. First, motorists require automobile insurance for protection against financial hardships or ruin from liability suits. Second, automobile insurance may be required by the government in order for a driver to legally operate a vehicle. For most drivers, the purchase of automobile liability insurance is the only practical way to meet the state's financial responsibility or compulsory insurance law. Thus, motorists generally believe they should have an unequivocal right to buy automobile insurance.

However, because of the underwriting goal of profitability, automobile insurers do not make available to the public unlimited amounts of automobile insurance. Automobile insurance is not available to all drivers in the standard markets since some drivers with a high loss potential are rejected by insurers based on their underwriting standards. Other drivers may be able to obtain the insurance only by the payment of substantially higher or surcharged premiums.

The conflict between the public's belief that it has a right to buy automobile insurance and the insurer's goal of profitability is often resolved by government intervention. As a condition for doing business in a state, the state may require automobile insurers to make available certain minimum amounts of liability insurance so that some drivers who ordinarily would be refused insurance can obtain some protection. The influence of government is widely reflected in the development of shared market plans.

Restrictions on Cancellation and Nonrenewal

All states have laws that restrict the insurer's right to cancel or not renew an automobile insurance policy. These laws reflect the government's desire to protect the public because of actions by some insurers that are perceived as being unfair to policyowners, such as canceling a driver after a single claim; withdrawal from a certain geographical area; a decision to stop writing automobile insurance for certain groups, such as younger drivers; or a decision to discontinue the writing of automobile contracts for a particular agent.[18]

Restrictions on Cancellation. Restrictions on cancellation generally do not apply to *new policies* that have been in force for less than a certain period (such as sixty days). During this period, insurers can generally cancel new policies, which gives them time to complete their initial underwriting and investigation of the applicant. However, after the new policy has been in force for a certain period, cancellation is permitted only for reasons specified in the law. The reasons vary from state to state, but cancellation generally is permitted for the following reasons:[19]

- Nonpayment of premiums
- Suspension or revocation of a driver's license
- Submission of a false or fraudulent claim
- Material misrepresentation
- Conviction for certain offenses, such as drunk driving
- Violation of policy terms or conditions

Notice of cancellation is required (such as twenty days). Most states also require that the reason for cancellation must be included in the notice or provided upon request. In addition, most states require the cancellation notice to indicate that coverage may be available from an automobile insurance plan or from some other shared market facility.

Restrictions on Nonrenewal. The preceding restrictions generally do not apply to the nonrenewal of an existing automobile policy. Insurers generally have the right to refuse renewal of an existing policy for another term, subject to certain restrictions. First, the insured must be notified that the policy will not be renewed. Most states require at least thirty days' advance notice that the policy will not be renewed. Second, many states require the insurer to give the reason for not renewing in the notice or to provide the reason on request. Finally, some states forbid insurers to refuse renewal of a policy solely because of age, residence, race, color, creed, national origin, occupation, or because another insurer has refused to write the policy or has canceled or refused to renew an existing policy.

Cost of Automobile Insurance

The factors that determine the cost of automobile insurance are discussed below. The discussion is confined to general principles since the actual rating systems vary in detail from insurer to insurer.[20]

Primary Rating Factors. The major or primary rating factors for determining the cost of automobile insurance are the following:

- Territory
- Age, sex, and marital status
- Use of the auto
- Good student discount
- Driver education

All of these factors may not be permitted to be used in all states, however.

Territory. Territory is one of the most important rating variables. A base rate for automobile liability insurance and physical damage insurance is first determined. The base rate is determined largely by the territory where the vehicle is used and garaged. Each state is divided into various rating territories that may include whole cities or parts thereof, the suburbs, and rural areas.

Automobile insurance is more expensive in densely populated territories because the number of accidents is directly related to the number of vehicles within the territory, medical care is more expensive in cities, automobile repair costs are higher, and jury awards in cities are likely to be higher than in rural areas.

Age, Sex, and Marital Status. *Age* is an extremely important rating factor since younger drivers are involved in a disproportionate number of automobile accidents. Drivers under age twenty-five account for about 19 percent of the total drivers in the United States, but they are involved in 32 percent of all accidents.

All insurers classify younger drivers. One example of such a system is the following:

- No youthful operator
- Female operator only, ages thirty to sixty-four
- Principal operator, age sixty-five or over
- Unmarried females under age twenty-five
- Married males under age twenty-five
- Unmarried males under age twenty-five who are not owners or principal operators
- Unmarried males under age thirty who are owners or principal operators

Young, unmarried male drivers who are the principal operators or owners of automobiles pay the highest rates since this group has the highest accident rate. Because of intense competition, automobile insurers have developed rating systems that consider the driving experience of younger drivers. Under these systems, the rates are scaled downward as the driver gets older.

Sex of the driver is also an important rating factor. Younger, unmarried female drivers tend to have better driving records and fewer accidents than unmarried male drivers in the same age bracket.

Finally, *marital status* is also important because young, married male drivers tend to have relatively fewer accidents than unmarried male drivers in the same age bracket.

Although these have been traditional rating factors, several states no longer permit their use.

Use of the Auto. Use of the auto is another important rating factor. Insurers classify vehicles based on use. The following is an example of this type of classification:

- *Pleasure use.* The vehicle is not used in business or customarily driven to work unless the one-way mileage to work is less than three miles.
- *Drive to work.* The vehicle is not used in business but is driven three to fifteen miles to work each day.
- *Drive to work (over fifteen miles).* The vehicle is not used in business but is driven fifteen or more miles to work each day.
- *Business use.* The vehicle is customarily used in business.
- *Farm use.* The vehicle is garaged on a farm or ranch and is not used in any other business or driven to school or used in other work.

Farm use has the lowest rating factor, which is followed next by pleasure use. If the vehicle is driven to work or used in business, higher rates are required.

Good Student Discount. Many companies make available a *good student discount* that can reduce premiums by as much as 25 percent. The good student discount is based on the premise that good students are better drivers. To qualify for the discount, the insured must be a full-time student in high school or college, at least age sixteen, and meet one of the following scholastic requirements:

- Rank in the upper 20 percent of the class
- Have a B average or the equivalent

- Have at least a 3.0 average
- Be on the Dean's List or honor roll

A school official must sign a form indicating that one of the scholastic requirements has been met.

Driver Education.   If a young driver completes an approved driver education course, he or she may be eligible for a *driver education credit.* The credit is commonly 10 percent. The rate credit is based on the assumption that driver education classes for teenage drivers can reduce teenage accidents and hold down rates.

Secondary Rating Factors.   The following secondary rating factors are also used to rate automobile insurance lines:

- Type of automobile
- Number of vehicles
- Driving record

Type of Automobile.   The type of automobile is another important rating factor. Considered as part of this factor are performance, age of the vehicle, and damageability because they affect the cost of physical damage coverage.

Performance of the car is an important rating factor. Sports cars, high performance cars, and foreign specialty cars are more expensive to insure for a physical damage loss than is a standard sedan. Thus, a Porsche and a BMW require higher physical damage premiums than a Chevrolet Caprice.

Age and original cost of the vehicle are also considered by many companies in their rating system. The cost of insuring a new Cadillac is more than the cost of insuring a new Chevrolet sedan. As the car gets older, the rates decline, and in general, automobiles five or more years old have the lowest rates. However, the rate reduction as the vehicle gets older is relatively less each year since the cost of repairing an older car generally is not less than the cost of repairing a newer car. In addition, it takes less damage to an older car to have a constructive total loss. For these reasons, the rate reduction for physical damage insurance on older cars is relatively modest as the car ages.

Finally, insurers now rate the make and model of new automobiles on the basis of *damageability and repairability.* Certain vehicles are more easily damaged and more costly to repair than others. In general, automobiles that are damage resistant and relatively easy to repair have lower rates.

Number of Vehicles.   If the insured owns two or more vehicles, a *multi-car discount* is available. The discount generally ranges from 10 to 25 percent. A multi-car discount is based on the assumption that two vehicles owned by the same insured will not be driven as frequently as one vehicle owned by that person. As a result, the exposure to the insurer is less for two cars owned by the same person as compared with two cars owned by two different people.

Driving Record.   The driving record of the owner or operator of the vehicle is another important rating factor. Most insurers use an individual's driving record to determine if the applicant for automobile insurance is acceptable at standard or preferred rates. Most insurers also impose a surcharge on the insured's premium, that is, multiply the base premium by a given percentage, for a chargeable accident that exceeds a certain amount. The surcharge generally lasts three years.

Finally, many insurers have *safe driver plans* in which the premiums paid are based on the insured's driving record. Accident points are assessed for chargeable accidents and traffic violations, and premiums are surcharged accordingly. Points are charged for speeding citations, drunk driving, failure to stop after an accident, driving with a suspended or revoked license, homicide or assault involving an automobile, and other offenses. The actual premium paid is based on the total number of chargeable points.

Other Factors.　Other factors such as the following are also important in determining rates:

- Deductibles
- Liability limits
- Other available discounts and credits

Deductibles.　The amount of the deductible for a collision loss and an other than collision loss has a significant effect on the cost of physical damage insurance on automobiles. Increasing the collision deductible from $100 to $200 reduces the collision insurance premium by 10 to 20 percent in many companies, and the premium would be reduced even more if a $500 or $1,000 deductible were selected. The actual reduction depends on the age and make of the vehicle, where the vehicle is garaged, and characteristics of the principal operator or owner (such as age, sex, and marital status).

Liability Limits.　For standard drivers, substantial amounts of liability insurance can be purchased without a proportionate increase in the premium. This can be illustrated by a simple example. Assume that the premium for $25,000 bodily injury liability insurance in one particular territory is $101. Additional amounts of liability insurance can be purchased as follows:

Liability Limit	Premium
$ 25,000	$101
50,000	115
100,000	136
300,000	154
500,000	164
1,000,000	185

The major reason that liability premiums do not increase proportionately with higher limits is that the probability of a large claim is considerably lower than the probability of a smaller claim. For example, the number of bodily injury claims under $25,000 is substantially higher than the number of $1 million claims.

Other Available Discounts and Credits.　In addition to the good student discount, driver education credit, and multi-car discount, other discounts and credits that can reduce premiums may be available. Insurers commonly give discounts for anti-theft devices, passive restraints, completion of a defensive driving course, and students' attendance at schools that are a specified distance from home. Discounts also may be given to senior citizens, farmers, nonsmokers, and females between the ages of thirty and sixty-four who are the only driver in the household.

SUMMARY

The automobile insurance problem consists of the following components— the high frequency of auto accidents, the costs of auto accidents to individuals and society, the substantial underwriting losses of auto insurers, the acts of irresponsible drivers, and the public's desire for coverage that is both available and affordable.

Traditionally, persons injured in auto accidents through the negligence of others have relied on the tort liability system to collect damages. In an effort to ensure that negligent drivers carry insurance to pay for such damages, various states have enacted financial responsibility laws and compulsory insurance laws. Some states have established unsatisfied judgment funds to provide compensation for auto accident victims. Uninsured and underinsured motorists coverages carried by the injured individual also are sources of recovery for some accident costs caused by negligent drivers.

In contrast to these traditional approaches to compensating auto accident victims, twenty-six states have enacted no-fault auto insurance laws. Under no-fault insurance, each injured party in an automobile accident collects from his or her own insurance regardless of fault. Under a no-fault add-on plan, there is no restriction on the right to sue. Under a modified no-fault plan, an injured victim can sue only if the monetary threshold is exceeded or the verbal threshold is met.

The personal injury protection (PIP) endorsement adds no-fault coverage to the personal auto policy. Benefits are paid, as specified in the law of the insured's state, for economic losses such as medical expenses and loss of earnings resulting from bodily injury to the insured. Noneconomic losses, such as pain and suffering, inconvenience, and mental anguish, are not paid under the PIP endorsement. However, all of the no-fault laws currently in effect allow for recovery of noneconomic losses from the negligent party after a monetary or verbal threshold is exceeded.

Several types of shared or residual automobile insurance market plans are available in the various states. The most common form of shared market plan is the automobile insurance plan. In addition, a small number of states have a joint underwriting association (JUA) for high-risk drivers. A few states have a reinsurance facility that allows the insurer of a high-risk driver to reinsure the business in a reinsurance facility supported by all auto insurers in the state. Maryland has its own state auto insurance fund supported by private insurers.

In rating auto insurance, individuals with similar characteristics are placed in the same underwriting class, and each person is charged the same rate. Thus, rates may be reduced for better-than-average drivers and increased for below-average drivers.

Through laws and regulations, states control the rates charged for auto insurance. Rates must be adequate, reasonable (not excessive), and not unfairly discriminatory. Rate regulation may involve the use of prior approval laws, file-and-use laws, open competition, or mandatory state or bureau rates.

The states may expand the public's right to purchase insurance in the voluntary and shared markets through laws and regulations. States may also restrict the insurer's right to cancel or not renew insureds except in specified situations.

Numerous factors determine the cost of automobile insurance. Primary rating factors include territory; age, sex, and marital status; use of the auto; good student discount; and driver education credit. Secondary rating factors include the type of automobile, number of vehicles, and driving record. Other factors affecting the cost of insurance include deductibles, liability limits, and a variety of specific discounts and credits.

Chapter Notes

1. *1990 Property/Casualty Insurance Facts* (New York: Insurance Information Institute, 1990), pp. 74-79.
2. National Safety Council, *Accident Facts*, 1988 edition (Chicago: National Safety Council, 1988), pp. 52, 61.
3. *1990 Property/Casualty Insurance Facts*, p. 74.
4. *1990 Property/Casualty Insurance Facts*, p. 79.
5. *1990 Property/Casualty Insurance Facts*, p. 22.
6. General Accounting Office, *Issues and Needed Improvements in State Regulation of Insurance Business* (Executive Summary) (Washington, DC: U.S. General Accounting Office, 1979), Table 6, p. 40.
7. *1990 Property/Casualty Insurance Facts*, p. 76.
8. This section is based largely on material drawn from *Fire, Casualty & Surety Bulletins*, Personal Lines Volume, Personal Auto Section; George E. Rejda, *Principles of Insurance*, 3rd ed. (Glenview, IL: Scott, Foresman and Company, 1989), Chapters 9, 11-12; Glenn L. Wood, Claude C. Lilly III, Donald S. Malecki, Edward E. Graves, and Jerry S. Rosenbloom, *Personal Risk Management and Insurance*, 4th ed., vol. I (Malvern, PA: American Institute for Property and Liability Underwriters, 1989), Chapters 2-3; and David L. Bickelhaupt, *General Insurance*, 11th ed. (Homewood, IL: Richard D. Irwin, Inc., 1983), Chapter 19.
9. This section on damages is based on James H. Donaldson, *Casualty Claim Practice*, 4th ed. (Homewood, IL: Richard D. Irwin, Inc., 1984), pp. 78, 752.
10. The section on no-fault insurance laws is based largely on the sources cited in note 8.
11. Summary of the major defects of the tort liability system in automobile liability lawsuits can be found in U.S. Department of Transportation, *Major Vehicle Crash Losses and Their Compensation in the United States, A Report to the Congress and the President* (Washington, DC: Government Printing Office, 1971), pp. 15-100. The statistics cited in this section are based on this study.
12. The material in this section and statistics cited are based on Brian W. Smith, "Reexamining the Cost Benefits of No-Fault," *CPCU Journal*, vol. 42, no. 1 (March 1989), pp. 28-35 and "Brother Can You Spare A Tort?" *Journal of American Insurance*, vol. 65 (Third Quarter 1989), pp. 16-19.
13. Material on shared market plans for high-risk drivers is based largely on the sources cited in note 8.
14. *Policy Form & Manual Analyses*, Casualty Coverages, Automobile Liability Section, (Indianapolis, IN: Rough Notes, 1986), 224.5-2.
15. Rejda, *Principles of Insurance*, p. 229.
16. Wood *et al.*, *Personal Risk Management and Insurance*, vol. I, p. 152.
17. Rejda, *Principles of Insurance*, pp. 581-582.
18. Frederick G. Crane, *Insurance Principles and Practices*, 2nd ed. (New York: John Wiley & Sons, 1984), p. 121.
19. Crane, pp. 121-122.
20. This section is based on Wood *et al.*, *Personal Risk Management and Insurance*, vol. I, pp. 153-160 and Rejda, *Principles of Insurance*, pp. 229-231.

Chapter 10

Life Insurance

The preceding chapters have focused on property and liability loss exposures. Individuals and families are also exposed to other loss exposures, such as the premature death of a wage earner, poor health, or insufficient income during retirement. This chapter focuses on life insurance, which is designed to address the financial consequences associated with premature death.

Several aspects of life insurance are discussed in this chapter. The need for life insurance is examined, followed by a discussion of the various types of life insurance. The chapter also describes major life insurance policy provisions and riders that may be used to modify coverage. The chapter concludes with discussions of life insurance underwriting and group life insurance.

THE NEED FOR LIFE INSURANCE

In the economic sense, death can be considered premature when it occurs during a person's financially productive years, usually before age seventy.[1] The results of premature death usually include outstanding or unfulfilled financial obligations such as a mortgage, family members to support, or children to educate. The need for life insurance is a function of the costs of premature death. The amount of life insurance to own is a function of family financial needs.

Costs of Premature Death

At least four costs are associated with premature death. First, the deceased's earning power is terminated, and the family's share of that income is lost forever. Second, additional expenses may be incurred for burial costs, a last illness, probate and estate settlement costs, and federal estate taxes for large estates. Third, because of insufficient income, some families may be forced into poverty, which may result in the payment of public assistance or other welfare benefits. Finally, certain noneconomic costs are also incurred, such as the grief of a surviving spouse and loss of a role model, counselor, and guide for children.

Life insurance can be used to alleviate the financial consequences of premature death. The purchase of life insurance can be economically justified if the insured has an earning capacity and others are dependent on that earning capacity for at least part of their financial support. If a family wage earner dies prematurely, life insurance can be used to restore the family's share of the lost earnings.

A life insurance policy is not a contract of indemnity but a valued policy that pays a stated sum to a named beneficiary. The insured event is the *uncertain time of death*. While everyone will die, the time of each death is uncertain.

Amount of Life Insurance to Own

Many families are inadequately insured. The average amount of life insurance in force per family in 1988 was $87,600, which represents only about twenty-eight months of disposable income per family.[2] The proper amount of life insurance to own is, however, an individual matter since family needs, goals, and circumstances vary widely. In the past, certain arbitrary rules have been proposed for determining the amount of life insurance to own, such as five or six times annual earnings. However, these rules do not consider that needs, goals, and circumstances vary from family to family. One method used to estimate the proper amount of life insurance to own is the *needs approach*.[3]

Under this approach, the family's financial needs are estimated after taking into consideration any social security benefits that may be paid. The amount of current assets available for meeting these needs is then calculated. Life insurance and any other survivorship benefits are included in this calculation of current assets. Current assets are then subtracted from the family's financial needs to determine the additional amount of life insurance needed, if any, to meet these needs.

For an example of the needs approach, assume that the Jones family consists of Bob, age thirty-two; Mary, age thirty; and their son, age three. Bob earns $35,000 annually and Mary does not work outside the home. The Jones family's needs are typical of the needs of many families.

1. *Estate settlement fund.* Cash is needed immediately for burial expenses, expenses of last illness, installment debts, estate administration expenses, and estate taxes. Jones family estimate: $10,000.
2. *Income during readjustment period.* This is the one- or two-year period following a family wage earner's death during which the family continues to receive the same amount of income it received when the wage earner was alive. Jones family estimate: $50,000.
3. *Income during dependency period.* This period follows the readjustment period and typically lasts until the youngest child reaches age eighteen. Jones family estimate: $180,000.
4. *Blackout period.* Income is needed during the *blackout period* when social security benefits to a surviving spouse are temporarily terminated. Social security survivor benefits can be paid to a surviving spouse with eligible children under age sixteen. The benefits paid to the surviving

Exhibit 10-1
Illustration of Needs Approach

Bob Jones, age 32	**1. Family Needs**	
Mary Jones, age 30	Estate settlement fund	$ 10,000
Son, age 3	Readjustment period fund	50,000
	$1,000 monthly for 15 years	
	to supplement Social Security benefits	180,000
	$500 monthly for 17 years—Mary	
	(age 43 to age 60)	102,000
	Mortgage redemption fund	63,000
	Education fund	25,000
	Emergency fund	10,000
	Retirement fund for Mary	50,000
	Total family needs	$490,000
	2. Current Assets	
	Individual life insurance—Bob	$ 50,000
	Group life insurance—Bob	35,000
	Mutual fund shares	25,000
	Lump sum employer pension benefit—Bob	20,000
	Checking and savings account	10,000
	Less current assets	−$140,000
	3. Additional Life Insurance Needed	$350,000

spouse are terminated when the youngest child attains age sixteen and will not be resumed until the spouse attains age sixty. The children's benefits, however, continue until the youngest child attains age eighteen. Jones family estimate: $102,000.

5. *Special needs.* There may be three special needs: (a) a *mortgage fund* to pay off a mortgage, (b) an *education fund* for the children, and (c) an *emergency fund* for unexpected events. Jones family estimate: $98,000.

6. *Retirement fund.* There also may be the wish to provide a retirement fund for the surviving spouse. Jones family estimate: $50,000.

Exhibit 10-1 illustrates how the Jones family's needs can be compared with their current assets to determine the amount of additional insurance needed on Bob Jones's life. In estimating the amount of life insurance needed, it is assumed that the life insurance proceeds can be invested at a rate of interest that exactly equals the inflation rate. This is a conservative assumption and overstates somewhat the amount of life insurance needed.

TYPES OF LIFE INSURANCE

There are three basic types of life insurance: term insurance, whole life insurance, and endowment insurance. Because endowment insurance is rarely used, the following discussion of life insurance will focus primarily on term and whole life.

Term Insurance

Term insurance is the most basic type of life insurance. Term insurance is referred to as pure protection because it is priced to reflect only the probability that the insured will die during the policy period, or term. It may be helpful to think of term insurance pricing as similar to that of property and liability insurance in that the premium is determined on the basis of the probability that the insured will suffer a loss during the policy term. In 1988, term insurance accounted for the largest dollar amount of individual life insurance sold—34 percent of the $995 billion in new coverage written.[4]

Basic Characteristics.   Term insurance has four characteristics. First, term insurance provides only temporary protection such as one, five, or ten years, or until the insured reaches a specified age, such as sixty-five or seventy. If the insured is still alive at the expiration of the term period and the policy is not renewed for another term, the insurance protection expires.

Second, term insurance policies have no cash value or savings element. The insurance provided is pure protection, and cash values are not accumulated. However, some long-term contracts develop a small reserve, which is used up by the end of the period.

Third, most term insurance policies are renewable and convertible. *Renewable* means that the policy can be renewed for additional periods without evidence of insurability. To minimize adverse selection, insurers typically do not allow renewal after age sixty-five or seventy. *Convertible* means that the term insurance policy can be exchanged for some type of cash value life insurance with no evidence of insurability.

Fourth, term insurance premiums increase with age. Term insurance premiums are based on the mortality, or death, rate. Since the death rate increases with age,[5] term insurance premiums must also increase. For example, based on the 1980 Commissioners Standard Ordinary Mortality Table, the death rate for men at age twenty-five is 1.77 for each 1,000 lives. If 100,000 individuals at age twenty-five are insured for $1,000 each for only one year, the insurer must expect to pay 177 death claims or $177,000. Thus, ignoring expenses and compound interest, each insured must pay a pure premium of $1.77 ($177,000/ 100,000 = $1.77), which is the same as the death rate. Although the pure premium is relatively low in the early years, it increases substantially in later years. For example, at age forty-five, the pure premium per $1,000 is $4.55; at age sixty-five, it is $25.42; and at age eighty-five, it is $152.95.

Types of Term Insurance.   A wide variety of term insurance policies are sold today. The most widely used types are described below.

Yearly Renewable Term.   Yearly renewable term is issued for one year. The policyowner has the right to renew for successive one-year periods.

Five-, Ten-, Fifteen-, or Twenty-Year Term.   Term insurance policies can be issued for a specified period, such as five, ten, fifteen, or twenty years, or even longer. The premiums remain level during the policy term. However, if the policy is renewed at the end of the term, the premium will increase.

Term to Age Sixty-Five or Seventy.   Term to age sixty-five or seventy provides insurance to a stated age. The premiums remain level during the policy term, and the insurance expires when the stated age is reached. The policyowner usually has the right to covert the term insurance to a cash value policy, but the insurer may specify that the policy must be converted at some time prior to the expiration date. For example, insurers minimize adverse selection under a term to age sixty-five policy by requiring the policyowner to convert before age sixty.

Decreasing Term.   Under a decreasing term insurance policy, the premiums remain level during the policy term, but the face amount of insurance gradually declines over time. For example, a $50,000 policy issued for thirty years may gradually decline to $25,000 by the end of the twentieth year, and to zero by the end of the thirtieth year. Decreasing term policies can be issued for specified periods, such as ten, twenty, twenty-five, or thirty years. Decreasing term to age sixty-five or seventy also is available in many companies.

Reentry Term.   Reentry term is another type of term insurance. The premiums are based on a low-rate schedule. To remain on the low-rate schedule, the insured must periodically demonstrate evidence of insurability, such as every one to five years, depending on the company. Rates are substantially increased if the insured cannot provide satisfactory evidence of insurability.

Whole Life Insurance

Whole life insurance has level premiums, provides lifetime protection to age 100, and has a savings element. There are two basic types of whole life insurance: ordinary life insurance and limited payment life insurance. These two types of whole life insurance accounted for 48 percent of the individual life insurance policies sold in 1988 and 23 percent of the dollar amount of coverage written.[6]

Ordinary Life Insurance.   Ordinary life insurance is a form of whole life insurance in which the premiums are level, and lifetime protection is provided, to age 100. If the insured is still alive at age 100, the face amount is paid to the policyowner.

Under an ordinary life policy, the premiums paid during the early years of the policy are higher than necessary to pay death claims, while the premiums paid during the later years are lower than necessary for paying death claims. In effect, the policyowner is overcharged for the insurance protection during the early years and is undercharged during the later years. The significance of the level premium method can be illustrated by Exhibit 10-2, which compares the net premiums under an ordinary life policy with premiums for yearly renewable term insurance for a $1,000 policy issued at age twenty-five. A level premium is possible because the excess premiums paid during the early years are invested at compound interest and are used later to supplement the inadequate premiums paid during the later years of the policy. In contrast, premiums for yearly renewable term insurance are relatively low during the early years but increase sharply in the later years.

Exhibit 10-2

Comparison of Yearly Renewable Term Insurance Premium
with Level Premium for an Ordinary Life Policy Issued at Age 25

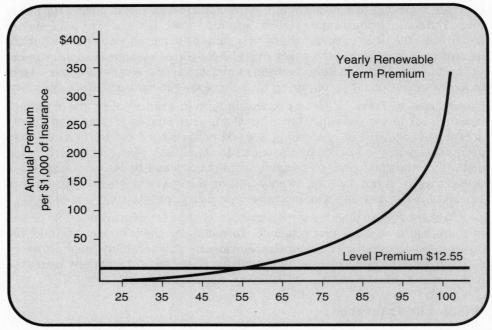

Reprinted with permission from George E. Rejda, *Principles of Insurance,*
2nd ed. (Glenview, IL: Scott, Foresman & Co., 1986), p. 332.

Legal Reserve. An ordinary life policy and other permanent life insurance
contracts develop a legal reserve, which arises out of the level-premium method
and redundant premiums paid during the early years of the policy. A *legal
reserve* is a liability item on the company's balance sheet. The reserve formally
reflects this redundancy of premiums paid. Assets must be accumulated by the
life insurer to offset this legal reserve liability.

Cash Values. An ordinary life policy also has *cash values* (the savings
element), which should not be confused with the legal reserve. Cash values are
below the legal reserve for many years and eventually equal the legal reserve
after an extended period, such as fifteen years. Like the legal reserve, cash
values result from the overpayment of premiums during the early years. If a
policyowner no longer wants insurance protection, the policy can be surrendered
for its cash value. The values can also be borrowed under a policy loan provision.
Although the cash surrender values are relatively low during the early years,
they accumulate to sizable levels over time. For example, a $100,000 ordinary
life policy issued at age twenty-five will have at least $50,000 in cash value at
age sixty-five.

Limited-Payment Life Insurance. Limited-payment life insurance is another form of whole life insurance. The premiums are level but are paid only for a certain number of years. After that time, the policy is paid up. For example, Hubert may purchase a twenty-year limited payment policy in the amount of $100,000. After twenty years, no additional premiums are required, and the policy is completely paid up.

Limited-payment policies can be issued for various time periods, such as ten, twenty, or thirty years. A policy that is paid up at age sixty-five or seventy is also available. Since the premiums paid under a limited-payment policy are considerably higher than for an ordinary life policy, the cash values are also higher.

Endowment Insurance

An endowment policy is the third basic type of life insurance. An endowment policy pays the policy proceeds to the named beneficiary if the insured dies within a certain period; if the insured survives to the end of the stated period, the policy proceeds are paid to the policyowner.

Although endowment insurance once was a popular financial planning tool, the purpose it served is now being met by other tax-favored investment products. The decline in interest in endowment insurance is illustrated by the following figures. In 1978, endowment policies represented 6 percent of individual life insurance sales and 3 percent of the dollar amount of new coverage written. By 1988, endowment policies accounted for less than 0.5 percent of both categories of sales.[7]

OTHER LIFE INSURANCE POLICIES

Various other types of life insurance policies are designed for certain needs or specific groups. These contracts frequently combine term insurance with whole life insurance.

Universal Life Insurance

Universal life insurance is a form of whole life insurance that has increased in importance. Universal life insurance was first widely introduced in the early 1980s; by 1988, it accounted for 19 percent of the new policies written and 27 percent of the dollar amount of new coverage provided.[8] Universal life policies are often sold as investments that combine insurance protection with savings. Universal life insurance can be defined as a flexible premium deposit fund combined with monthly renewable term insurance. The policyowner pays a specified initial premium. The gross premium less expenses, if any, is credited to the policy's initial cash value. A monthly mortality charge for the pure insurance protection is deducted from the cash value. The remaining cash value is then credited with interest at a specified rate.

Universal life insurance has several basic characteristics:

- Two forms available
- Separation of protection, savings, and expense components
- Stated investment return
- Considerable flexibility
- Cash withdrawals permitted

Under the first form of universal life, the initial death benefit is level. As the cash value increases, the amount of pure insurance protection declines. Under the second form, the death benefit is equal to the face amount of insurance plus the cash value. For the same policy face amount, premiums are higher for this second type of policy.

A second characteristic of universal life is that the policyowner receives detailed information regarding the allocation of the premiums paid and the status of the cash accumulation in the policy. An annual disclosure statement shows the portion of the premium used to (1) purchase pure protection, (2) increase savings, and (3) pay for insurer administrative expense.

A third characteristic is that the interest rate credited to the cash value is stated and known. Two rates of interest are typically stated. First, there is a *guaranteed minimum rate* such as 4 or 5 percent stated in the policy. Second, *excess interest* also is paid at a rate periodically determined by the company. Excess interest is the difference between the guaranteed rate (say 4 percent) and the current quoted rate based on current market conditions (say 8 percent).

Another characteristic is that universal life insurance provides considerable flexibility. Premiums can be increased or decreased; premium payments can be skipped as long as the cash value is sufficient to cover mortality costs and expenses; the death benefit can be increased (with evidence of insurability) or decreased; the policyowner can add to the cash value at any time subject to certain restrictions; policy loans are permitted; and additional insureds often can be added to the policy.

A final characteristic is that cash withdrawals are permitted. Depending on the provisions of the policy, the death benefit may be reduced by the amount of the withdrawal. Many policies also have a surrender charge for cash withdrawals, which declines over time. The period over which a surrender charge is applied can be as long as twenty years.

Variable Life Insurance

Inflation can quickly erode the real purchasing power of life insurance. For example, at 6 percent inflation, the real purchasing power of a $100,000 policy is reduced to $50,000 in only twelve years. With a variable life insurance policy, the face amount of insurance varies according to the investment experience of a separate account maintained by the insurer. The premiums are invested in stocks or in other investments. If the investment experience is favorable, the face amount of insurance is increased. If the investment experience is unsatisfactory, the amount of insurance may automatically be reduced. However, the amount of insurance can never be reduced below the original face amount. The purpose of a variable life policy is to maintain the real purchasing power of the death benefit.

Variable-Universal Life Insurance

A variable-universal life insurance policy combines the features of variable and universal life insurance. The basic policy characteristics are similar to those of a universal life insurance policy. However, there are two major differences. First, there are no guarantees with regard to the accumulation of cash values. The amount credited to the cash value of the policy is determined by the investment experience of a separate account maintained by the insurer. The second major difference is that the policyowner chooses the type of separate account in which premiums are to be invested—stocks, bonds, fixed income, etc.

A variable-universal life insurance policy combines the flexibility of a universal policy with the opportunity to achieve greater increases in the policy's cash value (and face amount, depending on the type of policy) when the selected investment fund is performing well. If the investment experience is unsatisfactory, however, the policy's cash value can decline.

Adjustable Life Insurance

Adjustable life insurance is a whole life policy that permits changes to be made in the amount of life insurance, period of protection, amount of premium, and duration of the premium-paying period. Adjustable life insurance is frequently referred to as "life cycle" insurance since certain policy changes can be made to conform to the different periods in the insured's life.

The adjustable life policy is designed to provide considerable flexibility to meet changing insurance needs over time. Within certain limits, the policyowner can make the following adjustments as the situation warrants:

- Increase or reduce the face amount of insurance
- Lengthen or shorten the period of protection
- Increase or decrease the premiums paid
- Lengthen or shorten the period for paying premiums

A cost-of-living provision also can be attached to an adjustable life policy to maintain the real purchasing power of the insurance.

The major advantage of adjustable life insurance is that within one policy the insurance can easily be adjusted to the insured's needs as they change over time. The disadvantage is that the policy is more expensive and more complex than a traditional term or ordinary life policy.

Modified Life Insurance

A modified life insurance policy is a whole life policy in which the premiums are reduced for some initial period, such as three to five years, and are higher thereafter. The initial premium paid is slightly higher than for term insurance but is substantially lower than the premium paid for an ordinary life policy issued at the same age.

There are different versions of modified life contracts. Under one version, term insurance is used for the first three to five years, which then converts automatically into an ordinary life policy at a premium higher than the premium paid for a regular ordinary life policy issued at the same age.

A second approach is to redistribute the premiums by charging lower premiums during the early years of the policy but higher premiums thereafter. For example, premiums can be gradually increased each year for five years and then remain level thereafter.

The purpose of a modified life policy is to allow policyowners to purchase permanent life insurance even though they cannot currently afford the higher premiums for a regular policy. Modified life insurance can be attractive to persons who expect their incomes to increase in the future.

Family Policy

The *family policy* is a whole life policy that insures all family members under one policy. The policy usually is sold in units that state the amount and types of life insurance on the family members. For example, one unit may consist of $5,000 of ordinary life insurance on the family head, $2,000 of term insurance to age sixty-five on the other spouse, and $1,000 of term insurance on each child to some stated age, such as twenty-five. The term insurance can be converted to some form of permanent insurance. The children are typically allowed to convert up to five times the amount of insurance on their lives with no evidence of insurability. Finally, there is no additional premium if another child is born.

LIFE INSURANCE POLICY PROVISIONS

Life insurance policies contain a number of important contractual provisions. Some of the major policy provisions that appear in life insurance contracts are examined in this section.

Ownership Clause

The owner of a life insurance policy can be the applicant, the insured, or the beneficiary. In most cases, the same person is the applicant, the insured, and the policyowner. Under the *ownership clause,* the policyowner possesses all contractual rights in the policy while the insured is still alive. These rights include the selection of a settlement option, naming and changing the beneficiary designation, election of dividend options, and other rights. These contractual rights can typically be exercised without the beneficiary's consent.

In addition, the ownership clause provides for a *change in ownership.* The policyowner can designate a new owner by filling out an appropriate form with the company. The insurer may require that the life insurance policy be endorsed to show the name of the new owner.

Incontestable Clause

Under the *incontestable clause,* the company cannot contest the policy after it has been in force two years during the insured's lifetime. The insurance company has two years to discover any irregularities in the contract, such as a material misrepresentation or concealment. If the insured dies after that time, the death claim must be paid. For example, if Joseph conceals a cancer operation when the application is filled out and dies after expiration of the incontestable period, the death claim must be paid.

The purpose of the incontestable clause is to protect the beneficiary if the insurance company tries to deny payment of the death claim years after the policy is issued. Since the insured is dead, allegations by the insurer concerning statements made in connection with the application cannot be easily refuted. After the incontestable period has expired, with few exceptions, the company must pay the death claim.

Suicide Clause

A typical *suicide clause* states that the face amount of the policy will not be paid if the insured commits suicide within two years after the policy is issued. The only payment is a refund of the premiums. The purpose of the suicide clause is to reduce adverse selection against the insurer by providing the insurer some protection against an individual who purchases a life insurance policy with the intention of committing suicide.

Grace Period

A *grace period* is another important contractual provision. A typical grace period gives the policyowner thirty-one days to pay an overdue premium. The life insurance remains in force during the grace period. If death occurs during the grace period, the overdue premium is usually deducted from the policy proceeds.

Reinstatement Clause

If the premium is not paid during the grace period, a life insurance policy may lapse for nonpayment of premiums. The *reinstatement clause* allows the policyowner the right to reinstatement of a lapsed policy under certain conditions:

- The insured must provide evidence of insurability, a condition that insurers often waive for lapses of less than two months.
- All overdue premiums plus interest must be paid.
- Any policy loan must be repaid or reinstated.
- The policy has not been surrendered for its cash surrender value.
- The lapsed policy must be reinstated within five years.

If the policyowner wishes to continue the same type of life insurance coverage, it usually is more economical to reinstate a policy than to buy a new one. This is because a new policy is likely to have a higher premium since it will be issued when the insured is older.

Misstatement of Age

The insured's age may be misstated in the application. Under the *misstatement clause,* the amount paid in the event of death is the amount of life insurance that the premium would have purchased at the insured's correct age. For example, assume that Mary's correct age is thirty but is recorded in the application as twenty-nine. Assume that the premium for an ordinary life policy at age twenty-nine is $14 per $1,000 and $15 per $1,000 at age thirty. If Mary has $15,000 of ordinary life insurance and dies, only 14/15 of the proceeds, or $14,000, will be paid.

Beneficiary Designation

The beneficiary is the person or party named in the policy to receive the policy proceeds. Following are the beneficiary designations in life insurance:

- The *primary beneficiary* is the first party who is entitled to receive the proceeds at the insured's death.
- The *contingent beneficiary* is the beneficiary entitled to the policy proceeds if the primary beneficiary is not alive.
- A *revocable beneficiary* designation means that the policyowner has the right to change the beneficiary designation without the beneficiary's consent.
- An *irrevocable beneficiary* designation means that the policyowner cannot change the beneficiary without the beneficiary's consent.
- A *specific beneficiary* designation means that the beneficiary is named and can be identified. For example, Mary Jones may be specifically named to receive the policy proceeds if her husband should die.
- A *class beneficiary* designation means that a specific individual is not named but is a member of a group to whom the proceeds are paid. One example of a class beneficiary designation would be "children of the insured."

Exclusions and Restrictions

A life insurance policy contains few exclusions and restrictions. The major exclusions or restrictions are as follows:

- The *suicide clause* excludes payment of the policy proceeds if death occurs within two years of the issue date.
- An *aviation exclusion* clause may be present in the policy. For instance, some companies exclude aviation deaths unless the insured is a fare-paying passenger on a regularly scheduled airline.
- Certain dangerous activities, such as sky diving, flying a hang glider, or automobile racing, may be excluded or covered only by payment of an additional premium.

In addition, to control adverse selection, companies may insert a war clause in the policy that excludes payment if death occurs as a result of war.

Assignment Clause

A life insurance policy can be assigned to another party if the policyowner desires. There are two types of assignments.

- An *absolute assignment* transfers all ownership rights in the policy to a new owner.
- Under a *collateral assignment*, the policy is assigned to another party as collateral for a loan. Under this type of assignment, only certain policy rights are transferred to the creditor to protect its interest.

LIFE INSURANCE OPTION PROVISIONS

Life insurance policies often contain provisions that give the policyowner, and to a limited extent the beneficiary, the right to choose among several options in the event of specified circumstances. Option provisions typically apply to (1) the manner in which the death benefit is to be paid, (2) continuation of coverage if the policyowner discontinues premium payments on a fixed-premium policy with accumulated cash value, and (3) the use of policy dividends.

Settlement Options

In life insurance, the payment of benefits following the insured's death is referred to as the settlement of the policy. A life insurance policy's *settlement options* describe the various methods by which the *policy proceeds* may be paid to the beneficiary or beneficiaries. The policy proceeds include the amount of the death benefit with the possible addition of any accumulated dividends or additional amounts of insurance purchased and possible deductions for any policy loans or unpaid premiums.

The policyowner has the right to select among the various settlement options at any time prior to the death of the insured. If the policyowner does not designate a settlement option before the death of the insured, the beneficiary has the right to select a settlement option following the insured's death. The policyowner may feel that he or she should select the settlement option if the beneficiary is a minor or an adult who is not able to handle money matters. In most cases, however, allowing the beneficiary to select the settlement option gives the beneficiary the ability to choose the method of payment that best meets his or her financial needs.

One Sum Settlement. Under this method, often referred to as a lump sum settlement, the beneficiary receives the policy proceeds in a single payment upon the death of the insured.

Proceeds at Interest. This settlement option provides that the insurer will hold the policy proceeds and make interest payments to the beneficiary. A minimum interest rate is specified in the policy, and the insurer may pay a higher rate at its discretion. Under this settlement option, as well as the other settlement options that do not guarantee a lifetime income, the beneficiary has the right to

Exhibit 10-3
Fixed Years Installments Table: Monthly Payment Amount per $1,000 of
Proceeds at 4.5 Percent Interest

Years	Payments	Years	Payments
1	$ 85.34	8	$ 12.38
2	43.61	9	11.32
3	29.71	10	10.32
4	22.76	15	7.60
5	18.60	20	6.28
6	15.83	25	5.51
7	13.86	30	5.01

withdraw all or part of the proceeds of the policy at any time. If the beneficiary
should die, the remaining proceeds are paid to the beneficiary's estate.

Fixed Years Installments. Under this settlement option, the insurer
pays out the proceeds in a series of equal monthly payments. The person select-
ing this option, the policyowner or beneficiary as the case may be, chooses the
number of years for which payments will be made. The amount of the monthly
payment depends on the amount of the policy proceeds, the number of years for
which payments are to be made, and the interest rate paid by the insurer, as
shown in Exhibit 10-3.

Fixed Amount Installments. Under this settlement option, the insurer
makes equal payments per month, or at longer intervals, in an amount chosen
by the policyowner or beneficiary. Interest is earned on the balance of the
proceeds held by the insurer. Assuming that the monthly payment is greater
than the monthly interest earned, the balance of the proceeds held by the insurer
decreases each month until the total proceeds and interest finally are paid out.

Life Income. This settlement option provides equal monthly payments
to the beneficiary for life. The amount of the monthly payment depends on the
amount of the policy proceeds, the beneficiary's sex and age at the time payments
begin, and whether payments are guaranteed for a *period certain*. Period certain means that payments will be made for the specified number of years regardless of whether the beneficiary lives to the end of that period. In the event that
the beneficiary dies during the period certain, payments will be made to the
beneficiary's designated successor. Examples of life income benefits payable
with and without a period certain are shown in Exhibit 10-4.

Under this settlement option, the beneficiary typically does not have the
right to discontinue the monthly payments and withdraw the value of the remaining payments. However, when benefits are guaranteed for a period certain
and the beneficiary dies within that period, the beneficiary's successor usually

Exhibit 10-4
Life Income table: Monthly Payment Amount per $1,000 of Proceeds
for Male and Female Payees Ages 50 to 75, With and Without
Ten-Year Period Certain

Age Last Birthday	Life		Life With 10 Years Certain	
	Male	Female	Male	Female
50	$5.06	$4.81	$5.02	$4.78
55	5,47	4.17	5.40	5.09
60	6.03	5.57	5.89	5.48
65	6.82	6.16	6.56	6.01
70	7.99	7.02	7.42	6.71
75	9.80	8.30	8.44	7.61

may elect to continue to receive monthly payments to the end of the period certain or to be paid the value of the remaining payments in a one sum settlement.

Joint Life Income. When this settlement option is chosen, equal monthly payments will be made as long as either one of two payees is alive. This option might be chosen by an insured who contributes toward the support of his or her parents. In the event of the insured's death, the parents, as beneficiaries, would receive monthly income for the rest of their lives. The amount of the monthly benefits would depend on the amount of the policy proceeds and the parents' ages at the time they began to receive the monthly payments.

Nonforfeiture Options

Life insurance policies that build up cash values contain provisions that protect the policyowner from forfeiting these cash values in the event that the policy is discontinued. If the policyowner decides to stop making premium payments on a policy, he or she may elect to use the policy's cash value in any one of several ways.

Cash Surrender. The policyowner may surrender the policy and request the insurer to pay the policy's *cash surrender value*. The cash surrender value is equal to the policy cash value, plus the cash value of any paid-up additions and any dividends, and less any policy loan or accrued loan interest. All coverage ceases when the policyowner surrenders the policy.

Reduced Paid-Up Insurance. The policyowner may request that the cash surrender value of the policy be used to purchase a reduced amount of paid-up insurance coverage under the same policy. The amount of paid-up death benefit that can be purchased will depend on the amount of the policy's cash surrender value and the insured's sex and age at the time the policyowner discontinues premium payments. The reduced amount of insurance purchased stays the same for the insured's lifetime. In addition, the policy continues to have a cash value and may pay dividends.

Extended Term Insurance. The policy cash surrender value may also be used to purchase term insurance coverage in the same amount as that provided under the original policy. While the amount of the death benefit remains the same, the coverage applies only for a limited term. The term or number of years and days of coverage will depend on the amount of the policy's cash surrender value and the insured's sex and age at the time premium payments were discontinued. This extended term insurance has no cash value.

Other Uses of Cash Surrender Value. The cash surrender value of a life insurance policy may also be used for policy loans or to pay premiums that are due.

Policy Loan. The policy loan provision allows the policyowner to borrow from the insurer an amount up to the policy's cash value. In older contracts, the rate of interest is likely to be specified in the policy. In newer contracts, the interest rate is likely to be tied to the prevailing market interest rate. There is no repayment schedule for policy loans. The policyowner may repay a policy loan when and if he or she chooses. If the policy becomes payable because of the insured's death, or if the policyowner surrenders the policy for its cash value, the amount of a policy loan and any interest due is subtracted from the policy proceeds prior to payment.

Automatic Loan Provision. The policyowner may authorize the insurer to make an automatic loan from the policy's cash value to pay any premium not paid by the end of the grace period.

Dividend Options

Some life insurance policies contain a provision under which the insurer may pay an annual dividend to the policyowner. Policies that pay dividends are referred to as *participating policies* because the policyowner participates in the earnings of the insurer through the dividend payment. The dividend options in a participating policy give the policyowner a choice among several ways in which dividends may be used.

Cash Payment. When this dividend option is chosen, the insurer sends the policyowner a check in the amount of the dividend payment.

Reduction of Premium. Under this dividend option, the policyowner's premium for the upcoming year is reduced by the amount of the current year's dividend.

Accumulation at Interest. Dividends may be held by the insurer to accumulate with interest paid at a rate specified in the policy. The insurer may pay a higher rate at its discretion. The policyowner may withdraw the accumulated dividends and interest at any time. If left on deposit with the insurer until the insured's death, the accumulated dividends and interest become part of the policy proceeds.

Paid-Up Additions. If this option is chosen, dividends are used to purchase additional amounts of paid-up life insurance under the policy. The additional insurance purchased will be of the same kind and subject to the same provisions as the original policy. Upon the insured's death, the paid-up additional insurance becomes part of the policy proceeds.

One-Year Term. Some policies allow dividends to be used to purchase one-year term coverage. In the event of the insured's death, the amount of the one-year term coverage would be added to the basic policy death benefit in determining the total proceeds payable.

LIFE INSURANCE POLICY RIDERS

In life and health insurance, the word rider is used instead of endorsement. The effect is the same, however, and life insurance riders modify the coverage under the basic policy. Three frequently used riders in individual life insurance deal with (1) waiver of premium payments in the event of disability, (2) accidental death and dismemberment benefits, and (3) the guaranteed right to purchase additional insurance.

Waiver of Premium

If the insured becomes totally disabled for longer than a specified period of time, often six months, the insurer waives the payment of premiums during the period of disability. Any premiums paid during this waiting period are refunded. Policies may use one of several definitions of "total disability," which are examined in Chapter 11 in the discussion of the disability peril. Waiver of premium is the most frequently used life insurance rider, and its provisions are included directly in some life insurance contracts.

Accidental Death and Dismemberment Benefits

Some riders provide only accidental death benefits, while others provide benefits for both accidental death and dismemberment.

Accidental Death. The accidental death benefit usually is the same amount as the policy's normal death benefit. Therefore, if the insured's death is the result of an accident, the beneficiary receives twice the face amount of the policy. This often is referred to as an accidental death *double indemnity* payment despite the fact that life insurance is a valued policy rather than a contract of indemnity.

Most accidental death riders also require that, for benefits to be paid, death must occur within a limited time after the accident. The period specified typically ranges from 90 to 180 days. Coverage usually terminates when the insured

Exhibit 10-5
Schedule of Benefits Under Dismemberment Coverage

Loss of	Benefit
Both hands	Principal sum
Both feet	Principal sum
Sight of both eyes	Principal sum
One hand and one foot	Principal sum
One hand and sight of one eye	Principal sum
One foot and sight of one eye	Principal sum
One hand	1/2 Principal sum
One foot	1/2 Principal sum
Sight of one eye	1/2 Principal sum

reaches a specified age, such as sixty-five or seventy. However, some riders provide lifetime accidental death benefits.

Dismemberment. When dismemberment coverage applies, payment is made to the insured, rather than the policy beneficiary, in the event of specified traumatic bodily injuries. The benefits payable are listed in a schedule within the rider and are stated in terms of the policy face amount or *principal sum*, as shown in Exhibit 10-5. The loss must occur within a specified period, often up to one year, following the accident. Loss caused by amputation is excluded unless medically necessary and as the result of an accidental injury.

Guaranteed Purchase Option

The guaranteed purchase option rider is used most frequently in connection with whole life insurance rather than term. Under the provisions of the rider, the insurer guarantees to issue additional coverage on the life of the insured *without evidence of insurability*, at specified intervals, until a given age. For instance, the rider may guarantee the issuance of additional coverage at the policy anniversary date nearest the insured's birthday for ages twenty-five, twenty-eight, thirty-one, thirty-four, thirty-seven, and forty. The total amount of additional coverage that may be purchased typically is equal to the original policy face.

LIFE INSURANCE UNDERWRITING

Life insurance underwriting practices are aimed at developing a profitable and growing book of business for the insurer. To accomplish this goal, life insurance underwriters attempt to provide coverage for a group of insureds whose expected mortality rate is lower than the expected mortality rate of the population as a whole. If it is successful in its underwriting efforts, the insurer will avoid the consequences of adverse selection and achieve an average or better spread of exposures on the lives it insures.

Underwriting Factors for Individual Coverage

Individual life insurance is priced on a class basis. Prospective insureds are classed on the basis of a number of factors that insurer experience has shown to predict expected mortality rates. The principal rating factors are age, sex, health, and occupation.

Age. Mortality rates, often expressed in terms of deaths per 1,000 persons, increase with age. For this reason, the cost of purchasing a life insurance policy increases as a person's age increases.

Sex. On average, women in the United States live seven years longer than men. Therefore, all other things being equal, the cost of life insurance for a woman is lower than for a man of the same age.

Health. An applicant's personal health and, to some extent, the health history of his or her family help indicate to a life insurance underwriter whether the applicant presents an average or better than average "risk" for the insurer. In evaluating an individual's health, insurers consider whether the applicant or several family members have had illnesses such as cancer, heart disease, hypertension, or diabetes. On average, persons with a health history including these diseases are likely to have a higher than normal mortality rate.

In assessing an individual's current health, life insurers may use information supplied by the applicant as well as the applicant's physician and hospital records. The applicant may also be asked to have a physical examination that includes blood and urine tests and an electrocardiogram (EKG). Because of the link between smoking and lung and heart disease, most insurers offer lower rates to nonsmokers.

Occupation and Avocation. Some occupations are more hazardous than others. Likewise, some hobbies such as flying and scuba diving are more dangerous than others. On average, applicants with hazardous occupations or avocations are likely to have a higher than normal mortality rate.

Personal Habits. When a large amount of coverage is requested, life insurers frequently investigate the personal circumstances of the applicant's life. Such an investigation might seek information on potential problem areas such as alcohol or drug use, poor driving record, or financial troubles.

Foreign Travel or Recent Immigration. Persons who have traveled or resided outside of the United States shortly before applying for life insurance coverage may have been exposed to diseases not commonly found in this country. Also, mortality rates may be different in other countries. An insurer may require special medical tests or a postponement of coverage for such persons.

Underwriting Actions

On the basis of information provided by the applicant and the other sources noted above, life insurance underwriters take one of three actions. First, the applicant may be rated "standard" and charged the normal premium for the desired coverage. More than 90 percent of life insurance applicants qualify for coverage on this basis. Second, the applicant may be rated as "substandard" and charged a higher premium. About 4 percent of life insurance applicants are rated substandard. Finally, about 3 percent of life insurance applications are declined because the chance of loss is too great to provide the requested coverage.[9]

In addition to these three basic underwriting actions, many insurers also identify "preferred risks" for whom they will provide standard coverage at a reduced premium. To be rated as a "preferred risk," an individual must be in excellent health and meet or exceed the insurer's other underwriting criteria. As noted above, most life insurers also classify nonsmokers as preferred risks for whom lower premiums are charged.

GROUP LIFE INSURANCE

Up to this point, the discussion of life insurance has focused on individual life insurance—contracts purchased by individuals to provide security for themselves and their families. However, for many families, a substantial part of the life insurance on the family wage earner(s) is provided by group life insurance.

Differences Between Individual and Group Life Insurance

There are several major differences between individual and group life insurance.[10] These differences are related primarily to the underwriting, marketing, and administration of group insurance plans, rather than significant differences in the basic kinds of protection available to the insured.

Underwriting Criteria. The underwriting of individual life insurance focuses on the characteristics of the individual insured. In group insurance, the underwriter evaluates the characteristics of the group of persons to be insured. With the exception of very small groups, the individual characteristics of the persons in the group are not considered in underwriting a group policy.

Policyowner. In individual life insurance the policyowner is an individual, often the insured or a family member. In group life insurance the policy or *master contract* is issued by the insurer to the group insurance plan sponsor. For instance, when an employer provides group life insurance as part of its employee benefits plan, the parties to the master contract are the employer and the insurer. While an employee covered under the plan has certain rights, such as naming his or her beneficiary, the employee receives a *certificate of insurance,* not an insurance policy.

Marketing and Administration. Individual life insurance policies are sold on a one-to-one basis, with a substantial part of the first years' premiums allocated for marketing expense. In addition, each policy requires individual record keeping and billing by the insurer. In group life insurance, the marketing and insurer administrative expenses, even though higher than for an individual policy, may be spread over the premium charged for hundreds or thousands of persons insured under one group policy. In addition, the group plan sponsor often undertakes some of the day-to-day record keeping responsibilities. The net result is that the overall cost of group life insurance usually is lower than that of comparable individual coverage. However, the benefits provided generally are predetermined by the plan without regard to the insured's needs, and the advice and service provided by the life insurance producer are absent.

Rating. Individual life insurance policy premiums are determined on the basis of class rates. Premiums for group policies, especially those covering a large number of insureds, are based on experience rating. Under experience rating, past losses sustained by the group are considered in determining the policy premium. As a general rule, the larger the group size, the more predictive value is placed on its previous loss experience, and the greater will be the effect of this loss experience on the overall cost of coverage.

Groups Eligible for Coverage

State insurance regulations specify the kinds of groups that are eligible for group life insurance coverage. While there are differences between the states, the following kinds of organizations usually may sponsor a group plan:

1. *Employers.* Persons eligible for coverage include current and retired employees of the business firm and its subsidiaries, directors of a corporation, partners, sole proprietors, and independent contractors. Some states also allow dependents of employees to be covered.
2. *Unions.* Union members may be covered under a master contract issued to a union.
3. *Creditors.* Organizations in the business of making loans, such as banks, mortgage companies, credit unions, and finance companies, may provide life insurance coverage for persons who borrow money from them. The cost of coverage is paid by the borrower. The amount of coverage typically is equal to the unpaid balance of the loan and is payable to the creditor to satisfy the debt in the event of the insured debtor's death.
4. *Other Groups.* Professional, trade, and veterans associations as well as alumni, religious, and social groups may also act as sponsors of group life insurance plans.

Group Life Insurance Underwriting

State insurance regulations, many of which are based on the National Association of Insurance Commissioners Model Group Life Insurance Bill, often set requirements that must be followed by insurers in underwriting group life insurance. In addition, insurers evaluate a number of characteristics of a group in underwriting group life policies.

Statutory Requirements. While regulations vary from state to state, the following requirements often are imposed on group life insurance underwriting.

Insurance Incidental to the Group.   To avoid adverse selection against the insurer, the purchase of group insurance must be incidental to the purpose of the group. This is because a group whose underlying purpose was to purchase group life insurance would most likely consist largely of persons whose health or other personal characteristics precluded them from purchasing individual coverage at standard premiums.

Minimum Size.   Many states require that a group consist of at least ten persons under an employer-sponsored plan. Larger group sizes may be required for other types of plan sponsors. Some states do not require a minimum group size, leaving this decision to life underwriters.

Minimum Participation Percentages.   Under employer-sponsored plans for which the employer pays the full premium, 100 percent of eligible employees may be required to be covered under the plan. Such plans are referred to as *noncontributory* because employees do not contribute to the cost of coverage. Under a *contributory* plan, one in which employees contribute toward the cost of coverage, a minimum of 75 percent of eligible employees is usually required to participate in the plan.

Insurer Requirements.   Insurers underwriting group life insurance have a number of concerns, in addition to the statutory requirements, as they decide whether to provide coverage and, if so, at what premium. These concerns include the composition of the group and other factors.

Composition of the Group.   Insurers consider the age and sex of group members because the death rate is higher at older ages, and men have a higher death rate than women of the same age. The average income of the group may also be considered because of differences in expected death rates between low and high income groups.

Flow of Persons Through the Group.   Ideally, a group should be composed of persons of a variety of ages, with younger people joining the group from time to time as older people leave it. If the average age of the group remains relatively constant, the group's loss experience also will remain relatively stable over time. This allows the insurer to more accurately predict its loss costs and required premiums.

Group Size and Persistency.   An insurer's ability to predict long-term loss costs is enhanced when the group size is large and when the coverage extends over a multi-year period. Therefore, large groups, which are expected to persist into the future and to continue their coverage with the insurer, are more desirable than small groups with doubtful persistency.

Sponsor Cooperation and Participation.   Insurers favor groups in which the holder of the master contract is willing and able to (1) provide effective assistance in the day-to-day operation of the plan and (2) share in the cost of coverage for plan members, thereby gaining an incentive to control the overall cost of the plan.

Group Life Insurance Coverage

Most group life insurance is written under a yearly renewable term insurance policy. Like its counterpart in individual life insurance, this policy provides pure protection with no savings element and is renewable on a yearly basis. Up to $50,000 of yearly renewable term coverage may be provided by an employer to an employee without any income tax consequences to the employee. For employer-paid coverage in excess of $50,000, the employee must pay federal income tax on the value of the premium for the excess coverage.

Continuation of Coverage

Group life insurance policies contain provisions that allow the insured to continue coverage upon termination of employment or retirement *without providing proof of insurability.*

Conversion Privilege. The employee may purchase an individual life insurance policy—most often a whole life policy—from the insurer that provides the employer's master contract. The application and payment for this individual policy must be made to the insurer within thirty-one days of termination of employment. The amount of coverage may not exceed the amount provided under the group plan. The policy premium is based on the benefit amount, type of policy purchased, and the insured's age and rating class. A separate, more restrictive conversion privilege often applies if coverage is terminated because the master contract is canceled.

Extension of Coverage. Coverage under the master contract automatically applies to the thirty-one-day period following the termination of employment regardless of whether the employee applies for individual coverage. If the insured dies within thirty-one days of termination of employment, the group policy's benefits are payable in full.

Reduced Benefits on Retirement. Some plans provide reduced benefit amounts to retired employees. One approach provides all retired employees with a fixed amount of coverage for life. Under another approach, benefits are gradually reduced each year after retirement until they reach a specified percentage of the insured's preretirement benefit amount.

SUMMARY

In an economic sense, premature death means that a person dies with outstanding unfulfilled financial obligations, such as a mortgage, family members to support, and children to educate. The costs of premature death include the income loss to the family, additional family expenses, possible costs to the welfare system, and noneconomic losses. Life insurance is one method of alleviating the economic consequences of premature death. One method for estimating the amount of life insurance a family should have is the needs approach.

The three basic types of life insurance are term, whole life, and endowment. Term insurance policies develop no cash value and offer only temporary protection; however, they may be renewable and also convertible to whole life coverage. In addition, the premium for term insurance increases with age. Term insurance includes policies that provide level benefits for terms of up to twenty years or until age sixty-five or seventy as well as policies with decreasing benefits over terms of ten to thirty years.

Whole life insurance may be divided into the categories of ordinary and limited payment. Under ordinary life insurance, premiums are payable for life up to age 100. Limited payment life insurance policies require premium payments only for a specified number of years. All whole life policies develop a cash value because the premiums collected during the early years of the policy are in excess of the amount necessary to fund the insurer's net amount at risk.

Endowment policies pay proceeds to the named beneficiary if the insured dies during the policy period, and to the policyowner if the insured survives that period.

Several variations on the whole life insurance product have been developed to give the policyowner more flexibility in meeting his or her overall financial and estate planning objectives. These life insurance products include (1) universal life, (2) variable life, (3) variable-universal life, (4) adjustable life, and (5) modified life. In addition, insurers offer the family policy to provide life insurance coverage on all members of an insured's immediate family.

Life insurance policies contain a number of provisions that are important to understanding the nature of the life insurance contract: ownership clause, incontestable clause, suicide clause, grace period, and reinstatement clause. Other important policy provisions deal with misstatement of age, beneficiary designation, exclusions and restrictions, and policy assignment. Life insurance policies also contain provisions that give the policyowner, and to a limited extent the beneficiary, options as to how specified situations may be handled. These option provisions apply to the settlement of the policy, use of policy cash value if premium payments are discontinued, and the use of dividends under participating policies. Three frequently used riders that modify basic policy provisions are waiver of premium, accidental death and dismemberment benefits, and the guaranteed purchase option.

In underwriting life insurance, insurers seek to develop and maintain a growing and profitable book of business. The selection and rating of applicants in an effort to meet this objective requires consideration of a potential insured's age, sex, health history, occupation and avocations, personal habits, and other matters. Based on the insurer's evaluation of an applicant, it may be decided to provide insurance at either standard or substandard rates, or to decline the application.

Group life insurance differs from individual life insurance in terms of the underwriting criteria used, the ownership of the policy, marketing and administration, and rating methods. Group coverage may be sponsored by employers, unions, creditors, and other groups. Group life insurance is most commonly funded by yearly renewable term insurance. All group policies contain provisions for the continuation of an insured's coverage in the event that the insured leaves the covered group or the group master contract is canceled.

Chapter Notes

1. George E. Rejda, *Social Insurance and Economic Security*, 4th ed. (Englewood Cliffs, NJ: Prentice Hall, 1991), Chapter 3.
2. *1989 Life Insurance Factbook Update* (Washington, DC: American Council of Life Insurance, 1989), p. 12.
3. The material on life insurance in this chapter is based on Glenn L. Wood, Claude C. Lilly III, Donald S. Malecki, Edward E. Graves, and Jerry S. Rosenbloom, *Personal Risk Management and Insurance*, 4th ed., vol. II (Malvern, PA: American Institute for Property and Liability Underwriters, 1989), Chapters 8 and 9; and George E. Rejda, *Principles of Insurance*, 3rd ed. (Glenview, IL: Scott, Foresman and Company, 1989), Chapters 16-18.
4. *1989 Life Insurance Factbook Update*, p. 7.
5. The death rate actually declines from birth to age ten and then increases at an increasing rate as the person gets older.
6. *1989 Life Insurance Factbook Update*, p. 7.
7. *1989 Life Insurance Factbook Update*, p. 7.
8. *1989 Life Insurance Factbook Update*, p. 7.
9. *1989 Life Insurance Factbook Update*, p. 54.
10. This comparison of group and individual coverages is based on Davis W. Gregg and Vane B. Lucas, *Life and Health Insurance Handbook*, 3rd ed. (Homewood, IL: Richard D. Irwin, 1973), pp. 352-353.

CHAPTER 11

Health Insurance

Health insurance provides protection to individuals and families for financial losses resulting from sickness and accidental injury. Health insurance may be divided into two broad categories—medical insurance and disability insurance. Various kinds of medical insurance policies are available to pay for the cost of care by physicians and other medical professionals, hospital charges, laboratory fees, and other related medical expenses. Disability insurance policies typically pay benefits when injury or illness prevents the insured from working.

As with the life insurance policies treated in Chapter 10, there are no "standard forms" of health insurance policies comparable to the ISO homeowners and personal auto policies examined earlier in this text. Each health insurer prepares its own policy forms in which the coverages offered are tailored to meet the insurer's underwriting and marketing objectives. There are, however, certain coverages, limitations on coverage, and exclusions that appear in most health insurance policies of a given kind. In addition, there are uniform policy provisions, some that state insurance regulations require in all health insurance contracts and others that are optional. The discussions of health insurance policies in this chapter focus on those provisions found in a "typical" policy providing a specific kind of coverage as well as the uniform provisions set forth in state insurance regulations.

This chapter begins by examining the various kinds of medical insurance policies. The next section of the chapter focuses on disability insurance. As noted above, both medical and disability insurance policies contain a number of similar provisions, many of which are required by state law. These health insurance policy provisions are examined in the next major section. The chapter concludes with a look at health insurance underwriting and the providers of health insurance, including private insurers, service associations such as Blue Cross and Blue Shield, and health maintenance organizations.

MEDICAL INSURANCE

Medical insurance can be purchased to provide coverage for virtually any kind of necessary medical expense. In medical insurance, the perils insured against are sickness and accidental bodily injury. Sickness or injury can lead the insured to incur a wide variety of medical costs. One major difference between the various kinds of medical insurance policies is the specific types of medical costs for which each kind of policy provides benefits. Three categories of medical insurance are examined here: (1) medical expense insurance, (2) dental expense insurance, and (3) limited medical policies.

Medical Expense Insurance

Medical expense insurance, like many other life and health coverages, may be written on an individual or group basis. At one time, broad medical expense coverages were available only when written on a group basis. Today, however, broad medical expense coverage is also available to medically qualified individual insureds. Some restrictions may apply to such individually written coverages, and the coverage flexibility and experience rating found in the group coverage are absent. Nevertheless, the medical expense coverages now available to both individuals and groups are very similar. For this reason, the following discussions of medical expense insurance coverages apply to both individual and group policies unless otherwise specifically noted.

Medical expense insurance policies can be written to provide coverage for an individual insured or for an insured and his or her immediate family. Family members qualifying for coverage typically include the insured's spouse and any unmarried dependent children until they reach a specified age—frequently age nineteen. Some policies extend coverage for unmarried dependents up to age twenty-three or twenty-four if they are full-time college students. In addition, most policies continue coverage for an insured's physically handicapped or mentally retarded child after the child's nineteenth birthday. To be eligible for continued coverage, an incapacitated child must meet the following criteria: (1) be insured under the policy and become incapacitated before reaching age nineteen and (2) remain incapacitated, unmarried, and a dependent of the insured.

Medical expense insurance written by private insurers typically provides worldwide coverage. These policies usually do not contain any definition of the "territory" in which coverage applies, and they do not require that insureds receive medical treatment from specified physicians or treatment facilities. There are, however, some limitations on the selection of physicians and hospitals as well as on geographic coverage areas under medical insurance plans offered through some other health care coverage providers. These limitations will be discussed when the various kinds of health care coverage providers are examined later in this chapter.

There are two types of medical expense insurance policies—those which provide *basic medical expense coverages* and those which provide *major medical expense coverage*.[1] More than 180 million persons in the United States have either one or both of these medical expense coverages.[2]

Basic Medical Expense Coverages. Basic medical expense insurance may include coverage for one or more of the following three kinds of medical expense: (1) hospital expense, (2) surgical expense, and (3) physicians expense (also referred to as regular medical expense). Hospital expense insurance and surgical expense insurance can be purchased separately or together in one policy. Physicians expense coverage is usually available only when written in connection with one of the other basic medical expense coverages.

Basic medical expense coverages have traditionally provided benefits on a *first-dollar basis*. This means that coverage applies to the first dollar of medical expense incurred. In recent years, however, insurers have begun to write basic medical expense policies with deductibles of $100 or more. Unlike a property insurance deductible, which typically applies separately to each covered loss, a medical expense deductible frequently applies on a policy-year or calendar-year basis. (Some individual policies do apply the deductible on a per-sickness basis.) After an insured pays his or her own medical expenses in the amount of the deductible during the year, the insurer pays the balance of covered medical expenses in full, up to the policy limits. However, payments may be subject to *inside limits* in the policy. A health insurance policy's inside limits state the maximum amount that the policy will pay for specified expenses. For instance, hospital expense coverage may have an inside limit of $250 per day for hospital room and board charges. An insured who desires lower or higher inside limits in a basic medical expense policy often may obtain that coverage by purchasing a more costly version of the policy.

Hospital Expense Coverage. The typical hospital expense policy provides coverage for hospital room and board, including treatment in an intensive care unit, operating room fees, laboratory tests, and other medically necessary hospital services and supplies. In addition, coverage often is provided for hospital emergency room treatment within a limited time (twenty-four to seventy-two hours) after an accident. Other coverages may include treatment in a skilled nursing facility or at home by a health care agency, following a covered hospital confinement. Auxiliary services such as ambulance fees and a wide range of other expenses related to an insured's hospitalization may also be covered. Covered room and board charges are usually limited to the cost of a semi-private room unless a private room or treatment in an intensive care unit is medically necessary. Not covered are an insured's personal expenses such as television rental and telephone charges.

Surgical Expense Coverage. This coverage pays for physicians fees related to surgery. A surgical expense policy providing narrow coverage may pay only the fee of the physician actually performing the surgery. However, many surgical expense policies also pay for related physicians fees, such as those charged for administering anesthesia during surgery.

Most surgical expense policies have inside limits. Some policies contain a *surgical schedule* that lists the maximum amounts payable for various kinds of operations. A second method of limiting the amount payable for a particular type of operation is based on what is called a *relative value schedule*. Policies with this kind of limit also contain a comprehensive list of surgical procedures. However, rather than listing a maximum dollar amount for each procedure, the relative value schedule lists a numerical value or weight for each procedure. Simple operations have lower numerical values, and more complicated operations have higher values. To determine the dollar amount of coverage for a given operation, the number representing the relative value of that operation is multiplied by a dollar amount based on the current level of surgeons fees in the geographical area where the surgery is being performed. A third method of determining the amount payable for various procedures also attempts to recognize geographical differences in surgical fees. This method of stating surgical fee limits provides that the policy will pay an amount up to the *reasonable and customary* charges prevailing in the insured's area for a particular type of surgical procedure.

Physicians Expense. This coverage pays for physicians fees for treatment other than surgery. Physicians expense insurance was originally written to provide coverage only for in-hospital doctor visits. Today, physicians expense coverage provided under group plans often pays doctor bills for medical treatment that occurs in the hospital, the doctor's office, and even in the home. Some individual policies continue to provide only the in-hospital benefit. The costs of diagnostic X-rays and laboratory tests are also often covered under physicians expense insurance.

Inside limits typically apply. Each policy usually lists dollar limits for the various types of doctor visits they cover. Coverage under both individual and group policies is typically limited to doctor visits for the treatment of sickness or accidental injury. Routine physical examinations, flu shots, immunization for foreign travel, and other medical expenses within the control of the insured are not usually covered.

Major Medical Expense Insurance. Major medical expense insurance is designed to cover serious illnesses and accidents that are expensive to treat. Major medical coverage is characterized by high policy limits—lifetime limits of $250,000 to $1 million are common. Some major medical policies provide coverage with no lifetime limit. Because the intent is to provide protection against catastrophic medical expenses, coverage under these policies is always subject to a deductible. In addition, major medical expense coverage includes a coinsurance or participation provision that requires the insured to pay for part of the cost of covered medical expenses.

Types of Policies. Major medical insurance may be provided in one of two ways. A *supplementary major medical expense* policy may be written to "wrap around" basic medical expense coverages provided in a separate policy, in much the same way that a personal liability umbrella policy supplements the basic liability protection provided by an insured's auto and homeowners policies. When major medical expense insurance is provided on a supplementary basis, coverage under the insured's basic medical expense policy provides the primary protection in the event of loss. The supplementary major medical expense policy covers the cost of medical treatment in excess of the limits of the underlying basic medical expense policy. In addition, a supplementary major medical expense policy may provide payment for some medical expenses not normally covered under basic medical expense insurance.

The second type of major medical expense coverage is provided under a *comprehensive major medical expense* policy. This policy includes coverage for the basic hospital, surgical, and physicians expenses, plus major medical expenses, together in one policy.

Covered Expenses. Major medical expense insurance provides coverage for necessary medical expenses with few exclusions. All of the hospital costs, physicians fees, and related medical expenses covered under the three basic medical expense coverages also are covered under a major medical expense policy. In addition, this type of policy may include payment for medically necessary private-duty nursing care, the cost of prescription drugs, and hospice care for the terminally ill.

Major medical expense policies typically have fewer inside limits than basic medical expense policies. Hospital room and board charges are usually payable on a semi-private room basis unless care in a private room or intensive care unit is medically necessary. Physicians fees for medical and surgical treatment are typically payable on the basis of reasonable and customary charges. Fee schedules, such as those found in basic surgical and physicians expense policies, are not usually found in major medical expense policies. Inside limits may apply to items such as physicians fees for hospital admittance and discharge, and fees charged by assisting surgeons. As with basic hospital expense coverage, items of personal expense incurred during hospitalization are not covered.

Deductible. Both comprehensive and supplementary major medical expense policies include deductible provisions. The amount of the deductible can range from $100 up to $1,000 or more. As with property insurance, a higher deductible will result in a lower premium for comparable coverage. In individual policies, the deductible often applies to all covered expenses that the insured incurs during the one-year policy term. However, in some individual policies that provide narrower coverage, the deductible applies separately to each covered sickness or accidental injury. Group policies usually apply the deductible to all covered expenses within a calendar year.

The deductible applies in a slightly different manner depending on whether coverage is provided on a comprehensive or supplementary basis. For purposes of illustration, assume that a $300 deductible applies to a major medical policy covering only one insured. If the policy is written on a comprehensive basis, the insured will bear the full cost of the first $300 of covered expenses within the policy or calendar year. Coverage under the comprehensive policy will apply only to those expenses in excess of $300.

If coverage is provided under a supplementary policy, the deductible does not come into play until after the insured's medical expenses exceed the limits of liability of the underlying basic medical expense coverages. The following example illustrates the application of the deductible under a supplementary major medical expense policy. Assume that an insured has a basic hospital expense policy that provides first-dollar coverage for up to $10,000 of covered expenses. The insured also carries a supplementary major medical expense policy with a $300 deductible and a $1 million limit. If the insured incurs $11,000 in hospital expenses covered under the two policies, benefits will be paid in the following manner. The first $10,000 of the insured's covered charges will be paid in full by the hospital expense policy. The insured will have $1,000 of remaining expenses to be covered under the supplementary major medical expense policy. The supplementary policy's $300 deductible will apply to this $1,000, leaving $700 in expenses covered under the policy. (The insured's actual recovery under the supplementary policy will be less than $700 because of the operation of the policy's coinsurance provision, which is described below.) Because a supplementary policy's deductible applies when the transition is made between the basic coverages and the major medical expense coverage, it often is referred to as a *corridor deductible*.

Several other provisions regarding deductibles are found in major medical expense policies and are applicable to coverage written on a comprehensive or supplementary basis. In the example above, coverage was assumed to apply only to one insured. When coverage is provided for a family, the policy typically requires that a separate deductible apply to the medical expenses incurred by each insured, but with a cap on the family's total deductible. Such a provision might stipulate that a $100 deductible shall apply to the medical expenses of up to three family members during the policy period or calendar year. After three family members have incurred covered expenses of $100 each, no further deductible would apply to the covered medical expenses of any family member during the policy period or calendar year.

In addition, major medical expense policies usually contain a *common accident clause*, which provides that if two or more family members are injured in the same accident, the deductible for only one insured will apply to all covered medical expenses arising from the common accident.

An additional deductible provision is typically included in comprehensive policies that apply the deductible on a calendar-year basis. This provision allows insureds to carry over covered but unreimbursed medical expenses from the last three months of the prior calendar year to meet the current year's deductible. This is called a *deductible carry over provision*. For example, assume that an insured is covered under a policy with a $300 calendar-year deductible and had only the following covered medical expenses during the prior year: $50 in May, $125 in October, and $100 in December. Because the insured's total covered expenses of $275 were less than the policy deductible, no payment would have been made under the policy during the prior year. However, under the carry over provision, the insured would be allowed to apply $225 of unreimbursed expenses from the months of October and December toward the current year's deductible.

Coinsurance.   The major medical expense *coinsurance provision* is also referred to as the *percentage participation clause*, because it requires the insured to participate in, or pay for part of, the cost of covered expenses. Unlike the property insurance coinsurance provision that applies only when an insured does not carry adequate coverage limits, the major medical expense coinsurance provision applies regardless of the policy limits carried by the insured. Under the most frequently used coinsurance provision, the insured pays 20 percent of covered expenses above the deductible, and the insurer pays the remaining 80 percent.

In the event of a serious illness or accident resulting in substantial medical expenses, a coinsurance provision that applies to *all* covered expenses above the deductible would result in financial hardship for most families. Consequently, major medical expense policies typically include a *stop loss provision*, which limits an insured's participation in the total cost of the medical treatment. Two forms of stop loss provisions are commonly used: (1) the *dollar limit* and (2) the *covered expenses limit*. Under a dollar limit stop loss provision, the policy's coinsurance requirement no longer applies *after the insured has paid a speci-fied dollar amount*, such as $1,000 or $2,000, toward the cost of a covered illness or accident. Amounts paid by the insured under both the policy's deductible and coinsurance provisions are counted toward the stop loss limit specified in the policy. Under a covered expenses limit, the insured's participation stops *after the total amount of covered expenses in excess of the deductible reaches a specified limit* such as $5,000 or $10,000.

Medical Expense Coverage Limitations. Basic and major medical expense policies are likely to include limitations on coverage for the following:

- Maternity in individual policies
- Mental illness
- Alcohol or drug dependency

Maternity. Many individual medical expense policies do not include mater-nity benefits. However, maternity benefits may frequently be obtained by adding a maternity benefit rider at an increase in premium. Group medical expense plans sponsored by employers with fifteen or more employees are required by federal law to include maternity benefits on the same basis as benefits provided for covered illnesses. Smaller group plans may place some limitations on mater-nity benefits.

Medical expense policies that limit maternity benefits differentiate between maternity benefits and the cost of medical expenses arising out of complications due to pregnancy. Maternity benefits are typically defined to include physicians fees for prenatal and postnatal care, and physicians and hospital charges in connection with a normal delivery, surgical delivery, miscarriage, or abortion. These types of medical expenses may be excluded or limited under some medical expense policies. However, all medical expense insurance covers expenses that result from complications due to pregnancy, such as nonelective Caesarean section, toxemia, Rh factor problems, and similar conditions.

When maternity benefits are included in an individual or small group policy, there usually are limitations on coverage intended to reduce the effects of ad-verse selection. One commonly used limitation is a *waiting period*. In health insurance, a waiting period is a specified amount of time after a person is insured under a policy during which coverage for certain expenses does not apply. A waiting period of twelve to twenty-four months is common in policies that limit maternity benefits.

Mental Illness. Coverage for mental illness is subject to limitations because, to some extent, the insured has control over the costs incurred under this cover-age especially when treatment consists of a series of office visits. Coverage may be limited in a number of ways:

- Limiting the total amount of expense payable under the policy
- Making an inside limit on the covered amount per office visit
- Limiting coverage to a specified number of office visits, such as one per week or a total of ten during the coverage period
- In major medical expense policies, applying a 50-50 coinsurance provision to office visits

Coverage for hospital treatment of mental illness usually is provided on the same basis as coverage for any other illness. However, the limit on total expense for the treatment of mental illness would still apply.

Alcohol and Drug Dependency. Coverage for alcoholism, chemical dependency, and drug addiction is usually limited to inpatient treatment at a state-licensed residential treatment center or hospital to which the insured is admitted on the recommendation of a physician. Benefits are typically payable for a limited number of days of treatment, ranging from thirty to forty-five days. Otherwise, the benefits payable are comparable to those for inpatient treatment of other diseases.

Cost Containment Provisions. In recent years, many insurers have added provisions to both basic hospital and surgical expense policies and major medical expense policies that are designed to encourage insureds to be more selective in the medical expenses they incur. The goal of these provisions is to reduce the overall cost of medical care and to eliminate expenses for medical procedures that may not be necessary.

Cost containment provisions are designed to encourage insureds to use such services as the following:

- Preadmission testing
- Outpatient surgery
- Hospice care
- Second surgical opinions

Use of the above services is encouraged by providing a higher level of reimbursement to the insured than ordinarily would be available under the policy. Payment is often subject to no deductible and may be reimbursed at 100 percent rather than 80 percent.

Preadmission Testing. When surgery is scheduled, routine tests can often be performed on an outpatient basis before the insured is admitted to the hospital for surgery. The full cost of preadmission testing often qualifies for 100 percent reimbursement.

Outpatient Surgery. Outpatient surgery is performed on a patient who is not admitted to a hospital for an overnight stay. An insured who elects to have outpatient surgery may need to have outpatient testing a day or two before surgery and be able to recuperate at home. However, by complying with the policy's cost containment provisions, the insured's hospital expenses and surgical fees may be paid at a higher rate or in full.

Hospice Care. Hospice care is special care provided to the terminally ill, usually cancer patients, and includes counseling services for the patient and family members. Hospice care may involve the administration of drugs or the operation of life-support devices, but it does not require the full range of medical services available in a hospital. Benefits are frequently paid at a higher rate if hospice care is provided outside of the hospital setting either at home or in a hospice care center.

Second Surgical Opinion. Payment for second opinions at 100 percent, with no deductible, is a commonly used cost containment provision. The cost of second surgical opinions is often paid for such operations as back surgery, bone surgery of the foot, breast removal, cataract removal, coronary bypass surgery, gall bladder removal, hysterectomy, knee surgery on cartilage, prostate removal, reconstruction of the nose, and tonsillectomy and/or adenoidectomy.

In addition, some major medical expense policies contain what amounts to a penalty provision if the insured elects to have a listed type of surgery performed without obtaining a second surgical opinion. One such penalty provision reduces the insurer's payment for covered expenses from 80 percent to 50 percent. This penalty provision does not apply, however, when there is a malignancy or when hemorrhaging or other traumatic conditions are present.

Medical Expense Exclusions. Medical expense policies typically exclude coverage for expenses arising out of elective treatment, hazardous activities, situations in which the insured incurs no expense, and types of treatment for which other insurance is available. The following exclusions often are found in medical expense policies:

- *Workers compensation.* Illness or injury for which the insured is eligible for coverage under any workers compensation or occupational disease act is excluded.
- *Intentional injury.* Treatment required as a result of self-inflicted injury or attempted suicide is excluded.
- *Drugs.* Treatment required as the result of the use of drugs or other controlled substances, except as prescribed by a physician, is excluded.
- *Dental.* Routine dental care is excluded. However, coverage often is provided for treatment of accidental injury to natural teeth and for oral surgery.
- *Other than as fare-paying aircraft passenger.* Some policies specifically exclude injuries resulting from the operation and use of private aircraft.
- *War.* Injury or sickness resulting from war, declared or undeclared, or war-like acts is excluded.
- *Military service.* No coverage is provided if the insured becomes a member of any military service. Individual policies typically provide for a refund of premium if the insured joins the military.
- *Eye exams.* No coverage is provided for routine eye exams, glasses, or contact lenses. The costs of fitting and purchasing hearing aids are also excluded.
- *Cosmetic surgery.* Coverage for cosmetic surgery is provided only when it is required following a covered injury or to correct a congenital anomaly of a covered child.

- *Infertility.* Treatment for infertility, artificial insemination, and reversal of sterilization are excluded.
- *Not authorized by a physician.* Treatment not authorized or performed by a licensed physician is excluded.
- *Government facilities.* No coverage is provided for treatment in government facilities or by a physician who is a member of the insured's family if the insured would not have been required to pay for the treatment in the absence of medical insurance.

Dental Expense Insurance

Dental expense insurance is offered almost exclusively as part of group insurance plans. Prior to 1960, relatively few group medical benefit plans included dental expense coverage. Today, however, over 95 million people in the United States are covered by dental expense insurance.[3]

Dental Expense Coverage. Benefits under dental expense insurance may be provided on a *comprehensive basis* or *schedule basis*. When coverage is provided on a comprehensive basis, the approach to coverage is similar to that under a comprehensive major medical expense policy. A comprehensive dental expense policy covers most dental procedures including dentists' fees for oral surgery, root canal work, dentures, bridges, and braces. Payment under a comprehensive policy is typically made on the basis of reasonable and customary charges prevailing in the insured's area. Covered expenses are subject to deductible and coinsurance provisions similar to those in comprehensive major medical expense policies. The deductible provisions usually include a cap on the total annual deductible per family and a single-accident provision. An 80-20 coinsurance provision is most frequently used. Comprehensive dental insurance may be written under a separate policy, or it may be integrated within a major medical expense insurance plan. When written on an integrated basis, medical and dental expenses often may be combined to satisfy the policy's deductible provision.

Dental expense insurance provided on a schedule basis is similar in its approach to coverage to a surgical expense policy containing a schedule of covered expenses. A schedule within the policy lists the maximum amount payable for various kinds of dental services. Covered dental expenses under this type of policy may also be subject to deductible and coinsurance provisions similar to those in comprehensive dental expense policies.

In addition to covering dental treatment, dental expense policies usually also include coverage for routine dental checkups and cleaning. As an incentive to insureds to have regular dental checkups, some dental plans waive the policy deductible, the coinsurance provision, or both for one or two checkups per year.

Limitations on Coverage. Dental expense coverage is often subject to an annual limit, such as $1,000 per covered person. Dental expense policies usually have inside limits that apply to items such as dentures, bridges, inlays, crowns, and braces. A lifetime, per-person limit, such as $1,000, may apply to braces. Another approach to limiting recovery is to make the payment for such items subject to a 50-50 coinsurance provision. In addition, coverage for braces, gold inlays, and other charges within control of the insured may be subject to both an inside limit and a 50-50 coinsurance provision.

The exclusions in dental expense insurance are similar to those in major medical expense insurance. Dental coverage also typically excludes crowns installed for cosmetic purposes, procedures designed to improve the insured's appearance, and kinds of treatment that do not meet the standards of practice accepted by the American Dental Association.

Limited Medical Policies

As compared with medical expense policies, which usually provide worldwide coverage for sickness or injury with few exclusions, limited medical policies provide coverage that applies only for specified causes of loss or types of loss, and in limited dollar amounts. In addition, coverage may apply only in the United States.

State insurance regulations require insurers to include a statement in bold type on the first page of these policies notifying the insured of the limited nature of the coverage. Limited medical policies include the following:

- Travel accident—coverage only for accidental injury when traveling, sometimes only within the United States and while using specified forms of transportation
- School and other "accident-only" policies—provide relatively low limits of coverage only in the event of accidental injury, which duplicates coverage under almost any other medical expense policy carried by the insured
- Dread disease—coverage only for treatment of specified diseases, such as cancer
- Hospital income (indemnity)—pays a specified amount, ranging from $50 to $200 per day for each day the insured is hospitalized
- Credit—makes installment loan payments on behalf of a covered person in the event of a disabling illness or injury

DISABILITY INSURANCE

The most common type of disability insurance is disability income insurance, which may provide individual or group coverage. There are other types of disability insurance that meet the special needs of some business owners.

Disability Income Insurance

When *disability* resulting from a *covered cause* keeps an insured from earning his or her normal income, disability income insurance pays an *income replacement benefit*. This brief statement contains three elements that need to be examined for a fuller understanding of the kinds of coverage that are available in this line of insurance.

First, *disability* may be defined in several ways. The definition of disability used in a particular policy governs whether the kind of "disability" an insured suffers is covered under the policy. Second, the *cause* of the insured's disability must be covered if the insured is to recover under the policy. Third, disability income policies provide several different kinds of *income replacement benefits*. The amount and kind of benefit an insured receives as the result of a "covered disability" will depend on the kind of income replacement benefit the policy provides. To the extent that there tend to be differences among these key elements with respect to individual and group coverage, these differences will be noted in the following discussion.

Disability. Disability income policies may define disability in several ways:

1. The inability of the insured to perform the duties of his or her occupation
2. The inability of the insured to perform the duties of any occupation for which he or she is fit on the basis of experience, education, or training
3. The inability of the insured to perform any kind of work

From the insured's viewpoint, the first definition above is the most liberal in that the test of disability is whether the insured can do the kind of work he or she has done in the past. The second definition requires that the insured not be able to do any kind of work he or she is reasonably fit to perform. The third definition is not often used in private disability insurance sold today.

In disability income policies that provide benefits for extended periods, both the first and second definitions may be used in the same policy. The first definition will typically apply during the first one to three years of disability. The second, more restrictive definition will apply in the years thereafter.

Most disability income policies provide coverage only for *total disability*, while others may provide benefits for *partial disability*. The concepts of total disability and partial disability are further refinements of the three preceding definitions of disability, not substitutes for them. Total disability means that the insured is unable to perform *any of the duties* of an occupation. Partial disability means that the insured is unable to perform *one or more of the significant duties* of an occupation. For instance, under the first definition of disability above, a policy that provides coverage only in the event of total disability would require that the insured be unable to perform *any of the duties of his or her occupation*. A policy that paid benefits at a reduced rate for partial disability would require that the insured be unable to perform *one or more significant duties of his or her occupation*. The concepts of total disability and partial disability also can be applied under the second definition of disability given above. Policies using the third definition, the inability to perform any kind of work, are written on a total disability basis.

In recent years, some insurers have begun to provide coverage for *residual disability*. Residual disability is measured in terms of an insured's loss of income following disability, rather than the inability to perform the duties of an occupation. This kind of coverage can be particularly important to professionals in individual practice. For instance, an attorney in individual practice who is disabled for several months is likely to find that his or her income upon returning to work is lower than it was prior to the disability, even if recovery from the disability is complete. While the attorney was disabled, some clients would have found other attorneys whom they preferred, and no new clients would have come into the practice. So, despite full recovery and the ability to perform all of the duties of his or her occupation, the attorney could be expected to experience a residual loss of income for some time as a result of the disability. A policy providing residual disability coverage would provide benefits to the attorney as a result of this loss of income.

Covered Causes of Disability. Disability income policies are usually written to provide coverage for disability resulting from both accidental injury and sickness. However, some policies provide coverage only for disability resulting from accidental injury. In either case, the insured is typically required to be under the care of a physician, and the insurer maintains the right to have its own physicians confirm the findings of the insured's physician.

Disability income policies typically contain provisions that exclude or reduce benefits when the cause of disability makes the insured eligible to receive benefits under a state workers compensation law. If a disability income policy excludes coverage when workers compensation applies, it is referred to as a *nonoccupational* policy. Coverage under a nonoccupational policy applies only to disability resulting from accidental injury or illness that is not work-related. On the other hand, an *occupational* disability income policy provides coverage regardless of whether the disability is work-related. Occupational policies cover most causes of disability with few exclusions. However, they do not ignore the fact that an insured may be eligible for workers compensation benefits for some injuries or illnesses. Occupational policies typically contain a provision that reduces benefits paid to the insured to the extent of disability income benefits payable under workers compensation.

The excluded causes of loss in disability income insurance are similar to those in the medical expense policies, described earlier in this chapter. Typically excluded are disability resulting from intentional injury, drug use, injury in noncommercial aircraft flights, war, and military service. Additionally, nonoccupational policies specifically exclude accidental injury or illness for which workers compensation benefits are payable.

Benefits. Disability income insurance is intended to replace a substantial part, but not all, of an insured's loss of income. There are several reasons that the intent is to replace only a portion of the income loss. First, when an insured is disabled, he or she no longer incurs expenses associated with employment, such as meals and transportation costs. Overall expenses may increase because of medical bills, but provision for medical expenses is outside of the scope of disability income insurance. Second, disability income benefits under policies purchased by individual insureds are tax-free, and benefits may be tax-free or only partially taxable under group plans. Because the insured will have no taxes, or fewer taxes, to pay on disability income benefits, the benefits can be lower than the insured's normal, taxable income and provide the same amount of spendable income. Third, if disability benefits match or exceed an insured's (after-tax) pre-disability income, they may encourage malingering. An insured with a relatively high income during disability may attempt to extend the period of disability, thus postponing the return to work.

Disability income insurers generally limit benefits payable to between 60 and 70 percent of an insured's normal income. In individual policies, this is accomplished by requiring a prospective insured to provide verification of his or her income. The insurer then determines the maximum amount of monthly benefit it will provide under the policy, and the insured may purchase coverage up to that limit. In group disability income policies, the benefit is usually expressed as a percentage of the insured worker's normal salary. The benefit is often set at 60 percent of normal salary.

Both individual and group policies contain other insurance provisions aimed at preventing an insured from "profiting" from the disability. Individual policies often contain a provision stating that the insurer will consider all disability income sources and will pay no more than an amount that would bring the insured's disability income up to a specified percentage of his or her normal income. Group policies are likely to reduce the amount paid under the policy by any amounts payable under social security, state nonoccupational disability funds, and workers compensation.

In addition to specifying the amount of weekly or monthly benefits to be paid, disability income policies also specify the period during which payments will be made. This is done by stating the *elimination period* that applies to covered disability and the *benefit period* for which payments will be made. The elimination period is a period of time, measured from the onset of disability, during which no benefits are paid. This elimination period acts as a deductible expressed in time rather than dollars. The benefit period for which payments will be made may be expressed as a certain number of months or years, or until the insured reaches a specified age. The benefit period is measured from the end of the elimination period.

Group disability income policies have traditionally been divided into the categories of *short-term* and *long-term*. Short-term disability income policies are characterized by short elimination periods and benefit periods ranging from thirteen weeks up to two years. Group short-term policies also frequently apply different elimination periods depending on whether disability results from injury or sickness. It is common under these policies to provide immediate coverage (no elimination period applies) for disability resulting from accidental injury. Elimination periods of one or two weeks are typical for disability resulting from illness.

Long-term disability income policies are characterized by longer elimination periods and benefit periods greater than two years. Elimination periods ranging from several months up to a year or more are common. The same elimination period applies regardless of whether disability results from accidental injury or illness. The term of coverage may extend for five to ten years or until the insured reaches age sixty-five or seventy if still gainfully employed.

The traditional distinctions between short-term and long-term policies have become somewhat blurred as disability income insurers have introduced policies that can be tailored to the needs of the individual or group for which protection is provided. Subject to the underwriting guidelines of the insurer, insureds often have flexibility in choosing the benefit amount, elimination period, and term of coverage. All other things being equal, the cost of coverage will be greater when a higher benefit amount, shorter elimination period, or longer benefit period is chosen.

In addition to providing benefits related to loss of income, some disability income policies also provide *lump sum benefits*. A lump sum benefit is an amount specified in the policy that is payable if the insured suffers certain permanent injuries or accidental death. The benefit is similar to the life insurance accidental death and dismemberment benefit discussed in Chapter 10.

Riders. Two riders or endorsements that commonly are available to insureds purchasing individual disability income policies are the cost of living rider and the guaranteed purchase option. Both riders require the payment of an additional premium. The cost of living rider provides for an automatic increase in the benefit payable as the cost of living increases. The guaranteed purchase option allows the insured to purchase increased monthly benefits, subject to the insurer's underwriting guidelines, without having to show evidence of insurability.

Other Types of Disability Insurance

Individuals who own their own businesses may face additional disability-related loss exposures. Business overhead expense insurance and disability buy-out insurance are designed to provide protection for these special business-related exposures. When appropriate, they would be purchased in addition to the insured's long-term disability income coverage.

Business Overhead Expense Insurance. A sole proprietor or professional practitioner (doctor, attorney, and so on) who becomes disabled faces not only loss of income, but also the need to pay continuing business expenses during the period of disability. For the covered insured who becomes disabled, business overhead expense insurance will pay the cost of continuing expenses such as rent, utilities, insurance premiums, necessary repairs to business property, employee salaries, and other customary and normal costs of operating a business or professional practice. The monthly coverage amount is based on the average of the insured's normal monthly business expenses. Coverage may be subject to an elimination period of thirty days or more. The benefit period typically ranges from twelve to eighteen months.

Disability Buy-Out Insurance. Disability buy-out insurance can be purchased by business partnerships, closely held corporations, or their owners to fund buy-sell agreements between the partners/owners in the event that one of them becomes disabled and can no longer actively participate in the business. A buy-sell agreement drawn up for this purpose would spell out the conditions under which the disabled partner/owner would be required to sell his or her share of the business to the other owners. The agreement would also indicate the terms of the sale and that funds for the purchase were to be provided by disability buy-out insurance.

HEALTH INSURANCE POLICY PROVISIONS

The specific coverage-related provisions of medical and disability income policies have been examined in the preceding sections of this chapter. This section focuses on the policy provisions common to both medical and disability coverages. These provisions can be grouped in the following three categories:

- Commonly used provisions
- Uniform mandatory provisions
- Uniform optional provisions

Some of the commonly used policy provisions have developed through industry tradition. Others are required by the insurance regulations of a number of states, which has led to their general use.

The uniform policy provisions, both mandatory and optional, are found in the model Uniform Individual Accident and Sickness Policy Provisions Law developed by the National Association of Insurance Commissioners (NAIC) in 1950. The provisions of this NAIC model law have been included in the insurance regulations of most states. Insurers are not required to include these provisions in their policies word-for-word—wording that conveys substantially the same meaning or provides more favorable treatment to the insured also may be used.

Commonly Used Policy Provisions

Some of the commonly used health insurance policy provisions apply only to individual policies. Provisions dealing with coverage for preexisting conditions are included in both individual and group policies.

Ten Day Right to Examine.   This provision is also referred to as the "ten day free look." It grants the insured ten days, after the receipt of a policy, to examine the policy and return it to the insurer or its agent for a full refund of premium. If the policy is returned within the ten-day period, it is deemed void from its effective date. This provision is included in individual policies, but not group policies.

Preexisting Conditions.   Health insurance policies contain wording that restricts coverage to injuries and sicknesses that occur during the policy period. The intent is to exclude coverage for *preexisting conditions*. Preexisting conditions are medical or health conditions that existed prior to the effective date of the policy. Some policies will provide coverage for preexisting conditions, but only after a waiting period that may range from three months to two years.

A number of states require that when a group health policy is written to replace an existing group health plan, the replacement policy may not exclude coverage for health conditions for which an insured was covered under the previous policy. Such regulations are referred to as *no-loss, no-gain* provisions. No-loss, no-gain provisions have the effect of waiving the replacement policy's preexisting conditions provisions. They typically require that the replacement group health policy provide coverage for preexisting conditions on the same basis as that provided under the previous policy. For example, assume a replacement policy pays disability benefits based on 65 percent of salary and the previous policy's disability benefit was 60 percent of salary. The replacement policy would be required to pay only 60 percent of salary for a worker who became disabled because of a preexisting condition after the employer's group coverage was changed over to the replacement policy.

Waiver of Premium. Individual health insurance policies frequently waive the insured's premium payments during a period of total disability. As discussed, the definitions of total disability vary from policy to policy. A waiting period of one to six months often applies before the waiver takes effect. Any premiums paid by the insured during the waiting period are refunded to the insured once the waiting period is satisfied.

Policy Continuation—Renewability. Individual health insurance contracts are written for a one-year term and may contain any one of six renewability provisions. The insured's ability to renew a health insurance policy becomes very important if he or she contracts an illness that requires long-term treatment. If an insured were forced to seek new coverage while suffering from such an illness, coverage likely would be unavailable, available only at an increased premium, and/or subject to a long waiting period during which coverage for preexisting conditions would be excluded. Of course, for policies that limit or prohibit nonrenewal by the insurer, the insured will pay a higher premium than would be charged when the insurer retains the right not to renew.

The six kinds of individual health policy renewal provisions, listed in ascending order in terms of the renewability protection they provide the insured, are as follows:

● Cancelable
● Nonrenewable
● Renewable at the insurer's option
● Conditionally renewable
● Guaranteed renewable
● Noncancelable

The kind of renewability provision a health insurance policy contains also affects the insurer's right to increase premiums at the renewal date. For this reason, the following examination of renewal provisions also deals with the insurer's right to increase premiums on renewal.

Cancelable. Relatively few cancelable health insurance policies are written today because of the lack of security they provide to the insured. Also, some states prohibit their use. This type of policy contains a cancellation provision similar to that found in most property-liability insurance contracts. Unless a longer time is required by state law, the insurer may cancel on five days' notice. The insured's premium is refunded on a pro rata basis.

Nonrenewable. Nonrenewable policies cannot be canceled by the insurer during the policy term. However, they contain no provision for renewal.

Renewable at the Option of the Insurer. In a health insurance policy with this provision, the insurer has the right to cancel the policy, but only at the annual renewal date. Insurers are typically required to give an insured at least thirty-one days' notice of their intent not to renew. Health policies with this renewal provision typically contain no restrictions on the insurer's ability to increase the insured's premium upon renewal.

Conditionally Renewable. When a health insurance contract contains this provision, the insurer promises to allow the insured to renew the policy unless certain specified conditions occur. The insurer's withdrawal of a particular type of policy from all insureds in the same class or state is usually listed as one such condition. The insured can be nonrenewed with thirty-one days' notice if one of the policy nonrenewal provisions applies. Under a conditionally renewable policy, the insurer also has the right to increase the insured's premium annually, so long as the premium increase applies equally to all insureds in the same class.

Guaranteed Renewable. Under a contract with this continuation provision, the insurer cannot cancel the policy and the insured is guaranteed the right to renew the policy annually up to an age specified in the contract. The insurer has the right to increase premiums annually so long as the premium increase applies equally to all insureds in the same class.

Noncancelable. Policies with this continuation provision are often referred to as "noncancelable and guaranteed renewable." Whether this longer phrase, or simply the word "noncancelable" is used, the policy has the same continuation provision. Noncancelable policies, like guaranteed renewable policies, cannot be canceled and may be renewed annually at the insured's option until the insured reaches the age specified in the contract. The difference between the two policies is that under the terms of a noncancelable policy, the insurer cannot increase the policy premium, not even for a class of similar insureds. The insured pays the premium indicated in the policy for as long as the policy remains in effect. Noncancelable policies are written primarily in disability insurance in which the benefit amount is stated in the policy. Faced with the constantly increasing costs of medical treatment, insurers cannot offer noncancelable medical expense policies with a fixed premium for years into the future.

Uniform Mandatory Provisions

There are twelve uniform mandatory provisions that apply to individual policies. These provisions are not required in group health insurance contracts.

Entire Contract. This provision states that the policy plus any papers attached to it—such as the insured's application and any endorsements—constitute the entire contract between the insured and insurer. It also provides that no agent of the insurer has the authority to change or waive any policy provisions. To be valid, any changes or amendments to the policy must be (1) in writing, (2) approved by an executive officer of the insurer, and (3) attached to the policy.

Time Limit on Certain Defenses. This provision limits the period of time during which the insurer may seek to deny coverage by questioning the truth of the insured's statements on the application for insurance. Depending on state law, insurers may designate either a two- or three-year period. After the policy has been in effect for the specified number of years, the insurer may not contest the insured's coverage on the basis of the insured's omissions or misrepresentations in the application unless the insurer can prove that such omissions or misrepresentations were made with the intent to defraud the insurer. Because this provision limits the insurer's right to contest the policy, it often is referred to as the *incontestable provision*.

Grace Period. The grace period is the time after a renewable policy expires during which the insured may pay the renewal premium and continue to have uninterrupted coverage without providing evidence of insurability. When premiums are paid annually, the grace period usually is thirty-one days. Policies for which premiums are paid on a weekly, monthly, or quarterly basis typically have shorter grace periods.

Reinstatement. If an insured fails to renew a policy within the grace period, the policy may often be renewed under the terms of the reinstatement provision. However, this provision grants the insurer the right to request a statement from the insured regarding health conditions; the insurer may also require the insured to have a physical examination to verify insurability. On the basis of this information, the insurer may place restrictions on or deny approval of a reinstatement of coverage. In addition, the time limit on certain defenses provision applies to any statements made by the insured as part of the reinstatement process. Thus, misrepresentations or omissions on the reinstatement application would allow the insurer to void coverage during the subsequent two or three years. If the insured submits a request for reinstatement, the insurer has forty-five days within which to request updated underwriting information or to deny reinstatement of the policy. If the insurer takes no action within forty-five days after a request for reinstatement and the insured has paid the premium, coverage is automatically reinstated.

Notice of Claim. This provision requires the insured to provide notice of a claim to the insurer or its agent within twenty days, or as soon as reasonably possible, after an accidental injury or the beginning of a covered sickness. Long-term disability income policies may also include a provision requiring that if an insured is collecting disability benefits, the insured must submit notice of continuing disability to the insurer every six months.

Claim Forms. The insurer is required to provide claim forms to the insured within fifteen days after receiving the insured's notice of claim. If the insurer does not provide the necessary forms, the insured may comply with the policy's proof of loss requirements, described immediately below, by writing to the insurer and providing information about the occurrence and the character and extent of the loss.

Proof of Loss. The insured is required to submit written proof of loss to the insurer within ninety days of the occurrence of a medical expense loss or within ninety days after returning to work following a disability income loss. If a proof of loss cannot be submitted within ninety days, it may be submitted as soon as reasonably possible thereafter. All claims must be submitted within one year except in the event of legal incapacity of the insured.

Time of Payment of Claims. This provision states that medical expense benefits are payable to the insured as soon as the insurer receives a written proof of loss. For disability income payments, the insurer is required to indicate in the policy the frequency of payments. Disability income payments must be made at least monthly.

Payment of Claims. This provision allows the insurer to discharge its responsibilities on behalf of the insured by making payment to persons or organizations other than the insured under specified circumstances. This includes payments to hospitals and physicians for medical services and payments to the insured's estate in the event of death.

Physical Examinations and Autopsy. The insurer is granted the right to require the insured to have physical examinations at reasonable intervals at the insurer's expense. In addition, unless prohibited by state law, the insurer has the right to request an autopsy in the event of the insured's death.

Legal Actions. An insured has the right to take legal action against an insurer to resolve coverage disputes. This provision states that such legal action may not be taken less than sixty days after the insured has submitted a written proof of loss, or longer than three years after the time at which the proof of loss was furnished or should have been furnished.

Change of Beneficiary. Unless the insured has named an irrevocable beneficiary under the policy, the insured has the exclusive right to change the policy beneficiary, surrender or assign the policy, and make any other changes in the policy. Changes in the policy regarding coverages or limits would, of course, be subject to the insurer's approval.

Uniform Optional Provisions

The NAIC model statute also includes a number of uniform optional provisions for use in individual policies.

Change of Occupation. Disability income insurance premiums are based, in part, on the insured's occupation. This provision deals with situations in which an insured becomes disabled while working in an occupation for which the premium is different from the premium for the insured's occupation at the time when coverage was purchased. If the insured is engaged in a more hazardous occupation at the time of loss, the policy will pay the benefit amount that the insured's premium would have purchased if the insured had been rated for the more hazardous occupation. If the insured is engaged in a less hazardous occupation at the time of loss, the policy will pay the benefit amount the insured purchased. Any excess in premium paid by the insured after changing to the less hazardous occupation will be refunded.

Misstatement of Age. The insured's age also is a determining factor in the premium charged in health insurance. If the insured's age is misstated on the application, the policy will pay the benefit amount that the premium paid would have purchased at the insured's correct age.

Other Insurance With Same Insurer. If an insured has duplicate coverage with the same insurer, the insurer may limit payments to an aggregate amount of indemnity or to the maximum amount payable under one policy selected by the insured to provide coverage. The excess coverage is considered void, and any excess premiums paid are returned to the insured.

Insurance With Other Insurers. This provision is used in medical expense policies, and its effect is essentially the same as the pro rata liability provision in property insurance. In general, if duplicate individual coverage applies, the insurer will only be responsible for its pro rata share of benefits payable. This provision applies to coverage with other insurers that the insured had but did not disclose to the insurer prior to a covered loss. Any excess premiums paid are refunded to the insured. This provision does not typically apply to "duplicate coverage" provided under group insurance, automobile medical payments insurance, workers compensation insurance, or to recovery as the result of a liability action against a third party. The uniform optional provisions contain two slightly different wordings of this provision. One is worded to apply to indemnity payments. The other is worded to apply to coverage provided on a services basis, as in Blue Cross/Blue Shield contracts.

In group health insurance, the counterpart of the insurance with other insurers provision is the *coordination of benefits provision*. In the event that coverage is provided by more than one group policy, the insured's total recovery under all applicable policies is limited to 100 percent of covered expenses. The coordination of benefits provision also designates the order in which multiple health insurers are to pay benefits.

Relation of Earnings to Insurance. This provision is used in individual disability income policies and provides for pro rata payment of benefits under certain circumstances when an insured carries more than one policy. If the total amount of disability benefits payable under all of an insured's applicable policies exceeds either (1) the insured's monthly income at the time of disability or (2) the average of the insured's monthly income for the two years prior to disability, then the total monthly payment is limited to the greater of these two amounts and is made on a pro rata basis by the various policies providing coverage. Because of the way the cap on benefits is determined, this provision is often referred to as the "average earnings clause." Unless otherwise stated in the policy, this provision does not apply to benefits that may be payable under workers compensation, employers liability insurance, or group disability income plans.

Unpaid Premium. If an insured suffers a covered loss and owes the insurer part of the premium on the policy, this provision grants the insurer the right to deduct the amount of the premium due from the loss payment.

Cancellation. This provision is used in health insurance policies that may be canceled by the insurer. The uniform optional cancellation provision allows the insurer to cancel the policy on five days' notice within the original policy term and at any time if renewed beyond the original term. However, many states require thirty-one days' notice of cancellation in either case. If a health insurance policy is canceled by either party, the insurer is required to pay all covered claims originating before the cancellation date. If the insurer cancels, premiums must be refunded to the insured pro rata. If the insured cancels, the return of premium may be made on a *short-rate basis*. When premiums are returned on a short-rate basis, the insurer is allowed to retain a portion of the unearned premium to compensate it for its administrative expenses. The refund of premium the insured receives is calculated on the basis of short-rate tables on file with the state insurance department.

Conformity with State Statutes. This is essentially the same provision found in many property-liability insurance contracts. It states that if any policy provision is in conflict with a state law, the policy is automatically amended to conform with the minimum requirements of that law. Many states require that this provision be included in all health insurance policies.

Illegal Occupation. This provision states that the insurer shall not be responsible for the payment of benefits if an otherwise covered injury or sickness results from the insured's commission of a felony or occurs while the insured is engaged in an illegal occupation.

Intoxicants and Narcotics. This provision excludes coverage for injury or illness that stems from the insured's being intoxicated or from the use of any narcotic unless administered on the advice of a physician.

HEALTH INSURANCE UNDERWRITING

The overall goal of health insurance underwriting, as with underwriting in other lines of insurance, is the selection and maintenance of a profitable, growing book of business. In the underwriting of individual health insurance policies, this requires careful evaluation of the characteristics of the applicant. Likewise, underwriting group health insurance involves evaluating the characteristics of the group of persons to be insured. In both instances, the underwriter must try to build a book of business composed primarily of insureds who face an average chance of loss. An underwriter who meets this objective will minimize the consequences of adverse selection. With regard to individual applicants or groups that are likely to have greater than average losses, the underwriter must decide under what conditions, if any, the insurer should provide the desired health insurance coverage.

Underwriting Individual Health Insurance

Underwriting and Pricing Factors. Each of the following characteristics of an individual applicant may be considered in underwriting individual health insurance.

Age. Older insureds are likely to suffer more frequent and longer term illnesses than younger insureds. For this reason, health insurance premiums increase as insureds grow older.

Sex. As a group, women tend to incur more frequent and larger medical expenses and more frequent and longer disability income losses. Consequently, premiums for medical expense and disability income insurance for women are higher than for men.

Health History. If an applicant has a poor health history or suffers from a chronic illness, he or she can be expected to incur higher than average medical expenses and disability claims in the future. A higher premium may be charged to reflect such an insured's expected loss costs.

Occupation. Persons employed in certain occupations have a higher than average rate of claim frequency and severity. Health insurers may charge higher premiums to insureds in some occupations and may be unwilling to provide coverage for persons in other occupations.

Personal Habits. Insurers often offer a discount to nonsmokers because, on average, they are less likely than smokers to suffer from lung and heart disease. Insurers may investigate other aspects of an applicant's personal habits including use of alcohol, community status, and home life. Heavy drinking, an unconventional life style, or a troubled family life may indicate a greater than average chance of future medical expense or disability losses.

Underwriting Actions. In addition to accepting an applicant at the standard premium or rejecting the application, the health insurance underwriter may accept the applicant subject to modifications in premium or coverage.

If an applicant has a marginal health history but no chronic medical problems and is acceptable in all other respects, standard coverage may be provided at an increased premium. If the applicant has suffered recent medical problems but otherwise has a good health history, standard coverage may be provided. However, a waiting period of one to two years may be imposed on coverage for the preexisting condition that caused the recent medical problem.

If the applicant has a health problem that is likely to continue, a policy may be issued with an impairment rider. An impairment rider lists the health condition(s) for which the policy does not provide coverage.

Another approach to limiting coverage, used in short-term disability income insurance, is to increase the elimination period for specified causes of disability. For instance, if an insured has a medical problem that flares up occasionally and causes the insured to be out of work for a week or two, the elimination period for this particular condition may be increased to thirty or sixty days.

Underwriting Group Health Insurance

The underwriting practices in group health insurance closely parallel the group life underwriting practices examined in Chapter 10. For this reason, the discussion here focuses on the additional factors considered in group health underwriting. These additional factors are particularly important when group health insurance includes disability income coverage.

Working Conditions. Many group plans provide long-term occupational disability income coverage. As a result, the hazards of the workplace must be taken into account when underwriting and pricing such coverage.

Employment Patterns. Some businesses are more likely than others to employ workers on a seasonal basis or to periodically lay off workers. Health insurers are concerned about such employment patterns because some employees may attempt to replace their lost wages during unemployment by submitting unwarranted disability income claims.

HEALTH CARE COVERAGE PROVIDERS

Health insurance has traditionally been provided by private insurers and by service associations such as Blue Cross and Blue Shield. Health maintenance organizations and preferred provider organizations offer alternative methods of health care coverage and financing.

Private Insurers

Health insurance is sold by health, life, and casualty insurance companies. All of the kinds of health insurance described so far in this chapter are written by private insurers, and many coverages are available on both an individual and group basis.

Private insurers typically issue medical expense policies that provide for payment of claims on an *indemnity basis*. This means that the insurer directly indemnifies or reimburses the insured for medical expenses, subject to any limitations within the policy. Many hospitals and some physicians accept an *assignment of benefits* from the insured and submit bills directly to the insurer for payment. If an insured chooses this payment option, the insurer will directly pay the provider of health care services to the extent of coverage provided under the policy. The health care provider will then bill the insured for the difference, if any, between the total cost of treatment and the payment received from the insurer.

Service Associations

Service associations, such as Blue Cross and Blue Shield, typically provide only the basic and major medical coverages. These associations are nonprofit organizations, usually formed by health care providers. Blue Cross associations originally provided hospital coverage, while Blue Shield associations provided surgeons and physicians coverage. Today these associations are often jointly administered, and the coverages they offer are commonly referred to as Blue Cross/Blue Shield plans. Blue Cross/Blue Shield plans are written on both an individual and group basis, but individual insureds are often accepted only periodically during "open enrollment" periods.

The basic and major medical coverages offered under service association plans typically parallel the coverages offered by private insurers. The two primary differences between service association plans and private health insurance relate to the manner in which benefits are paid and the way in which this payment procedure may limit the insured's choice of health care providers.

Service association plans do not provide indemnity to the insured for incurred medical expenses. Instead, they make payment directly to the hospital or physician providing treatment. Service associations negotiate with these health care providers to accept direct payment from the plan at a reduced rate of compensation. Hospitals and physicians that have agreed to accept these direct payments are referred to as *participating providers*. If an insured chooses to receive treatment from a physician or hospital that is not a participating provider, the insured must typically pay for treatment at the provider's standard rate and accept reimbursement from the service association at the reduced rate it would normally pay to a participating provider. To some extent, this practice limits the insured's choice of health care providers.

Health Maintenance Organizations

A health maintenance organization (HMO) combines health care delivery and health care financing. HMO coverage typically is available only on a group basis. For a monthly fee, the HMO guarantees to provide all of the necessary covered medical services that the insured requires. Most HMOs originally operated on what is called a *closed panel* or group practice basis. Under a closed panel HMO, the insured is required to secure all routine medical treatment at the HMO's medical office. Many HMOs now operate on what is called an *open panel* basis. Under an open panel HMO, the insured may choose a private physician who is participating in the HMO and may designate this physician as his or her primary physician. The insured is then required to secure all routine medical treatment from this primary physician.

Under either type of HMO, the insured is required to obtain a referral from his or her HMO physician for treatment by specialists and for surgery or hospital admission. The cost of these services is covered by the HMO plan, but only when preauthorized by the insured's HMO physician. Treatment by a non-HMO physician and hospital treatment that is not preauthorized are covered only when required in an emergency. Follow-up care to emergency treatment must be provided through the HMO.

An HMO medical plan typically provides coverage comparable to, but somewhat broader than, a comprehensive major medical expense policy. Additional coverages often provided under an HMO plan include routine physical examinations, immunizations, hearing and vision tests, limited reimbursement for glasses and hearing aids, and participation in wellness programs for weight loss and smoking cessation.

HMO plans often require the insured to make a nominal copayment toward the cost of routine medical care, such as $2 to $5 per office visit. Copayments and inside limits also typically apply to treatment of mental illness. Coverage for alcohol and drug dependence commonly is subject to restrictions. Otherwise, HMO plans tend to cover 100 percent of necessary medical expenses with no deductible or copayment requirement.

Preferred Provider Organization Plans

In recent years, private health insurers have established preferred provider organization (PPO) plans in an effort to control health care costs and to compete with service associations and HMO plans for group health insurance business. PPO plans have two basic characteristics. First, a private insurer enters into contracts with selected physicians and hospitals to provide medical services according to specific guidelines at a reduced fee. These physicians and hospitals are the "preferred providers" under the PPO plan. The second basic characteristic of a PPO plan is that the insurer offers incentives to its insureds to use the plan's preferred providers when they need medical care. For example, if an insured is treated by a preferred provider, the insurer often pays 90 to 100 percent of the cost of treatment, rather than 80 percent as it would under the normal 80-20 coinsurance arrangement. In addition, coverage under the plan typically includes cost containment provisions similar to those discussed earlier in this chapter.

Large employers that self-fund their employee health care benefits also have developed PPO plans. Under this type of PPO plan, the employer makes arrangements directly with the preferred providers and typically provides an increased benefit amount when a covered employee receives treatment from one of the plan's preferred providers.

SUMMARY

Health insurance encompasses both medical insurance and disability insurance. Medical insurance policies are designed to cover the cost of medical care resulting from sickness and accidental injury with few exclusions. Disability insurance provides benefits when the insured is unable to work because of sickness or accidental injury.

Medical insurance policies include both basic and major medical expense coverages, dental coverage, and various kinds of limited coverages provided under what are referred to as limited health insurance policies. Basic medical expense policies may be written to cover the insured's expenses arising out of hospital, surgical, and physicians treatments, often on a first dollar basis. Major medical expense insurance can be provided on a supplementary or comprehensive basis. This type of policy is characterized by high limits and broad coverage subject to few exclusions, but the insured is required to participate in the cost of treatment through the use of deductible and coinsurance provisions. Dental expense policies cover a wide range of dental procedures, including preventive care, with internal limits that apply to certain elective procedures. Limited medical insurance policies provide narrow coverage under which benefits are provided only for specified causes of sickness or injury, and often in limited amounts.

Disability income policies provide benefits when the insured becomes disabled. Several different definitions of disability are used in these policies. Some policies pay benefits only in the event of total disability, while others provide partial disability and residual disability benefits. Coverage may be provided on an occupational or nonoccupational basis, and some policies provide for integration with other disability income sources such as workers compensation insurance and social security. Other kinds of disability policies may be used to meet an insured's business needs. These include business overhead expense insurance and policies designed to fund disability buy-out agreements.

State insurance regulations require that individual health insurance policies include the uniform mandatory policy provisions or wording of comparable intent. The NAIC model bill on which these mandatory uniform provisions are based also includes a number of uniform optional provisions. Other standard health insurance policy provisions have come into use through custom or because they are required in a number of states.

The underwriting and pricing of individual health insurance policies is based in part on the applicant's age, sex, health history, occupation, and personal habits. In addition to accepting an applicant at a standard premium or rejecting the application, a health underwriter may accept substandard risks by charging a higher premium or by using an impairment rider or longer elimination period. Group health insurance underwriting is similar to group life underwriting except for the consideration of the additional factors of working conditions and employment patterns.

Health care coverage is provided by private insurers; service associations, such as Blue Cross and Blue Shield; health maintenance organizations; and preferred provider organizations. All of the health insurance coverages described in this chapter are offered through private insurers. Service associations provide both basic and major medical expense coverages, while HMOs provide somewhat broader coverage than that found in the typical comprehensive major medical expense policy. Both private insurers and service associations write policies for individuals and groups. HMO coverage typically is available only on a group basis. Private insurers provide benefits on an indemnity basis. Service associations and HMOs provide a service benefit with some limitations on the insured's ability to choose among health care providers. In recent years, private insurers have established preferred provider organization (PPO) plans designed to control health care costs and to meet the competition for group insurance business offered by service associations and HMOs.

Chapter Notes

---

1. John S. Thompson, Jr., "Individual Medical Expense Insurance," *Life and Health Insurance Handbook* (Homewood, IL: Richard D. Irwin, 1973), p. 291.
2. *1988 Update, Source Book of Health Insurance Data* (Washington, DC: Health Insurance Association of America, 1988), p. 3.
3. *1990 Source Book of Health Insurance Data* (Washington, DC: Health Insurance Association of America, 1990), p. 27.

CHAPTER 12

Government Insurance for Personal Losses

Numerous government insurance programs are in operation at the federal and state levels. These programs are extremely important in providing financial security to individuals and families. This chapter examines the major government insurance programs that provide indemnification for personal losses. Three areas are emphasized. The chapter begins by briefly reviewing the major government insurance programs in the United States and examining the reasons government insurance programs are considered necessary. The second section focuses on the basic characteristics of social insurance programs in the United States. The chapter concludes by examining the major features of other government insurance programs that provide considerable protection for certain personal losses.

OVERVIEW OF GOVERNMENT INSURANCE PROGRAMS

This section provides an overview of social insurance programs and other government insurance programs, which are the two categories into which government insurance programs are generally classified. Also discussed are the reasons for government insurance and the role of the government as an insurer.

Social Insurance Programs

Social insurance programs are compulsory government insurance programs with certain characteristics that distinguish them from other government insurance programs. The basic characteristics of social insurance are examined later in the chapter. Major social insurance programs in the United States include the following:

1. *Social security.* The Old-Age, Survivors, Disability and Health Insurance program (OASDHI), commonly known as social security, provides valuable protection against the financial consequences of premature

death, disability, old age, and catastrophic medical expenses incurred by the aged and certain other groups.

2. *Unemployment insurance.* All states have unemployment insurance programs that pay weekly cash benefits to workers who are involuntarily unemployed.

3. *Workers compensation.* All states have workers compensation programs that provide benefits to workers who are injured or disabled by a job-related accident or disease.

4. *Temporary disability insurance.* Six jurisdictions have compulsory temporary disability insurance laws that provide for the partial replacement of wages that may be lost because workers are temporarily disabled.

Other Government Insurance Programs

In addition to social insurance programs, other government insurance programs provide protection against certain losses experienced by specific groups. They include the following:

1. *FAIR plans.* FAIR (Fair Access to Insurance Requirements) plans are in operation in twenty-seven states, the District of Columbia, and Puerto Rico. FAIR plans provide basic property insurance coverages to property owners who are unable to obtain coverage in the normal markets.

2. *Federal flood insurance.* Federal flood insurance is available in all states to indemnify property owners for flood and mudslide losses.

3. *Federal crime insurance.* The federal government provides burglary and robbery insurance to individuals and business firms at subsidized rates in certain jurisdictions where the Federal Insurance Administration has determined that crime insurance is not available at affordable rates.

4. *Federal crop insurance.* Federal crop insurance provides coverage for most crops against many unavoidable perils, such as drought, excess rain, insects, disease, and hail.

5. *Federal Deposit Insurance Corporation (FDIC).* The Federal Deposit Insurance Corporation insures depositors against loss resulting from the failure or insolvency of commercial banks and savings and loan associations.

6. *National Credit Union Administration (NCUA).* The National Credit Union Administration insures depositors against loss resulting from the failure or insolvency of federal and some state credit unions.

7. *Government life insurance.* The federal government has numerous life insurance programs for members of the armed forces and for veterans. Wisconsin also has a state fund that provides life insurance.

Reasons for Government Insurance

Although the United States has a highly developed private insurance industry, government insurance programs are also needed. Government insurance programs are considered useful for the following reasons.

Promote Social Objectives. Government insurance programs are often established *to deal with complex social or economic problems.* For example, the social security program was initiated in 1935 in response to the problems of massive unemployment and widespread poverty caused by the Great Depression. Another social objective is to provide a *base or layer of financial security* to the population. Again, the social security program provides a base of financial protection to most Americans against the financial consequences of premature death, disability, old age, and medical expenses incurred by the aged. *Prevention of poverty* is another important social objective of the social security program.

Make Insurance Available. Government insurance programs are established to make otherwise unobtainable insurance available to individuals and families. For example, flood insurance on buildings and on most personal property in flood zones cannot be provided by commercial insurers without financial assistance from the federal government because of the problems of *catastrophic loss* and *adverse selection.* A flood can damage a great deal of property in an area, creating a catastrophic loss for property owners and insurers. Adverse selection is a serious problem since only property owners in flood zones are likely to seek protection. Because of these problems, the federal flood insurance program was created to make flood insurance available to property owners in flood zones.

Unemployment is another peril that is difficult to insure privately. Large numbers of workers may be laid off at the same time during a business downswing; thus, a catastrophic loss may result. Also, expected losses are difficult to predict in the short run, which makes it difficult to calculate a correct premium. In order to address these problems, government unemployment insurance programs that restore part of the wages lost by workers who are involuntarily unemployed have been enacted into law in all states.

Make Insurance Affordable. Government insurance programs are established to make insurance affordable. For example, as noted earlier, the peril of flood is difficult to insure privately because of the problems of a catastrophic loss and adverse selection. The premiums for property insurance in flood zones would be too high for most persons to pay without a government subsidy. Thus, flood insurance is heavily subsidized by the federal government so that the insurance can be purchased at affordable rates.

Another example is the crime exposure in high-crime-rate areas. This exposure is difficult to insure privately because of (1) the relatively high frequency and severity of losses, (2) adverse selection created by business firms and individuals who are likely to be robbed or burglarized and want crime insurance, and (3) the moral and morale hazards created by the making of false claims or a careless attitude toward protecting property. Federal crime insurance is provided at subsidized rates in certain jurisdictions where private crime insurance is not available at affordable rates.

Supplementary Medical Insurance (Part B) of the Medicare program is also heavily subsidized by the federal government so that the aged can more easily afford the protection. Part B of Medicare pays for doctor bills and other related medical expenses. Because of limited incomes and a higher frequency and severity of claims, many elderly persons would be unable to purchase private health insurance at the actuarially required premiums. However, general revenues of the federal government pay about three-fourths of the costs of Supplementary Medical Insurance, which sharply reduces the monthly premium the elderly must pay for the protection.

Supplement Private Insurance. In some cases, government insurance programs are enacted to supplement the amount of protection from private insurers. For example, some workers who become disabled may not be covered under an individual or group disability income insurance plan. However, in those jurisdictions with state-provided temporary disability insurance, weekly disability income benefits can be paid to eligible disabled workers.

Crop insurance sold earlier by private insurers generally covered loss from only a small number of perils, such as wind, hail, frost, and freezing. However, the establishment of the federal crop insurance program made it possible for private insurers to offer multiple-peril crop insurance since the federal government acted as a reinsurer under the program. Thus, the federal program supplemented the private protection.

Yardstick to Measure Insurer Performance. Government insurance programs can also be used as a yardstick to measure the performance of private insurers. For example, a competitive workers compensation state fund can be used to measure and evaluate the performance of private insurers that compete for the same business. Likewise, the performance of state funds may be compared with the performance of private insurers.

Role of Government

In this overview of government insurance programs, it is worthwhile to examine more specifically the role of government in the field of insurance and the various relationships that exist between government and private insurers.

Insuring Function. Governmental insurers have two major insuring functions. They may serve as a primary insurer or as a reinsurer.

Primary Insurer. When the government functions as a primary insurer, it is the actual insurer for the program; that is, the government provides the coverage and pays all claims and expenses. The federal government is the actual insurer for the social security program, as well as for the federal crime and federal crop insurance programs. When flood insurance is placed directly with the federal government under the National Flood Insurance Program (NFIP), it is also the actual insurer.

A state government also may be a primary insurer. State government is the actual insurer for a state unemployment insurance program and a monopolistic or competitive workers compensation state fund.

Reinsurer. Government functions as a reinsurer, for example, under the write-your-own federal flood insurance program, in which participating private insurers are reimbursed by the federal government for flood losses that exceed premiums and investment income. In addition, the Federal Crop Insurance Corporation acts as a reinsurer for a number of private insurers that offer the same coverage that the federal crop insurance program now provides.

Relationship of Government Insurers to Private Insurers. Government insurers can affect the private insurance industry in at least three ways. Government can be a partner of private insurers, it can be a competitor, or it can be the insurer of last resort, providing insurance on perils that are not considered commercially insurable.

As a Partner. Government can act as a partner with private insurers in making insurance available and affordable. This is particularly true when complex social or economic problems require close cooperation between government and the private sector. For example, with respect to FAIR plans, private insurers provide the basic protection, and the federal government acts as a partner since insurers that participate in approved FAIR plans are permitted to purchase federal riot reinsurance.

As a Competitor. Government insurers can also compete with private insurers. For example, state workers compensation funds compete with private insurers. Critics of government insurance programs often argue that this type of competition is unfair to private insurers since the state fund is heavily subsidized by taxpayers and does not pay the taxes that private insurers must pay.

As the Insurer of Last Resort. Government insurers frequently write insurance on perils that are not commercially insurable. The perils of war and unemployment can illustrate this point. Losses resulting from war are not commercially insurable because such losses can be catastrophic and expected loss is impossible to predict. However, the federal government has provided war risk insurance to address these problems since it has the ability to create money and impose taxes to finance expenditures. Unemployment is not commercially insurable for similar reasons. As a result, federal-state unemployment insurance programs have been enacted into law to provide weekly cash benefits to eligible unemployed workers.

OLD AGE, SURVIVORS, DISABILITY AND HEALTH INSURANCE (OASDHI)

The social security program is the most important social insurance program in the United States. It is a massive public income maintenance program that provides considerable financial security to individuals and families. More than nine out of ten workers are working in occupations covered by social security. Monthly benefits are paid to about 39 million beneficiaries, or about one in six Americans.

Basic Characteristics of Social Security

Social insurance programs have certain characteristics that distinguish them from other government insurance programs. These characteristics of social insurance programs can be illustrated by analyzing the basic characteristics of the social security program. They include the following:[1]

- Compulsory
- Minimum floor of income
- Emphasis on social adequacy
- Benefits loosely related to earnings
- Benefits prescribed by law
- Self-supporting
- Full funding unnecessary
- Benefits based on presumed need

Compulsory.   With few exceptions, social security is a compulsory program. This means most employers and employees must contribute to the program. As a means of achieving social goals, a compulsory program has two major advantages: (1) the social objective of providing a base of financial security to the population can more easily be met, and (2) adverse selection is generally reduced or eliminated since all healthy and unhealthy lives are essentially covered.

Minimum Floor of Income.   The social security program provides only a minimum floor of income with respect to covered losses. Individuals are expected to supplement this minimum floor of income with their own personal program of savings, investments, and private insurance.

Emphasis on Social Adequacy.   The social security program pays benefits based on social adequacy rather than individual equity. *Social adequacy* means the benefits should provide a certain socially adequate standard of living to all beneficiaries. To accomplish this objective, social security benefits are heavily weighted in favor of certain groups who are unable to pay the full actuarial cost of their protection, such as people with low incomes, elderly people who are retired, and people with large families. These groups receive benefits that substantially exceed the actuarial value of their tax contributions.

The emphasis on social adequacy helps achieve the social objective of providing a minimum floor of income to all covered groups in the population. If low income persons were to receive social security benefits actuarially equal to the value of their modest tax contributions, the benefit paid would be too small to provide a minimum floor of protection.

In contrast, the *individual equity principle* is followed in private insurance. Individual equity means contributors receive benefits that are directly related to the actuarial value of their premiums; the actuarial value of the premiums paid is closely related to the actuarial value of the benefits purchased. The social security program does not completely ignore individual equity in the payment of benefits; however, the benefits are paid largely on the basis of social adequacy.

Benefits Loosely Related to Earnings.   Social security benefits are loosely related to the worker's earnings. The higher the covered earnings, the greater the benefits that are received. Although the relationship between benefits and earnings is loose and disproportionate, it does exist. Thus, some attention is given to the individual equity principle.

Benefits Prescribed by Law. Social security benefits are based on federal law, not on a contract. The benefit amounts, benefit formulas, eligibility requirements, method of financing, and other details are established by law.

Self-Supporting. Another important characteristic of the social security program is that it is financially self-supporting. The sources of its funds are the payroll tax contributions of employers, employees, and the self-employed; interest on the trust fund investments; and revenues derived from the taxation of part of the social security benefits.

Full Funding Unnecessary. The social security program is not fully funded. A fully funded program means that the value of the assets already accumulated under the plan is sufficient to discharge all liabilities for the benefit rights accrued to date under the program. A fully funded social security program is considered unnecessary for several reasons:

- The program is expected to operate indefinitely.
- Since social security is compulsory, new entrants will always pay taxes to support the program.
- If the program has financial problems, the federal government can use its taxing and borrowing powers to raise additional revenues.

Benefits Based on Presumed Need. Social security benefits are based on *presumed need.* This means that the benefits are never automatically paid, but are paid only as the result of certain occurrences and when the eligibility requirements have been met. For example, social security benefits are never automatically paid at the normal retirement age (now sixty-five) but only upon retirement. An earnings test (discussed later) is used as an objective measure of retirement. A gainfully employed worker is presumed not to need the benefits since he or she has not lost any earned income. However, when the worker retires and no longer has earned income, it is presumed that the benefits are needed.

Also notice that a formal needs test is never required. A *needs test* requires the applicant for benefits to show that his or her income and financial assets are below a certain level. A needs test is always used to determine if applicants are eligible for public assistance or welfare benefits. However, applicants for social security benefits have a statutory right to the benefits if they meet the eligibility requirements discussed later.

Covered Occupations

Most occupations are covered on a compulsory basis. However, certain groups can elect coverage, and other groups are covered only by meeting special requirements.

Compulsory Coverage. The major groups covered on a compulsory basis include the following:

1. *Employees in private firms.* The social security program is compulsory for virtually all gainfully employed workers in private firms.
2. *Federal civilian employees.* Federal civilian employees who were hired after 1983 are covered on a compulsory basis. Federal civilian employees who were hired before 1984 are covered by the Civil Service Retirement System and are not required to contribute to the OASDI portion of the total OASDHI program. However, such employees are required to contribute to the hospital insurance portion of the Medicare program. These employees also have the option to switch over to the new Federal Employees Retirement System (for new employees hired after 1983) and would then be covered for both OASDI and hospital insurance.
3. *Religious, charitable, and educational nonprofit organizations.* Workers who are employed by a religious, charitable, or educational nonprofit organization are covered on a compulsory basis if they are paid $100 or more during the year.
4. *Self-employed persons.* Self-employed persons are covered on a compulsory basis if their net annual earnings are at least $400. This category also includes farm operators if their net annual earnings are at least $400.
5. *Other groups.* Other persons covered on a compulsory basis include the following:

   - Ministers unless they elect out because of conscience or religious principles.
   - Persons on active duty in the armed forces.
   - Railroad workers subject to the Railroad Retirement Act. These workers are not required to pay OASDHI taxes directly; however, because of certain coordinating provisions between the two programs, railroad employees in essence are covered under the social security program.

Elective Coverage.   Certain groups have the right to elect coverage. *State and local government employees* can be covered if the state voluntarily enters into an agreement with the federal government. In addition, *U.S. citizens and residents who are employed by a foreign affiliate outside the United States* can be covered if the U.S. employer has at least a 10 percent interest in the foreign affiliate and elects coverage for the employees.

Special Eligibility Requirements.   Certain groups must meet special eligibility requirements to be covered. They include the following:

1. *Domestic workers* if they receive cash wages of $50 or more in a calendar quarter from one employer
2. *Farm workers* if they are paid cash wages of $150 or more during the year or are employed by an employer who pays at least $2,500 in wages during the year

Excluded Occupations.   In most states, police officers with their own retirement systems are excluded. Other excluded occupations are student nurses, students employed by educational institutions, newspaper carriers under age eighteen, and children under age twenty-one employed by their parents in an unincorporated business.

Insured Status

To become eligible for social security benefits, a worker must have credit for a certain amount of work while employed in a covered occupation. For 1990, a worker received *one quarter of coverage* for each $520 of covered annual earnings. A maximum of four quarters of coverage can be earned during one calendar year. The amount of covered earnings needed for a quarter of coverage will automatically increase as average wages in the economy increase. To become eligible for the various benefits, a worker must attain an insured status. There are three types of insured status.

Fully Insured. A worker is fully insured if he or she has (1) forty quarters of coverage or (2) one quarter of coverage for each year after 1950 (or after age twenty-one, if later) up to the year he or she dies, becomes disabled, or attains age sixty-two. A minimum of six quarters is required under the second test. Workers who have forty quarters of coverage are fully insured for life even if they never work again.

Currently Insured. A worker is currently insured if he or she has at least six quarters of coverage out of the last thirteen quarters ending with the quarter in which death, disability, or entitlement to retirement benefits occurs. Currently insured status enables survivors to collect some benefits even if the worker is not fully insured.

Disability Insured. A worker is disability insured if he or she is fully insured and also has at least twenty quarters of coverage out of the last forty quarters ending with the quarter in which the disability occurs. Special rules apply to younger workers and to the blind to make it easier for them to qualify for disability benefits.

Types of Benefits

The social security program has four major benefits:

- Retirement benefits
- Survivor benefits
- Disability benefits
- Medicare benefits

Old age, survivors, and disability income benefits (OASDI) are paid on a monthly basis and are funded somewhat differently from Medicare benefits. For this reason, the immediately following sections focus only on OASDI benefits and financing. Medicare benefits and financing are examined separately.

Retirement Benefits. All monthly retirement benefits are based on the worker's *primary insurance amount* (PIA). The PIA is the monthly amount

Examples of Monthly OASDI Payments*

Benefit Category	January 1990 Payment
Maximum benefit to a worker retiring at age 65	$ 975
Average monthly benefit, retired worker	566
Aged couple, both receiving benefits	966
Widowed mother and two children	1,173
Aged widow living alone	522
Disabled worker, spouse, and children	975
All disabled workers	555

*Based on information from the Social Security Administration.

paid to the worker at the normal retirement age or to a disabled worker. The PIA is based on the worker's *average indexed monthly earnings*. The worker's actual earnings are indexed or updated to take into account changes in average wages since the year the earnings were received. The adjusted earnings are then averaged for purposes of determining the benefit amount. The purpose of the indexing method is to ensure that workers who retire today and workers who retire in the future will have about the same proportion of their earnings restored by social security benefits.

After the worker's average indexed monthly earnings are computed, they are then applied to the benefit formula for determining the worker's primary insurance amount. As noted earlier, the PIA benefit formula is heavily weighted in favor of low income groups.

Cost-of-Living Adjustment. The monthly cash benefits are automatically adjusted each year for changes in the cost of living, which maintains the real purchasing power of the benefits. Whenever the Consumer Price Index increases from the third quarter of the previous year to the third quarter of the present year, the benefits are automatically increased by the same percentage for the December benefit (payable in early January). For example, the January 1990 benefit payment reflected a 4.7 percent benefit increase based on the cost-of-living provision.

Normal Retirement Age. The normal retirement age for full benefits is now sixty-five. However, starting in the year 2003, the normal retirement age will be gradually increased until it reaches sixty-seven in 2027. The new retirement age will affect people born in 1938 and later.

Early Retirement Age. People can retire as early as age sixty-two with actuarially reduced benefits. At present, the benefit normally payable at age sixty-five is reduced 5/9 of 1 percent for each of the first thirty-six months that the person is below the normal retirement age of sixty-five. For example, a worker retiring at age sixty-two receives only 80 percent of the full benefit.

The actuarial reduction in benefits for early retirement at age sixty-two will also gradually be increased from 20 to 30 percent when the new higher normal retirement age provisions become fully effective.

Delayed Retirement Credit. To encourage working beyond age sixty-five, a credit is given for delayed retirement. For 1991, the worker's PIA increased 3.5 percent for each year of delayed retirement (7/24 of 1 percent monthly) beyond the normal retirement age (now sixty-five) and up to age seventy. The delayed retirement credit will gradually be increased until it ultimately reaches 8 percent (2/3 of 1 percent monthly) for workers who reach the normal retirement age in 2009 (then age sixty-six).

Monthly Retirement Benefits. Monthly retirement benefits can be paid to the following persons:

1. *Retired worker.*
2. *Spouse of a retired worker* if he or she is at least age sixty-two and has been married to the retired worker for at least one year. A divorced spouse is also eligible for benefits if he or she is at least age sixty-two and the marriage lasted at least ten years.
3. *Unmarried children of a retired worker who are under age eighteen* or under age nineteen if full-time elementary or high school students.
4. *Unmarried disabled children of a retired worker* who are age eighteen or over if they were severely disabled before age twenty-two and continue to remain disabled.
5. *Spouse of a retired worker at any age with dependent children under age sixteen* or disabled children as defined above.

Survivor Benefits. Survivor benefits can be paid to the dependents of a deceased worker. The worker must be either fully or currently insured at the time of death, but for certain survivor benefits a fully insured status is required. The following persons are eligible for survivor benefits:

1. *Unmarried children under age eighteen* or under nineteen if full-time elementary or high school students.
2. *Unmarried disabled children* as defined above.
3. *Surviving spouse with children under age sixteen* or unmarried disabled children as defined above.
4. *Surviving spouse age sixty or over* if the deceased worker is fully insured. A surviving divorced wife age sixty or older is also eligible for survivor benefits if the marriage lasted at least ten years.
5. *Disabled widow or widower, ages fifty through fifty-nine* if disabled at the time of the worker's death or became disabled no later than seven years after the worker's death, or within seven years after the mother's or father's benefits end. The deceased must be fully insured. A surviving

divorced spouse must have been married to a deceased spouse for at least ten years.

6. *Dependent parents* age sixty-two and over if the deceased worker is fully insured.

7. *An eligible surviving spouse or entitled child* also is paid a lump-sum death benefit of $255.

Disability Benefits. The third major benefit is the payment of disability income benefits to disabled workers who meet the following eligibility requirements:

- Are disability-insured
- Meet a five-month waiting period
- Satisfy the definition of disability

The definition of disability is strict. The worker must have a physical or mental condition that prevents him or her from doing any significantly gainful work, is expected to last (or has lasted) at least twelve months, or is expected to result in death. In determining whether a person can do significantly gainful work, his or her age, education, training, and work experience can be taken into consideration. If the disabled person cannot work at his or her own occupation but can engage in other significantly gainful work, the disability claim will not be allowed.

The monthly disability income benefit is equal to the worker's full primary insurance amount. Benefits also can be paid to unmarried children under age eighteen; unmarried disabled children age eighteen or older who became disabled before age twenty-two; a spouse at any age if he or she is caring for a child who is under age sixteen (or who is disabled); and a wife or husband age sixty-two or older even if there are no children present.

Loss or Reduction of OASDI Benefits. Social security monthly cash benefits can be terminated or reduced under certain situations.

Earnings Test. If a beneficiary has earned income that exceeds the annual maximum limits, he or she will lose part or all of the monthly benefits. The purpose of the test is to restrict the payment of monthly benefits to people who have lost their earned income and to hold down the cost of the program.

For 1990, beneficiaries age sixty-five through sixty-nine could earn a maximum of $9,360 with no loss of monthly cash benefits; beneficiaries under age sixty-five could earn a maximum of $6,840 without losing any benefits. The annual exempt amount is automatically increased each year based on the increase in average wages in the national economy if there is a benefit increase for the preceding December.

Part or all of the benefits will be withheld if the beneficiary's earnings exceed the exempt amount. For beneficiaries age sixty-five through sixty-nine, $1 in benefits is withheld for each $3 of earnings above the exempt amount. However, the benefit reduction is relatively higher for beneficiaries under age sixty-five with excess earnings. For them, $1 in benefits is withheld for each $2 of earnings above the exempt amount.

The earnings test has three major exceptions. First, persons age seventy and older can earn any amount and receive full benefits. Second, the earnings test does not apply to investment income, dividends, interest, rents, or annuity payments. The purpose of this exception is to encourage private savings and investments as supplements to social security benefits. Finally, a special monthly earnings test is used for the *initial year of retirement* if it produces a more favorable result than the annual test. Under this special test, the monthly exempt amount is one-twelfth of the annual exempt amount. For the initial year of retirement, regardless of total earnings for the year, full benefits are paid to a beneficiary who neither earns more than the monthly exempt amount ($780 in 1990 for persons aged sixty-five through sixty-nine and $570 for those under age sixty-five) nor performs significant services in self-employment. The purpose of the special monthly test is to pay full retirement benefits, starting with the first month of retirement, to the worker who retires in the middle or near the end of the year.

Blackout Period. The *blackout period* refers to the period of time when social security survivor benefits are not paid to a surviving spouse. Social security benefits to a surviving spouse are temporarily terminated when the youngest child reaches age sixteen and generally are not resumed again until the surviving spouse attains age sixty.

Other Situations. Other situations including the ones listed below can also result in the loss of benefits.

- Mothers and fathers lose their benefits when they are no longer caring for an eligible child under age sixteen (or are no longer caring for a disabled child).
- Children lose their benefits when they attain age eighteen (or age nineteen if in school full time).
- Death or recovery from disability also causes the benefits to terminate for a particular person.
- Benefits generally terminate if a beneficiary marries a person who is not receiving dependents' or survivor benefits. However, a widow or widower age sixty or older can remarry without losing benefits.
- If a spouse or surviving spouse who is receiving social security benefits as a dependent or survivor also receives a public pension from a job in government not covered by social security on the last day of employment, the social security benefit is reduced by two-thirds of the public pension benefit.

Taxation of OASDI Benefits. Part of the monthly cash benefits is subject to federal income taxation if the beneficiary's income exceeds a certain specified amount. Up to half of the monthly benefits is subject to the federal income tax if the beneficiary's adjusted gross income, plus nontaxable interest income, plus half of the social security benefits exceed certain base amounts (see the "sidebar" on the next page). The base amounts are $25,000 for a single taxpayer, $32,000 for married taxpayers, and zero for married taxpayers filing separately if they have lived together for any part of the year. The purpose of

How Are Social Security Benefits Taxed?

For purposes of taxation, the beneficiary must add together his or her adjusted gross income plus any tax-free interest income plus half of the social security benefits. *The amount of social security benefits subject to taxation is the lower of (1) one-half of the social security benefits or (2) one-half of the excess of the taxpayer's combined income over the base amount.*

Example: A married couple filing jointly has an adjusted gross income of $30,000, tax exempt interest of $1,000, and annual social security benefits of $10,000. They must report $2,000 of the social security benefits as taxable income.

Adjusted gross income	$30,000
Tax exempt interest	1,000
50% of the social security benefits	5,000
Combined income	36,000
Less: Base amount	−32,000
Difference	4,000
Less: 50% of difference	− 2,000
Taxable benefit	$ 2,000

this provision is to improve the long-range financial solvency of the program by taxing part of the benefits paid to upper income taxpayers.

OASDI Financing. The OASDI program is financed by payroll taxes, a relatively small amount of investment income on the trust funds, and revenues derived from taxation of part of OASDI monthly benefits. Each covered worker pays a payroll tax on earnings up to some maximum limit, and the amount is matched by an identical contribution from the employer. The self-employed pay a contribution rate that is equal to the combined employee-employer contribution rate.

In 1990, the worker paid a tax contribution rate of 7.65 percent on a maximum taxable earnings base of $51,300. This amount is matched by an identical contribution from the employer. (Note: these amounts represent contributions to both OASDI and the hospital insurance portion of Medicare.) The self-employed paid a gross rate of 15.3 percent on the same earnings base.[2] The earnings base will automatically increase in the future if benefits are increased according to the cost-of-living provisions. The earnings base will increase based on changes in average wages in the national economy.

Medicare Benefits. The fourth major social security benefit is the payment of Medicare benefits to eligible persons. Almost all persons age sixty-five and older are eligible for Medicare benefits. Medicare benefits can also be paid to disabled persons under age sixty-five who have been entitled to social security disability benefits for at least twenty-four calendar months (they need not be continuous). Persons under age sixty-five who need long-term kidney dialysis treatment or a kidney transplant are also covered by the Medicare program. The Medicare program consists of two parts—Hospital Insurance (Part A) and Supplementary Medical Insurance (Part B).

Hospital Insurance (Part A). Hospital Insurance (HI) provides four major benefits: (1) inpatient hospital care, (2) skilled nursing facility care, (3) home health care, and (4) hospice care.

Inpatient hospital care is provided to a patient in a hospital for up to ninety days for each benefit period. A benefit period starts when the patient first enters the hospital and ends when the patient has been out of the hospital for sixty consecutive days. Coverage is subject to an initial deductible, after which covered hospital expenses are paid in full for the first sixty days. For the sixty-first through ninetieth day of hospitalization, a daily coinsurance charge must be paid. If the patient is still hospitalized after ninety days, a *lifetime reserve* of sixty additional days can be used. The lifetime reserve coverage is subject to a daily coinsurance charge that is twice the amount of the daily coinsurance charge applicable to the sixty-first through ninetieth days. The deductible and coinsurance charges are automatically adjusted each year to reflect changes in hospital costs.

Inpatient care in a skilled nursing facility is also available. The patient must be hospitalized for at least three days to be eligible for coverage, and confinement in the skilled nursing facility must be for medical reasons. Custodial care is not covered. A maximum of 100 days of coverage is provided. The first twenty days of covered services are paid in full. For the next eighty days, the patient must pay a daily coinsurance charge.

Charges for *home health care services* provided in the patient's home by visiting nurses, physical therapists, speech therapists, and other health professionals are also covered. The number of visits is unlimited.

Hospice care for terminally ill beneficiaries is covered if the hospice is certified by Medicare.

Supplementary Medical Insurance (Part B). Supplementary Medical Insurance (SMI), or Part B of Medicare, is a voluntary program that covers physicians' fees and other related medical services. Most persons covered under HI are automatically enrolled for SMI unless they voluntarily refuse the coverage. The 1990 monthly premium for the coverage was $28.60. The balance of the cost of SMI is paid for out of federal general revenues.

SMI pays for several types of medical services when they are medically necessary. First, *physicians' services* are covered in the doctor's office, hospital, or elsewhere. Second, *outpatient hospital services* for diagnosis and treatment are also covered, such as care in an emergency room or outpatient clinic, or diagnostic services received as an outpatient. Third, Part B provides for an unlimited number of *home health visits* for such services as physical or speech therapy. Finally, *other medical and health care services* are covered, such as durable medical equipment used at home and supplies for fractures.

Supplementary Medical Insurance pays 80 percent of the *approved charges* for covered medical services after the patient pays a $75 calendar-year deductible. Recognized or approved charges are updated annually according to an economic index formula that considers both the costs of maintaining a medical practice and increases in general earnings levels. However, because of a time lag in the determination of approved charges and high rates of inflation, the amounts approved are often less than actual charges of doctors and suppliers.

Because of the rapid increase in physician fees, physicians will be reimbursed in the future under a new method called a "resource-based relative-value scale." The new method will gradually be phased in over a five-year period beginning January 1, 1992. Under the new system of reimbursement, a complex national fee schedule will determine fees based on the time and resources that physicians devote to each medical procedure. Congress is optimistic that the new method will slow down the rate of increase in physician fees.

Financing Medicare.   The HI (Part A) coverage is financed largely by the payroll tax on covered earnings (described earlier in connection with OASDI financing), plus a relatively small amount of general revenues. All HI contributions are deposited into the Hospital Insurance Trust Fund. The SMI (Part B) program is financed by monthly premiums paid by insured persons and general revenues of the federal government. SMI premiums are deposited into the SMI Trust Fund.

UNEMPLOYMENT INSURANCE

Unemployment insurance programs are federal-state programs that pay weekly cash benefits to eligible workers who are involuntarily unemployed. Each state has its own program.

Unemployment insurance programs have several important objectives:

- Pay weekly cash benefits to workers involuntarily unemployed
- Help unemployed workers find jobs
- Encourage business firms to stabilize their employment
- Provide stability to the economy[3]

Several practices are incorporated into unemployment insurance programs to ensure that these objectives are achieved. For example, applicants for unemployment insurance benefits must register for work at local public employment offices, and the personnel at these offices provide information to the workers about jobs for which they are qualified. Through experience rating, businesses with stable employment histories are assessed at a reduced rate for unemployment insurance taxes.

Covered Occupations

Most *private firms* are covered for unemployment insurance benefits. A private firm is covered if it employs one or more workers in each of at least twenty weeks during the calendar year or preceding calendar year, or if the firm pays wages of at least $1,500 during a calendar quarter of either year.

Most employees in *state and local government* are also covered for unemployment insurance benefits. State and local governments are not required to pay the federal unemployment tax; however, the state must make unemployment insurance benefits available to most state and local government employees.

Nonprofit organizations of a charitable, educational, or religious nature are covered for unemployment benefits if the nonprofit organization employs four or more workers for at least one day in each of twenty weeks during the current or prior year. Nonprofit organizations are not subject to the federal unemployment tax; however, nonprofit organizations have the right either to pay the unemployment tax under the state's law or to reimburse the state for any unemployment benefits paid.

An *agricultural firm* is covered if it has a quarterly payroll of $20,000 or more, or the firm employs ten or more workers for at least one day in each of twenty weeks during the current or prior year.

Finally, *household workers* in domestic employment are covered if the household employer pays wages for domestic employment of at least $1,000 in a calendar quarter.

Eligibility Requirements

Unemployed workers must meet the following eligibility requirements:

- Have qualifying wages or work during the base period
- Be able to and available for work
- Actively seek work
- Meet a waiting period
- Be free from disqualification

Qualifying Wages. One requirement is that a worker must have earned qualifying wages during the *base period*, or must have worked a certain number of weeks or calendar quarters during the base period, or have some combination of both. The base period generally is a fifty-two week or four-quarter period prior to the period of unemployment. The purpose of this requirement is to limit benefits to workers who are currently or recently part of the labor force.

Able to and Available for Work. A person must also be physically and mentally capable of working and must be available for work. Available means that the individual is ready, willing, and free to work.

Actively Seeking Work. Registration for work at a public employment office provides evidence that someone is actively seeking work.

Waiting Period. In most states, workers are required to satisfy a one-week waiting period to qualify for benefits. The waiting period acts as a deductible, reduces short-term claims and administrative expenses, and provides time to process a claim.

Free From Disqualification. A worker must also be free from disqualification. Disqualifying acts include quitting a job without good cause, refusing suitable work, being discharged for misconduct, or participating directly in a labor dispute.

Unemployment Insurance Benefits

Unemployment insurance programs provide regular benefits and extended benefits to eligible workers.

Regular Benefits. A weekly cash benefit is paid for each week of total unemployment. The benefit paid is based on the worker's wages earned during the base period, subject to minimum and maximum dollar amounts. The maximum duration of regular benefits in virtually all states is twenty-six weeks.

Extended Benefits. A permanent federal-state program is now established that pays additional benefits to unemployed workers who exhaust their regular benefits during periods of high unemployment. Under the extended benefits program, unemployed workers can receive up to thirteen additional weeks of benefits, or up to one-half of the total amount of regular benefits, whichever is less. There is an overall maximum limit of thirty-nine weeks for combined regular and extended benefits. The costs of the extended benefits program are paid equally by the states and the federal government.

Financing Unemployment Insurance

Regular state unemployment insurance programs are financed by a payroll tax paid by covered employers on the covered wages of the employees. Five states (Alabama, Alaska, New Jersey, Pennsylvania, and West Virginia) also require the employees to contribute. All payroll taxes are deposited in the federal Unemployment Trust Fund. Each state has a separate account, and unemployment benefits are paid out of the state's account.

In 1990, covered employers paid a federal unemployment tax of 6.2 percent on the first $7,000 of annual wages paid to each covered worker. However, the employer can credit toward the federal tax any contributions paid under an approved state unemployment insurance program and any tax savings under an approved experience rating plan. The maximum employer credit is limited to 5.4 percent. The remaining 0.8 percent is paid to the federal government and is used for administrative expenses, for financing the federal government's share of the permanent extended benefits program, and for a loan fund from which the states can borrow when their reserves are depleted.

Because of a desire to maintain fund solvency and to strengthen their unemployment reserve accounts, the majority of states now have a taxable wage base that exceeds the federal standard of $7,000 of annual wages paid to each covered worker.

WORKERS COMPENSATION

To address the problem of occupational injury and disease, all states have enacted workers compensation laws. The fundamental principle on which workers compensation is based is the *liability-without-fault principle*. This means that employers are held absolutely liable for the occupational injury or disease incurred by workers regardless of who is at fault. Losses covered are limited to those arising out of and occurring in the course of employment. Injured workers are not required to sue their employers and prove negligence to receive benefits but instead are paid according to a schedule of benefits established by law.

Workers compensation insurance may be purchased by employers to pay for the benefits prescribed by state law. Retention (self-funding) of workers compensation claims is permitted in forty-seven states. Six states have monopolistic state funds, and covered employers must purchase the coverage from the state fund. Thirteen states have competitive state funds that compete with private insurers in providing workers compensation coverage.

Workers compensation laws provide four major benefits: medical care, disability income benefits, death benefits, and rehabilitation services. These benefits are briefly described in the following paragraphs. A more detailed discussion of workers compensation insurance is presented in INS 23.

Medical care costs are paid in full in all states without any waiting periods or deductibles. There are usually no limits on the duration of benefits or on their amount.

Weekly disability income benefits are also paid after a short waiting period that usually ranges from three to seven days. Most states pay benefits retroactively if the worker is still disabled after a certain number of weeks or days.

A burial allowance can be paid if the worker dies from a job-related accident or disease. In addition, weekly cash benefits based on a proportion of the deceased worker's wages can be paid to eligible dependents such as a surviving spouse or dependent children.

Rehabilitation services such as vocational retraining are available in all states. These services help restore disabled workers to productive employment.

TEMPORARY DISABILITY INSURANCE

Six jurisdictions (California, Hawaii, New Jersey, New York, Rhode Island, and Puerto Rico) have enacted social insurance programs that pay disability income benefits to covered workers who are temporarily disabled because of a *nonoccupational accident or disease*. The coverage also applies to eligible unemployed workers who become disabled while unemployed.

Eligibility Requirements

Temporary disability laws generally cover employees in private industry. However, disabled workers must meet certain eligibility requirements to receive benefits.[4] They must (1) meet an earnings or employment requirement, (2) be disabled as defined in the law, and (3) satisfy a waiting period.

Earnings or Employment Requirement. An applicant for benefits must have earned a certain amount of qualifying wages or must have worked for a certain number of weeks to be eligible for benefits. The purpose of the earnings requirement is to limit benefits to workers who are currently part of the labor force.

Disability as Defined in the Law. The worker must be disabled as defined in the law. Disability is generally defined as the inability of the worker to perform his or her customary work because of a mental or physical condition. However, New Jersey and New York impose stricter requirements for disability that occurs during unemployment. Also, some jurisdictions deny payments for a disability resulting from a self-inflicted injury or an illegal act.

Waiting Period. A waiting period of seven consecutive days is required before disability income benefits are paid. In California and Puerto Rico, the waiting period is waived if the worker is in the hospital.

Temporary Disability Benefits

Weekly cash income benefits are paid to eligible disabled workers and are intended to replace at least one-half of the weekly wage, subject to some maximum and minimum weekly amount. The maximum duration of benefit payments is twenty-six to thirty-nine weeks.

Financing

Temporary disability benefits are financed by a payroll tax paid by employees on covered wages up to some maximum limit. In four of the six jurisdictions, covered employers must also contribute to the program.

OTHER GOVERNMENT INSURANCE PROGRAMS

FAIR Plans

The basic purpose of FAIR plans is to make basic property insurance available to property owners who cannot obtain coverage in the normal markets.[5] The plans cover loss from fire and what are traditionally known as the "extended coverage perils" such as windstorm and hail, smoke, explosion, and vehicles. All plans also cover vandalism or malicious mischief; crime and sprinkler leakage coverages are provided in a few states.

Inspection of Property. The property the applicant wants to insure must first be inspected, and if it meets certain underwriting standards, it can be insured. If a building is substandard, it may still be insurable at higher premiums. In some cases, the property owner may be required to make certain improvements before the policy is issued. Finally, the insurance application may be denied if the property is considered uninsurable. However, the insurance cannot be denied solely on the basis that the property is located in a riot-prone area or is exposed to environmental hazards.

Role of Private Insurers. Each FAIR plan has a placement facility that assigns the approved applications to participating insurers. The applications are assigned on the basis of a formula that considers the proportion of premiums written in the state by each participating insurer. The participating insurers then pay their proportionate share of losses and expenses.

Federal Flood Insurance

Federal flood insurance is available in all states, the District of Columbia, Puerto Rico, Guam, and the U.S. Virgin Islands. The original program was established by the National Flood Insurance Act of 1968 and is administered by the Federal Insurance Administration. The basic purpose of the act is to provide flood insurance at subsidized rates to property owners in flood areas.

Write-Your-Own Program. In late 1983, the federal government changed the flood insurance program to a program called the "write-your-own program." Under this program, private insurers sell the flood insurance under their own names, collect the premiums, retain a specified percentage for commissions and expenses, and pay their own claims. If the insurers' losses are not covered by the premiums and investment income, they are reimbursed for the difference by the federal government. Any profits, however, go to the federal government.

Eligibility Requirements. Most buildings and their contents can be insured if the community agrees to enforce sound flood control and land use measures. When a community first joins the program, property owners in flood areas are allowed to purchase limited amounts of insurance at subsidized rates under the *emergency* portion of the program.

The federal government then prepares a flood insurance rate map that divides the community into specific zones to determine the probability of flooding in each zone. When the map is prepared and the community agrees to adopt more stringent flood control and land use measures, the community enters the *regular* phase of the program. Higher amounts of flood insurance can then be purchased at actuarial rates.

Amount of Insurance. The maximum amount of insurance that can be purchased at subsidized rates under the *emergency* program is $35,000 on a single-family dwelling (higher limits are available in Alaska, Hawaii, Guam, and the U.S. Virgin Islands) and $10,000 on the contents. For other residential structures, the maximum amount is $100,000.

The maximum amount of insurance that can be purchased at actuarial rates under the *regular* phase of the program is $185,000 for a single-family home and $60,000 on the contents. Other residential structures can be insured for a maximum of $250,000.

A $500 deductible applies separately to the buildings and contents. Higher deductibles are available. There is also a $250 aggregate limit on jewelry, precious metals, and furs. A similar $250 limit applies to paintings and other art objects.

Federal Crime Insurance

The federal crime insurance program was established in 1970 and became operational in 1971. This program provides crime insurance at subsidized rates in areas where the Federal Insurance Administration has determined that crime insurance is not available at affordable rates. Federal crime insurance is available in about half the states, the District of Columbia, Puerto Rico, and the U.S. Virgin Islands.

The insurance is sold by licensed agents and brokers. The crime insurance contracts are issued and maintained by participating private insurers. A servicing insurer has a contract with the Federal Insurance Administration to perform the various service functions in selling the insurance. The Federal Insurance Administration, however, is the actual insurer.

There are two federal crime insurance contracts: (1) a residential policy and (2) a commercial crime policy.

Residential Crime Insurance. The residential crime policy covers the loss of personal property as a result of burglary, larceny, and robbery (including observed theft) while the property is on the insured premises or in the presence of the insured. For example, if a thief breaks into an apartment and steals a television set, the loss is covered. Likewise, if an insured is mugged in a subway and a wallet is stolen, or if a thief grabs the handbag of an insured and runs, the loss is covered.

The residential crime policy also covers damage to the insured's living quarters, including damage to insured personal property or to insured property away from the premises by vandalism or malicious mischief. Damage to the building, however, is covered only if the insured owns the building or is legally liable for damage to the building.

The maximum amount of crime insurance is $10,000, and the minimum is $1,000. To qualify for the insurance, home owners or renters must maintain certain protective devices, such as door and window locks that meet certain specifications.

All covered losses are subject to a deductible of $100 or 5 percent of the amount of the gross loss, whichever is higher. The purposes of the deductible are to encourage insureds to protect their property and to eliminate small claims.

Commercial Crime Policy. The commercial crime policy insures industrial, commercial, nonprofit, and public property against certain types of crime losses.

Federal Crop Insurance

Federal crop insurance provides multiple-peril coverage at subsidized rates for unavoidable crop perils, including drought, hail, wind, excessive rain, freezing, snow, plant disease, flood, and earthquake.

The insured is guaranteed a certain amount of crop production expressed in terms of bushels, pounds, or other commodity unit. If the insured's actual production is less than the guaranteed amount, a loss payment is made for the lost production based on a price selected by the insured before the growing season starts. Federal crop insurance, however, does not guarantee full production, but only a maximum of 75 percent of the average production over a representative period of years. A lower percentage guarantee of 65 or 50 percent can be elected with a reduction in premiums. For example, assume that a farmer's average production on a particular crop is 12,000 bushels, and that the 75 percent guarantee on that crop is 9,000 bushels. If a farmer produces only 3,000 bushels because of a drought, the loss is 6,000 bushels multiplied by the price selected earlier. Thus, if the farmer had selected a price of $3 per bushel, the amount of indemnity would be $18,000 (6,000 bushels × $3), less any premium due.

Federal Deposit Insurance Corporation (FDIC)

The Federal Deposit Insurance Corporation (FDIC) is an independent federal agency that provides protection against the loss of depositors' funds because of the failure or insolvency of an insured bank or savings and loan association. The FDIC currently insures the deposits in national banks, most state banks, commercial banks, mutual savings banks, and federally insured savings and loan associations.

The account of an individual depositor is insured up to a maximum of $100,000. A valid joint account by a husband and wife (or two or more persons) in the same insured bank is separately insured up to a maximum of $100,000 for the account. Deposits into an individual retirement account (IRA) or Keogh plan for the self-employed are also separately insured up to $100,000. Therefore, a person with an individual account, a joint account, and an IRA account all in the same bank could have up to $300,000 of FDIC coverage with a maximum of $100,000 per account.

National Credit Union Administration (NCUA)

The National Credit Union Administration is an independent federal agency that insures the savings accounts of depositors in federal and some state chartered credit unions. Federal chartered credit unions are required to have this protection; state chartered credit unions may elect to have this protection or, in some states, may be required to have this protection. Protection for depositors is comparable to that provided by the FDIC for commercial bank depositors.

Government Life Insurance

Congress has enacted numerous life insurance programs for members of the armed forces and for veterans. Below are two current federal programs:[6]

- Servicemen's Group Life Insurance (SGLI)
- Veterans' Group Life Insurance (VGLI)

Servicemen's Group Life Insurance (SGLI). In 1965, Servicemen's Group Life Insurance was enacted into law to provide life insurance to members of the armed forces on active duty. Since that time, the program has been expanded and liberalized.

Eligibility Requirements. Persons eligible to purchase the insurance are members of the armed forces on active duty, qualified members of reserve units including the National Guard, and retired reserve members who have completed twenty years of creditable service.

Amount of Insurance. Service members on full-time active duty are automatically insured for a maximum of $50,000 unless the person elects in writing not to be insured or wants a smaller amount of insurance, such as $40,000, $30,000, $20,000, or $10,000. No other choices are available. Retired reservists are not automatically insured; they must apply for the insurance and pay the first premium before the insurance is effective.

Payment of Premiums. The federal government pays the administrative expenses and the extra cost due to the increased risk of military duty. The balance is paid by insured service members.

Role of Private Insurers. The insurance is underwritten by a pool of commercial insurers. One company acts as the primary insurer, and the remaining companies participate as reinsurers. The program is administered by the Office of Servicemen's Group Life Insurance under the supervision of the Veterans Administration.

Conversion Right. When the service member leaves the military or is no longer eligible for coverage, the insurance is automatically converted to Veterans' Group Life Insurance. The automatic conversion, however, is subject to the timely payment of the initial premium.

Veterans' Group Life Insurance (VGLI). Service members who leave active duty can convert their SGLI to VGLI with no evidence of insurability. VGLI is *nonrenewable,* five-year term insurance. The premiums are paid entirely by the veteran who converts. The term insurance can be converted to a cash value policy with any private insurer that is participating in the program.

Wisconsin Life Fund

At the state level, the Wisconsin State Life Fund was created in 1911 to provide low-cost life insurance to persons residing in Wisconsin when the insurance is purchased. The fund is administered by the state treasurer and is supervised by the state insurance commissioner. No agents are used. Applications for the insurance are taken by state banks and by designated public officials who then forward them to the state insurance commissioner.

The insurance sold is generally low-cost protection because no agents are involved, commissions are not paid, the state provides a subsidy since the fund pays no rent or officers' salaries, and lapse rates are relatively low.

SUMMARY

The purposes of government insurance programs are to promote social objectives, make insurance available, supplement private insurance, and serve as a measure of insurer performance. The government may be a primary insurer or a reinsurer. It can be a partner or competitor to private insurers or an insurer of last resort by writing "uninsurable" loss exposures.

The social security program has the following characteristics. It is generally compulsory, provides a minimum floor of income, and emphasizes social adequacy. Benefits are loosely related to earnings and are prescribed by law. The OASDI program is financially self-supporting and is not fully funded. The benefits are based on presumed need. By working in a covered occupation, a worker becomes insured and eligible for benefits. Benefits are paid when a worker retires, dies, or becomes disabled.

Medicare includes Hospital Insurance (Part A) and Supplementary Medical Insurance (Part B). Medicare Part A is financed largely by payroll taxes. Part B is financed from premiums paid by insured persons and general revenues of the federal government.

Unemployment insurance funds are joint federal and state programs that pay weekly cash benefits to eligible workers who are involuntarily unemployed.

All states have enacted workers compensation laws to meet the problems of occupational injury and disease. Benefits are paid on a liability-without-fault basis and include payment of medical expenses, disability income benefits, death benefits to survivors, and rehabilitation services. Six jurisdictions also provide temporary disability insurance resulting from nonoccupational accidents or disease.

FAIR plans make basic property insurance available to property owners who cannot obtain coverage in normal insurance markets. Underwriting is based on an inspection of the building itself without regard to "environmental hazards."

Flood insurance provides protection at government-subsidized rates to property owners in areas subject to floods. Federal crop insurance provides multiple-peril coverage for unavoidable perils to crops. Private insurers writing this coverage are reinsured by the federal government.

Deposits in banks and savings and loan associations are protected, up to a certain amount, by the Federal Deposit Insurance Corporation. The National Credit Union Administration provides insurance on deposits with credit unions.

Life insurance is also available to certain segments of the public through federal and state government programs.

Chapter Notes

1. This section is based on George E. Rejda, *Social Insurance and Economic Security*, 4th ed. (Englewood Cliffs, NJ: Prentice Hall, Inc., 1991), Chapters 2, 5, 6, and 9 and George E. Rejda, *Principles of Insurance*, 3rd ed. (Glenview, IL: Scott, Foresman and Company, 1989), Chapter 24.

2. The self-employed tax rate is now equal to the combined employer-employee tax rate. However, the base to which the tax rate is applied can be reduced by two deductions. First, net earnings from self-employment are reduced by an amount equal to half of the total self-employment tax. This is similar to the way that employees are treated since the employer's portion of the total social security tax is not considered taxable income to the employee. Second, half of the self-employment tax can be deducted as a business expense. This is similar to the deduction allowed to employers for the taxes they pay on behalf of their employees.

3. The material on unemployment insurance is based on Rejda, *Social Insurance and Economic Security*, Chapter 14 and Rejda, *Principles of Insurance*, Chapter 24.

4. Rejda, *Social Insurance and Economic Security*, Chapter 9.

5. The section on FAIR plans and other government insurance programs is based partly on material from Rejda, *Principles of Insurance*, pp. 142-145.

6. This section is based on *Federal Insurance Benefits* (Cincinnati, OH: The National Underwriter Company, 1989), Section 18, pp. 28-34.

Bibliography

Bickelhaupt, David L. *General Insurance.* 11th ed. Homewood, IL: Richard D. Irwin, Inc., 1983.

"Brother Can You Spare a Tort?" *Journal of American Insurance,* vol. 65, Third Quarter 1989, pp. 16-19.

Crane, Frederick G. *Insurance Principles and Practices.* 2nd ed. New York: John Wiley & Sons, 1984.

Donaldson, James H. *Casualty Claim Practice.* 4th ed. Homewood, IL: Richard D. Irwin, Inc., 1984.

Explanatory Memorandum. New York: Insurance Services Office, 1985.

Fire Casualty & Surety Bulletins, Personal Lines Volume and Management Sales Volume. Cincinnati, OH: The National Underwriter Co.

Federal Insurance Benefits. Cincinnati, OH: The National Underwriter, 1989.

General Accounting Office. *Issues and Needed Improvements in State Regulation of Insurance Business* (Executive Summary). Washington, DC: U.S. General Accounting Office, 1979.

Gregg, Davis W. and Lucas, Vane B. *Life and Health Insurance Handbook.* 3rd ed. Homewood, IL: Richard D. Irwin, 1973.

Hollingsworth, E.P. and Launie, J.J. *Commercial Property and Multiple Lines Underwriting.* 2nd ed. Malvern, PA: Insurance Institute of America, 1984.

Homeowners Policy Program (1991 Edition) Manual. New York: Insurance Services Office, 1991.

Keeton, R.E. *Cases and Materials on Basic Insurance Law.* 2nd ed. St. Paul, MN: West Publishing Co., 1977.

Launie, J.J. "The Incidence and Burden of Punitive Damages." *Insurance Counsel Journal,* January 1986, pp. 46-51.

National Safety Council. *Accident Facts,* 1988 edition. Chicago: National Safety Council, 1988.

1988 Update, Source Book of Health Insurance Data. Washington, DC: Health Insurance Association of America, 1988.

1989 Life Insurance Factbook Update. Washington, DC: American Council of Life Insurance, 1989.

1990 Property/Casualty Insurance Facts. New York: Insurance Information Institute, 1990.

1990 Source Book of Health Insurance Data. Washington, DC: Health Insurance Association of America, 1990.

Policy Form & Manual Analyses, Casualty Insurance Volume and Property Insurance Volume. Indianapolis, IN: The Rough Notes Company.

Rejda, George E. *Principles of Insurance.* 3rd ed. Glenview, IL: Scott, Foresman and Company, 1989.

_____. *Social Insurance and Economic Security.* 4th ed. Englewood Cliffs, NJ: Prentice Hall, 1991.

Smith, Barry D.; Trieschmann, James S.; and Wiening, Eric A. *Property and Liability Insurance Principles.* Malvern, PA: Insurance Institute of America, 1987.

Smith, Brian W. "Reexamining the Cost Benefits of No-Fault." *CPCU Journal,* vol. 42, no. 1, March 1989, pp. 28-35.

U.S. Department of Transportation. *Major Vehicle Crash Losses and Their Compensation in the United States: A Report to the Congress and the President.* Washington, DC: Government Printing Office, 1971.

Wood, Glenn L.; Lilly, Claude C. III; Malecki, Donald S.; Graves, Edward E.; and Rosenbloom, Jerry S. *Personal Risk Management and Insurance.* Volumes I and II, 4th ed. Malvern, PA: American Institute for Property and Liability Underwriters, 1989.

Index

A

Abandonment of property condition, *42*

Absolute assignment, *235*

Absolute liability, *7*

Abuse or sexual molestation, *57*

Accident victims, compensation of, *196*

Accidental death, *239*

Accidental death and dismemberment benefits, *239*

Accidental discharge or overflow of water or steam, *31*

Accumulation at interest dividend option, *238*

Actions, underwriting, *271*

Actual cash value—mobilehome endorsement, *97*

Additional coverages, homeowners, *33* homeowners liability, *60*

Additional insured—residence premises endorsement, *88*

Additional living expense, *32*

Additional residence rented to others endorsement, *87*

Additional vehicle, *147*

Additions and alterations, *45*

Add-on plans, *204*

Adjustable life insurance, *231*

Adverse selection, *279*

Age, misstatement of, *234, 269* retirement, early, *286* normal, *286*

Age and original cost of auto as rating factor, *218*

Age, sex, and marital status as rating factor, *216*

Age as underwriting factor for health

insurance, *271*

Age as underwriting factor for life insurance, *241*

Agreement, PAP, *146*

Aircraft, damage from, *30* exclusions to, *57*

Alcohol and drug dependency as medical expense coverage limitation, *256*

"All-risks" coverage, under PEF, *127*

Amount of coverage, *22*

Amount of insurance, *22*

Appraisal, *40* PAP Part D, *171*

Appraisal award, *40*

Approved or recognized charges, *292*

Arbitration, *161*

Assault and battery, *6*

Assignment of benefits, *272*

Assignment clause, *235*

Auto, covered, *147* nonowned, *166* performance of as a rating factor, *218* type of as a rating factor, *218*

Auto policies, two or more, *176*

Automatic loan provision, *238*

Automatic termination provision, PAP, *175*

Automobile accidents, high costs of, *194* high frequency of, *194*

Automobile insurance, availability and affordability of, *196* cost of, *216* primary rating factors for determining, *216* no-fault, *204* personal, underwriting and rating, *213*

Automobile insurance discounts and

305

D

E

G

H

Uninsured vehicles, *158*
Unit, definition of, *48*
Unit-owners exposures, *49*
Unit-owners insurance, *48*
Universal life insurance, *229*
Unpaid premium, *269*
Unsatisfied judgment funds, *201*
Unscheduled personal property, *26, 123*
Use of auto as rating factor, *217*
Using a vehicle without reasonable
    belief of permission, *152*

V

Vacation mobilehomes, *96*
Vandalism and/or malicious mischief,
    23, 30
Variable life insurance, *230*
Variable-universal life insurance, *231*
Vehicle, additional, *147*
    newly acquired, *147*
    temporary substitute, *147*
Vehicle furnished or available for
    regular use, *152*
    of any family member, *153*
Vehicles, eligible, for PAP, *143*
    motorized, with fewer than four
        wheels, *152*
    number of, as a rating factor, *218*
    uninsured, *158*
Verbal threshold, *204*
Veteran's Group Life Insurance (VGLI),
    300
Volcanic eruption, *32*
Volcanic eruption period, *43*

W

Wages, qualifying, for unemployment
    insurance, *293*

Waiting period limitation, *255*
Waiting period for unemployment
    benefits, *293*
Waiver of premium, *239*
War, *26, 57*
Warranties, in personal yacht policy,
    134
Water damage, *25*
Waterbed liability, *48*
Watercraft, exclusions to, *56*
    insurance on, *128*
    physical damage coverage for under
        homeowners, *128*
    physical damage for under personal
        auto policy, *129*
Watercraft endorsement, *85*
Watercraft package policies, *131*
Weight of ice, snow, or sleet, *31*
Whole life insurance, *227*
Windstorm or hail, *29*
Wisconsin Life Fund, *300*
Work, able to and available for, as
    requirement for unemployment
    insurance, *293*
    actively seeking, as requirement for
        unemployment insurance, *293*
Worker, currently insured, *285*
    disability insured, *285*
    fully insured, *285*
Workers compensation, *278, 295*
Working conditions as underwriting
    factor for group health insurance,
    272
Write-your-own program, *297*

Y

Yearly renewable term policy, *226*